NEW DUBLINERS

NEW DUBLINERS

Urbanization and the Irish Family

Alexander J. Humphreys

NEW YORK
FORDHAM UNIVERSITY PRESS

First published in the U.S.A. 1966
by Fordham University Press
Bronx, New York 10458

Copyright Alexander J. Humphreys 1966

Library of Congress Catalog
Card Number 66–15773

Printed in Great Britain

Foreword

by George C. Homans

NOT LONG AGO the study of the varieties of family organization was the domain of social anthropologists, working in non-literate or at least non-Western societies. Modern Western societies belonged to the sociologists, and they were less interested in family structure than in family statistics: divorce statistics, for example. Recently the situation has begun to change from both sides. Anthropologists have begun to study kinship in Western societies, and sociologists to take a broader view of what is interesting about families, including their characteristic cultural patterns.

Though the focus shifted to modern Western families, it remained for a time on families in those sectors of society that most resembled the groups the anthropologists studied: the traditional rural areas. An early and classic example is the book by Conrad Arensberg and Solon Kimball, *Family and Community in Ireland* (Cambridge, Massachusetts: 1940). Only in the last few years has systematic attention been paid to family structures in modern Western urban areas. Yet surely the urban areas are the ones that make the difference, for good or ill.

Of this most recent trend the present book is a distinguished example. It is a study by a professional sociologist of characteristic family structures in modern Dublin. The book would be interesting enough if we were interested in Ireland alone, for, taken together with the work of Arensberg and Kimball, it allows us to understand how the rural Irish family maintains but modifies its traditions over the generations as it moves to a very different setting. And this would be much, in view of the enormous contribution Irish immigration has made to the social life of modern cities all the way from Sydney to Boston and to Manchester.

But the book is not enlightening simply to students of the great race of the Gael. It tells us much of prime importance about kinship in the West at large and indeed in any industrialized society. It analyses the changes in normal family patterns as determined by migration from rural, agricultural, uniform, and traditional conditions to urban conditions of high population density, high social

v

mobility, and a wide and changing range of occupations. The book also analyses the variation in family patterns between different social classes, another feature marking off the urban from the old rural milieu. Surely these are changes we really must understand if we are to extrapolate into the future the development of any modern society.

The present author's research was distinguished not just in what he undertook to do, but also in his manner of doing it. Partly, no doubt, because of his position in the Catholic Church, Father Humphreys was able to establish unusually close relations with the families he studied, and gather unusually rich material on their family life and its social setting and on their own attitudes towards both. He allows us to see the society of a great modern city with the sympathy and insight of a native without ever losing the detachment and rigour of a social scientist.

Contents

Contents

ACKNOWLEDGEMENTS

TO DEAL WITH THE IDEAS and to dig up the data needed for a study such as this is to dig oneself deeply into debt to many people. I am particularly indebted to George Homans and to Peter Rossi who collaborated in directing the thesis which is the basis for this work. Both were constantly generous with their time and invigorating and encouraging with their criticism and advice. Talcott Parsons throughout contributed invaluable suggestions not only as to theoretical matters but also in regard to problems connected with the fieldwork. Gordon Allport was a perennial source of assistance, and for help in resolving certain specific problems I owe thanks to Carle Zimmerman, Harvey Locke, the late Samuel Stouffer and the late Clyde Kluckhohn. Finally I must thank John V. Kelleher, Professor of Irish History and Literature at Harvard University, for frequent and enlightening discussions of historical matters relative to my subject; and Conrad Arensberg.

I shall have occasion in the text to acknowledge most of the people in Ireland who in various ways helped me in the fieldwork. But besides these, special thanks are also due to Mr. Seamus Delargy, Director of the Irish Folklore Commission, and to one of his research assistants, Mr. Tadgh Murphy, particularly for aiding my work in the rural areas; Dr. Eammon F. O'Doherty, Professor of Psychology at University College, Dublin; the late Canon John Hayes, Chairman of Muintir na Tíre, a national organization of parish councils; Rev. Thomas Counihan, S.J., a member of the Emigration Commission; Rev. Edward Coyne, S.J., Chairman of the Irish Agricultural Organization Society and Professor of Moral Theology at the Jesuit Theologate in Dublin; Dr. Raymond C. Geary, former Director, and M. D. McCarthy, present Director of the Central Statistics Office of Eire, as well as Brendan Broderick, its Assistant Director; and Mr. John Ingram, of the Labour Commission.

Acknowledgement is also given to Houghton Mifflin Company, for permission to use, in Chapter I, some of the material which originally appeared in 'The Family in Ireland' in *Comparative Family Systems*, edited by Meyer F. Nimkoff, and published in Boston 1965.

Finally, for their generous help in the preparation of the manuscript, and in facilitating publication, I wish to thank Jack Sweeney, Mrs. Pat Zawadsky, Mary Jergens, Jean Cook, Grace Tevis and Maynard Smith.

ALEXANDER J. HUMPHREYS, S.J.

Loyola University
Los Angeles, California

'For me the initial delight is in the surprise of remembering something I didn't know I knew.'

ROBERT FROST

From 'The Figure a Poem Makes'
in *Complete Poems of Robert Frost*,
p. vi (Holt, Rinehart and Winston,
New York, 1949).

Introduction

THIS WORK IS a study of the effects of urbanization upon human life and behaviour in Ireland. In particular, it examines the changes wrought upon human life at the level of the family, and the relations to kin and neighbours with which the family traditionally has been integrated.

The process of urbanization which, going hand in hand with modern industrialization, has been rampant in Western society during the last century and a half is now spreading to the rest of the world. It has had profound repercussions upon human life which some have praised and other bewailed. It is perhaps wiser simply to acknowledge that it confuses us and challenges us to understand it. For it has modified and changed important human relations at all levels, given rise to novel institutions and forms of human organization, begotten new ideas and values, and created unforeseen and complex social and economic problems on the international as well as on the national scale. Philip M. Hauser has written:

> It is becoming increasingly clear . . . that urbanization and urbanism, as such, are complex and confounded variables which must be further analysed into elements. . . . [There exists for] the sociologist the need to reconsider some of the perhaps too hasty generalizations of the past.[1]

This study tries to contribute to such an elemental analysis and to examine some of these generalizations.

Urbanization is such a complicated development that the social sciences must of necessity study it from many angles and at many different levels. But none is more important nor perhaps more illuminating than the level of family life. In the first place, the family group is small enough to permit a study in depth of human behaviour and of the effect of urbanization upon it. And second, as the most basic of human groups, the family is so centrally located that it can provide special perspectives on urban life on all sides. On the one hand, it is intimately bound up with all the major groups in the urban community and so strongly influenced by them that it is impossible to study the urban family without at the same time increasing our

[1] 'World Urbanism: An Editorial Forward', *American Journal of Sociology*, LX No. 5 (March 1955), 427.

1

knowledge of these crucial urban institutions. On the other hand, since the family is the major formative factor in the life of the individual, no group can shed more light on the impact urban living has upon the psychological development of human personality.

Despite the fact that Ireland is still predominantly an agricultural country, there are good reasons for choosing to study urbanization there. Although most Irish cities are quite small by English and American standards, Dublin as the nation's capital has grown into a truly modern metropolis, especially since Ireland gained her national independence in 1922, and it has been the main Irish terminal for a large and steady migration from the countryside. Looking forward to her likely entry into the European Economic Community, Ireland since 1958 has adopted policies which have fostered substantial investments by foreign capital. These have greatly increased the nation's rate of industrialization and, perforce, of urbanization. As a result, Dublin, the industrial centre of Ireland, is an extremely rewarding community in which to study this process that is transforming the traditional social structure of the Emerald Isle.

Moreover, the Irish field possesses other decided advantages for studying the effects of urbanization. To ascertain the results of this process clearly and precisely it is virtually a necessity to compare urban society with rural society within the same culture. Such a comparison is all the more fruitful the more consistent it is in its general theoretical framework and in the methods used in investigating the rural and urban communities. Ireland not only provides the cultural uniformity, but circumstances made it relatively easy to achieve this desired technical consistency there. For the rather copious literature about rural Ireland, though quite diversified, contains a series of exceptionally systematic and objective studies of the Irish family and community written between 1935 and 1940 by Conrad Arensberg and Solon T. Kimball.[2] These works have been our major source of information for the structure of the rural family and community. The present study, for which the field research was done from 1949 to 1951, is directly correlative with the research of these authors in the rural community.

First, their work enabled me to verify and to supplement their findings by studying several typical communities of small farmers in

[2] These are: Conrad M. Arensberg and Solon T. Kimball, *Family and Community in Ireland* (Cambridge, Mass., 1940); Conrad M. Arensberg, *The Irish Countryman* (New York, 1937); S. T. Kimball, 'The Tradesman and His Family in the Economic Structure of an Irish Town' (unpublished Ph.D. thesis, Harvard, 1935). Among other useful sources, some of the most helpful have been T. W. Freeman, *Ireland* (London, 1950); E. E. Evans, *Irish Heritage* (Dundalk, 1949); and, despite its regional focus, J. M. Mogey, *Rural Life in Northern Ireland* (London, 1950).

Tipperary and Limerick and especially in Kerry and Mayo. During the period of almost twenty years between these earlier studies and the present one, a number of changes have occurred in the rural community that have affected the family life of country people. I have attempted to take these into account and to compare the family in Dublin with the rural family as it was when I made this study. But, as we shall see, up to that moment transformations in the rural community had been relatively slow and small, and the countryman's family retained the essential features that Arensberg and Kimball have so ably described and analysed.[3] Furthermore, since it is people from precisely such rural areas as these authors analysed who have been thronging into Dublin during the last half-century, it was possible in studying the families of their children in the city to trace them back to the exact rural community of their origin and to ascertain that it was similar to the communities Arensberg and Kimball had described. Finally, since I accept substantially the same general theory of the social system as these two authors, it was possible, as far as the urban conditions allowed, to take the same fully rounded view of family life in Dublin as they had taken of the rural family and community, and to use similar methods in gathering the data needed to compare the two.

One obvious advantage of being able to make this kind of continuous study is the fact that the countryman who leaves the farm for Dublin stays in Ireland and so in a cultural sense stays home. One can, of course, learn much about urbanization by studying the fate of the countryman who has migrated across the seas and settled in one of the great industrial centres in England, the United States or elsewhere as, to cite but one example, Thomas and Znaniecki did in *The Polish Peasant in Europe and America*.[4] But such an immigrant from Ireland, fresh from the farm, must not only adjust himself to city life. Fresh from Ireland, he must also adjust himself to a new and different general culture. In his case, therefore, it is often hard to tell which of the many changes that occur are due to the novel way the city organizes his life, and which are due to his encounter with new ideologies and ultimate values in the urban community—if, indeed, these two distinguishable influences can effectively be sorted out at all. By contrast, the countryman who settles in Dublin remains within his native culture and so never radically feels like a Ruth among the alien corn. For he finds in Dublin the same over-arching Irish culture that, like the sky, is common to countryside and city and that softens and tends to integrate the differences between them. And thus the

[3] v. ch. i, *passim*, and ch. vii, pp. 233–34.
[4] W. I. Thomas and Florian Znaniecki, *The Polish Peasant in Europe and America*, 5 vols. (Boston, 1918–20).

3

changes that take place in his life and in his children's, and that mark them both as different from the people of the countryside, are not due to any great ideological variations they have experienced, but are clearly the effects of the distinctive way the modern city organizes its life.

Consequently, the focus of this study is a sample of twenty-nine Catholic families whom, with a tip of the hat to James Joyce, I have called New Dubliners.[5] The New Dubliners are first-generation urbanites: the sons and daughters of immigrants, born, raised and living their married life in Dublin. Different from his immigrant parents in some respects, the New Dubliner also differs in other respects from those Dubliners whose families have resided in the city for many generations. In the colourful Irish idiom, the latter are the 'Dublin jackeens', whom I shall refer to more prosaically as the Old Dubliners. Of course, all of these Dubliners appear upon our stage, for naturally the New Dubliners do not of set policy marry only New Dubliners. They marry Old Dubliners and immigrants as well, and such intermarriage profoundly affects the speed of the process of urbanization. But in every family here studied at least one of the spouses is truly a New Dubliner and I have therefore felt justified in referring to them all as New Dubliner families, even though some of them could just as well be called families of immigrants or Old Dubliners.

Of all these, however, the New Dubliner holds a strategic middle position for an understanding of the transition from country to city life. Dermott Malone is a case in point. His father, Seamus, is a brewery foreman who was born and bred on a farm in Cork and came to Dublin at the age of fifteen. Inevitably, Seamus has been deeply conditioned by his rural upbringing in his struggle to fit into the city's life. Dermott, on the other hand, has been affected only indirectly by his father's rural background. As a child of the city, his direct experience has been entirely of the city except for two occasions when Seamus took him down to the farm in Cork during the summer holidays. In Seamus's words: 'Dermott knows of trams and cinema houses, not of cattle and barns.' Dermott is thus more of a 'citizen' than Seamus—more versed in city ways, impregnated with city views and values, and confronted with city problems.

To be sure, a person like Maureen Gallagher, the wife of an eminent surgeon and a descendant of families who have lived in Dublin since the eighteenth century, is even more urbane in the root sense of the word than Dermott. But she is not quite as rewarding a subject

---

[5] Originally, thirty families were included in the sample, but due to unforeseen developments one family had to withdraw from the study when it was too late to replace it.

as Dermott for the study of the contemporary shift from country to city life. Her origins are lost in the mists of time so that we cannot be certain that they were rural to begin with, and even if they were, they have long lost their force. The changes which have undoubtedly affected her ancestral families in the course of the last hundred years are not so much the result of a transition from the rural to the urban community as of the normal pattern of living in a city which itself has been constantly changing. But Dermott's historical tie with the country is clearly traceable through Seamus. And in his case, as with all the New Dubliners, we can determine the contemporary type of rural community his parents came from and be sure that in him we are observing the effects of urbanization upon a person of recent country stock.

The fact that New Dubliners can also put us in touch with their immigrant parents themselves is another great point in their favour. For the immigrants patently are invaluable sources of information about the countryman's adjustment to city life, and especially about the problems country-bred people have had in raising urban children. Even where his immigrant parents are dead, the New Dubliner's first-hand account of life with his immigrant father and mother can be immensely illuminating. By concentrating on the New Dubliners, then, we can get important insight into how the process of urbanization begins in the immigrants and, by comparing the immigrant's family life with that of their married children in Dublin, we can learn something about those elements in family life that first yield and change under the pressure of the city, and those elements that tend to resist and endure.

That I selected New Dubliner families that were Catholic was virtually inevitable in view of the fact that the Republic of Ireland as a whole is over 94 per cent Catholic and Catholics make up over 90 per cent of the population of Dublin. As we shall see, urbanization produces very important effects upon Irish Catholic attitudes and practices. It does not, however, involve on a broad scale the radical religious clashes, transformations and even decay which it often brings about elsewhere and which have sometimes been claimed as among the principal results of urban life. Furthermore, since Irish culture is overwhelmingly Catholic in the city as well as in the country —or, as the sociologist is prone to say, since the religious variable in Ireland is substantially constant—the major effects of urbanization which emerge there clearly are not mainly religious in origin. It is intensely interesting to observe and analyse these changes since, especially in popular literature, many of them have often been attributed to religious factors.

The number of families studied directly is limited because I desired to make as complete a case study of each family as possible. I felt that such treatment would yield the best sort of detailed information for a fruitful, systematic comparison of urban and rural life. At the same time, the sample had to be large enough to provide significant insight into the general pattern of family life in Dublin and yet include a representative selection of New Dubliners from each of the important class levels in the city. As a result of these considerations, I chose eleven families of artisans, and six families each from the employer-managerial class, from the clerical class and from the class of general labourers.[6]

Although it is convenient to designate them by occupational status, these classes are not merely abstract occupational categories. The other factors used in trying to determine the class structure of Dublin and the class position of the New Dubliners were their income, residence and education; their relative social power, their privileges and obligations; their general style of life; and the amount of inter-action between them on the basis of all these. On these grounds Dubliners appear to fall into two main classes, one of which, however, is made up of several sub-classes. One major class is the *employer-managerial* class composed of those who own or at least control relatively large productive or service enterprises. To this group, of course, belong the higher free professionals, especially doctors, solic-itors and barristers. The other large class consists of employees below the managerial level, whether they are salaried or work for a wage. But within this second group there appear to be three dis-tinguishable classes. The first is the *clerical* group which includes hired professionals—such as schoolteachers, laboratory technicians and the like—as well as the white-collar workers in public adminis-tration and on the staffs of industrial and commercial firms. in many important ways the life of these people differs from that of the skilled workers in the trades and of the lowest echelon of administrators such as foremen, all of whom make up the *artisan* class. Finally, the *general labourers*, who are largely semi-skilled and unskilled workers, again differ in significant respects in their manner of living from either of these latter groups.[7]

There are, of course, shadings and transitional areas at various

[6] v. Appendix I, pp. 264–65, *infra,* for a fuller discussion of the representative quality and the class composition of this sample.

[7] One other category of people is scattered through two, or possibly three, of these levels in proportions that we are not able to determine. These are small business people, the most numerous of which are shopkeepers. Although they own their own businesses, these people range from those who, according to the indices of class we have used, are on the same level as the better paid white-collars to those who are on the level of the artisan, and even in the case of the poorer shopkeepers, of general labourers.

levels of this class structure. Furthermore, when the study was made, data were not yet available to determine accurately how Dubliners in general, let alone New Dubliners, were distributed through these classes. Consequently, the class proportion of the sample had to be determined on the basis of several months' observation, a great deal of discussion with informed Dubliners, and realistic practical considerations. Since it was impossible to get complete correspondence between the class proportions of the city and the sample, I decided to include enough families of New Dubliners from each class to get a real taste of life at every level. As there were good reasons to believe that the largest portion of people in Dublin were artisans, I decided to select more families from that class and an equal number from the other three classes. The class composition of this sample of New Dubliners, then, is necessarily biased to a certain extent. But it is not so far out of kilter with the general class distribution to distort the reality seriously, and still it provides enough data on each class to give significant insight into the principal differences between them.[8]

The players in this drama of city life in the employer-managerial class are the families of the president and part owner of a large food-processing company with three plants and several stores in Dublin; the president and part owner of one of the city's largest insurance companies; a stockbroker, a surgeon, a solicitor and a barrister. The families of a chief librarian in the Dublin Public Library; a senior administrator in the city's government—officially entitled the Dublin Corporation; a chief cashier, and three clerks in various business concerns are the clerical people in the cast. The artisan families are those of four foremen, two coopers, an electrician, a carpenter, a baker, a rate collector for the Electrical Supply Board and an assistant headwaiter in one of the large Dublin hotels. Three of these families are marginal to the clerical class on the one side, and one is marginal to the general labouring class on the other. Finally, the general labourers we are to meet are the families of a bus driver, a boilerman in a large downtown building, a cement worker and three dock workers. Again, one of these families is marginal to the artisan class.

These leading families had a very large supporting cast, for they put me into contact with their friends, neighbours and relatives who make up the most intimate sector of the social setting in which they live. All of these related people and families were indispensable for the study of the New Dubliners. But, as we have anticipated, in one respect at least the most important of all were the grandparents. For

[8] A year after the field research was completed, Census data for the year 1946 were published which indicate that the bias necessarily introduced by this method of sampling was not very great. v. ch. ii, pp. 61–2, *infra.*

the history of the grandparents clearly shows that the majority of these New Dubliners were children of people who had come from the small farms and small rural towns that hold the bulk of the Irish population. From the one hundred and sixteen parents of the fifty-eight spouses included in our sample, only thirty-one were born and raised in Dublin, and only six in towns with a population of 2,500–5,000 in 1926. Sixty-seven of them were children of farmers; nine were children of farm labourers; and twelve were raised in towns whose population in 1926 was under 2,000. Furthermore, their roots reached into every part of the country since they came from each of the four Provinces, and from twenty-one of the twenty-six counties of the Irish Republic.

I met these families in several different ways. In many cases my first contact was quite formal. Thus Professor George O'Brien, Professor of Economics at University College, Dublin, kindly introduced me to Sir Charles Harvey, managing director of Guinness's Brewery, who most liberally put the facilities of that famous concern at my disposal and arranged meetings with employees at the Brewery where I first interviewed them on company time. The president of another large Dublin concern did the same thing. More often, I travelled the ancient road of mutual friendship, surely the widest, fastest and most pleasant in Ireland. My Jesuit colleagues co-operated nobly by introducing me to friends who were formerly their pupils, and I was fortunate enough to make many friends on my own. Such friendships opened many doors in Dublin, indeed; and in several instances families whom I had incorporated into the project in turn introduced me to other families who consented to participate in the work.

With all of these families I had a minimum of six very long interviews, both with individual family members and with the family as a group. The fact that I was a priest and a member of a religious order had one drawback for my relations with these people, since it required me to live with my own religious community and so limited the amount of direct observation I would have had if I could have resided with one or more of them. But apart from that my priesthood was, I am sure, a distinct advantage for our communication with each other. The New Dubliners were delighted to have a priest in their homes who would let them talk openly and fully about their lives, and they spoke very frankly on many subjects where, I believe, they would have been quite reserved had I not been a priest. One indication of this was the fact that they had no objections to my open note-taking during these interviews. But perhaps the most vivid sign of the fullness of our rapport was the informal relations which in increasing measure grew out of our first formal dealings and which led to many visits with these families for the sake of sheer friendship. Surely the best way to study a family is to be at home with them and I have never felt more at home than I did with the New Dubliners. I trust that the following pages which describe and analyse their family life will do justice to their hospitality and co-operation.

As a concrete study of urbanization in Ireland this study must smack of Ireland and things Irish as the wine must taste of its own grapes. And it inevitably does so because as far as possible I have let the people of Dublin speak for themselves—and few can speak better. Certainly no apology need be made for a study of Ireland. It is an important and interesting country in its own right because it has been and continues to be an integral, yet distinctive, part of Western European civilization, and because of the significant influence its people have had upon human society in the New World and in the Old. But the central focus of our attention in this study is not upon the peculiarities of Irish society, even though they are vital to our task, but upon behaviour that is commonly human.

As a result, the author here has attempted, as far as possible, not to evaluate Irish society on any scale of ultimate values, nor to pose as an expert on Irish matters eager to make recommendations on the conduct of Irish affairs. If in this work by a foreigner who lived closely with them for a year and a half the Irish people find anything that is helpful to them in dealing with the problems they face, I shall feel most grateful for being able thus in some small way to repay their warm generosity without which this work would have been impossible and which I would not dare abuse. The responsibility of solving their own problems, of course, lies with the Irish people themselves and their long, hard battle for the freedom to exercise that trust is surely some warrant of their capacity to do so.

The ultimate aim of this book, then, is wider than an understanding of Ireland as a particular society, however important that may be. Rather, it is to describe as objectively and as systematically as possible the uniform and common changes that take place in the process of urbanization and the order in which they take place; and to analyse the observable causes of these transformations in the hope that this will broaden our knowledge of this constantly developing feature of modern society. Even deeper than that, this study seeks to throw further light on the basic characteristics of human interaction in society in general. In the end, our main preoccupation is with our central theoretical position that human society is meaningfully and creatively integrated in a systematic way so that change in human behaviour in one sphere leads to changes in human behaviour in other spheres. We seek here to understand more thoroughly how this process works. In a word, our interest in the Dublin people is engaged not only because they are Irish and city folk and Western Europeans, but above all because they are human beings who can help us better to understand ourselves and other men in society everywhere.

Chapter I

COUNTRYMEN AND NEW DUBLINERS

THE MAZE OF relationships that make up the family is so intricate that it is very easy to lose one's way in trying to trace it. This is particularly true in the present case where there is need to compare two family systems, the rural and the urban. Clarity is at a premium here and so it will be best, perhaps, to come to the point immediately and to make a descriptive comparison of the family life of the Irish countryman with the family life of the New Dubliner. To discuss the recent history and the structure of Dublin as a city, to present the fascinating details of the New Dubliners' life which are the source and justification of the sketch to be drawn in this chapter, and to analyse the process of urbanization as this comparison reveals it will then be the task of the remainder of this book.

THE COUNTRYMEN

To be at home with the Irish countryman as his friend for any reasonable length of time is to come to know virtually every family in the rural community. This is due to the essential structure of that community and an enlightening clue to its nature. For in rural Ireland the farm family is typically small, yet in nearly every rural community the small farm family is the centre of power.[1] Indeed, a rural community for the most part is a group of interlocking small farm families tied together by bonds of kinship and neighbourliness, and these mainly mould the structure of the place.

Other non-familistic groups are found there, of course. Nearly every community has its church and resident clergy, and its school and schoolteachers. It may also boast of a resident doctor and lawyer

[1] Thus of all male farmers occupied in Ireland in 1951, 69 per cent worked farms of less than fifty acres and 88·5 per cent ran farms under one hundred acres. These percentages were compiled from data given in *Census of Population, 1951*, III, Pt. 1 (Dublin, 1954), Table 6A, 104–5.

11

and administrative government agencies, such as a post office, a police station or a local office of the Land Commission. More rarely it may contain a factory, though productive concerns are quite few in the rural areas partly because Ireland's industrial resources are relatively meagre, and partly because the Irish government's policy of industrial decentralization has not notably succeeded. Among business concerns the most numerous and important are the shops and stores which serve the rural community. Some of these are situated at cross roads in the agricultural areas of the community, but most of them are located in a nearby town which serves as the community's commercial centre.

Despite the presence of groups such as these, the most numerous and strongest ties in the typical rural area are familistic in nature and they generate a high degree of solidarity between the members of the community. Perhaps nothing better illustrates the strength of familistic relations in the rural community than the extent to which considerations of family, kinship and neighbourliness affect and modify business activity which in theory is classically impersonal. The shops that serve the rural community are normally family enterprises so geared in with the families of the farmers and farm labourers that their operation more nearly approaches the operation of the small farm itself than that of the large, impersonal stores located in a city such as Dublin. For instance, the clientele of a draper in a rural community will consist largely of the families in the area who are related to him by blood or marriage, and of his old friends and their old friends. So sure is he of their trade because of the mutual obligations of friendship, and for the same reasons so sure of their customers are his fellow drapers in the same community that they can hardly be said to be competitors in the usual economic sense of the word.[2] Similar familistic considerations in diverse ways profoundly modify the function of the law, the school and the Church. In short, the small farm families, taken collectively, hold and exercise the largest measure of power in the rural community and other, non-familial organizations are relatively subordinate to them. Consequently the overall structure of the rural community is such as to secure and foster the family's traditional organization and to reinforce and support its ideals and values.

The root of the family's power lies in its ownership, control and direct operation of the principal form of productive property in the community—the farm itself. The control and operation of economic production give the farm family its own intrinsic measure of independence from non-familial organizations. For it makes the family a collective productive unit and thereby makes the homestead the

[2] Kimball, op. cit., *passim*, discusses this relationship at length.

prime centre of each individual's total activity, economic and otherwise. At the same time, family control of production leagues each farm family with other local families in a strong communal alliance which strengthens the independence of each in regard to non-familial organizations.

The collective working of the farm normally requires that the father of the family, and his grown sons and daughters prior to their marriage, all labour on the homestead. This results in a balanced distribution of direct domestic responsibilities of all kinds between all the members of the family.[3] Such balance is reflected in the equal subordination of all the children to their parents and especially in the equal division of labour that exists between the farmer and his wife.

In the economic sphere, a farmer's wife has an important share in the productive activity which creates income. She not only may help her husband in the open field at sundry times when the pressure of work demands, but regularly she assists him in the care of the stock, and normally she has charge of the vegetable garden and the poultry which are important, if secondary, sources of income for the farm family. The services that must be performed daily and seasonally for the family and for the homestead, and the exchange activities of buying and selling are likewise rather equally divided between husband and wife. It is the farmer's responsibility to repair the house, barn, fences, drains and heavier furniture and gear; to handle the sale of the heavier stock at the fair; and to purchase the major pieces of furniture and equipment. On the other hand, his wife not only provides the traditionally wifely services of cooking, cleaning and mending, but she also sells eggs and poultry and is the purchasing agent for food, clothing and the lighter necessities.[4]

This balance of responsibility in economic matters is the ground on which grows a similar balance in respect to all the other spheres of family life. In the matter of authority over family affairs in general, of course, the farm wife is subordinate to her husband because as an important economic enterprise the farm requires strong centralized control in rural Ireland as in any other rural society. But in practice, especially in regard to the children, both parents actually exercise

[3] As used here, direct domestic responsibilities are those that are fulfilled by activity which terminates immediately in the home or in some member of the family or in the family as a group; for example, a father repairing family furniture or helping his son with his lessons. Indirect domestic responsibilities, on the other hand, are those that are fulfilled by activities which terminate immediately outside of the home and the family group altogether, although they may be of crucial importance for the family's benefit and welfare. Work done in an office for a salary is an instance of the latter.

[4] Arensberg and Kimball, op. cit., pp. 46–50.

authority in roughly equal measure. In the daily round, as the girls are immediately under the jurisdiction of their mother, so the boys likewise are directly subject to the supervision of their father. When immediate disciplinary action is called for, especially where the boys are concerned, the farm wife rarely has to have recourse to the lame threat of punishment 'when your father gets home', since father is home to administer it here and now.

The affectional rapport between parents and children is also balanced in a manner that parallels the exercise of parental authority, although the pattern of the relationship is necessarily reversed. Since the exercise of direct authority demands considerable restraint between superior and subject, the warm, intimate relationships wherein affection is concretely conveyed flow more strongly from mother to son and from father to daughter. Neither the farmer nor his wife is placed in the exasperatingly ambivalent position of having to be for one and the same child the central source of authority and at the same time the haven of confidence and love. And so the Irish countryman's family manifests the pattern that is common throughout the rural communities of the Western world. The mother favours her sons while the father favours his daughters.[5]

The socialization of children, however, involves much more than satisfying the children's need for affection and exercising adequate authority over them. Just as important are the effective models of adulthood which parents provide in their own persons in the living context of family life. For it is mainly from these parental models, and as much by observation as by precept, that children learn the roles they are expected to fulfil as adults in their society. Here again there is a clear balance in the countryman's family. For the boys are in the same close association with their father that the girls are with their mother. And so they can learn not only the technical skills needed to manage a farm, but the more important general social skills, habits and attitudes that become a man, because they are in a position constantly to observe their father dealing as an adult man with other adult men and women and, indeed, with children.[6]

The distinction between economic and other forms of social activity which we have made here for purposes of description does not effectively exist in the minds of the country folk. For in their lives these activities merge into full, integrated roles that are simply designated by the terms husband and wife, father and mother, son and daughter. If we think, then, of the total role of father and mother we may further note that the status each enjoys in the rural community is roughly equivalent. The fact that a wife has subordinate authority to

[5] Ibid., pp. 57–9.
[6] Ibid., pp. 51–5.

14

her husband, much less the fact that the rural community defines that she should not invade spheres that are properly male any more than he should assume female activities and responsibilities, does not militate against this statement. On the contrary, since these are necessary consequences of a functional division of labour within the family upon which the status of the whole family and each of its members depends, the more faithfully she observes these role restrictions the more fully does she contribute to the family's status in the community. Consequently, the functional role of a farm wife and that of her husband combine and become identified with the family status in which each equally share. So much so that in the minds of the country folk '. . . the work of his [the farmer's] wife is complementary to his, and in its own sphere of as great importance to the livelihood and organization of the family unit'.[7]

This balanced integration of family life, which is the inner source of the small farm family's power, is bolstered by the integral solidarity of the families which make up the larger local community. No family is self-sufficient and must depend upon outside groups for help in many ways. But from a given rural family the lines of dependence span out in complex fashion, like the strands of a web, to other families in the rural community much more than to the other persons and groups which have intruded on the community from the greater outside world. With the latter the rural family tends to maintain relations that are largely impersonal and formally contractual. With the former there is a far fuller solidarity which arises from the extension to all of these families of the same sort of relationships that prevail between the members of the individual family itself. Indeed, such relationships are grounded on ties of kinship between families, and to a lesser extent upon the fact of long cohabitation in the same community. 'Friendliness' is the word by which the countryman summarizes these relationships, and friendliness is the force that fashions and conditions them.

Relationships of friendliness constitute a set of reciprocal obligations between farm families which, even when they mainly concern economic activities, are never motivated by purely economic incentives but by sentiments that span the full range of the social nature of the countryman. They govern a great many matters and are the basis for the co-ordination of the community's activity. For this co-ordination is largely determined by the clique of old men who make the crucial decisions about local affairs. These are the male heads of the families in the community, and in Frederic Le Play's apt phrase they are the true 'local authorities'. In their informal but regular meetings they discuss local personalities, problems, procedures and

[7] Ibid., pp. 48, 50.

15

policies, and their decisions carry the greatest weight in determining the course of community affairs.[8]

This clique also serves as a recreational and congeniality group for the older men of the community. It is but one of several such groups, all of which are similarly based upon age and sex. Thus, the young, unmarried men discernibly flock together in pursuit of their common recreational interests, as do the young unmarried girls. By the frequency and kind of interaction each carries on, these two groups are clearly distinguishable from each other and from the clique of older men.[9] As a result, recreational activity in the rural community is enjoyed largely by people whose families are all known, and in various ways related, to each other. And it goes on within a framework of age-sex groups which are projections of the age-sex divisions that characterize the family itself. The 'social' life of the countryside is mainly centred in these familial groupings and by comparison with these the recreational importance of the cinema or the dance-hall even today is decidedly secondary.

Friendliness is also the foundation for extensive economic co-operation. Perhaps the most graphic instance of this occurs during the spring ploughing, harrowing and sowing, and during the summer harvest when families related by kinship, whether immediate or extended, mutually help each other. Such help is accorded according to the principle that a favour received is a favour to be returned according to the measure in which it has been given. But such co-operation goes on through the full round of the year and, indeed, of life. As circumstances demand, it reciprocally binds the families of the community to provide tools, food, clothes and at times stock and even money. It requires families to supply personal services at times of childbirth, sickness, death and at important festive occasions. It governs the important matters of visiting and hospitality, and may often motivate a family to take in and raise the child of a deceased relative or friend. So deeply do these obligations bind that failure to fulfil them is normally countered by sanction—by estrangement, and even in extreme cases by virtual ostracism.[10]

This network of relationships is not limited to the families of the small farmers only, but reaches out to include nearly all the families of the rural community regardless of their status. To that extent it overlays class lines and contains and subordinates class distinctions. This is least true in regard to those people that occupy the highest station in the community—the clergymen, schoolteachers and other professionals, and the large landowners wherever they are present.

[8] Ibid., ch. x. Also Arensberg, *The Irish Countryman*, ch. iv.
[9] Arensberg and Kimball, op. cit., pp. 179–80, 193–201.
[10] Ibid., pp. 70–8.

The relations of the rest of the community to this group are somewhat more formal and segmental. But the number of people and families on this level are very few in the typical rural area, and the families below them comprise the great core of the community. Here at its heart the class structure of the community is relatively simple. In Ireland the occupations that are nearly wholly rural are those of the farm owner-operator and farm labourer, and these make up the bulk of the community. Intermingled with these are the owners of cross-roads' shops, contractors, a small variety of craftsmen—the most notable of whom are the smiths—the masons and the carpenters, and sundry non-farm labourers, such as creamery workers, navvies, and construction workers. Due to a combination of factors some of these, particularly shopkeepers, contractors and smiths, enjoy a status that roughly equals that of the small farmer, while the rest approximate the position of farm labourers. As a result, the class structure of the community is virtually restricted to these two levels.[11]

In this closely knit world, there is relatively little mobility from one class to another. Because land is scarce and his income meagre, a labouring man rarely has the chance to buy a farm and only with great difficulty can he muster sufficient dowry to marry a daughter into a farm. On the other hand, the farm family takes great pains to secure for its children in occupation and marriage the same status level in the community that it enjoys itself. If this cannot be done, parents and children alike are generally agreed that the children 'must travel', that is, migrate from the community. If emigration results in a son achieving success in the business world or in the professions, or in a daughter making a socially successful marriage, the reflected glory of their achievement may enhance the family's status and prestige in the community. In most cases, however, family status remains relatively stable from generation to generation. At the same time, there is also little residential movement within the community itself, so that virtually all the families in the place live in a house that their ancestral family has occupied for several generations. As a result, apart from emigration, which takes people out of the community altogether, the amount of social mobility within the community itself is very slight.

The class distinctions that mark the rural families are jealously guarded and are the subject of much comment in the conversation of the country people. But they are small, and the countrymen recognize them as such and commonly refer to manifestations of class consciousness in humorously belittling terms. And they are broken down in a thousand ways by the overriding 'friendliness' which is much more important and powerful in the rural community than class considerations. Much thicker than the water of occupational and

[11] Ibid., ch. xii.

17

economic differentiation is the blood of kinship and of the customary obligations woven by the immemorial interaction of neighbouring families who have resided in the same community for untold decades.[12]

Few of the features of family life so far described are peculiar to the Irish rural family and community. Nearly all of them, with some variations in detail, are found in the peasant family and community anywhere in Western Europe. Emigration from the rural community is perhaps the major exception to this statement. It is exceptional, and to that extent distinctively Irish, not so much by reason of the fact that it exists, as that for over a century the incidence of emigration from rural Ireland and from Ireland as a whole has been higher than for any other country in the Western world. This high rate of emigration from the land, together with a whole host of traits that characterize the Irish countryman, in turn are related to a complicated set of practices concerning marriage and inheritance whose pattern is peculiarly Irish.

The farm family in Ireland is, quite naturally, concerned about its own continuity on its holding from one generation to another. Since the farm is normally too small to make further subdivision economically feasible, family continuity demands that the farm pass from the parental to the filial generation intact. In effect, this means that only one son can inherit the homestead, while the other children must leave the family home whether or not they remain in the rural community. In Ireland as a whole the customs governing inheritance do not specify which of the sons shall be heir to the land. There is no nationally uniform practice of primogeniture nor of ultimogeniture, and the only general rule is that the farmer himself chooses the son who is to succeed him.[13] Although, presumably, this empowers the father to decide when he shall designate his heir and when he shall hand over to him the ownership and management of the farm, by customary practice and in the normal course of events he abdicates only at his heir's marriage. A partial reason for this is that custom also imposes on the farmer the obligation to dower his daughters as far as possible—an obligation which, in the event of his premature death, may devolve upon his heir. A major source of the money needed for this comes from the dowry of the heir's wife which goes, not to the newly married couple, but to the heir's father and which he in turn uses for his daughters' dowries.

This peculiar combination of customs enables the small farm family to achieve continuity on its holding and thus to retain its

---

[12] Thus the same sort of social co-operation which farm families give to each other also exists, on a somewhat diminished scale, between the families of the labouring man and of the farmer. Ibid., pp. 263–74.

[13] Ibid., pp. 63, 107–9.

identity and status in the community. The conjunction of the heir's marriage with his accession to the farm, as well as the use of his wife's dowry for the dowries of his sisters, makes it possible for the family to effect a smooth and realistic transfer of a delicately balanced group enterprise from one generation to another.[14]

Such a benefit costs a price, but it is one the farm family is willing to pay. For all the children who remain at home, it inevitably results in their continued subordination to their parents and so in the postponement of their occupational and full social adulthood until the marriage of the heir. The marriage of the heir is, consequently, the central event in the cycle of the rural family. Upon it depends the marriage of the daughters of the family, the dispersal of the other sons from the family homestead to take their lives in their own hands elsewhere, and the virtual retirement of the farmer and his wife, though they usually continue to dwell on the farm till they die. Therefore, it is of the greatest significance that this crucial event occurs extremely late in the lives of the Irish countrymen. For the stark fact is that on the average farmers do not marry until they are about thirty-six years of age.[15]

To explain why this practice of very late marriage has arisen in rural Ireland is difficult, largely because we have not yet sufficient knowledge of the great social transformation that occurred there between 1840 and 1880 when the present rural family system evolved.[16] But in any case, its effects on family and community relations, rather than its causes, interest us here. For granted that this practice exists and together with the other elements that comprise the rural system of marriage is considered traditional, it is understandable that a man, himself under severe and extensive subordination to his father until his mid-thirties, is not likely to relinquish the responsibility and power of his man's estate until he is in his mid-seventies, so that the cycle constantly perpetuates itself. In these circumstances, the early marriage of the heir would constitute a premature displacement of parental power and would disrupt the delicate balance of the group

---

[14] Ibid., ch. vii.

[15] In 1946 the average age at marriage for men in all rural areas in Ireland was 34·7 years. For farmers and farm managers it was 36·9, while for agricultural workers it was 32·1. *v. Memorandum on the Age at Marriage, 1946*, issued in mimeographed form by the Central Statistics Office, Dublin, 1952, Table 1A, p. 2 and Table 6, p. 11. *v.* ch. iii, pp. 68–9, 75.

[16] It may be well to note that the present system is traditional, but not in the sense that it stretches back over centuries in Ireland. It is, in fact, something less than one hundred years old. For an illuminating analysis of the quite different system of family life that prevailed in Ireland prior to 1845, *v.* K. H. Connell, *The Population of Ireland 1750–1845* (Oxford, 1950), ch. iii; and George O'Brien, *The Economic History of Ireland from the Union to the Famine* (London, 1921).

enterprise. Similarly the early marriage or emigration of any of the other sons tends to diminish that power and impair that balance.

In the nature of the case, this complex of relationships of father and son relative to the land, if considered only in itself, constitutes a strong centrifugal thrust that tends to drive the sons away from the family and, indeed, from the rural community altogether. To enumerate the centrifugal factors present in the structure of the rural farm family is to appreciate their force: the lack of any binding custom specifying which son will succeed to the holding; the father's tendency to conceal his selection of the heir and to postpone long into his old age the transfer of the farm; the consequent necessity for the sons to remain celibate and at the same time extremely subordinate to their father who treats them as boys and refers to them as 'boys' even when they are in their thirties; and finally, a son's fear that he may sustain all this in vain if the father designates a brother as an heir.[17] Such a combination of circumstances constitutes a powerful motive for sons, often enough all of them, to take life in their own hands, to leave the land and its frustrations, and, as so many do, to make their own way in Dublin or Birmingham or Boston.

However, there is a counteracting centripetal mechanism built into the fabric of the rural family. This is the strong, preferential love of the rural mother for her sons. She is the magnetic centre of the family and her cohesive power is affection. This love, which leads her 'to slave' for her sons and to demand that her daughters do likewise, cushions the son's hard lot. It mollifies the constant rub of his subordination to his father. It bars overtures to a marriage that would, from the viewpoint of the family's interest, be premature. At the same time it compensates for the long postponement of adulthood both sexually and in the assumption of manly responsibility. Furthermore, the bond of affection between mother and son bridges the distance emigration creates between the emigrant and his family, and insures that in the city or on alien soil he will not forget to contribute financially to the family by remittance. But its primary effect is to prevent the emigration of all the sons from the land and, in regard to the sons who must eventually migrate, to postpone that event as long as possible. There is little doubt that without this cohesive relationship between mother and sons male emigration from the land would be even greater in rural Ireland than it has been. This relationship has other drawbacks, however. Domination by affection often gives greater power than domination by authority and generates equal reluctance to let that power lapse. Hence, it is not infrequent in rural Ireland that even after the father dies, maternal affection obstructs the marriage of the inheriting son, even to the point of endangerign

[17] Arensberg and Kimball, op. cit., p. 56.

20

the continuity of the family on the holding. This is the basis for the conflict between mother-in-law and daughter-in-law that is so intense in Ireland, the prospect of which leads so many sons to refuse 'to bring another woman in on my mother'. This is evidenced by the remarkable number of men in the countryside working the farm for their widowed mother through their forties and even into their fifties, who will not marry until she dies and who, by then confirmed bachelors, may never marry at all.[18]

This entire web of circumstances also conditions the relationships between rural parents and their daughters. It works indirectly to delay the daughter's marriage since her dowry is in great part supplied out of the dowry of the wife of the inheriting son. As the same set of conditions and attitudes towards marriage is rife among the unmarried men of the community, the daughter's opportunities on the local marriage mart are meagre.[19] This constitutes another centrifugal push acting upon the daughters also to leave for the town or city and, indeed, at an earlier age than the boys because of the natural premium put upon earlier marriage for a girl. As there is less expectation that a girl will fall heir to the holding, the forces binding her to her home are correspondingly weaker. A girl, too, comes in for a large share of affection. She is more openly favoured that way by her father than are the boys. Her brothers, whom she serves well, are fond of her. And she does not deeply resent the favour her mother shows her brothers for she appreciates that, while his role in the family's future is crucial, a boy's lot under his father is hard and in sympathy and family loyalty she is willing to try to ease it. Between her sister and herself there are little grounds for rivalry. They are all in the same boat, and they will all be adequately dowered, in the normal course of events, by their father or inheriting brother. Furthermore, her mother loves the daughter well for all her favouritism towards her sons, and through that love, as well as through the living proof from her life of the power so to be gained, she impresses on her daughter a strong attachment to the mother-wife ideal. All of this makes up the emotional ground of filial piety which, in certain circumstances, will keep a girl at home to care for a widower father or a widowed mother—especially if all the boys are gone—or even a bachelor brother who has succeeded to the holding. But not all this compounded love for a daughter reaches the restraining pitch and

[18] Ibid., pp. 54–60, 127–8.

[19] This is evidenced by the late age at which rural women marry. The average age at marriage for women in all rural areas in 1946 was 28·7 years. *v. Memorandum on Age at Marriage, 1946*, Table 1B, p. 3. It is further manifested by the fact that in 1951 fully a quarter of the women in all rural areas are unmarried by the age of forty. *v. Census of Population of Ireland, 1951*, II, Pt. II (Dublin, 1953), Table 7C, 33. *v.* ch. iii, pp. 67–70 and Appendix I, pp. 255–6, *infra*.

force of maternal love for the sons. The total result is that normally a girl is even freer than the boys to migrate from the land and likewise more susceptible to the lure of the city. This appears in the predominance of single women among the migrants to Dublin and the emigrants abroad.[20]

Obviously, the total structure of family relationships which we have described concentrates the maximum of power in the hands of the aged and in effect makes the Irish rural community a gerontocracy. This has had profound repercussions on the national social structure of Ireland and, as we shall see later, it creates an important area of tension between rural Ireland and Dublin where the pattern of life tends to redress this balance of power in favour of the young.

In view of the organization of the rural family and community, we can now begin to understand and appreciate the sentiments and values which are characteristic of the Irish countryman. A substantial set of these values stems directly from the way in which his life is organized and is related to the maintenance and the smooth functioning of the family and community organization.

Like every European countryman whose family and community life is rooted in the working of a small farm holding, the Irish countryman has a deep love of the land and a strong desire for the continuity of the traditional family holding. In his mind, therefore, the family as a group has a certain relative pre-eminence over the individual, and this is reflected in the obligations of filial piety which are geared to secure the perpetuity of the family on the land and its position in the community. While he is not indifferent to any opportunities for improving his own and his family's status, this status is largely acquired rather than achieved and he is principally concerned with preserving it. Since his family's welfare and status are so intricately bound up with the familial relations of his own family to those of his kin and his neighbours in the local community which have been elaborated in the long informal process by which custom comes into being, he puts his trust in the personal and particularistic ties that make up the web and woof of the community and in the accumulated wisdom of tradition.

Values such as these the Irish countryman has in common with countrymen everywhere in Europe. But in addition he has other values which are distinctively his own and which flow directly from aspects of family and community organization which are peculiarly Irish. The uniquely advanced age at which parents marry and accede to control of the farm, and in turn relinquish it to their successors, has profound and singular effects upon the obligations of filial piety. It makes for a pronounced glorification and veneration of the aged, especially of the authority of the father and the affection and devotion

[20] Arensberg and Kimball, op. cit., pp. 65-7.

of the mother. And this, in the total situation we have described, leads to the sanctioned expectation of prolonged celibacy, subordination to parental control and, in special circumstances, of the sacrifice of individual achievement through occupation and through marriage in the interests of family welfare. This has resulted in the creation of a process of socialization of the children which instils in them a deep sense of inferiority, of submissiveness and many other notable juvenile traits.[21] And these in turn so intensify the traditionalism and conservatism common to countrymen everywhere that the Irish countryman is among the most conservative and wary of innovation of any people in the Western world.

All of these values of the countryman are clearly derived from the way he organizes his family and community and they directly support and implement that organization. But the values of the countryman are not limited to these. First of all, there are values among country people in Ireland whose source lies on levels of national organization beyond the family level and in historical contacts with other people. This is particularly true of the countryman's high respect for the professions and the premium he puts on locating a son in one of them, as well as his acceptance of certain class values and norms of behaviour which are characteristically English and Anglo-Irish. More certainly, perhaps, the countryman's distrust and jaundiced view of government in general, and even of his own government, today appears to be a traditional attitude spawned in long years of oppression under an alien power whose rule he constantly considered as unjust, illegal and evil.

Another category of rural values still persists in the Irish cultural stream and their presence appears to be due to social inertia, whatever may have been their origin. These are the whole set of superstitious beliefs about fairies and the 'wee people' and their pishogues which the countryman, though in constantly lessening measure, still entertains. An interesting attempt has been made to interpret these beliefs as symbolically and functionally related to the social structure of the rural family and community. However this may be, it is certain that they are residues of the long period when education was virtually non-existent in rural Ireland.[22]

But there is another set of values of paramount importance to the countryman which are not merely instrumental to the organization of his family and community, but which have become imbedded in his historical tradition because they have been accepted by generations of countrymen—and indeed by virtually all Irishmen—as supreme in-

---

[21] Ibid., pp. 51–60. Is it too bold to suggest that the traits of the 'Fighting Irish' simply confirm this statement?

[22] *v.* Arensberg, *The Irish Countryman*, ch. vi; and ch. ii, pp. 27–8, *infra.*

trinsic values and goods in their own right. These are the Catholic beliefs and values which make up his religion and which have such a constant modifying effect upon the organization of his family and community that without them the Irish countryman and his family can never be fully understood.[23] The countryman is not entirely un-affected by the secularism of the Western world with which Ireland is in contact and which we shall have to discuss when dealing with life in Dublin. But the influence of secularism on the rural community in Ireland has been relatively small and has not seriously changed the countryman's traditional Irish Catholic beliefs.

The Irish countryman believes unquestioningly that the Roman Catholic Church is a divinely created institution whose objective is to bring all men to their divinely appointed last end which is eternal life. Eternal life, as his Church teaches, consists in a special knowledge and love of God whose culmination is in the direct face-to-face vision of God in Heaven. The countryman is aware that by nature man can only know and love God indirectly; that is, through his knowledge of creatures. By nature, therefore, man has neither the right to the direct vision of God nor the native powers to receive it. Consequently, the countryman believes that eternal life is a supernatural state—literally, *above* man's nature. As such, it is a gratuitous gift of God to man.[24] This gift, first given to man at his creation and lost by Adam's

[23] Although a great deal has been written about the subject in general literature dealing with Ireland, the effects of the religious tradition of the Irish, let alone of the countryman, upon the social behaviour and attitudes of the people has never been systematically studied from a sociological point of view. Arensberg and Kimball leave the matter virtually untouched. The present analysis, then, except where it refers to essential and universal Catholic teaching, must be by way of a suggestive working hypothesis. But it is not on that account unsupported by empirical evidence. The attitudes and practices of immigrants into Dublin as reported by their children and often by themselves are one source of evidence, and this evidence we shall consider in our study of the New Dubliners. The reports from the rural people whom I interviewed, but which I cannot present in their entirety here because of spatial limitations, are another source.

[24] It is essential to the understanding of any Catholic society to keep in mind this precise meaning which the term 'supernatural' has in Catholic teaching. This meaning is not identical with that attached to the term in modern anthropological and sociological literature which has broader connotations. Cf., for example, T. Parsons, *The Social System* (Glencoe, and London, 1951), pp. 369–70. In Catholic doctrine the supernatural does not refer to the transcendence of God which is a natural attribute of divinity. Neither does it refer primarily to the miraculous intervention of God in the processes of nature which He has created. The supernatural is not an order of causes invoked to explain natural events, even though in practice it is so invoked often enough, in Ireland as elsewhere. In the constant, universal teaching of the Catholic Church, the supernatural order means that God has gratuitously destined man for a final activity that is beyond the powers of human nature or of any created nature, namely, to know and love God directly as He knows and loves Himself. The achievement of this end requires

24

original sin, is bestowed on man today through the merits of Jesus Christ who is the natural Son of God made man. The Irish country-man therefore is convinced that those who believe in Christ and obey His commandments will continually possess eternal life by preserving within themselves the gift of sanctifying grace and its accompanying gifts which make them adopted children of God and thereby entitled to share in the life proper to God. Such persons, he believes, form the society of the faithful who are members of the Kingdom of God and of the Mystical Body of Christ which is the Church. Christ, however, has given this society a definite form and institutional structure. On the one hand, He has vested in the Pope as the successor to Peter, and in the bishops, the authority to teach His doctrine authentically and to govern the Church through legislative, judicial and executive powers. On the other, He has established the sacraments as the normal, institutionalized channels through which men may receive an increase of sanctifying grace, or regain it if they have lost it through grievous or mortal sin.

All this the Irish countryman believes in common with all Catholics everywhere. But within the range of this commonly held and orthodox doctrine, there are in the Catholic Church many distinctive schools of thought which differ among themselves in regard to the numerous problems which this rich core of basic doctrine contains. Such theo-logical currents have great sociological importance and the socio-logist who ignores them does so at his peril. For historically these different theological streams have gained greater currency and in-fluence in different Catholic societies, and they account for many of the notable differences that are to be observed between the social structures and cultures of societies which are all Catholic at base. The specific doctrinal tradition to which Ireland and the Irish countryman in particular has fallen heir is the Augustinian.[25]

that God supplement the human powers of knowledge and love by special action of His own, namely, grace, to which nature of itself has no claim. This doctrine of the *donum gratis datum*, despite popular distortions and misunderstandings, is the most essential element in the conception of life that a Catholic society entertains, and it influences the entire structure of such a society. To overlook it or to misinterpret it, would cause serious distortions.

[25] As a stream of theological thought Augustinianism (also called Augustinism) is made up of a wide variety of doctrinal movements. Indeed, no Western Chris-tian theology has been unaffected by St. Augustine. Still, Augustinianism can be distinguished on many counts from other theological schools, the most notable of which is Thomism. *v.* A. A. Cayre, 'The Great Augustinism', in *Theology Digest*, I & II (1953–54), 169–73. E. Portalie, 'Augustine of Hippo', in *The Catholic Encyclopedia* (16 vols., New York, 1907–14), II, 84–104; 'Augustinisme', in *Dictionnaire de Théologie Catholique* (15 tomes in 37 vols., Paris, 1925–), Tome II, Pt. II, cols. 2501–61; and 'Augustinianisme', ibid., cols. 2485–2501. H.-X. Arquillière, *L'Augustinisme Politique* (Paris, 1934). J. Forget, 'Jansenius', in *The*

By comparison with other orthodox views within the general framework of Catholic doctrine, the Augustinian tradition lays relatively greater emphasis on the weakness and evil to which human nature is prone as a result of original sin. By the same token, it attributes relatively less efficacy to natural knowledge and human action and relatively more validity to God's revelation and more power to the action of God's grace. Under the impact of this particular Catholic conception of life, aided and abetted by the traditionalism characteristic of the rural areas, the Irish countryman has acquired a more than average distrust of native human reason. As a Catholic he cannot and does not deny the validity of rational thought, but he tends to be quite suspicious of the pride of the mind and so wary of ultimate rationalism that he shies away from reasoned discussions of high truths, especially about matters of faith. The tradition he inherits tends towards a certain historical and theological positivism in regard to the major truths and values of life, and, together with other historical factors, has led him to an intensified reliance upon the teaching power of the Church as voiced by the clergy. At the same time, while appreciating the need for positive good works, he is inclined to place relatively greater emphasis on those which are directly concerned with obtaining grace and relatively lesser store by simple ethical behaviour. And finally, although he is certain that man's bodily nature with its emotions is at root good, he is rather more suspicious of it and deals with it somewhat more severely. As a result he inclines to a jaundiced view of sex and a generally ascetic outlook which places a high premium upon continence, penance and, in most spheres of life, on abstemiousness.[26]

Catholic Encyclopedia, VIII, 285–94. A. Gaudel, 'Peché originel', in *Dictionnaire de Théologie Catholique*, Tome XII, Pt. 1, cols. 275–606.

For Augustinian influence in Ireland, see John Ryan, *Irish Monasticism* (New York, 1931). L. Gougaud, *Christianity in Celtic Lands* (London, 1932). Eoin MacNeill, *St. Patrick* (London, 1934). J. B. Bury, *The Life of St. Patrick* (New York, 1905). Philip Hughes, *A History of the Church* (3 vols., New York, 1934–47), II, *passim*. Máire and Liam de Paor, *Early Christian Ireland* (London, 1958), chs. i and ii.

[26] Generally speaking, Arensberg and Kimball attribute the countryman's attitude towards sex almost exclusively to the structure of life in the rural community. *v.* Arensberg and Kimball, op. cit., ch. ix. Granted the profound influence social structure has on such a basic matter, a purely structural-functional analysis is hard put to explain adequately the quite ascetic sexual morality of the Irish countryside. If the family system of rural Ireland is essentially that of all northern and western Europe as well as of the United States, as these authors declare, why is such a strong code characteristic of the Irish community, but notably less characteristic of other rural communities equally Catholic, such as those in Italy, Spain, Austria, Bavaria? If one retorts that these are not 'equally as Catholic' as Ireland, he really cedes the point for they are all about equally rural and similar in social structure. More pertinently, as we shall see, an attitude

All of these values which do not derive directly from the countryman's family and community organization, religious and non-reli-
gious alike, are nevertheless integrated with that organization and
contribute their share of influence upon it. They redouble its traditional character. They also account for the organizational emphasis
that is placed by the rural community on formal religious and especially sacramental activity. And at least partly, they influence the
general tendency of the countryman to identify the sphere of individual and family morality with that of public morality. Above all,
these religious values especially buttress family and community organization in its strong enforcement of continence. They also probably contribute to the lack of communal festivities and the consequent
drabness of life which is notable in rural Ireland and which is a real, if
not precisely measurable, force motivating countrymen to leave the
land for Dublin's fair city.

THE NEW DUBLINERS

If you come into Dublin on a train out of the West, as the average
immigrant from the countryside does, the confluence of railroads and
highways from all over the country, the compacted houses, factories
and ornate public buildings that slide by your window, the activities
in the harbour and on the Liffey River and the incessant traffic in the
streets overwhelmingly impress upon you the fact that here life is
organized on quite a different basis than in the small, quiet, rural
community you have left. All of these things make for a very palpable
realization of what the incoming countryman has known only in an
abstract way: that it is in its organization that Dublin differs most
from the countryside. For Dublin is truly a modern metropolis where
the great organizations of government, industry, commerce, education, communication, art and entertainment are centred and mesh.

Actually, of course, Dublin appreciably differs from the countryside in other, less tangible respects of which the incoming countryman
initially, perhaps, is not so aware. Just because it is the capital and the
one major metropolis in the Irish Republic, Dublin is much more in
contact with the world outside of Ireland. As a result it has been
penetrated much more deeply than the countryside by that world and
has become much more intimately engaged with ideas and values that
stem from that world. These ideological currents that wash into

similar to that of the countryman is far from uncommon in a city such as Dublin
—and among New Dubliners and Old Dubliners to boot—whose social structure
differs so radically from that of the countryside. Structural-functional explanations of attitudes do hold up to a point. But world-views and their ethical consequences also have their special effect.

Dublin through diverse channels are many and varied. But the current whose force has been most strongly felt in modern Dublin is that of rationalistic secularism which has been associated with the modernization of Dublin itself.[27] For Dublin's recent development has been directly influenced by the growth of industrialization in Europe and particularly in England in the last one hundred years. Thus it has occurred at a time when English society, having already passed through the several phases of religious thought associated with the earlier stages of the Industrial Revolution, has given wide acceptance to secularism. In Dublin conflict between basic systems of value is now mainly between traditional Irish Catholic views and secularistic views rather than traditional Protestant conceptions.

The major values which secularism embodies are the supremacy of human nature, reason and action, and the sufficiency of human nature to perfect itself by its own unaided powers. This necessarily entails a rejection of any supernatural dimension in life, and therefore of the notion of original sin and of redemption by God through Christ, as well as of the existence, let alone the efficacy, of any supernatural influence such as grace. It likewise includes the repudiation of a transcendent, yet personal and provident God; or if it concedes the possibility of the existence of such a Being, it doubts God's involvement in man's life or, at any rate, man's capacity to know how and in what direction God may influence human affairs. Man's destiny, in consequence, resides entirely within himself and must be achieved without reference to any putative moral law originating with a personal and concerned God. As a result, secularism assesses religion as having only therapeutic value, whether sublimational or opiate, whereby it may contribute to organizational efficiency by insuring,

[27] I use the word 'secularism' here because of its appropriateness in designating the substance of the views and values to which I refer. These conceive the temporal process of the observable cosmos as the only reality extant or, at least, knowable and therefore of relevance to human life and society. Consequently, 'secularization' here means the process whereby such a set of views becomes accepted on a widening scale. Such usage has precedent in sociological and anthropological literature. For instance, 'secularization' is used in this sense by Robert Redfield in *The Folk Culture of the Yucatán* (Chicago, 1941), esp. ch. ix. So is 'secularism' by Harry Elmer Barnes as edited by Becker in Howard Becker and Harry Elmer Barnes, *Social Thought from Lore to Science* (2nd ed., 2 vols.; Washington, D.C., 1952), I, 540. But we should note that the term 'secular' has a wider meaning as used in the sacred-secular theory of Becker, Hill and others where it signifies 'readiness to accept or initiate social change'. See Becker in ch. 6, 'Current Sacred Theory and Its Development', in Howard Becker and Alvin Boskov (eds.), *Modern Sociological Theory in Continuity and Change* (New York, 1957), p. 142. I am sure that secularism as I have defined it is included in Becker's formulation. But I use it in this restricted sense only and not in the expanded sense which identifies secular society with rapidly changing society, as opposed to 'sacred' society which is traditionalistic and relatively impervious to change.

for those who happen to need it, mental and emotional health and by promoting effective morale. But it discounts religious knowledge as being in any way valid knowledge of objective reality and so, except for purely therapeutic purposes, it tends to isolate religion from the political, economic and educational spheres of life and, more and more, from the family and the community altogether. Finally, although man is to achieve his destiny alone, probably the more prevalent secularistic view of man is mechanistic rather than humanistic. Man does not carve out his niche in the universe by the force of his will which asserts his inalienable self, but by finding through the good offices of reason the laws inherent within him which determine the proper equilibrium of his native forces that will yield the healthy personality and the good society.

Of the major forms of secularism the one that, up to the moment, has had the greatest impact on Dublin has been the individualistic variety which has grown out of the classical liberalism of nineteenth-century England rather than the socialism which stems largely from Marx and which has had wider acceptance on the continent. Dublin has not been impervious to socialist influence particularly through the agency of the labour union movement and especially during the first quarter of the century. But generally speaking conservative liberal forces have made greater headway than socialistic movements in the Irish capital. Consequently, the more current species of secularism in Dublin makes the primary agent of naturalistic perfection, both of the human person and of the human community, the human individual rather than the human group. As a result, in theory at least, it tends to subordinate the group—government, business, the family—to the individual.

Merely to describe this complex of ideas is to indicate how forcefully it clashes with the Irishman's system of Catholic ideas and values. The fact that these secularistic values are given much more effective voice in Dublin than in the countryside means that the conflict between the two sets of values is much sharper in Dublin than in rural Ireland and we shall eventually have to appraise the effects of this conflict upon the New Dubliners.

But the countryman entering Dublin undoubtedly is not as aware of this conflict as he is of the more tangible difference between Dublin and the rural community which lies in the organizational structure of the city. For in Dublin the primary influence upon community life and affairs is no longer exerted by the family and groups that are kindred to the family to which the countryman is accustomed, but by large, impersonal and non-familistic organizations, particularly of business and of government.

Whether they be governmental or economic, these large-scale organizations in Dublin have for their goal the production of goods and services according to a specific rational code of efficiency.[28] Both the economic concerns which are motivated by profit, and the governmental agencies which, theoretically at least, are not so motivated, have in common the express aim of producing the maximum of quality goods or services at a minimum of cost and labour. This is judged by a complex set of standards that are determined by objective analysis of the facts of experience. Although this goal is never perfectly realized, its legitimacy is as commonly accepted in Dublin as it is elsewhere in modern industrial society and with the same result. As a consequence, the ascendancy of power and control over community organization and affairs has shifted from private families linked together by ties of kinship and common residence to foster familial ideals and interests, and has passed into the hands of a comparatively small number of large impersonal organizations which are interlocked for quite a different purpose. The manner in which these large-scale corporations are internally organized, as well as the manner in which they are mutually interrelated, are central factors in producing the differences that are to be found between the family of the countryman and the New Dubliner.

The clearest indication of this shift in power is to be found in the ownership and control of property devoted to production and service. There are in Dublin, perhaps more than in any other comparable city in Great Britain or the United States, shops and stores that are family owned and operated, but even in Dublin the number of these are relatively few. In the course of time, productive property and its administration has almost wholly passed out of the hands of private families and has come under the control of a relatively small group of large corporations, public and private.

Internally, these corporations are organized on the basis of a formal rational analysis of the most effective way of relating to one another material, machines, men and their operations in order to reach the end of the greatest practicable productivity and service. The criterion

[28] By 'rational' I here refer to what Max Weber defines as a course of action based on consciously reasoned 'expectations as "conditions" or "means" ' for the ends chosen by an individual or a group. There often seems to be a tendency in modern sociological literature to limit the term 'rational' to this meaning which Weber called *zweckrational*. But this does not exhaust the meaning of the word. In addition, action may also be called rational 'in terms of rational orientation to an absolute value . . . involving a conscious belief in the absolute value of some ethical, aesthetic, religious, or other form of behaviour, entirely for its own sake and independently of any prospects of external success'. This Weber called *wertrational*, and I shall use 'rational' in this sense later when discussing the approach of New Dubliners to religious ideas and values. *v.* Max Weber, *The Theory of Social and Economic Organization*, trans. A. M. Henderson and Talcott Parsons (New York, 1947), pp. 115–18; 184–6; 337–9.

whereby this effectiveness is judged is the pragmatic crucible of observable qualities and experience. It is no argument against this to note that many a concern in Dublin, especially newly founded concerns, simply try to ape the patterns of organization which have been successful elsewhere and so tend to accept them on traditional grounds, for the industrial tradition embodies the need to adhere to this formal code of efficiency. Neither is the fact that in every case, especially in Dublin, a host of other factors—and principally familial factors—are at work to modify these central organizational principles so that they are never realized in all their abstract perfection. Despite these limitations, in each case this set of principles has the primacy in fixing the general structure of these organizations and their relationships to one another.

All of this is simply saying that in the main the business concerns and governmental bodies of Dublin organize themselves according to established principles of economic organization and of public administration current in the industrial nations of the West. But it is worth spelling this out in order later to appreciate in detail the transforming impact these principles have on the family of the New Dubliners. Each public or private corporation, even the quite modest one, divides its jobs and their interrelationships, and especially its offices of authority and their hierarchy, on the basis of an empirically tested analysis of the pattern logically most likely to achieve its purpose. The same rule is applied to the choice of persons who are to fill these offices and perform these tasks. As a result, the corporation rarely employs an already established group and almost never a family. Rather, it selects individuals who are assigned to their position, given their rank in the company and promoted according to their individual ability as established by objective, impersonal tests and records of achievement.

In such circumstances, the force of age and sex as the grounds for the division of labour and authority sharply declines. Seniority remains important, but more as an evidence of proven competence and ability than as a claim on the corporation's gratitude for loyal services that can no longer be as effectively tendered as before. On the other hand, because it tends impersonally to select the competent individual, the corporation in Dublin has opened up jobs and occupational careers for women on a hitherto unprecedented scale, and employment and promotional policies that are still discriminatory against women stem less from any internal principle of organization within the corporation than from the requirements of outside groups, and especially of the family.

The same general principles of efficiency largely determine the relationships between the various corporations in Dublin, and these in

31

turn profoundly affect the structure of the entire Dublin community. It is more economical in every sense of the word for corporations which are constantly dealing with each other—governmental as well as private—to set themselves up near each other in one central locale. And it is precisely this geographic centralization of productive and service facilities and of labour that has made Dublin the economic and political capital of Ireland and the large metropolis that it is.

However, as we have already noted, these principles of efficient organization are affected in many ways by the needs of familial organization and by familial values. The combination of these two produces another striking feature that distinguishes Dublin from the rural community. On the one hand, the bureaucratic system of ranks within the corporation establishes between the people who occupy them a complex set of differentials in income, prestige and power. On the other hand, principles of family organization require that these differentials be shared by the families of the individuals employed by the corporation. Because the levels of rank in Dublin corporations are many, the result is that the class levels in the community also become more numerous and heterogeneous. Thus the class structure of Dublin is more complex than that of the rural community.[29] At the same time, because the system of ranks within the corporation is open and the corporation fosters the promotion of capable individuals, there is considerable movement of families from one class level to another; and in the Dublin community at large the amount of social mobility, which usually involves residential mobility, is very great by contrast to the relative class rigidity of the countryside.

On the whole, then, the manner in which the large corporations of Dublin organize themselves and their mutual relationships has, by comparison with the rural community, changed the fundamental form of community solidarity. Where the solidarity of the rural community is pre-eminently inter-familial and rests on intense interaction between families which is particularistic and diffuse, the structure of Dublin promotes the co-operation of specialized individuals who interact in a universalistic, specific, impersonal and segmental way.[30]

[29] The process of stratifying people into a complex class structure and the expansion of the bases of co-operation between individuals to grounds other than kinship and friendliness begins in towns much smaller and less differentiated than Dublin. *v.* Kimball, op. cit., pp. iv–v, 253.

[30] The concepts signified by the terms 'particularistic' and 'universalistic' are those of Talcott Parsons and are familiar to the professional sociologist. For the benefit of the general reader, a particularistic relationship is one that is based upon who a particular person is relative to another particular person or object, such as, for example, the relationship expressed when a man says: 'I must help him because he is my brother.' On the other hand, relationships that are independent of such particular, personal considerations and are based upon objective,

This does not, of course, mean that inter-familial solidarity ceases in Dublin altogether. But it does mean that inter-familial solidarity declines sharply and that the most extensive relationship in the city becomes the interaction of specialized individuals.

Geared to this world, the New Dubliner's family differs significantly from that of the countryman in its internal structure. The most glaring difference is that typically the New Dubliner's family does not own and operate property productive of income and as a result it not only has lost central control over such productive activities, but has ceased to be a collective domestic unit of production. The activities of its members upon which its livelihood depends are not, as in the countryman's family, performed together at home but are dispersed and performed individually outside the home. Because of this elemental change among the New Dubliners, the wife in the usual case no longer participates in activity which produces income, while the husband is taken out of the home and away from the family for the major portion of the working day. This economic mutation radically transforms the balance of labour and responsibility between family members which is so characteristic of the countryman's family. On the marital axis, the New Dubliner husband and wife no longer share direct domestic responsibilities in roughly equal fashion, but the major portion of these now falls upon the wife's shoulders.

Despite the fact that the New Dubliner wife no longer engages in productive activity, she must perforce assume the major portion of the total economic load. Unlike the rural wife whose husband divides these activities with her, the New Dubliner wife with few exceptions is responsible for virtually all of the exchange and service activities so important for the family. She manages the budget, does nearly all the buying, is responsible not only for the cooking and cleaning, but also for the household repairs and entertainment, and for the most part is the actual representative of the family to the immediate local community. More significantly, the wife carries the greater responsibility in the matter of raising the children. In the actual exercise of authority and discipline, it is she who has to watch, admonish, give orders and apply the sanctions which usually must be administered here and now—for she alone is here to do it now. She also has the greater responsibility in providing the children with adult example and, in regard to her sons, this presents her with an especially harassing problem. The association of mother and daughter that we have noted in the rural family remains much the same and the New Dubliner

impersonal characteristics and norms such as those between doctor and patient, employer and employee, etc., are universalistic. *v.* Talcott Parsons, *Essays in Sociological Theory Pure and Applied* (Glencoe, Ill., 1949), pp. 192, 195–7; and *The Social System*, pp. 61–5.

mother can be an effective role model for her girls. But her sons, as they grow into adolescence, cannot look to her as an adult model for the simple reason that she is a woman and they are going to be men. Within the normal New Dubliner household, where the husband comes home tired from an exhausting day, there is no adequate model of manhood for the sons to contemplate and to imitate and they must, often without complete success, look outside of the home for substitute guides as to what a man should be.

Inevitably, in this situation the wife's authority over family affairs increases considerably and her relationship to her husband changes significantly. Where the rural wife is generally subordinate to her spouse, the New Dubliner wife has equal authority with her husband and, though technically he is still the 'head of the house', both husband and wife feel, act and speak of themselves as 'partners'. This very fact modifies the delicate set of affectional relationships between parents and children. Because he no longer exerts constant daily authority over his sons in the rural fashion, the New Dubliner father, while maintaining essentially the same relationship with his daughters, is much more companionable with his sons in their late adolescence and they in turn are much more relaxed, open and frank with him. But in regard to all of her children, and especially her sons, the New Dubliner wife is in an ambivalent position. By position and by cultural definition she, above all, is supposed to be the source of warmth, affection and intimate, friendly relations, and she strives to maintain this role especially, like the rural mother, with her sons. Yet force of circumstance puts her in the central position of authority and this tends to reduce intimacy between her and her children and to beget restraint and even, under certain conditions, resentment.

But the increased responsibilities which devolve upon the New Dubliner wife do not result in a corresponding increase in her status as such in the community. On the contrary, since the primary grounds for status in Dublin, as in all the industrial nations of the West, normally lies in income-producing activity which she no longer shares with her husband, the status of wife and mother is generally lower in Dublin than it is in the countryside. As a result, as we shall see, there is a tendency among New Dubliner women to attempt to redress the balance by activities which are often in conflict with the traditional role of mother and wife in much the same fashion as women do elsewhere in the industrial West.

Internally, then, the New Dubliner's family by comparison with the family of the countryman is unbalanced in the distribution of direct family responsibilities in the sphere of economic activity, and consequently in the spheres of parental authority and example, of affectional relationships between family members, and of the individual status of husband and wife. The most notable consequences of this transformation in Ireland are the decline in the range of parental control and the power of the older generation, and in the earlier age at which children reach full social adulthood.

Under urban conditions where the family no longer controls and operates a productive holding, the patterns of inheritance change appreciably because there is no longer any need to transfer the family holding intact to one son, or to dower the daughters in the rural fashion. At the same time, the family economy ordinarily requires that the sons before marriage work outside the home and not at home under the direction of their father, and the Dublin community normally supplies enough occupational opportunities that they can do so without having to leave the city. As a result, the marriage of the inheriting son, so central in the cycle of the rural family, simply ceases to be as crucial a factor in the lives of the New Dubliners as it is for the country family. Without having to leave Dublin, all the sons can and generally do enter an occupational field in late adolescence, achieve occupational adulthood in early manhood and in many cases can climb to a higher occupational and social level than that of their father. Simultaneously, they are able to marry earlier without jeopardizing the family's interests and usually are in an independent economic position to do so. The daughters likewise, save in exceptional circumstances, no longer depend upon a dowry, find ample occupational openings in Dublin, and can marry earlier than the girls of the countryside. Often they have the opportunity, particularly through occupational contacts, to improve their social position by marriage. In short, New Dubliners of both sexes can and, as a rule, do achieve full social adulthood at an earlier age than the country people, and have better chances for social advancement to boot.

In preparing their children for this world, parents must inevitably yield to outside agencies a far greater measure of influence than rural parents. Having ceased to be a collective unit of production, the New Dubliner family tends to become less of a collective unit in certain other respects. As productive activities, so educational, recreational and courtship activities tend to become more individualized and dispersed throughout the Dublin community. The school, the shop or office where the young people learn their trades and skills, and the peer groups in which they recreate and meet their mates and which are no longer, as in the country, based on inter-familial ties—all of these are much more vital factors in moulding the children's attitudes, values and standards of behaviour than in the rural community.

The greater range, and the greater importance, of relationships that family members have with large, impersonal organizations and with groups that are not familial in character signalize another major change which accompanies the internal alterations in the structure of the family which urbanization produces. This is the decline and the weakening of inter-familial solidarity on the basis of kinship and neighbourliness. City life not only affects the inner equilibrium of the family; it also tends to isolate the family from those families that are neighbours and kin, with which the rural family has such deep and crucial ties.[31]

This is evident from the fact that on every class level and with few exceptions almost every form of co-operation between neighbours and kin found in the rural community has diminished among the New Dubliners and in some cases has disappeared entirely. The major forms of co-operation between New Dubliner families are regular visiting and recreation, recurrent exchanges of gifts, help in times of crisis such as sickness and death, financial aid in periods of distress, and assistance in getting a relative a job. New Dubliner families, especially those related by kinship, may also jointly impose sanctions upon a miscreant member, particularly one who neglects his obligations to his family, but the social pressure neighbours or kin are able to bring to bear is considerably weaker than in the rural community. But the regular and extensive co-operation in economic activities, the exchange of goods and services, the channelling of trade along familial lines so widespread between rural kin and neighbours have virtually disappeared among the New Dubliners. Finally, while the older men in a neighbourhood may still gather of an evening in the local pub, their meetings are largely recreational and their discussions and decisions have nowhere near the influence of the old men's cliques in the countryside upon the affairs of the neighbourhood, much less the larger community. This decline in inter-familial solidarity lessens the support the nuclear family can receive on a familistic basis and therefore forces the family to rely the more for such support upon non-familistic groups and agencies in Dublin.

These profound organizational changes in the inner structure of the family and in its relations with both familial and non-familial groups in the community inevitably result in far-reaching modifications in the sentiments and values which are directly connected with the organization of life. The New Dubliner is not, like the countryman, concerned about land and the continuity of his family on a homestead, nor content with the acceptance of acquired status. Rather he is concerned with wage security and with the achievement of status by means of occupational advancement and hypergamy. Consequently, filial piety—that set of sentiments and values that bind parents and children together—changes significantly in Dublin. While

[31] Parsons, *Essays in Sociological Theory*, pp. 237–8, has pointed out this phenomenon of the isolation of the conjugal family in urban America.

children there have a solid respect for their parents, there is among
the New Dubliners considerably less veneration and glorification of
the aged than among the country people. Generally speaking, as
there are greater equality and *camaraderie* between husband and wife,
so children are less fearful of their parents and are less dominated by
them. Both parents and children attach a much higher premium than
the countryman to the ambitions and the earlier emancipation of
youth from parental control. New Dubliners consider it right and
proper that children should enjoy freedom and assume adult responsibilities in respect to occupation, marriage and indeed the whole
range of life many years earlier than the rural community would
allow. As a consequence among New Dubliners the juvenile attitudes
towards sex and women, the sense of inferiority and of submissiveness
characteristic of the countryman are notably less pronounced and
tend to disappear altogether.

The shift from the countryside to Dublin also has had important
repercussions upon those values and attitudes which are not directly
connected with organization at the family level. The New Dubliners
retain the traditional Irish respect for the professions, but this has
been tempered by their increasing appreciation of business as a career
and their growing esteem of the role of business in the nation's
welfare. As a people who have had political independence and the
freedom to make their own way for little over a quarter of a century,
the New Dubliners still frequently take as models of class behaviour
the norms of the old Anglo-Irish Ascendancy. But the influence of a
more open and flexible occupational and class structure has seriously
altered these values and the New Dubliners are in the process of
evolving their own somewhat distinctive class norms. In like fashion,
while the New Dubliner is still quite sceptical of government and
politics in general, he is far less suspicious of this sphere of life than
his country cousin, perhaps because in the capital he has much wider
contacts with government agencies and personnel in action.

Of all the countryman's values, the most notable fatality in the
move to the city is superstition. Although their immigrant parents
may have brought the rural 'wee people' and pishogues with them
into the city, the New Dubliners, except to a moderate extent those
living in the slums, have lost these eccentric creatures and their ways.
This is almost certainly due to the direct and indirect influence of the
greater education which prevails in Dublin and to contact with a
more reasoned and analytical way of life.

But what is perhaps most striking of all is that the basic set of
religious values which the countryman accepts survives the transition
to the city and persists among the New Dubliners. The New Dubliner
entertains the same supernatural view of the universe as the country-

37

man and like him considers that activities that merit and preserve supernatural grace are paramount in life. And he has much the same tendency to be wary and suspicious of human nature and its inclination towards evil. Both in regard to his bodily appetites and the power of reason he is inclined to think, as one Dubliner put it, that man has been given a 'double dose of original sin'. This is abundantly clear, as we shall see, from the religious sentiments and attitudes which New Dubliners of every class express. It is also evident from their religious practice and observance. Urbanization has not produced a significant decline in devotion, in the reception of the sacraments and in the fulfilment of religious duties. If anything, city life has facilitated and increased such behaviour by bringing the New Dubliner into closer physical proximity to the Church which is its centre. In short, in spite of his many points of contact with modern secularism and his involvement with a modern industrial economy, the New Dubliner has not become secularized.

There is, then, essential religious continuity between the countryman and the New Dubliner. Nevertheless, many of the religious attitudes and sentiments characteristic of the Irish are tempered and modified by city life. In general, the New Dubliner tends to be less traditionalistic and more intelligent and reasoned in his approach to religion. Thus, points of religious doctrine are much more frequently matters of discussion among the New Dubliners than among the country folk. The New Dubliner also feels much freer to criticize the clergy and to seek convincing reasons from them for the standards of behaviour they hold up and the policies they advocate. At the same time he is more open and frank than the countryman in discussing sex and the problems of sexual instruction and morality, and he tends to take a more reasoned, rather than a sheer authoritarian, approach to the religious instruction of his children.

It is difficult to sort out and assess the independent influence of ideological factors on the one hand, and of the organization of city life on the other, in producing these variations in the religious attitudes of the New Dubliners. Probably these changes are the result of the combined influence of both. Undoubtedly, the rationalism of the secular view of life challenges the New Dubliner to become more informed about his religious beliefs and to seek the grounds which make them intellectually acceptable. At the same time, he is daily confronted with an economy organized in such a way as to put heavy premiums on rational analysis and decision. One therefore reinforces the other in stimulating him to take a more inquiring and critical approach to life in general and to religion in particular, as well as to his familial situation and its problems.

The effects of urbanization on the family in Ireland, then, are

38

extensive and quite swift. Despite certain radical continuities between the farm family and the family in Dublin, by the time the children of the immigrants from rural areas have reached full adulthood and founded their families the total round of change has reached the point where the distinctive pattern of the family life of the countryman is no more. The countryman has been transformed literally into a citizen.

Chapter II

DUBLIN: OLD AND NEW

THE LIFE SPAN of the oldest subject in this study covers the seventy years from 1880 to 1950. That span constitutes for Ireland a period of revolution and reconstruction. Dublin has been a major focal point for the changes that have occurred in this time and that have had profound significance for family life in the city in general and especial significance for the New Dubliners we are to meet. Some general historical survey of these years is, therefore, essential to the understanding of the family life of the New Dubliners.

Unfortunately, the general history of these years has not yet been written for the Republic of Ireland as a whole, let alone for the city of Dublin. Monographs on isolated aspects of it are only now beginning to appear. As we obviously cannot here attempt even an outline of this phase of Irish history in anything like its entirety, we can only select those features which bear most directly and intimately on the family life of the people we are to study. By this norm, it seems advisable to concentrate less on the distribution of power and the mode and direction in which it has been applied in Irish society, and to focus our attention on the major institutions which constitute the social context of Irish life.

PRE-TREATY DAYS: 1900–1922

Until the Irish Revolution of 1916, the most portentous event in Irish political history during the nineteenth century was the Act of Union of 1800. This Act terminated twenty years of Irish Home Rule under Grattan's Parliament and, while it formally created a legislative reunion of England and Ireland, in effect it reduced Ireland to the status of a colony with representatives at Westminster. The Irish party was in such a position in Parliament that it could only be effective either by following an obstructionist policy which became increasingly difficult after 1882 or by holding the balance of power which largely depended upon the vicissitudes of English politics. On the whole, representatives of English and Scottish interests predominated at Westminster, and for the greater part of the century they pursued a general policy, enforced by the English administration from Dublin Castle, which proved disastrous for the Emerald Isle.

Within Ireland itself, the presence of the Anglo-Irish Ascendancy had for centuries cleft the country into 'two races, two creeds . . . two spheres of economic interest and pursuit . . . socially two separate classes. . . .'[1] Rooted in the long years of Catholic disfranchisement and the Penal Code, and in the establishment of the Church of Ireland, the Ascendancy's power was vested primarily in the landlords and in the land system. But its dominance extended into industry, the professions, and the field of political patronage, and was most strikingly manifest in its virtual monopoly of higher education. Its privileged access to opportunity in a land where opportunities were few was a constant barrier to the social development of a strong Irish-Catholic middle class, and it aggravated economic depression as it implemented political subordination to England.

Against both these institutions many turbulent political movements surged during the nineteenth century. Representative of different segments of Irish society, these movements often differed in their objectives and, even more often, in regard to the means of achieving these objectives. For the most part they were short-lived, often illegal institutions until Sinn Fein arose in the later part of the century and ultimately won out. In any event, every movement had to bargain with the one institution which continuously had primary influence with the majority of the Irish people, the Catholic Church.

Considering the total situation, it was perhaps inevitable that in the nineteenth century the Church should have acquired a wide range of political power, for in view of the lack of an educated Catholic laity, priests and bishops had a corner on the intellectual equipment for leadership. In fact, they became political leaders with wider scope than the clergy of any other country in Europe. But while their power had as its general objective the bettering of the lot of Catholics in Ireland, they achieved little more cohesion and unity in pursuit of that goal than did the formal political movements which they, in turn, supported or opposed. In this ecclesiastical stream there are many eddies, but two main currents seem to have predominated in the course of the century. One of these, represented by such men as Archbishop McHale, Bishop Doyle, Archbishop Croke and Bishop Duggan, supported the peasants, sought land reform and tended on the whole to be nationalist. The other current, of which Archbishop Cullen in Dublin in mid-century was the most noted, while formally

[1] Sir Horace Plunkett, *Ireland in the New Country* (London and New York, 1905), p. 143.

41

nationalistic, opposed revolutionary movements such as the Young Irelanders and the Fenians, and generally favoured those segments of the middle class whose interests lay in what later was to be termed the 'connection with England'.[2] For a number of reasons, not the least of which was the fate of Parnell, the latter group gained the upper hand towards the end of the nineteenth century. In the midst of the revolutionary movements of the first quarter of the present century, conservatism thus became the uniform hallmark of the hierarchy, and reluctance characterized its nationalism.

What political movements and ecclesiastical influence in the nineteenth century in Ireland generally opposed, and England constantly promoted—with the half-willing, half-unwilling support of the Ascendancy—was a land system and a commercial and industrial policy which had made Ireland a virtual pariah among Western nations. In the south of Ireland and in contrast with Ulster, the land was controlled by landlords notable, during the first half of the century, for their absenteeism.[3] Under them the Irish peasantry existed as tenants without security of tenure, subject to tithes to the Church of Ireland, subject, too, to arbitrary and disproportionate increase in rent. As agriculture underwent a general shift from tillage to pasturage in the latter half of the century, the peasantry were also often victimized by wholesale eviction. The rural conditions of poverty were notorious.

On the other hand, under the influence of mercantilism, the British Parliament in the hundred years prior to 1779 had passed a series of acts restrictive of Irish trade the effect of which was to paralyse Irish industry, especially Irish manufacture of wool and cotton. When England adopted Free Trade in 1779, however, these restrictions were withdrawn. In 1782 the Irish Parliament in Dublin was granted legislative freedom over domestic affairs, and during the subsequent eighteen years of Home Rule Ireland experienced a marked industrial revival. The Act of Union of 1800 terminated this renaissance prematurely. Commercial bounties that had been granted to new Irish industries by the Irish Parliament were now cut off. Irish customs and

---

[2] While the Fenians, as a secret society, were generally condemned by Catholic Bishops, there is evidence that some of the less conservative clergy sympathized with them and even supported them secretly. And this is true of other nationalist movements *v.* W. S. Blunt, *Land War in Ireland* (London, 1912), pp. 130, 309, *et passim*. Also C. G. Duffy, *The League of North and South* (London, 1886); L. Paul-Dubois, *Contemporary Ireland* (Dublin, 1908), pp. 460–511; T. de Vere White, *Road to Excess* (Dublin, 1945), pp. 165–7; B. O'Reilly, *The Life of John McHale, Archbishop of Tuam* (2 vols., New York, 1890), II, 535, 545.

[3] Where the 'Ulster custom' was in force. This gave the tenant security and the right 'to leave to his personal representative or heir all interest in the farm which was recognized by custom to be in him'. G. O'Brien, op. cit., pp. 110–12.

duties were first reduced and eventually amalgamated with those of England. And Free Trade, which Grattan had vigorously promoted, now boomeranged to the detriment of Irish development. For, without protection, Irish industry could not compete with the advanced industrial production of England. The Industrial Revolution and the introduction of the factory system into England further weakened Ireland's competitive position, since impoverished Irish industry had not the capital to finance the installation of machines and factories.[4] Industrial decay, coupled with agricultural exploitation, left Ireland 'an economic slum at Britain's doorstep'.[5]

The famine of 1847, striking Irish society in such an anaemic condition, was a catalytic agent whose most serious effect was to make emigration a national institution. Largely, though not solely, as a result of this continuing exodus, Ireland in the last half of the century acquired the dubious distinction of becoming the only nation in Western Europe with a declining population. Whereas Ireland had grown from an estimated population of nearly five million in 1791 to over eight million by 1841, her population in 1911 had declined to 4,390,000.[6]

Nevertheless, a continuous struggle for emancipation from these sundry limitations had gone on during the nineteenth century with varying degrees of success. In the period, 1900–1922, each of the features we have discussed was in a different stage of transition. In 1829 the first battle was won through Catholic Emancipation which legally entitled Catholics to stand for Parliament and to hold public office generally. The same act, however, deprived the forty-shilling freeholders of the franchise which Grattan's Parliament had granted them. Power, therefore, still remained in the hands of the landlords

---

[4] *v.* G. Locker-Lampson, *The State of Ireland in the Nineteenth Century* (London, 1907), pp. 183–4. See also E. A. Murray, *A History of the Commercial and Financial Relations Between England and Ireland* (London, 1903), pp. 347 ff.; S. Gwynn, *Ireland* (London, 1924), pp. 75–7; O'Brien, *The Economic History of Ireland from the Union to the Famine*, pp. 202 ff. The linen industry in Belfast was exempted from this general attack. This permitted an accumulation of capital whereby Belfast was enabled to develop industrially in the nineteenth century. *v.* Murray, ibid.

[5] E. Strauss, *Irish Nationalism and British Democracy* (London, 1951), p. 275.

[6] These figures are for the whole of Ireland. The estimate for 1791 is a revision of the traditional estimates made by K. H. Connell, op. cit., p. 25. The figure for 1911 is that of the *Census of Population*, 1911. For the territory of the present Republic of Ireland, exclusive of the six north-eastern counties, the population in 1841 was 6,528,000 and in 1911, 3,139,000. *v. Census of Population in Ireland, 1946* (Dublin, 1950), I, 3. Emigration from Ireland had been continuous and strong in the years 1780–1841, when the population, nevertheless, doubled itself. The significance of the famine is not that it started emigration, but that it enormously increased it and crystallized a social situation in which emigration on a large scale became a national institution, as it remains today.

and the Ascendancy, who by practice and custom continued to exclude Catholics from political office and from the higher social positions.

The continued power of the Ascendancy and the constant struggle against it during the nineteenth century appears clearly in the history of the educational system. In 1831 a primary-school system was created which became unique in being at once public and theoretically undenominational, but in fact rigidly denominational. After 1892, attendance at primary school became legally compulsory, although the implementation of the law was not universal nor its enforcement strict. Still, by the turn of the century, primary education was available for everybody and in various localities, such as Dublin, was required of everybody. Secondary education, however, was a different case. Every secondary school in the country was a private school and remained such even after 1878 when some measure of government aid was granted the schools. But the curricula of these schools were badly adapted to the needs of a people who were destined to earn their livelihood in agriculture and the trades. Sir Horace Plunkett judged them as fit only 'to turn our youth into a generation of second-rate clerks. . . .'[7] Through the Department for Technical Instruction, Plunkett succeeded at the turn of the century in introducing some technical education. But on the whole, while secondary education was economically feasible for the Ascendancy, the expense and impracticality of private secondary education combined to prevent the vast majority of Irish Catholic children from receiving any secondary education whatever prior to 1922.

For Catholics, higher education was in even poorer state. The only established institutions of higher learning were Trinity College and, after 1845, the Queen's Colleges. Though the former was ostensibly non-sectarian after 1792, it was in fact Protestant and the intellectual stronghold of the Ascendancy. The Queen's Colleges, on the other hand, were not well received by the Irish, being dubbed 'Godless colleges' by Catholics and by a large segment of the Protestants as well. In an effort to provide university education suitable for Catholics, Rev. John Henry Newman (later Cardinal), on the authority of the Catholic Bishops of Ireland, founded the Catholic University in Dublin in 1854. But without charter, without subsidy, and because of dissension and even opposition on the part of the bishops themselves, it floundered and gave way to University College under the Jesuits in 1883. In 1879 the English Parliament established a Royal University of Ireland which granted a modicum of aid in the form of fellowships and which, as an examining board, conferred degrees upon candidates

[7] Plunkett, *Ireland in the New Century*, p. 128. *v.* Locker-Lampson, *The State of Ireland in the Nineteenth Century*, pp. 125–47.

from recognized colleges such as University College and others throughout the country. Thus constituted, the Royal University was not a full-fledged university at all. And no such university acceptable to Catholics existed in Ireland until 1908 when the National University was established.[8]

This last concession in the field of education had been preceded by three major blows which struck at the roots of the Ascendancy's power. In 1869, Gladstone secured the disestablishment of the Church of Ireland. He followed this up the next year by obtaining the passage of the first Land Act which inaugurated land reform. Finally, in 1898 Ireland was granted a system of local government that incorporated the principle of representation and so destroyed the monopoly of office previously enjoyed by the old aristocracy. The most important of these developments was the Land Act. For, while this Act did not immediately solve the intricate land question, it did establish the basis essential for that solution and paved the way for subsequent legislative measures culminating in the Wyndham Act of 1903 which set up effective machinery enabling tenants to acquire outright ownership of their farms.[9]

These developments, however, had little immediate effect upon Ireland's industrial position which at the turn of the century remained essentially unchanged. The British Tariff Commission, reporting in 1912, stated that in the past sixty years 'Irish industries in general . . . have suffered severely, though the rate of decline has slackened in recent years'. In substantiation of this, the commission noted that the numbers employed in manufacturing industries fell by 66 per cent between 1841 and 1901 as compared with a 46 per cent decline of population in the same period, while 'between 1881 and 1901 the decline was 14 per cent in population and 11 per cent in persons occupied in manufactures'.[10] The first British Census of Production (1907) showed that in all industries except agriculture the whole of Ireland had a net output of £22,777,000 and employed 291,304 per-

[8] *v.* S. O'Cathain, SJ, 'Education' in *Studies*, 40: 440–56 (December 1951); An Irish Christian Brother, *Edmund Ignatius Rice* (Dublin, 1926); F. McGrath, SJ, *Newman's University: Idea and Reality* (Dublin, 1951), pp. 16–39; Paul-Dubois, *Contemporary Ireland*, pp. 367–74; Locker-Lampson, *The State of Ireland in the Nineteenth Century*, pp. 473–5. Alfred O'Rahilly, 'The Irish University Question (1) and (2)', *Studies*, vol. L (1961), 225–70; 353–70; 'The Irish University Question (3)', *Studies*, vol. LI (1962), 147–70.

[9] 'The Wyndham Act owed its effectiveness to the fact that it gave the government power to force landlords to sell, and for the first time, provided adequate and attractive compensation. It was financed by a £100,000,000 bond issue and a £12,000,000 appropriation for bonuses.' *v.* E. A. Dalton, *History of Ireland* (6 vols., London, 3rd ed., date not given), VI, 453–6.

[10] Great Britain, Tariff Commission Report, *The Economic Position of Ireland and Its Relation to Tariff Reform* (London, 1912), p. 9.

sons. A full quarter of these industrial employees were accounted for by the linen industry which was almost entirely concentrated in Ulster.[11] Elsewhere industry was stagnant. Coupled with the increase of migration to the towns, this made for the frustration of potential middle-class elements in the urban population, restricted the number of skilled artisans, and begot a mass of general, unskilled labourers and unemployed struggling to maintain themselves on a subsistence level. It is not strange, therefore, that the pre-war years were marked by industrial strife which culminated in the great Dublin strike of 1913. Neither is it strange that in those Irish political movements which resulted in the revolution and the creation of the Irish Free State urban interests played a crucial role. It is highly symbolic that it was in Dublin City that the Easter Rising of 1916 occurred.[12]

In spite of industrial stagnation, but almost concomitant with land reform, two demographic trends began to appear. On the one hand, the rate of emigration began to decline. Thus, while the total decrease of population in southern Ireland between 1841 and 1951 has been 54 per cent, 47 per cent of that decrease occurred in the fifty years between 1841 and 1891 and only 7 per cent in the subsequent sixty. On the other hand, within the country there has been a shift in the distribution of the population whereby the rural population has declined while the population of the towns has greatly increased. Between 1841 and 1891 the town population paralleled the rural population in decline and reached a minimum in 1891; but between 1891 and 1951, while the rural population has sustained a further loss of 34 per cent, the town population has increased by 44 per cent.[13] The

[11] Great Britain, Board of Trade (Labour Department), *Sixteenth Abstract of Labour Statistics* (London, 1913), p. 57. Compare with C. Booth, 'The Economic Distribution of Population in Ireland', in Department of Agriculture and Technical Instruction for Ireland, *Ireland; Agricultural and Industrial* (ed. William Coyne, Dublin, 1901), pp. 55–61.

[12] *v.* N. Mansbergh, *Ireland in the Age of Reform and Revolution* (London, 1940), pp. 194–6; Strauss, *Irish Nationalism and British Democracy*, pp. 216–28; J. D. Clarkson, *Labour and Nationalism in Ireland* (New York, 1925), pp. 311–12.

[13] This is based upon comparative statistics for rural and town populations from 1840 to 1940 contained in an unpublished report of the Director of the Central Statistics Office of the Irish Government, Dr. R. C. Geary; and on the *Census of Population of Ireland, 1951, Preliminary Report* (Dublin, 1951), p. 10. The figures listed in the latter reference have been corrected and supplied to me by M. D. McCarthy, presently Director of the Central Statistics Office. The relevant figures in *thousands* are as follows:

Year	Town	Rural
1841	1002	5527
1891	853	2616
1951	1228	1733

growth of the urban population has not been steady in all instances and some urban areas have suffered with the country as a whole from emigration of people from Ireland. In other instances, urban increase has been due mainly to natural increase. But to a great extent the general growth of the town population, especially during the last fifty years, has been due to increased migration from the countryside into the towns.

As the country's capital, Dublin felt the impact of all these developments, but none more acutely than the effects of the shift in the movement of population. Unique among Irish cities by reason of its continuous increase after 1841, the rate of its growth quickened after 1871. This growth was remarkable in that it did not stem from industrial development for in the south Dublin had been the chief victim of industrial depression. The introduction of the railroads and the coming of the steamship lines in the nineteenth century had, indeed, increased the city's importance as a port and as a centre of distribution. They likewise contributed to the expansion of two existing Dublin industries, the brewing and distilling industry, and the biscuit industry. But the wool, cotton, silk, leather and shipbuilding industries, all of which were in blossom at the beginning of the century, had withered to relative insignificance or complete extinction. At the end of the century, Dublin's famous poplin industry experienced a mild revival from its previous decline, and a small shipbuilding concern was established at the mouth of the Liffey in 1902. Other than that, in the words of the Dublin Civic Survey Committee, pre-Treaty Dublin was 'a city of no particular character beyond being the typical capital of a country in economic subjection and suffering from economic decay'.[14]

Statistics about Dublin were apparently as underdeveloped as its industry. But from those available its industrial decadence is clearly reflected in the occupational structure of the city. According to the Census of 1911, out of a total population of 304,000, only 135,000 (or 44 per cent) were listed as having any definite occupation. The remaining 56 per cent of the population, of whom over 53,000 were males, were classified in the 'Indefinite and Non-Productive Class'. The whole working population was distributed according to the various 'classes' as follows: 14 per cent in the 'Professional Class' (which besides the bona fide professions, included clerks and 'those engaged in the general or local government service and in the defence of the country'); 14 per cent in the 'Domestic Class'; 1 per cent in the

[14] The Civics Institute of Ireland, *The Dublin Civic Survey* (London, 1925), p. 82. For a detailed account of Dublin's industrial history until 1912 *v.* J. J. Webb, *Industrial Dublin Since 1869 and the Silk Industry in Dublin* (London, 1914), pp. 13–27; Paul-Dubois, *Contemporary Ireland*, pp. 323–5.

'Agricultural Class'; and 71 per cent in the 'Commercial Class' and the 'Industrial Class' taken together. More than three-quarters of the persons placed in these latter two categories were listed under the 'Industrial Class', but this was the result of poor classification. Persons such as shopkeepers, grocers, fishmongers, etc., were counted in the 'Industrial Class' which was thereby padded at the expense of the 'Commercial Class'.[15]

However classified, a full third of the entire working population were unskilled labourers, whose extreme predominance over skilled artisans the Civic Survey Committee attributed to the fact that Dublin was 'much more a commercial than a manufacturing city'.[16] And the British Board of Trade, reporting on conditions in Dublin in 1908 likewise commented that:

> ... the large number of general labourers ... like the number of domestic servants to which attention is called in this and other Irish reports, is a characteristic of Irish life which has come into prominence since the decay of Irish industry. In English and Scottish towns there are large bodies of men similarly described, but their economic significance is entirely different. In England and Scotland this class has arisen out of the needs of the great trades, but in Ireland no such necessity exists to give the labourer a regular and useful place in the industrial society. The class of 'general labourers' largely consists of the men whom the famine and its attendant miseries displaced.[17]

This rough sketch of the occupational distribution of Dublin's population hardly gives us a precise picture of the class structure of the city. Complex as this was, it is both possible and useful to determine what were the various class strata of Dublin society. The highest level consisted of a few members of the aristocracy, the chief British Army Officers and the top officials of the Civil Service. Prior to 1916, the social centre of this group was the residence of the Lord Lieutenant in Phoenix Park; reception there was the essential mark of having status on this level. Next in line came people in the professions and the owners of the larger business enterprises, the most notable of which was Guinness' Brewery. Somewhat below these stood the smaller but solid business people and the better-salaried white-collars, such as the middle echelon of the Civil Service, senior bank clerks, the 'staff' at Guinness's, etc. The smaller shopkeepers, and the minor clerks in business and government were one more remove below these. Finally, there were the labouring people among whom, as

[15] Webb, *Industrial Dublin*, pp. 116–21.
[16] *The Dublin Civic Survey*, p. 58.
[17] Great Britain Board of Trade, *Report on Working Class Rents, Housing and Retail Prices in the Principal Industrial Towns of the United Kingdom, 1908* (London, 1912), p. 559.

already indicated, skilled craftsmen were few and unskilled workers greatly predominated.

Although we have no exact data on the proportion of the population on each level, the labouring class was the broad base of what was generally a pyramid. But this does not tell the whole story, for in that pyramid the top levels were dominated by the Ascendancy and more so, perhaps, in Dublin than elsewhere, for Dublin had always been the centre of the Pale.[18] Speaking generally, the highest-ranking Catholics were professional men, including certain prominent barristers in important positions. There was no prosperous Catholic middle class based upon business enterprise. The only exception to this were the vintners or publicans. Catholics, and especially immigrants into the city from the country, monopolized this trade which Protestants generally spurned. Many of these vintners achieved a relatively high degree of financial success, but their trade was socially stigmatized and they did not share the social prestige of other moderately successful business men. Among the white-collars, whether in the Civil Service or in business, only the lower grades in practice were open to Catholics. The only avenues of advance for Catholics were the professions, the vintner trade, and the Colonial Civil Service in which Catholics could and did attain high positions. But of these, the second was socially tainted, while the third brought advance at the cost of leaving the country. Conversely, below the third level mentioned above, there were virtually no Protestants—'a few derelicts, that was all'.[19]

A sketch such as this is necessarily a matter of black and white. In reality there was much grey. In the revolutionary and transitional climate which prevailed from 1870 onwards, the wall of demarcation between these two sectors was breaking down at many points and people from both sides interacted and co-operated not only in political movements, but in social and cultural movements as well. But, founded as it was on cultural differences which were centuries old, 'the wall of separation', generally speaking, still stood. Associated

[18] Thus non-Catholics comprised 16·9 per cent of Dublin's population in 1911 while they constituted only 10·4 per cent of the population as a whole. *v. Census of Population of Ireland, 1936*, III, Pt. I (Dublin, 1939), p. 15.

[19] Quoted from one of the many elderly informants to whom I am, in part, indebted for the foregoing description. This gentleman remarked: 'It was a known fact, for example, that the most a Catholic in Guinness' could look forward to was a position of junior clerk, while in the home Civil Service only the lower grades were open to the Irish. . . . Whatever middle class Catholics there were existed by patronage on the part of the Ascendancy who demanded rigid conformity at least to the external behaviour which they decreed; for example, the wearing of Eton suits, observance of Sabbatarian practices, etc.' Among published accounts, *v.* Gwynn, *Ireland*, pp. 65–80; Paul-Dubois, *Contemporary Ireland*, pp. 89–99.

with the depressed condition of the city, this subordination in political power and patronage, in economic position and wealth, entailed for the majority of Dubliners an extremely low standard of living and of education.

Writers have described often and graphically enough the notorious conditions of the Dublin slums. My informants themselves recall the great number of children who went about barefoot or were shod only in burlap, and the widespread squalor to which they mainly attributed the intemperance and rowdyism then rampant. The extent of this poverty is revealed by the hard fact that 'the majority of the labouring class and a substantial proportion of the artisan class' lived in the slums; to be precise, 87,000 Dubliners, or 29 per cent of the city's populace, in the year 1913.[20] Of these, a full third were housed in quarters which the Dublin Corporation described as unfit for human habitation, while the rest dwelt in houses classified as 'structurally sound but not in good repair' or in 'houses so decayed as are soon like to be unfit for habitation', while 17,500 heads of families received a weekly wage of less than twenty-five shillings.[21]

For people in such circumstances, education was an impossible luxury; 57,000 pupils were, indeed, enrolled in the primary schools of Dublin County in 1913, but truancy was rife. In 1920, for example, the National Irish Teachers' Organization found that the average daily attendance was only 50 per cent. There are no statistics available for the secondary-school enrolment in the years 1900–1925, but it is a reasonable estimate that the number was substantially below the 5,800 secondary students in Dublin in 1931. As for technical education, there were in the territory of present-day Dublin City only 5,000 in attendance in the year 1919–20, and of these all but 116 were attending part-time evening classes! Paradoxically, university education alone experienced a relatively wide expansion after the founding of the National University, but this was largely because it had previously been so limited. Thus University College Dublin, where less than 500 students were enrolled in 1908, numbered over 1,000 students in 1925. But the metropolitan middle class, still relatively small, was economically in too precarious a position to be the major source

[20] Eire, *Report of Inquiry into the Housing of the Working Classes of the City of Dublin. 1939-43* (Dublin, 1943), pp. 15, 28.

[21] *v.* Clarkson, *Labour and Nationalism in Ireland*, p. 242; *The Dublin Civic Survey*, p. 60; A. Wright, *Disturbed Dublin* (London, 1914), pp. 3–4, 28–9; S. O'Farrell, 'The Changing Patterns of Irish Life', in *Studies*, 40: 428–36 (December 1951). A more graphic description by an 'insider' is given by Sean O'Casey in the first two of his autobiographical works, *I Knock at the Door* (London and New York, 1939), and *Pictures in the Hallway* (London and New York, 1942), if the reader can stomach the style.

of this increase which, even in Dublin, stemmed mainly from the emergent middle class of farmers.[22]

This in broad outline was Dublin prior to 1922. A provincial capital, culturally divided, industrially stagnant, it was, in the words of one of my oldest informants, 'just an inherited body of poverty'.

POST-TREATY DAYS: 1922–1951

In the history of Europe, Ireland's revolution surely is among the most un-revolutionary. To be sure, the fighting involved in it and in the Civil War which followed it, seems bloody and costly enough. But self-government, once achieved, led to no radical or violent uprooting of established institutions. Rather, these thirty years were marked by a general institutional continuity, by conservatism in policy and by change, which though steady was slow.

This is illustrated by the course of self-government itself, which was the most radical innovation and the one which has made the most rapid progress. Despite Ireland's declaration of a Republic in 1918, the Treaty of 1922 forced upon it the acceptance of Dominion status and the partition of the country and it thereby limited the territorial jurisdiction of the Free State. It was fifteen years before the Free State, benefiting by the general change in the constitution of the Empire and the expansion of powers accorded to the Dominions, could under De Valera actually transform herself into a Republic in 1937. Even so Great Britain did not fully recognize her as such until 1949.[23] Partition, meanwhile, remained and still remains a thorn in Ireland's side.

The same conservative character of the revolution is even more clearly manifest in the fate of the old tottering Ascendancy. For them, Irish independence was the *coup de grâce*. Where once they were the beneficiaries of the advantages of a privileged minority, they are now a minority unprotected by any special political prerogatives. Yet on the whole, the signing of the Treaty did not bring the exploitation which, as reprisal for previous *pogroms* against the Catholics in

[22] The figures for primary and secondary schools are taken from the records of the Education Department and supplied to me by Mr. J. Close of that Department through the courtesy of Mr. J. Ingram, formerly of the Department of Education and in 1951 a member of the Labour Court. For the statistics on technical education I am indebted to Mr. M. Gleeson, Chief Executive Officer of the Vocational Educational Committee for the City of Dublin. *v.* O'Cathain, 'Education', pp. 438–9, 443–5, 451–2; Ireland, *Statistical Abstract*, 1947–48 (Dublin, 1949), p. 125.

[23] *v.* V. Grogan, 'Irish Constitutional Development', in *Studies*, 40: 385–98 (December 1951); D. O'Sullivan, *The Irish Free State and Its Senate* (London, 1940), pp. 301–18, 488–503.

Belfast and other historic injustices, many of the Ascendancy feared. Generally speaking, discrimination against non-Catholics has not been institutionalized.

The Constitution of 1937 recognizes the separation of Church and State and confines itself to defining the Catholic religion as the religion of the majority, while it also recognizes the other religious denominations existing in Ireland at the date of the passage of the Constitution and guarantees religious freedom for all. Non-Catholics are eligible for any office and Eire's first President, Mr. Douglas Hyde, was in fact a Protestant while the Lord Mayor of Dublin was recently a Jew. Non-Catholic schools are granted state aid on the same proportional basis as are Catholic schools.[24] More significantly, perhaps, the scions of the Ascendancy have been able to maintain competitive advantages in business which stem from their forebears' period of power. Thus, in a sample of over 62,000 families from the non-agricultural population taken in 1946, non-Catholics comprised only 8 per cent, yet they accounted for 22 per cent of the professional-employer-managerial class. Moreover, this class together with that of small business men and salaried employees contained 68 per cent of the non-Catholic families as compared with 43 per cent of the Catholic families.[25]

Nevertheless, this former Ascendancy has declined in power through the abolition of their erstwhile privileges and the consequent narrowing of the gap between themselves and Catholics in wealth and prestige. They have also lost power through decline in numbers, having dropped from 10·4 per cent of the population in 1911 to 7·4 per cent in 1926 and to 5·7 per cent in 1946.[26] And in the minds of many non-Catholics, the legal equality that they enjoy, despite its relatively wide range, has many important limitations. Beyond specific limitations which they cite, they fear, as the source of these and of further potential limitations, the influence of the Catholic hierarchy on government as being undemocratic and prejudicial to their full liberties.[27]

The role of the clergy in politics has undergone a radical change since the nineteenth century. The clergy no longer, as they did then, participate openly in the political arena. There are no clerical partisan leaders and no Catholic cleric has held public office in Ireland. Nevertheless, despite formal constitutional separation of Church and State, among pressure groups in Ireland today the hierarchy, perhaps in-

[24] Ireland, *The Constitution of Ireland* (Dublin, 1951), Article 44, pp. 144–6.

[25] *v. Census of Population, 1946, Fifth Interim Report* (Dublin, 1952), Table 30, pp. 39–41.

[26] *Census of Population of Ireland, 1946, Second Interim Report* (Supplement to the *Irish Trade Journal and Statistical Bulletin*. June 1950, Dublin). Table 1C, p. 9.

[27] For statements of specific grievances, *v. The Irish Times, The Liberal Ethic* (Dublin, 1950).

evitably, is in a unique position. Indirectly through its influence upon the Catholic majority, and directly through its influence upon Catholic members of government, it is without peer in terms of power.

The actual power of the clergy is complex and has two grounds of legitimation, both of which are recognized in Ireland. First, as bishops and priests, the clergy have the legal right, as they have the canonical obligation, to protect the doctrinal principles and the rights of the Church when they believe these to be jeopardized by governmental policy. But it is also accepted that, apart from this area of 'mixed' matters, the clergy, as educated leaders of a professional group with valid temporal interests and with citizens' obligations in regard to the national well-being, have as legitimate a role in the purely political sphere as any similar group. Virtually no one in Ireland would deny that in this latter capacity they may as properly exert pressure on government as business, professional or other groups in the country.[28]

In practice, however, the clergy rarely exercises the second type of power in clear separation from the first. Possibly because of fear of the charge of excessive clerical interference in political affairs, the clergy with few exceptions have not undertaken the responsibilities of leadership in this open political sphere. There they have been passive and even negative. By the same token, the hierarchy have also publicly invoked this formal episcopal authority only on rare occasions and only where they have believed that the doctrine and rights of the Church were involved. But in so doing, they have at times conceived the latter so broadly as to seem to include under it purely political matters. There is here a confusion of two kinds of political power. And the confusion is further compounded by the fact that the exercise either of strictly episcopal authority or of legitimate political pressure is often not public but takes the form of confidential correspondence with government officials. While it is, therefore, hard to assess the extent to which hierarchical influence on government is employed, its actual exercise is perhaps relatively rare because it is rarely necessary. Fear of hierarchical opposition carries such weight that the government has consistently been conservative in the face of it and has been wary of pressing its constitutional prerogatives. In effect, the hierarchy actually is in position to prevent the introduction of legislation unacceptable to it into the Dail and, should it be introduced, virtually to predetermine its course.

A pertinent case that illustrates all of these features of hierarchical influence in Ireland was the proposed Mother and Child Scheme sponsored in 1951 by Dr. Noel Browne, then Minister of Health, which was based on the Health Act of 1947. In this instance, the

[28] *v.* S. O'Faolain, 'The Browne Case', in *The Bell* (April 1951).

hierarchy in confidential correspondence with the Taoiseach, Mr. John Costello, while objecting to the proposed bill on the grounds that it was not in accordance with Catholic doctrine, also presented reasons designed to show that in itself the scheme was unsound social policy. But they presented these latter reasons in such a way as to imply that they were also matters of Catholic doctrine. Their opposition was sufficient to persuade the government to jettison the proposed legislation prior to parliamentary debate and resulted in the resignation of Dr. Browne who then made the correspondence public.[29]

This case has further significance, however. For the fact that it directly concerned family life and that the hierarchy primarily objected to it as investing the State with excessive power over families as

---

[29] The indiscriminate mingling of objections against the bill that were based on doctrinal grounds with others grounded on opinion about social policy is revealed in a letter of 10 October 1950 to the Taoiseach from the Bishop of Ferns officially representing the views of the Bishops and Archbishops of Ireland, published in *The Irish Times*, 12 April 1951.

Stating that the Bishops 'feel bound by their office to consider whether the proposals are in accordance with Catholic moral teaching', he summarizes the general position of the hierarchy thus: 'In their opinion the powers taken by the State in the proposed Mother and Child Health service are in direct opposition to the rights of the family and of the individual and are liable to very great abuse. Their character is such that no assurance that they would be used in moderation could justify their enactment. If adopted in law they would constitute a ready-made instrument for future totalitarian aggression.'

The Bishop then proceeds to state the specific reasons for this position in the following order: First, 'the right to provide for the health of the children belongs to the parents, not the State'. Second, 'it is not sound social policy to impose State medical service on the whole community on the pretext of relieving the necessitous ten per cent [*of the population*] from the so-called indignity of the means test'. Thirdly, 'the right to provide for the physical education of children belongs to the family and not the State'. Fourthly, while 'education in regard to motherhood includes instruction in regard to sex relations, chastity and marriage, the State has no competence to give instruction in such matters'. Fifthly, that in other countries gynaecological care is often interpreted to include provision for birth limitation and abortion and 'we have no guarantee that State officials will respect Catholic principles in regard to these matters'. Sixthly, that the proposed service, destroying the confidential relation between doctors and patients, makes all medical records public 'without regard to the individual's right to privacy'. Seventhly, that 'the elimination of private medical practicioners by a state-paid service has not been shown to be necessary or even advantageous to the patient, the public in general, or the medical profession'. In the concluding paragraphs the Bishop refers to the bill as a 'costly bureaucratic scheme of nationalized medical service'.

This reference, and the second and seventh reasons put forth, are clearly matters of political opinion and represent the views of the Irish Medical Association which the Bishops were quite within their rights in sharing. But the position of these reasons in the context of the letter is such as to imply that they are also matters of Catholic moral teaching which hardly can be sustained. The italicized words in the above quotations are mine.

well as individuals indicates the main direction in which episcopal influence is exerted. The primary and almost exclusive concern of the bishops has been to preserve Catholic moral standards of family life. What non-Catholics construe as restrictions upon their full religious liberty are virtually all confined to this sphere of social life.[30] In all other aspects, the constitutional principle of separation of Church and State has a very wide range of real application in Irish society even though, for the foregoing reasons, its implementation is far from perfect. As a result, in independent Ireland the political influence of the hierarchy has never been wielded, either directly or indirectly, to create an institutionalized ascendancy on a religious basis.

Undoubtedly, clerical concern for Catholic familial morality has contributed its share to the continuity of another institution which instances the conservatism of the Irish revolution—family law. Family law in Ireland is still fundamentally the common law of England as it was based on Canon Law prior to the Reformation. Parliament specifically exempted Ireland from the innovations concerning marriage and divorce which were introduced into England after 1857. Thus, while in that year the Matrimonial Causes Act legalized divorce *a vinculo* in England, a series of special acts from 1844 to 1871 continuously maintained the prohibition of divorce *a vinculo* in Ireland, and this has not been changed by any subsequent legislation. Indeed, the Constitution of 1937 fortified the extant legal position by proscribing the introduction of legislation permitting divorce and by nullifying the effect of foreign divorces and decrees of nullity, including papal decrees of nullity.[31] The effect of all this is that today Irish law recognizes only separation *a mensa et toro*. The only legislation affecting marriage in Ireland has been the Married Women's Property Act of 1882 which, in Ireland as in England, constituted a married woman a feme-sole as regards property and so capable of entering into contract even with her husband. As a result, husband and wife are able under the law to contract to live separately without judicial action. The great majority of legal separations in Ireland, in fact, are obtained in this manner today, both parties

[30] Indicative of this is the fact that the major complaints of some non-Catholics concern the clergy's stand against divorce and contraception, and their positive support of censorship of books and movies. In regard to the last item, complaints about the clerical position are not limited to non-Catholics by any manner of means.

[31] Papal decrees of nullity in marriages that are *ratum, non consummatum* which, though rare, are granted under certain circumstances, are simply not recognized in Irish law. Furthermore, a marriage between a Catholic and non-Catholic performed by a Protestant minister or a justice of the peace is null according to the Canon Law of the Catholic Church; according to Irish civil law it is valid. Canonically, both parties to such a match are free to contract valid marriages with other parties. Civilly, this is impossible.

E

contracting to live separately through a solicitor and without court hearing.[32]

Yet, despite the conservatism that has so far characterized the independent Republic of Ireland, important changes have accompanied self-government and have had significant impact upon the families we are to meet. The most immediate change has been the increase in jobs and economic opportunities. First of all, independence has opened up a whole range of government jobs to people for whom such jobs were previously non-existent. For the entire machinery of national government—the executive, the parliament, the courts, the Civil Service and, in latter years, the diplomatic service—are now in the hands of the Irish people themselves and are centred in Dublin as the capital. Indirectly, the government has pursued policies which, conservative though they may be, have nevertheless fostered industrial development and raised the general standard of living. The overall effect of these developments has been the gradual modernization of Ireland during the last twenty-five years although, in both rate and extent, modernization varies between the rural and urban population.

On the agricultural side, the various governments since 1922 have consistently pursued the general policy of land reform which was in operation immediately prior to the signing of the Treaty, and proprietorship of the land is now largely in the hands of small farmers. In other respects, however, successive governments have differed sharply in their policies. Generally speaking, while the Cosgrave government encouraged the rather extensive pasturage characteristic of Irish agriculture since 1870, De Valera after 1932, in pursuit of a policy of 'moderate self-sufficiency' which involved Ireland in an 'Economic War' with England, increased the area under tillage by compulsory legislation. The economic conflict with Great Britain was settled in 1938, but the outbreak of World War II in 1939 forced Ireland to continue the policy of increased tillage, and this remained its policy until 1948 when emphasis once more was placed upon pasturage.

During this period, the lot of the farmer has improved somewhat. According to Dr. Geary, '. . . solely on account of the favourable trend in prices in relation to living costs, the *real* income of the average agriculturalist increased by seventy per cent since 1938'.[33]

---

[32] N. Geary, *Marriage and Family Relations* (London, 1892), pp. 17–18, 78–9, 184–202, 562–6. v. *The Lawyer's Digest* (Cincinnati, 1945), pp. 1,717 ff. Everyone of the many barristers and solicitors I questioned on this subject assured me it would be futile to try to dig up the records of court separations, since the vast majority of separations are made by mutual consent through a solicitor and thus are not recorded in one central place.

[33] R. C. Geary, 'Irish Economic Development Since the Treaty', in *Studies*, 40: 409 (December 1951).

But at the same time the gross volume of agricultural output did not noticeably increase between 1925 and 1950. A programme of land reclamation designed to improve or reclaim four million acres which was inaugurated in 1949 with the aid of ECA dollars may improve production but its effect was not yet visible in 1951. Meanwhile, education in modern agricultural techniques has lagged, although it has received stimulus from the Parish Council and Young Farmers movements and from the ECA programme. In general, while the standard of living has risen as a result of increased income, government policy in the second quarter of the century effected no fundamental change in the traditional family system of small farms which Arensberg and Kimball have described. As a result, rural depopulation since 1925 has gone on apace, the rural population dropping from 2,008,000 in 1926 to 1,762,000 in 1951,—a decrease of 12 per cent.[34]

Although Arthur Griffith, following the lead of Parnell, had pledged industrialization as a major plank in the platform of Sinn Fein, the Cosgrave government proceeded with extreme caution to nail it down. The Shannon Electric power project was constructed between 1925–29, but protection of Irish industries through the imposition of duties was very limited until 1932 when the Fianna Fail Party came to power. Under De Valera, Fianna Fail adopted a strong protectionist policy which was intensified during the Economic War and which to a large extent was continued till quite recently. This policy of industrialization has generally stimulated light industry and served the needs of the home, rather than the foreign market. When this study was made, it had seen modest success. Whereas in 1925, 164,000 persons were engaged in production other than agriculture, 268,000 were so engaged in 1951. This represented a 27 per cent increase in industrial employment. Similarly, the gross volume of production in index numbers (to base 100 in 1938) swelled from 61·8 in 1926 to 159·2 in 1950. Very significantly, the index of productivity in manufacturing industries has risen continuously since the end of the last war; from base 100 in 1936 it had increased to 129 in 1950.[35]

[34] *Census of Population, 1946, Preliminary Report*, Table C, p. 9, and *Census of Population, 1951, Preliminary Report* (Dublin, 1951), Table C, p. 10. For the history of recent agricultural developments, v. John O'Donovan, 'Trends in Agriculture', in *Studies*, 40: 410–27 (December 1951). J. Johnston, *Irish Agriculture in Transition* (Dublin, 1951), pp. 3–87; J. Dillon, 'The Land Rehabilitation Programme', in *Economic Survey of the Republic of Ireland*, issued by *The Statist* (London, 1951), p. 14; T. W. Freeman, *Ireland*; European Recovery Programme, *Ireland: Country Study* (Washington, D.C., 1949); Arensberg and Kimball, op. cit., pp. 3–29.

[35] Geary, 'Irish Economic Development Since the Treaty', pp. 408, 415–16. v. Freeman, *Ireland*, pp. 208–37; D. Morrissey, 'Industrial Development in

Since 1958, however, the tempo of industrial growth in Ireland has greatly increased due to a new programme of encouraging foreign investment and has greatly improved the country's economic position as it has changed her economic character. Her gross national product 'rose 5% a year (much faster than Britain's) in 1960 and 1961 while industrial production climbed 7% and 9% respectively'.[36] These developments are bringing about an economic shift such that industry now has a much larger share in Ireland's gross national product than agriculture.

These figures undoubtedly reflect the effect of an important and novel educational development in the last twenty-five years. This has been the establishment of a new system of Vocational Schools by the Vocational Education Act of 1930. The Act set up schools which, though requiring small fees, are virtually public schools providing technical training in full-time courses of two years as well as in part-time courses for adults. By the year 1948–49 there were 157 such schools in Ireland, with 15,500 full-time students and 36,000 part-time students. Meanwhile, in other spheres of education, compulsory attendance at primary school has been made universal and its enforcement strict. And secondary schools, besides being granted government subsidies, have been empowered to introduce a Junior Course of two years as well as a Senior Course of four. As a result of these developments, as well as of the *per capita* increase in national income, secondary-school attendance since 1926 has increased by 75 per cent for boys and 150 per cent for girls.[37] At the same time and for similar reasons, the number of students in the Universities had grown from 3,159 to 7,000 in 1947, of whom over 5,000 were attending the National University and slightly under 2,000 were attending Trinity which is now subsidized by the government.[38]

While these developments have not solved Ireland's demographic problem, they have had a profound effect upon it and have altered its nature in many important ways. It is most significant that between 1926 and 1951 Ireland's population virtually ceased to decline and remained more or less stable at roughly 2,950,000 people. Its marriage rate, the lowest in the world, is compensated for by its fertility, which is one of the highest in the world, with the result that its birth rate is normal by international standards. As its death rate is also normal, failure of the population appreciably to increase between 1926 and

Ireland', in *The Statist, Economic Survey of the Republic of Ireland* (London, 1951), pp. 15–16; *The Census of Industrial Production, 1948 and 1947*, published in *Irish Trade Journal and Statistical Bulletin*, 25: 84–99 (Dublin, June 1950).

[36] *Business Week*, 30 June 1962 (no. 1,713), p. 63. George O'Brien, 'The Economic Progress of Ireland', *Studies*, vol. LI (1962), 9–26.

[37] O'Cathain, 'Education', pp. 453, 448, 443–7.

[38] Ireland, *Statistical Abstract 1947–48*, Table 150, p. 125.

1951 is accountable to emigration, the amount of which during this period almost exactly corresponds to the amount of natural increase.[39] Approximately half a million people were thus lost to Ireland in the second quarter of this century. Nevertheless, during this period emigration diminished greatly and the population declined by only 0·4 per cent. This was a decided improvement over the trend of population during the preceding seventy-five years. In the subsequent ten years between 1951 and 1961 emigration again seriously increased and population declined notably.[40] However, the new economic policy adopted during the last three years of this period has again reduced the rate of emigration so that in the year 1961 emigration had dropped to what it was in 1951, namely, virtually the same figure as the national increase in population.[41]

Moreover, between 1926 and 1951 migration within Ireland continued apace and significantly changed the internal structure of Irish society. As against rural decline, the numbers living in towns of 1,500 or more increased by 23 per cent between 1926 and 1951 in which year they constituted 41 per cent of the total population. The principle that 'he who has, gets' applies here and the larger the town the larger has been the proportionate increase. As a result, Dublin City and Dun Laoghaire increased in size by 28 per cent and in 1951 contained almost a fifth of the total population of the country. The other three largest cities, the County Boroughs of Cork, Limerick and Waterford, taken together increased by 6 per cent since 1925 and their combined total of 154,000 in 1951 was only a little more than a quarter of the 569,000 residents in Dublin and Dun Laoghaire.[42]

[39] Geary, 'Irish Economic Development', pp. 400–1. However, De Valera apparently did not agree with Dr. Geary and the data published by the C.S.O. in this matter. In August 1951 he claimed on the basis of 'the most reliable estimates' that between 1947–50 'the rate of emigration per thousand of the population is more than 50 per cent over what it was in the period 1936 and 1946, which includes the war years'. *v. Ireland*: Weekly Bulletin of the Dept. of External Affairs, No. 100 (Dublin, 3 September 1951), p. 4.

[40] Thus for the thirty-year period, 1851–81, Ireland's population declined by 26·2 per cent; and for the thirty-five-year period, 1891–1926, it declined by 14·4 per cent. Likewise, in the five-year period from 1951 to 1956 alone it declined by 2·1 per cent. These percentages were compiled from data given in the *Census of Population, 1956, Population, Area and Valuation of each District Electoral Division and of each larger Unit of Area* (Dublin, 1957), p. xi.

[41] *Business Week*, 30 June 1962, p. 63.

[42] *v. Census of Population, 1946, Preliminary Report*, Table C, p. 9, and *Census of Population, 1951, Preliminary Report*, Table C, p. 10 and Appended Table 3, p. 28. Between 1951 and 1956 the rural population continued to decline, dropping by 4·4 per cent. The town population continued to increase, but at the drastically reduced rate of only 1 per cent. At the same time, Dublin and Dun Laoghaire increased by 0·7 per cent and accounted for 22·4 per cent of the total population. Cork, Limerick and Waterford together increased by 2·6 per cent, accounted for

Part of Dublin's phenomenal growth in the second quarter of the century resulted from the expansion of the city's boundaries in 1930 and again in 1940 to include surrounding Urban Districts. But by far the major source of this growth has been the incoming countryman. At each census from 1871 to 1926 a full 30 per cent of Dublin's residents were reported as having been born outside the city of whom a certain proportion, of course, were then British administrative personnel and soldiery. But since the British have left over one-fourth of Dublin's population has constantly consisted of people born elsewhere in Ireland, including the six counties of the North.[43]

The pull exerted by Dublin on the rest of the country, which supplements the push exerted by rural life, has many causes. But certainly chief among them are the twin facts that, while retaining its old character as the main port and commercial hub of the south, Dublin has become the national capital and thus the administrative core of the country and that, at the same time, it has also become the country's industrial centre. The policy of industrialization inaugurated in 1932 formally embodied an attempt to decentralize industry. But, according to Dr. J. P. Beddy of the Irish Industrial Authority, the economy of centralization for a long time proved an insurmountable barrier to the policy, and this was coupled with the fact that 'a great many of our industrialists are Englishmen who think the west of Ireland is as uncivilized as your Wild West'.[44] As a result, centralization of government has been accompanied by centralization of industry in Dublin. Where 126,000 persons were listed in the 1926 Census as being 'at work' in Dublin City and County, the number was 216,176 for Dublin City and Dun Laoghaire alone in 1946. Of those at work in 1946 in Dublin City and County, one-third were engaged in industrial production and constituted one-third of all persons engaged in industry in the entire

6·7 per cent of the total population, and their combined population was about 30 per cent of the population of Dublin and Dun Laoghaire. Thus, while the rate of growth has slightly increased for these latter cities, that of the Dublin metropolitan area declined during this five-year period. *v. Census of Population, 1956, Population, Area and Valuation*, Table VII, p. xviii, Table V, Table VI, pp. xvi–xvii.

[43] For Dublin and Dun Laoghaire, the percentages of residents born elsewhere in all Ireland for 1926, 1936, and 1946 were respectively: 27·3 per cent, 26·2 per cent, 27·5 per cent. *v. Census of Population, 1926*, III, Table 7, p. 158; *Census, 1936*, III, Table 7, p. 154; and *Census, 1946, Second Interim Report*, Table 13A, p. 39. For a fuller discussion of the differential rate of decline and increase by size of town and city, *v.* S. T. Kimball, 'The Tradesman and His Family in the Economic Structure of an Irish Town', pp. 26–7.

[44] Statement made in an interview with the author.

country.[45] In the same year the net industrial output for the Dublin metropolitan area accounted for 52 per cent of the total industrial output of the country.[46]

The complex character of Dublin as the Irish capital, not only of government, but of industry, trade and finance, is revealed in the following table, which gives the percentage distribution 'of persons "at work" in broad Industrial Groups' for Dublin City and Dun Laoghaire in 1946:

Table I*

Percentage distributions of persons at work in Broad Industrial
Groups in Dublin and Dun Laoghaire in 1946

INDUSTRIAL GROUP	%
Agriculture	1·2
Other Production	32·2
Transport and Communication	7·2
Commerce and Finance	21·1
Public Administration and Defence	12·0
Professions	8·9
Personal Service	13·7
Others	3·7
Total	100·0

* This table, compiled for the writer by the Central Statistics Office, is derived from *Census of Population, 1946*, VII, Table 3, 6–9.

While these figures indicate the general types of occupational activity and the proportion of working Dubliners engaged in them, they do not tell us much about the class distribution of the city. However, data on a large sample of *families* according to social group taken from the country at large have been published and provide some clue as to the class structure of Dublin. Of 57,150 Catholic families listed as belonging to the non-agricultural population and as being 'gainfully employed', 13·4 per cent belong to the employer-managerial-professional class; 29 per cent are salaried employees and

---

[45] *v. Census of Population, 1936*, II, Table 24, p. 26, and *Census, 1946, Third Interim Report* (published as Supplement to *Irish Trade Journal and Statistical Bulletin*, September 1950), Table 5A, p. 19. The *Census of Industrial Production 1945–1947* (Dublin, undated) confirms this, although its figures differ from those of the *Census of Population* because it covered only concerns employing three or more persons, while the *Census of Population* covered all persons at work. According to the *Census of Industrial Production*, those who were employed in industrial production in Dublin in 1946 comprised 42 per cent of the total personnel engaged in industry in the entire country. *v. Census of Industrial Production*, 1945–47, Table 13, pp. 47–8.

[46] Ibid.

small businessmen working on their own; 32·5 per cent are non-manual wage earners (e.g., foremen) and skilled workers; and 24·9 per cent are semiskilled workers and general labourers.[47] In so far as the sample is drawn exclusively from the non-agricultural population, it probably represents in a fairly accurate way the class structure of the city. At any rate these figures, by comparison with those cited above for pre-Treaty Dublin, highlight the decline of the class of general labourers and the growth of skilled workers and especially of the white-collars, all of which are hallmarks of a modern, industrialized community.[48]

Naturally, this has led to a general improvement in the standard of living which is reflected, among other things, in the steady improvement of housing conditions in Dublin. Where in 1926, 'families' of four or more persons living in one-room tenements comprised 16·9 per cent of the city's population, such families were only 9·1 per cent of that population in 1946. Of no less significance is the fact that the percentage of persons in 'families' having more than two persons per room likewise declined from 45·3 per cent in 1926 to 27·3 per cent in 1946.[49] All of this has taken place despite the steady rise in housing standards. The improvement has been achieved both by private enterprise and the activities of the Dublin Corporation in clearing the slums. The problem is far from solved, and Dublin's slums are still notable. But progress has been remarkable and has resulted in the development of large new residential areas along the outer reaches of the city such as Drimnagh, Crumlin, Whitehall, West Cabra and Inchicore which we shall be visiting.[50]

Similarly, the extent of education has broadened considerably. In 1940 there were over 95,000 pupils in the 350 primary schools in

[47] These statistics were compiled from *Census of Population, 1946, Fifth Interim Report*, pp. 39–41. These are real families.

[48] *v.* pp. 47–8, above.

[49] These are not real families. In its housing statistics, the Census treats 'any person or group of persons included in a separate Census return as being in separate occupation of premises or part of premises . . . as a separate "family".' *Census of Population, 1946, Second Interim Report*, p. 6. For the figures quoted, *v.* Eire, *Report of Inquiry into the Housing of the Working Classes of the City of Dublin*, p. 28; *Census, 1946, Second Interim Report*, Table 18, p. 7, and Table 15, p. 33.

[50] Many of the homes in these new areas are owned, or are being purchased by the occupants. Although there are no statistics for 1926 available upon which to base a comparison, it is likely that such home ownership has increased during these twenty-five years in Dublin. In 1946, in Dublin City and Dun Laoghaire, roughly 25 per cent of the homes were owned or in the process of becoming owned by the families occupying them, while about 74 per cent were rented. I am again indebted to the Central Statistics Office for these unpublished data. To clarify references we shall be making to various parts of the city, a map of Dublin is appended at the end of this chapter.

Dublin County (15 per cent of the total population), while average daily attendance stood at 87·0 per cent. In the same year the combined vocational schools in Dublin City registered over 21,000 pupils of whom 3,500 were full-time day pupils. In the same year also there were 9,200 pupils registered in the fifty-eight secondary schools in the city, and this takes no account of twenty-nine suburban schools adjacent to the city whose total enrolment was over 3,500. Similarly, University College Dublin, had a student body of nearly 3,000 and a large portion of these came from the growing middle classes of the city.[51] Despite this substantial increase in school attendance at all levels, however, the law which compels attendance only till the age of fourteen, the requirement of fees for any sort of post-primary education and the need in working-class families for supplementary income, all continue to restrict the number of those who receive education in any form beyond the primary level. Thus, it has been estimated that in Dublin in 1950 only about 45 per cent of the children who finished primary school registered at secondary or vocational schools of any kind.[52]

In broad outline, this is the changing institutional framework of Dublin as it has grown into a modern metropolis. We have traced the effects of this transformation on migration from the country into Dublin itself, on the city's occupational and class structure, on educational opportunities and on living conditions because all of these have profound bearing upon the family life of the people we are to study and contribute to the differentiation of the life of the Dubliner from the life of the countryman. To discover and to understand the full range of differentiation between the rural and the city family we will have to dig deep into the internal structure of Dublin families. But first there are certain important differences between rural and urban people which appear in the statistics pertaining to marriage and the family that we must consider.

[51] These figures are taken from the records of the Department of Education, and of the Vocational Education Committee of the City of Dublin. *v.* p. 17, n. 22, above.

[52] This estimate was made by Mr. John Ingram, formerly of the Department of Education.

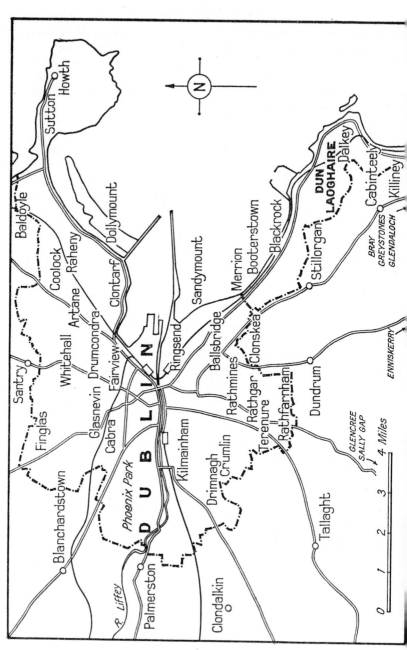

Dublin City and Dun Laoghaire

Chapter III

FAMILY SKETCH: STATISTICAL

STATISTICS ON MARRIAGE and family life in Ireland are not unlike a Gaelic illumination. The strands are many, they are intricately woven, and the whole configuration is certainly unique. For this reason, to bring out divergent patterns it is first necessary to observe the total design. Our main concern here is to compare the urban people with the people of the countryside. But the contrast between these two populations will be clearer if we first consider certain vital national characteristics of Irish family life.

THE NATIONAL PICTURE

Generally speaking, Ireland is distinctive among the nations of the Western world because in most matters pertaining to family life she tends to go to extremes. In the first place, since the beginning of the twentieth century, men have been more numerous than women in the Irish population. In 1951, the ratio was 956 females per 1,000 males. This sex ratio is notable because in virtually every other Western country females are more numerous than males.[1]

Furthermore, the age structure of the Irish population is also striking by comparison with other Western countries in that it has greatly favoured the older groups for a long period of time. Thus at every census since 1841 the proportion of people over sixty-five has increased while the proportion of those under that age has declined. During this period the vital working population between the ages of fifteen and sixty-four has fallen away to a point where in 1951 it was

[1] *Census of Population, 1951*, Vol. II, Pt. I, Table 5A, p. 14. In the United States the sex ratio is conventionally stated in terms of the number of males per 100 females. If we convert the Irish ratio into this form it becomes 105 males per 100 females. Donald J. Bogue, in *The Population of the United States* (Glencoe, Ill., 1959), Table 8–8, p. 163, gives a comparative listing of the sex ratios of selected nations with five million or more inhabitants at recent dates between 1948 and 1959. Ireland's sex ratio is higher than any European country and than any in the Western hemisphere in this list except Cuba and Argentina. *v.* M. D. McCarthy, 'Some Family Facts in Ireland Today', *Christus Rex*, V, No. 1 (January 1951), 49–50.

the smallest of all the nations of the West.[2] At the same time the group under fifteen years, which has been the feeder of a nation's population, has also steadily and constantly dropped. The appearance of this trend towards an ageing population at such an early stage in the industrialization of the West and its continued growth in a country that has remained predominantly agricultural is remarkable and poses problems we shall deal with later. But the relative preponderance of old people, as Arensberg and Kimball have shown, has crucial significance for family life in Ireland's rural areas and, as we shall see, in the urban population as well.

The age and sex structure of Ireland, of course, is intimately related to its marital statistics, and these are almost certainly unique in the international lists. For more people never marry at all in Ireland than in any other Western country and marriage there occurs at a later age than elsewhere.

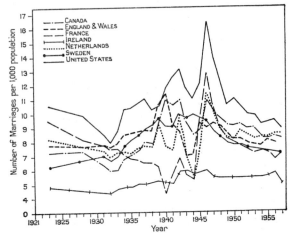

Although Ireland's marriage rate has increased a little since 1936, it still remains the West's lowest. From 1911 to 1926 the annual average marriage rate was only 5·0 per thousand of the population. This dropped to 4·6 from 1926 to 1936, then rose to 5·4 from 1936 to 1946,

[2] Between 1841 and 1951, the proportion of people under fifteen years of age fell from 38·0 per cent to 28·8 per cent, while that of people sixty-five years and over climbed from 3·1 per cent to 10·7 per cent. As a result, in 1951 only 60·5 per cent of the Irish population were in the age-bracket 15–64 years. *Census of Population, 1951*, Vol. II, Pt. I, Table 1, p. 2. This is a drop of 1·1 per cent from the percentage of 61·5 in 1946. By comparison, in the same period the percentages in age groups 15–64 were '. . . 69·4 in Belgium, 68·8 in England and Wales, 68·6 in Sweden, 67·7 in France, 67·0 in Denmark, 65·2 in the U.S.A. and 61·7 in Portugal'; McCarthy, op. cit., p. 48. *v.* Bogue, op. cit., Table 6–5, p. 105, for further comparative material.

and to 5·5 from 1964 to 1951.[3] The opposite figure, taken from a comparative study of selected modernized countries, graphically shows Ireland's low marriage rate.[4]

Similarly, the extent of Irish celibacy appears clearly in the fact that in 1951 almost one out of every three men, and one out of every four women, between the ages 55–64 had never married. For those who do marry the tendency towards late marriage is equally apparent. In that same year, within the age bracket 25–34, two out of every three Irish men, and more than two out of every five Irish women, were single.[5] And in the following graph, Kiser again shows the very low percentage ever married of Irish women aged 20–24.[6]

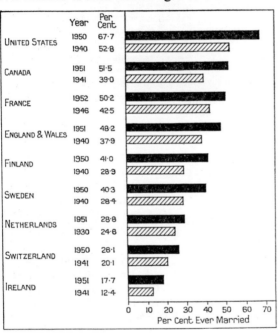

[3] *Census of Population, 1951*, Vol. I (Dublin, 1952), Table 3, p. 6.
[4] Taken from Clyde V. Kiser, 'Current Mating and Fertility Trends and their Demographic Significance', *Eugenics Quarterly*, VI, No. 2 (June 1959), 66. There appears to be a discrepancy between the rates from 1946 to 1951 cited by Kiser and those listed in the *Census of Population, 1951*, Vol. I, but it is small and does not change Ireland's low position. Cf. J. Hajnal, 'The Marriage Boom', *Population Index*, XIX, No. 2 (April 1953), Table 1, p. 81.
[5] The exact percentages of those aged 55–64 who had never married in 1951 were 28·8 for the men and 24·7 for the women. At the same time, 67·4 per cent of the men aged 25–34, and 45·6 per cent of the women, were unmarried. *Census of Population, 1951*, Vol. II, Pt. I, Table 7A, pp. 22–3. *v*. Appendix I, Table 2, p. 255.
[6] Taken from Kiser, op. cit., p. 69.

A study of first marriages, made by the Central Statistics Office of the Irish Government in 1946, more precisely revealed that in Ireland the average man then married when he was slightly over thirty-three years of age, while the average girl took the step when she was twenty-eight years old.[7] Again, the following graph demonstrates Ireland's extreme tendencies as to the average age at marriage for the

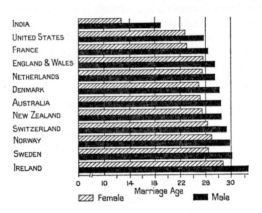

decade 1930–41.[8] The Irish bent to postpone marriage or to forgo it altogether is all the more remarkable because it is not a special trait of the higher classes but is common to all classes of the country. Thus Dr. M. D. McCarthy, Assistant Director of the Central Statistics Office, writes: '... the population unmarried at a given age *in specific occupations is lower in all cases* in England and Wales than in the Twenty-Six Counties'.[9]

These are not recent developments in Ireland but practices of long standing. There has been a steady trend towards increased celibacy since at least the last quarter of the nineteenth century, and since 1926 this trend has continued. Between 1926 and 1951, the percentage of single men and women aged 55–64 increased so that in 1951, 2·6 per

[7] The exact figures are 33·1 years of age for the men and 28·0 for the women. *Census of Population, 1946*, Vol. IX, *Fertility of Marriage* (Dublin, 1953), 226, 228. The figures are based on a study of over 14,000 couples in 1946 who were recorded as married for the first time and for less than a year. The study is treated in detail in *Memorandum on Age at Marriage. v.* ch. i, n. 15.

[8] Taken from *Population Index* (published by Office of Population Research, Princeton University; and Population Association of America, Inc.), XIX, No. 2 (April 1953), frontispiece. *v.* Hajnal, op. cit., Table 6, p. 91. For a comparison of *median* age at marriage in Ireland and other countries, *v.* Kiser, op. cit., figure 2, p. 68.

[9] McCarthy, op. cit., p. 54. The italics are mine.

cent more men and 1·1 per cent more women in this bracket were unmarried than in 1926.[10]

The trend towards later marriage in Ireland has also lasted a long time. It seems to have started shortly after the famine in 1845, although we do not have data exact enough to trace it accurately prior to 1891. However, between 1864 and 1890 the marriage rate in Ireland dropped 20 per cent which would seem to indicate that both celibacy and later marriage were on the increase during that period.[11] Between 1891 and 1936 the trend is clear, for in that period there was a national increase in both single men and women in almost every age bracket of the adult population.[12]

But interestingly enough, between 1936 and 1951 an opposite trend towards earlier marriage appears to have set in. The study of the age at marriage which we cited previously states: 'The average age at marriage of men has declined by 1·9 years and of women by 1·1 in the twenty years (*1926–1946*).'[13] This statement is true but it refers to this twenty-year period *as a whole*, since the last comparable study of the age at marriage made in Ireland prior to that of 1946 was made in 1926. There is fairly clear evidence, however, that this drop in the age of marriage is principally accounted for by people who married after 1936. During the period 1926–36 the proportion of single men and women in the ages 20–34 actually increased. But from 1936 to 1951 the proportion of single people of both sexes in this age bracket steadily declined.[14]

This latter development constitutes a recent reversal of a century-long trend, and we shall have to try to assess its significance later. Despite this, however, it is well here to stress the fact that marriage in Ireland still occurs at an uncommonly late date in a person's life. Indeed, the tradition of late marriage, which began with the famine in the middle of the nineteenth century, has become so embedded in

[10] *Census of Population, 1936*, Vol. V, Pt. I, pp. 26–7, and *Census of Population, 1951*, Vol. II, Pt. I, pp. 22–3. Cf. Rev. F. O'Briain, 'Rural Depopulation', in *Rural Ireland, 1949* (Tipperary, 1949), pp. 76–7.

[11] McCarthy, op. cit., pp. 54–5. *v.* Hajnal, op. cit., Table 3, pp. 84–5, and pp. 86–7.

[12] *v. Census of Population, 1936*, Vol. V, Pt. I, pp. 26–7.

[13] *Memorandum on Age at Marriage*, p. 5.

[14] Thus between 1936–51 the proportion of single men declined by 1·3 per cent among those aged 20–24, by 5·7 per cent among those aged 25–29, and by 5·6 per cent among those aged 30–34. Similarly for the respective age groups, the proportion of single women dropped by 4·1, 9·7, and 7·7 per cent. *Census of Population, 1936*, Vol. V, Pt. I, pp. 26–7; and *Census of Population, 1951*, Vol. II, Pt. I, pp. 22–3. *v.* Appendix I, Table 2, p. 255. *v.* Hajnal, op. cit., pp. 83–7; also graph of comparative marriage rates, p. 66, above. Estimated numbers of the population, according to age, sex and conjugal condition in 1956 supplied me by the Central Statistics Office, indicate that this trend was continuing as of that date.

Irish culture as to be looked on as the normal thing in life, or at least as an inescapable accompaniment of the Irish way of life.

But the Irish, at one extreme in being the most celibate and slowest to marry, are also at the other extreme in maintaining the highest marital fertility rate of all Western nations and probably in the world. In Kiser's comparative study of marital fertility for duration of marriage 15–19 years in 1950–51, Ireland's rate of 409 easily topped the countries listed, and far exceeded the rate of 322 set by her nearest competitor, the Netherlands.[15] The average number of children born per 100 married women for all durations of marriage is the national marital fertility rate for Ireland. It was 353 in 1946.[16] And inasmuch as this study concerns Catholic families, it is well to note that the same national rate for Catholics in 1946 was 361 children as compared to a rate of 245 children for other religious denominations.[17]

Yet it is true that fertility has declined in Ireland in the course of this century. Between 1911, when the last previous study of the country's fertility was made, and 1946 the *standardized* fertility rate had declined by 18 per cent. Whereas in the former year the standardized average number of children born of 100 married women aged 15–44 was 404, in 1946 the average was 331.[18] This decline in fertility naturally is reflected in a change in sizes of family. Thus in marriages of 30–34 years duration, in which fertility may be regarded as completed, 'the modal size of family . . ., which was eight children in 1911, fell to five children in 1946'. Similarly, in the same period and for marriages of the same duration, the percentage of families with four or less children went up from 26·7 to 47·5, while the percentage of families of ten or more children sank from 23·8 to 9·8.[19] Despite this decline, Ireland is still a country of large families and maintains her pre-eminence in marital fertility. More than two out of every three Irish families have from three to nine children.[20] And, as the

---

[15] *v.* Kiser's Table 2, p. 73, below.

[16] *Census of Population, 1946*, Vol. IX, Table 4A, p. 6.

[17] Ibid., Table 6, p. 8.

[18] *Census of Population, 1946, Fifth Interim Report*, p. 12. The discrepancy between this figure and that of 353 previously cited stems from the fact that it is a standardized rate whereas the former is not. The method of standardization is defined in a footnote to the text of the *Fifth Interim Report*, p. 12. *v.* McCarthy, op. cit., pp. 61–2.

We should also note that the 1911 Census covered the whole of Ireland whereas the censuses from 1926 to 1951 refer only to the Republic of Ireland. Furthermore, according to *Census of Population, 1946*, Vol. IX, p. x: 'It is not possible to derive from the available material fertility statistics for 1911 relating to the present area of the State. In view of this fact . . . only limited comparisons between the data for the two Censuses can be made.'

[19] *Census of Population, 1946, Fifth Interim Report*, p. 11.

[20] In 1946 fully 66·9 per cent of Irish families had from three to nine children. Ibid.

following graph shows, Ireland's fertility rate starts at a higher point in the earlier years of marriage than in other Western countries, and grows at a greater velocity through the succeeding years of marriage.[21]

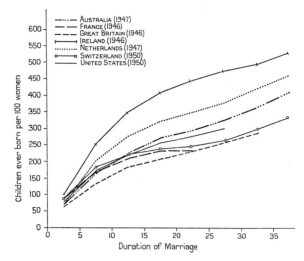

The result of this combination of Irish practices in regard to marriage and fertility is to put the Irish birth rate in a comparatively middle position among Western countries. Although suffering a decline in the years 1926–36, the Irish birth rate from 1891–1951 has averaged about 21·3 births per thousand population.[22] The consequence is the clearly central course Ireland holds relative to other countries, as the figure on p. 72 shows.[23]

Kiser states the case succinctly:

> Ireland is characterized by lowest marriage rate, oldest ages at marriage, lowest proportions married among women under 25. On the other hand, the fertility rates of the women who do get married probably outrank those of any other country in the Western world. Hence her crude birth rate and general fertility rates tend to be in a middling position despite the disadvantage of late age at marriage.[24]

And as shown in Table 2 on p. 73 he admirably summarizes most of the pertinent national Irish data about marriage and fertility and puts them in illuminating perspective against similar data from other countries.[25]

[21] Taken from Kiser, op. cit., p. 75.
[22] *Census of Population, 1951*, Vol. I, Table 3, p. 6.
[23] Taken from Kiser, op. cit., p. 71.
[24] Ibid., p. 80.
[25] Ibid.

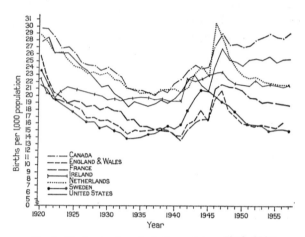

Crude birthrates in selected countries, 1920–1957

RURAL AND URBAN DIFFERENCES

We can now turn to the rural-urban differences in family practice and the causes underlying them which are the central concern of this study. We have already seen that as a result of internal population shifts during the second quarter of this century, two-fifths of the Irish population in 1951 resided in towns of 1,500 and over, and nearly one-fifth of the entire population lived in Dublin and Dun Laoghaire.[26] When we compare this urban population with the rural population in the matters bearing upon family practice under consideration we find that, with one notable exception, there is a marked disparity between them.

To begin with the sex ratio, where rural Ireland is man's country, Dublin and the towns generally belong predominantly to the women. Whereas in the aggregate rural areas in 1951 there were 115 men to every 100 women, the aggregate town areas had only 89·3. Significantly, the sex ratio of Dublin City at 87·7, and of Dun Laoghaire at 76·9, was lower than that of the general urban population.[27] This low

[26] *v.* ch. ii, pp. 46–7, above. This represents an 8·8 per cent increase in the urban population since 1926. *v.* United Nations, *Demographic Yearbook, 1952*, pp. 10–14. Ireland is far from being the most urbanized of Western countries. In fact, in Europe outside the Iron Curtain only Switzerland is less urbanized. Yet in a list of sixty-four countries of the world presented by Bogue, Ireland ranks twenty-seventh in the percentage of its urban population. Bogue, op. cit., p. 34, Table 2–4.

[27] *Census of Population, 1951*, Vol. II, Pt. I, pp. 14–16. *v.* McCarthy, op. cit., pp. 49–50.

Table 2

Recent Indices of Marriage and Fertility for Selected Countries

Country	Crude Marriage Rate (1957)[1]	Crude Birth Rate (1957)[1]	Median Age at First Marriage Circa (1950)[2]	Per Cent		Births Occurring to Women 15–24 (1954)[4]	General Fertility Rate		Cumulative Marital Fertility Rate by Duration of Marriage (1950–51)[4]	
				Ever Married Among Women 15–24 (1950–51)[3]	Ever Married Women 15–49 Who are 15–24 (1950–51)[3]		Women 20–24 (1954)[4]	Women 30–34 (1954)[4]	5–9 Yrs.	15–19 Yrs.
Australia	7·7	22·9	22·0b	27·7b	12·6b	37·1	198	122	164b	271b
Canada	8·2	28·6	21·7	30·2	13·8	35·6	220	160	—	—
England and Wales	7·9a	15·6a	22·0	27·3	10·2	36·0	136	85	134	209
Finland	7·2	19·8	22·9	23·2	11·1	31·6	154	123	210	320
France	7·0	18·4	21·9	24·4c	11·5c	32·7	156	110	169c	231c
Ireland	5·0	21·2	26·0	8·7	5·9	—	—	—	251	409
Netherlands	8·5	21·2	24·3	17·0	9·2	18·7	99	162	200	322
Norway	7·1	18·2	23·5	19·6	8·0	30·1	138	117	174	240
Sweden	7·0	14·6	22·8	23·0	8·5	37·5	125	86	—	—
Switzerland	8·1	17·7	24·5	14·3	6·8	26·1	105	110	182	237
United States	8·9	25·0	20·2	43·6	16·4	46·1	236	116	168	253

a Year 1956   b Year 1947   c Year 1946
[1] *Population Index*, July 1958, Vol. 24, No. 3, pp. 298–305.
[2] For explanation and source, see Figure 2.
[3] *Demographic Yearbook*, United Nations, 1955, Table 12, pp. 390–429.
[4] United Nations: *Recent Trends in Fertility in Industrialized Countries*, New York, 1958, pp. 23, 60, 135, 137.

sex ratio in the urban population of Ireland seems to parallel the trend in other Western industrialized countries. Indeed, it seems to be more pronounced in Ireland than elsewhere.[28]

In like fashion, while rural Ireland is relatively old in its age structure, Dublin and the towns are relatively young, and the age distribution of the urban population is more balanced. In 1951 only 8·1 per cent of the urban people were sixty-five years or over as contrasted with 12·4 per cent of the rural people. And the percentage of persons under fifteen years, and of persons 15–64 years was higher in the aggregate town areas than in the country.[29] Thus the ageing of the Irish population which we have noted is mainly attributable to the rural population. It is interesting to note that in the United States the percentage of urban people over sixty-five in 1950 was 8·2 or almost exactly the same as in Ireland, but that the percentage of rural farm people over that age is 7·6 which is considerably lower than in rural Ireland.[30] However, it should be noted that between 1936 and 1951 the age composition of the rural population remained about the same except for a small increase in males under fifteen years of age. But the town population during this period has grown older. Both for men and women there occurred a drop in those aged 0–14 and 15–54, and a definite increase in those over 55 years of age.[31] Thus while the urban population is younger than the rural in Ireland, it appears in recent years to be ageing while the rural is not.

The city folk are also more prone to marry than their country contemporaries. Caution must be used in making a comparison of the crude marriage rates of the urban and the rural population, since many rural people come into the cities for their weddings. Still, the crude marriage rates of each of the three largest County Boroughs—

[28] Thus, for example, in 1950 the sex ratio of the white urban population of the United States was 94·9 while that of the rural-farm population was 111·4. *v.* Bogue, op. cit., p. 159. Also United Nations *Demographic Yearbook, 1952*, p. 15, Table C.

[29] *Census of Population, 1951*, Vol. II, Pt. I, pp. 10–13. Children under 15 years comprised 29·4 per cent, and persons 15–64 comprised 62·4 per cent of the urban population as compared with percentages in the rural areas of 28·6 and 58·9 respectively. *v.* McCarthy, op. cit., p. 50.

[30] Bogue, op. cit., p. 101.

[31] The percentage of rural males over 55 was 21·1 in 1936 and 21·0 in 1951, while the percentage 0–14 went from 26·0 to 27·4. Rural women over 55 comprised 21·5 per cent of the female population in 1936 and 21·9 per cent in 1951, while the percentage aged 0–14 was 29·4 and 30·0 respectively. The changes are negligible in both cases save for the increase of 1·4 per cent of males aged 0–14. In contrast, men showed a decline in those aged 0–14 (of 0·5 per cent) and 15–54 (of 0·3 per cent), and an increase of 1·4 per cent in those over 55 years. The women likewise showed a decrease in the brackets 0–14 (of 1·3 per cent) and 15–54 (of 1·1 per cent), and an increase of 2·3 per cent in those over 55 years. These percentages were computed from *Census of Population, 1936*, Vol. V, Pt. I, Table 5, pp. 15–16; and *Census of Population, 1951*, Vol. II, Pt. I, Table 4A, pp. 8–9.

Dublin, Cork and Limerick—were notably higher in 1951 than the national rate of 5·5 per 1,000 population. Dublin County and County Borough together, which have the largest concentration of urban people, had a marriage rate of 7·4 that year, and no other county in the Republic was as high as 6·0.[32]

Much more significant than the comparison of the marriage rates is the fact that the national trend towards greater celibacy which we have noted is less pronounced in the town than in the rural population. Thus in the towns and cities from 1936 to 1951 the proportion of single men aged 55–64 decreased by 2·4 per cent in contrast to the 2·6 per cent increase of single men in these ages in rural areas. It is true that even in the towns the proportion of single women in this age group increased, but it was only about half as large as the increase in the proportion of single women in the country.[33] Particularly in the Dublin metropolitan area during the same period the decline in celibacy was greater than in the towns in general. Thus in Dublin City and County the proportion of the unmarried aged 55–64 declined by 3·5 per cent among men and 1·0 per cent among women.[34]

Not only do more people marry in the towns than in the rural areas, but as a general rule they marry at an earlier age. In 1946 the average Dublin man was marrying at thirty-one years of age, more than three years earlier than the average countryman who married at 34·7 years. The average Dublin woman was marrying more than a year earlier than the country girl—at 27·4 years as compared to 28·7 for the latter.[35] Consequently, there are proportionately more people married between the ages 20–34 years in the towns than in the country. The men are more responsible for this state of affairs than the women. In 1951 for the ages 20–24 and 30–34 there were actually less single women in the rural areas than in the city, while the proportion of single women aged 25–29 was the same in both cases.[36] But in each of these age brackets there were proportionately fewer bachelors in the town population than in the country, and the amount of difference

[32] *Census of Population, 1951*, Vol. I, p. 139. *v.* McCarthy, op. cit., pp. 55–6.

[33] To be precise, the increase was 0·4 per cent for women in towns and 0·7 per cent for rural women. *Census of Population, 1936*, Vol. V, Pt. I, pp. 32–4; *Census of Population, 1946*, Vol. V, Pt. I, pp. 36–7; and *Census of Population, 1951*, Vol. II, Pt. I, pp. 30–3.

[34] *Census of Population, 1951*, Vol. II, Pt. I, pp. 22–3.

[35] The average age at marriage is a bit later in the Dublin area than in the aggregate town areas where it was 30·9 for the men and 27·1 for the women. *v. Memorandum on the Age at Marriage*, pp. 2–3.

[36] Of women aged 20–24, 81·1 per cent of the rural women were single as compared with 83·2 per cent of the women in the towns. Of those aged 25–29 the percentage of single women was 54·4 for both town and country. Of those aged 30–34, 35·9 per cent of the rural women and 37·0 per cent of the women in towns, were single. *Census of Population, 1951*, Vol. II, Pt. I, pp. 30–3.

was much greater than the difference between the rural and urban women. Thus, for example, almost 25 per cent less men aged 30–34 were single in the towns than in the country.[37] This tendency for urban men to marry earlier than rural men, and for urban women to marry later than rural women appears also in the United States and may be common in Western countries.[38]

We have called attention to the national long-range trend towards later marriage in Ireland and to its recent reversal since 1936. In this matter, too, there is a significant difference between country and town. Prior to 1936, the trend towards later marriage and towards greater celibacy seems to have been more marked in the country than in the city, at least in the city of Dublin. Between 1891 and 1936 the proportional increase in single men and women in almost every age bracket was greater in the country at large than in Dublin City and County.[39] On the other hand, the reverse trend since 1936 is more pronounced in rural areas than in town areas. The towns, indeed, do show slightly greater decreases in single men in almost all ages under fifty-five, and smaller increases in bachelors over fifty-five than does the rural population. But this is more than counterbalanced by the comparatively greater decline in single women in the country, particularly among women aged 20–34. More important is the fact that Dublin City shows relatively lower decreases in single men and women than either the aggregate town or rural population, especially in the younger groups aged 20–34 years.

For during the period 1936–51 the proportion of unmarried men in the rural areas dropped 1·0 per cent in the group aged 20–34; 4·4 per cent for those aged 25–29; and 4·0 per cent for those aged 30–34. On the other hand, in Dublin unmarried men increased by 0·3 per cent in the 20–24 age group, and fell by 0·6 per cent and 0·1 per cent in the next two age groups. Meanwhile, the percentage decrease of unmarried women at these same ages was respectively 6·8, 12·4 and 9·3 in the country, as compared with a percentage increase of 0·9 for those aged 20–24, and a decrease of only 1·7 for the group aged 25–29, and 1·5 for the 30–34 bracket in Dublin City.[40]

Ireland in the past has been exceptional among Western nations by reason of the fact that rural women generally married later than

[37] In rural areas in 1951, 96·7 per cent of the men aged 20–24 were single as against 92·5 per cent in the towns. For the ages 25–29 and 30–34, the respective percentages for rural areas were 84·2 and 68·0 as compared to percentages of 66·4 and 42·2 for townsmen. Ibid.

[38] *v.* Bogue, op. cit., Table 10–6, p. 223, and Table 10–10, p. 227.

[39] *Census of Population, 1936*, Vol. V, Pt. I, pp. 26–7.

[40] *Census of Population, 1936*, Vol. V, Pt. I, pp. 34–5; *Census, 1946*, Vol. V, Pt. I, pp. 44–7; *Census, 1951*, Vol. II, Pt. I, pp. 30–3. The complete figures are given below in Appendix I, Table 3, p. 256.

urban women, whereas the reverse is true elsewhere. But rural women in Ireland had nearly caught up with urban women in age at marriage in 1946 and by 1951 were actually marrying earlier than women in the towns and cities. In this respect, then, the effect of the recent trend towards early marriage has been to bring the rural-urban pattern for women in Ireland into greater conformity to the general Western pattern. It remains to be seen if this new pattern will remain stable.

The increase in rural men who are marrying earlier is also notable. Indeed, it is almost as pronounced as among urban men. As a result, urban men in Ireland continue to marry about four years younger on the average than rural men in 1951. This difference between rural and urban men is similar to that which prevails in other Western countries and, in view of the factors which promote later marriage for men in rural areas, it is not likely that the Irish countryman will overtake his city counterpart. But it is significant that even rural Irish men have been marrying younger and that consequently in 1951 both men and women in town and countryside were marrying at an earlier age than a quarter of a century before.

These figures also indicate that in the last fifteen years there has been a slightly greater tendency in the towns than in the country for people who marry between the ages 20–34 years to marry in the later years of this bracket. The differences in this respect are too small to be completely significant, but they suggest that, although more people in the city as well as in the country are marrying between the ages 20–34, relatively more of the urban people are marrying between the ages 25–29 and 30–34 than previously. Within the younger groups of the urban population, then, there seems to be a countering shift towards later marriage.

One might be inclined to think that this recent counter trend towards marriage after twenty-five in the growing town population may be due to an increase of people in the higher classes who usually marry comparatively late. This is undoubtedly a factor but it is not the only one. While Ireland follows the general urban pattern of the Western world in that the higher social group tends to marry later than the lower, the general tendency of all Irish classes to marry late is quite marked, and the range of variation between the classes is notably narrow. We can see this by comparing class differentials in the average age at marriage in the town population. The average age at marriage for men in the aggregate non-agricultural population was thirty-one years in 1946. The greatest class difference was one of 2·6 years between the class of employers, managers and higher professionals whose average was 33·7 years, and that of the semi-skilled workers and general labourers whose average is 30·4 years. Women in these two groups also show the largest difference, but it is relatively small. Wives of general labourers marry only eighteen months younger on the average—at 26·9 years—than those in the highest class—at 28·4 years. Thus, the lower classes appear to contribute nearly as much as the upper classes to the late marriages characteristic of the urban Irish. Surely it is unique among Western urban populations that Dublin men in the working class marry as late as thirty years of age on the average, while their wives marry usually at twenty-six.[41]

But this recent trend towards earlier marriage, which seems to be changing the old rural and urban differentials, had not lasted long enough to change the long-standing marital composition of town and country in Ireland at the time this study was made. Despite developments since 1936, the urban population in the early 'fifties was made up of people in every class who had married several years younger than people in the rural areas.

Ireland is also similar to other Western nations in that the population of the Irish towns, and of Dublin in particular, is less fertile than the rural population. Here the crude birth rates must not be allowed to mislead us. The urban birth rate in 1951 was higher than the rural. In each of the four County Boroughs the birth rate was higher than the national crude rate of 22·2 per 1,000 population; and no county, except Kildare, had as high a rate as the County Boroughs of Dublin, Cork and Limerick. This has been true at each census since 1936.[42] But these rates make no allowance for differences in age, sex and marital condition. When such allowance is made and the rates are standardized, the rural population emerges as clearly more fertile than the urban.

Thus a United Nations study of 'children under 5 years per 1000 women aged 15–49 years in urban and rural areas' shows that in 1946 urban Ireland had 366 as compared with 461 for rural Ireland.[43] In a more refined statement, McCarthy writes: '. . . the standardized number of children 0–4 per 100 married women aged 15–44 was, in 1946, 106 in the towns and 134 in rural areas'. The corresponding figure for Dublin City and County was also 106, the same as that of

[41] *v.* Appendix I, Table 4, p. 257. It should be noted that the town population and the non-agricultural population in the Irish Census roughly, but not exactly, correspond to each other. While the town population is limited to people living in towns of 1,500 persons or over, the non-agricultural population goes beyond these to include persons living in rural areas whose occupation is non-agricultural; for example, a doctor or a teacher living in a small rural village. The number of these latter, however, is relatively small, and the town and non-agricultural population are nearly identical. For this reason, when data have not been available for the town and rural population, I have used data from the non-agricultural and agricultural populations respectively.

[42] *Census of Population, 1951*, Vol. I, p. 139. *v.* McCarthy, op. cit., p. 57.

[43] United Nations, *Demographic Yearbook, 1949/50*, p. 248, Table 10.

the towns in general.[44] If we consider only the Catholic population, this differential is confirmed by comparing the fertility data for Dublin City and Dun Laoghaire with those of the Provinces of the Republic of Ireland. The average number of children born per 100 Catholic married women according to all durations of marriage and all ages of wife at marriage in 1946 was 343 for Dublin City and Dun Laoghaire. It was 358 for the rest of Leinster, 359 for Munster, 381 for Connacht and 383 for the Republic's part of Ulster.[45]

But again it is necessary to stress the fact that however less fertile they may be when compared with their country cousins, the Irish townspeople without doubt have a higher marital fertility rate than people of any other Western nation. McCarthy states that while Portugal ranked next to Ireland in national fertility in 1946, the fertility of the Irish town population by itself exceeds the fertility of Portugal as a whole.[46] And it is almost certain that the marital fertility rate of the Catholics in Dublin for all durations of marriage and all ages of wife at marriage, which is 343, is the highest urban rate in the Western world.[47]

It is no wonder then that, on a comparative international basis, the size of Dublin families is quite large. It is true that the tendency for the large family to give place to the relatively smaller family, which we have noted for Ireland as a whole, is about the same in Dublin as in the rest of the country. Among families of women married thirty years or more, whose families could be considered as complete in 1946, Dublin had a higher percentage of childless families and families of one or two children than the country at large. And the increase in these categories has not been at the expense of families from three to five children, but rather at the expense of families with six or more children. Yet despite this decline in family size, fully 60 per cent of the families in non-agricultural population had from three to nine children.[48]

Within this town population itself there are differences in fertility according to class resembling class differentials in this respect in other Western countries. But, as with the age at marriage, the differences are noteworthy for being small. In 1946 the highest standardized fertility rate in the non-agricultural population was 442 and it belonged to the semi-skilled wage-earners. The general labourers were next with a rate of 435. As we move from these classes up through each ascendant class this rate successively declines until among the higher professionals it is 286. The only exception to this is the class of

[44] McCarthy, op. cit., pp. 59–60.
[45] *Census of Population, 1946*, Vol. IX, pp. 148–52.
[46] McCarthy, op. cit., p. 60.
[47] *Census of Population, 1946*, Vol. IX, p. 149.
[48] The full figures are given below in Appendix I, Table 5, pp. 257-8.

small business men, working on their own account, who have a higher rate than either the salaried workers or the non-manual wage-earners.

However, the most signal feature of these class differentials is that they are so small. Among the furthest deviants from the mean of the urban population—namely, the semi-skilled wage-earners and the higher professionals—the extent of deviation is 12 per cent and 15 per cent respectively. The fertility rates of all the other classes are covered by a range of only 8 per cent on either side of the mean.[49]

AN APPRAISAL OF THE NEW DUBLINERS

Before we try to draw any conclusions from the preceding data about the results of urbanization on marriage and family practice in Ireland, it may be well to see how our New Dubliners stand in this respect. For the effects of urbanization on the marriage practices of the Irish may well be greater than those indicated by the differences between townsmen and countrymen which we have just considered.

During the first half of this century fully a quarter of the population of Dublin have been first-generation immigrants into the city. Their presence undoubtedly has seriously affected the urban data on marriage and family practice in such a way as to reduce the degree of difference between rural people and fully urbanized people in these matters. Most of these immigrants were raised in the country, and it would be only natural for them to retain even in the city many of the attitudes and practices common to the countryside. It is also natural to expect that their children and the remainder of the Dublin population who were born and raised in the city may differ significantly from these immigrants in their marital practices.

In view of this, a comparative study of the immigrants on the one hand and of completely urbanized Dubliners on the other would yield a more exact picture of the effects of urbanization on marriage and family practice. Unfortunately, we cannot undertake such a study by direct methods since neither the immigrants nor the Old Dubliners are distinguished as groups in the census material, especially as concerns marital practice. But discreet use of data gathered from the New Dubliners may throw some light on this problem.[50]

[49] *v.* Appendix I, Table 6, p. 258.

[50] In regard to the familial matters discussed in this section, I gathered from the people interviewed not only data about themselves, but also about their mature siblings; and in some cases I was able to get data directly from these relatives themselves. What we are about to say concerning the New Dubliners is based on information which refers to 101 families. In certain matters the number of families is less than this because of the need to eliminate cases where the data are unreliable. These data require careful treatment, and their limitations, as well as the precautions necessary in their interpretation, are discussed in Appendix I, pp. 264–8.

Family Sketch: Statistical

We may profitably ask whether the general features of the town population, as contrasted with the rural population, are more pronounced among the New Dubliners than in the town population as a whole. If this is so, it seems logical to suppose that the differences between the New Dubliners and the general urban population are due to the presence in Dublin of the immigrants rather than to the presence of the older and more urbanized townsmen. For it seems reasonable to assume that the New Dubliners would tend to conform to the standards of the older townspeople rather than cling to those standards of their parents which are common to the countryside but which, in the townsman's definition of the situation, are less suitable to city life. And thus the New Dubliners may give us a more accurate picture of the effects of urbanization on marital practice.

On the whole, the New Dubliners in our sample not only display nearly all the features characteristic of the general urban population and of the Dublin population in particular, but in most instances they manifest them in a more marked degree. This is especially true of the decline in celibacy. As celibacy is less in the urban than in the rural population, so fewer New Dubliners ultimately remain unmarried than do urban people in general. Of men aged 55–64 in our group of New Dubliners in 1951 only 9·7 per cent were bachelors compared to 17·3 per cent of the men in that age bracket in Dublin City who were single. Among women in the same age bracket the difference is smaller, being 20·0 per cent unmarried for the New Dubliners as contrasted with 26·1 per cent unmarried for Dublin as a whole.[51] But it is worth noting that the percentage of single women at this age among the New Dubliners is even below that of the rural women. The fact that apparently fewer city-born women remained unmarried tends to confirm the view that the higher proportions of unmarried women in the later age brackets which are found in the city are in great part due to '. . . the drift of women, mostly unmarried, from the country to the towns and cities'.[52]

In like fashion, taking the group of New Dubliners as a whole, both men and women appear to marry earlier than do Dubliners in general. Thus, we may compare the proportion of persons in the urban population in 1926, 1936 and 1946 who were unmarried between the ages 25–29 with the proportion of New Dubliners who were unmarried at the same ages in the years 1925–27, 1935–37, and 1945–

[51] In the sample of New Dubliners three out of thirty-one men aged 55–64 were unmarried and six out of twenty-nine women. For the proportions unmarried at this age in the total Dublin population, v. Census of Population, 1951, Vol. II, Pt. I, pp. 30–1.

[52] McCarthy, op. cit., p. 52. The proportion of rural women unmarried at ages 55–64 is 22·3 per cent. v. Census of Population, 1951, Vol. II, Pt. I, p. 33.

47. In every instance, a smaller percentage of men and women among the New Dubliners were unmarried than in the total Dublin population.[53]

However, there is need for caution here. We have pointed out that prior to 1936 there was a long-range trend towards later marriage throughout Ireland, in the urban as well as in the rural population. This trend is reflected in the New Dubliners and again seems to be more pronounced among them than in the general urban population. Here we can make a comparison between the New Dubliners and the non-agricultural population in regard to the proportion of women married at the three five-year levels within the age bracket 20–34 years for durations of marriage 10–14, 24–28, 35–39, and 40 or more years. If we take the age brackets 20–24 and 25–29 together, both the general urban population and the sample of New Dubliners show a steady decline in the number of women married at these ages during this period, but the rate of decline is much greater among the New Dubliners than it is in the urban population as a whole. At the same time, the proportion of women in both groups who married between the ages 30–34 steadily increased, but again the rate of increase was higher among the New Dubliners than among urban women generally.[54] Data are not available for such a direct comparison between New Dubliners and urban men. But in our group of New Dubliners the men show the same tendency as the women and so it is likely that prior to 1936 they tended to marry later than the average urban male. For the same durations of marriage, the proportion of husbands aged 20–24 and 24–29 at marriage among the New Dubliners also dropped gradually from the earliest period and inversely rose for those who married between the ages 30–34.[55]

We have also pointed out that since 1936 an opposite trend towards earlier marriage appears in Ireland as elsewhere, and that it seems to be stronger in the rural than in the urban population. We cannot judge how New Dubliners may have been affected by this recent trend towards earlier marriage because the requirement of our study demanded a sample with a sufficient number of families that were fully developed and in which, therefore, most of the spouses were married before 1936. As a result, we do not have enough cases of couples married after 1936 to make an adequate comparison between Dubliners and New Dubliners. But it is interesting to note that the younger people in our sample of New Dubliners who married between 1945 and 1947 married later than either the general town population or that of Dublin. For the average age at marriage of

[53] *v.* Appendix I, Table 7, pp. 260-1.
[54] Ibid., Table 8, p. 261.
[55] Ibid., Table 9, p. 262.

New Dubliners who married during these years was later for both men and women of all classes than for the Dublin and non-agricultural population in 1946.[56]

On the other hand, the New Dubliners also tend to be like the urban population in regard to class differentials in the age at marriage. For the lower class of New Dubliners also appear to marry at an earlier age than the higher classes. This becomes clear if we combine the employer-managerial and salaried classes who married between 1945 and 1947 into one group and compare them with the group of wage-earners and general labourers who married at the same period. We find that the average age of marriage for the men was 35·9 years for the former as compared to 34·5 for the latter. Among the women, the average age at marriage was respectively 31·4 and 29·5 years. With one exception, similar differences between these classes of New Dubliners appear for both husbands and wives who were married between 1925–27, and between 1935–37, so that this tendency has been constant during the second quarter of this century.[57]

In regard to marriage and family patterns, then, the New Dubliners appear to move in the same direction as the general urban population but to do so a little more strongly. The one area which is an exception to this tendency to outstrip the general urban population is fertility. Among the New Dubliners fertility does not seem to differ to any significant degree from that of the Irish city people in general. A comparison by classes of the fertility rates of Catholic wives who are New Dubliners with wives in the non-agricultural population in 1946 aged 20–34 years at marriage for four selected durations at marriage shows that the scatter of differences between them is such as more or less to balance out. This comparison yields sixteen cases. In eight of these the fertility of the New Dubliners' marriages is lower than that of the non-agricultural population as a whole. In four it is higher, and in two it is at par. But where the group of New Dubliners lags in the marriages of shorter duration, they catch up to the general population in those of longer duration and vice versa. The one exception to this is the salaried class of New Dubliners. In this class alone the New Dubliners' fertility rate in all but one instance is lower than that of the salaried class in the general town population. But with this one exception the fertility rates of the New Dubliners and the non-agricultural population are quite similar to each other.[58]

[56] Ibid., Table 10, p. 263.
[57] Ibid.
[58] Ibid., Table 11, pp. 263-4.

THE IMPACT OF URBANIZATION

The data we have seen, and even the data we have not seen, which bear upon marriage and family life in Ireland indicate that urbanization there produces certain effects that are quite dissimilar to those it produces elsewhere in the Western world. Throughout the West urbanization has had the effect of weakening family stability, as shown particularly by the consistently higher urban divorce rate. In Ireland we cannot even refer to a divorce rate because there divorce is not only illegal, but unconstitutional.[59] In other Western nations the urban population is older than the rural, and urbanization thus seems to account for the ageing populations characteristic of industrial societies. In Ireland, as we have seen, the age structure of the urban population is clearly younger and better balanced than the rural. Similarly, the spread of cities in the West has generally produced a drastic decline in fertility. In Ireland the growth of the urban population has indeed brought about a decline in fertility, but one that is notable for being relatively very small. In all of these matters, urbanization in Ireland appears to have wrought unusual effects.

Certainly the impact of urbanization on fertility in Ireland is truly quite distinctive. For the fertility rates in all classes of the urban population are lower than the rates of the rural population by an uncommonly small margin. The United States, whose fertility rates are higher than those of many other Western nations, may serve here as a basis for comparison. It is not possible to find rates for Ireland and the United States that are completely comparable in every respect, but those we shall present are comparable enough to give us a very good approximation of the differences between the two countries.

Despite a steady decline in the rural-urban differential in fertility during the period 1800 to 1950, general fertility in rural farm areas in the United States in 1940 was about 45 per cent higher than in the urban population. In 1952 the standardized number of children ever born per 1,000 native white women 15–44 years ever married was almost 49 per cent lower in the urban than in the rural-farm population.[60] In Ireland in 1946, on the other hand, on the basis of the standardized number of children 0–4 years of age per 100 married women aged 15–44, McCarthy estimated 'the fertility of rural mar-

---

[59] *v.* ch. ii, pp. 55–6, nn. 31 and 32 above.

[60] The percentage difference for 1940 was derived from data presented by W. H. Grabill, C. V. Kiser, and P. K. Whelpton, in *The Fertility of American Women* (New York, 1958), Table 30, p. 88. Cf. U.S. Bureau of Census, *Population: Differential Fertility 1910–1940. Women by Number of Children Under 5 Years Old* (Washington, D.C., 1945), Table 5, p. 111. The figure for the differential for 1952 is based on figures presented by Grabill, *et al.*, op. cit., Table 31, p. 89.

riages to be by this measure between 25 and 30 per cent higher than in the towns'.[61] If we limit our consideration only to Catholics, who comprise over 90 per cent of the population in both rural and urban areas, the differences between these two areas in Ireland are even less than that. Among Catholics, the rate of the higher professionals, the least fertile of the Irish urban classes, is only about 24 per cent lower than the farmers and farm managers whose rate tops the Irish national scale. And this is emphasized by the fact that the fertility of the higher professionals is only about 23 per cent lower than that of the semi-skilled workers who are the most fertile of the urban classes. The higher professional class, in other words, is almost as far below the rest of the Catholic urban population as it is below Catholics in the rural community.[62]

The latter statement points to another unusual facet of urbanization in Ireland. There appears to be less differentiation in fertility between Irish urban classes than in the United States. In the United States, as elsewhere, there has been a long-standing inverse relationship in fertility according to occupation; the higher the occupation, the lower the fertility.[63] In the decade 1940–50 in the United States, however, changes in fertility occurred which reduced this differential. In that period there was a general increase in fertility in all urban classes, but the percentage increases tended to be highest for wives of professional men and lowest for wives of unskilled labourers.[64] Despite this development, however, the professionals in 1950 remained the lowest in fertility among the urban occupational groups, being over 33 per cent lower than the labourers who continued to have the highest fertility. Clericals and then proprietors were the next lowest in the urban population and were less fertile than the labourers by about 31 per cent and 26 per cent respectively.[65]

In the Irish urban population, the same inverse occupational differ-

---

[61] McCarthy, op. cit., p. 59. As the author notes, this figure is affected by infant mortality which is higher in rural areas than in the towns; hence the difference is greater than the approximately 21 per cent difference indicated by the actual number of children aged 0–4.

[62] These percentages have been computed from the 'standardised fertility rates per 100 married women for ages of wife 20–34 years at marriage and for different durations of marriage classified by social groups and religious denominations' given in *Census of Population, 1946, Fifth Interim Report*, Table XXVI, p. 13.

[63] This differential is very well established for Western nations. *v.* W. S. Thompson, *Population Problems* (New York, 1942), pp. 167–87; and the 1953 edition of the same work, ch. ix, especially pp. 194–5. Cf. Metropolitan Life Insurance Co., *Statistical Bulletin*, Vol. 26, No. 6 (June 1945) a. 'Fertility of American Women in Relation to Husband's Occupation', pp. 7–9; Grabill, *et al.*, op. cit., pp. 113–14.

[64] Grabill, *et al.*, op. cit., pp. 123–7.

[65] Ibid., Figure 25, p. 130, for the source of these percentage differentials.

ential appears. Indeed, at first blush, it appears to be just as great as in the United States for in 1946 the higher professionals, the least fertile in the urban population, were about 35 per cent below the semi-skilled labourers who were the most fertile. But if we compare the two occupational groups having the next lowest rates with the labourers, we find that the differences are considerably smaller than in the United States. Thus the fertility rate of employers and managers is less than 23 per cent lower than the labourers, and that of the lower professionals only about 19 per cent lower. Furthermore, the relative uniformity in fertility among urban occupational groups becomes even greater if we consider only the Catholic population. Here again the higher professional group has the lowest fertility, but it is only slightly less than 24 per cent below that of the semi-skilled labourers.[66] Clearly, then, while urbanization has decreased fertility in Ireland, it has done so to a much less extent than in other nations of the West, and its impact on the various urban classes has been quite different.

But aside from fertility, the other differences in the effects of urbanization are deceptive and may be more apparent than real. Indeed, if we make allowance for certain special Irish circumstances, and particularly if we concentrate on the Irish urban population itself and compare it with other Western populations, a different picture emerges. Then the Irish urban population shows in varying degrees virtually all the general features characteristic of urban populations in other Western countries.

Thus, while we cannot use divorce as a measure, urbanization may increase family instability in Ireland in a somewhat similar manner, if not to the same degree, as elsewhere. It is possible and likely that, as the urban population has grown, the amount of separation and desertion has also increased. But we cannot determine what the relative rural and urban rates for these matters are since the necessary data are not available for reasons stated above. The best qualified opinion among my informants in Ireland, however, was that both were greater in the city than in the rural areas.

Similarly, the urban population of Ireland is relatively young only because the age structure of the rural population is relatively so old. In itself the urban population of Ireland is old and, indeed, is older in its age structure than urban populations elsewhere in the Western world which in turn tend to be older than the rural populations. Furthermore, like others, the urban population of Ireland aged between 1936 and 1951, while the age structure of the rural population remained about the same. We may appropriately add here that the

---

[66] Source of these percentage differentials is *Census of Population, 1946, Fifth Interim Report,* Table XXVI, p. 13. The accompanying comments there are also quite pertinent.

urban population of Ireland is similar to others in its sex composition as well as its age structure, for its sex ratio is characteristically lower than that of the rural population.

In regard to marriage, urbanization in Ireland as elsewhere reduces the amount of celibacy among men, but increases it among women. And the latter result stems mainly from the same tendency found in other Western countries for unmarried rural women to migrate to the city. But the decline in celibacy among men seems to be relatively greater than among women. Taking men and women together, then, the total effect of urbanization seems to be to reduce general celibacy.

While the Irish urban population marries very late by international standards, on the whole and with a few interesting exceptions, urbanization in Ireland during the second quarter of this century has fostered earlier marriage. Irish developments in this matter again seem to be similar to recent trends in other Western societies.

Certain qualifications seem to be in order as to the effect of urbanization on the age at marriage. On the basis of the proportion of persons married in the earlier age brackets, urban men in the United States marry younger than rural males, and this is probably true of other Western industrialized countries. On the other hand, urban women in the United States and elsewhere marry later than rural women. And here again, in comparison to men the relatively greater proportion of urban women who marry later than rural women makes it probable that the total urban population marries later than the rural.[67] However, in the growing industrialized nations of the West the age of marriage for both men and women has been declining since 1936, and this suggests that urbanization does not, or does no longer, promote later marriages. It remains to be seen whether in advanced industrial society this trend will continue to the point where the urban population, female as well as male, will be marrying earlier than the rural population.[68]

[67] Thus in the white population of the United States aged 25–29 years in 1950, 4·6 per cent more rural than urban men were single, but 6·1 per cent more urban than rural women were unmarried. *v.* Bogue, op. cit., Table 10–6, p. 223 and Table 10–10, p. 227.

[68] The impact of urbanization on the age at marriage has not been definitely established. Previous conceptions about it seem to be undergoing significant changes.

The United States Bureau of Census in 1945 published a report on age at marriage and, for median age at marriage of white men and women who were married at the time of the 1940 Census, gave the following comparative figures for the whole United States:

	Males	*Females*
Urban	24·8	22·1
Rural-nonfarm	23·6	21·4
Rural-farm	24·7	21·2

G

In Ireland, urban men have consistently been marrying earlier than rural men during the first fifty years of this century. The studies of the average age at marriage made in 1926 and in 1946 show the decline for that period, and the proportion of men married at the ages 20–34 indicate it up till 1951. Furthermore, although the old national trend towards later marriage prior to 1936 affected the town population as well as the rural, the trend towards later marriage was less pronounced among urban men than among rural men and, from the evidence presented by the New Dubliners, it seems to have been even less marked the more urbanized the man. In addition, the national reversal towards earlier marriage since 1936 is slightly stronger among men in the urban population, although this is not true of the New Dubliners.[69]

But urbanization does not have such consistently similar effects on the age of marriage for women. First of all, as late as 1946 urban women in Ireland were marrying earlier than rural women and with them, as with the men, the trend towards later marriage prior to 1936 was less marked. Once more, the New Dubliners also appear to have been marrying even earlier than rural women during this period. This situation was the very reverse of that in other Western nations. But since 1936, while the Irish pattern has been changing towards earlier marriage throughout the country as a whole, the change has been greater among rural women to such an extent that a greater proportion of rural women than urban women aged 20–34 were married in 1951. Should this development continue, it would tend to bring the rural-urban differential in the age of marriage for women into conformity with the pattern common in other Western nations.

Urbanization, however, does produce the same effect as it does

(U.S. Bureau of Census, *Population—Special Reports Age at Marriage* [Series P-45, No. 7, Washington, 1945]).

An extensive study of this subject was made by T. P. Monahan, *The Pattern of Age at Marriage in the United States* (Philadelphia, 1951). On the basis of census material and statistics from several states, he concluded: 'Urban and industrial areas have a later marrying population than rural areas. . . .', p. 346. *v.* ibid., pp. 93–4, 125–8, 158–9, 164–73, 238–9.

On the other hand, from 1890–1951, a period of increasing urbanization in the United States, the median age at first marriage for both men and women has steadily declined from 26·1 to 22·6 years for males, and from 22·0 to 20·4 years for females. *v.* William E. Cole, *Urban Society* (Cambridge, Mass., 1958), pp. 281–2. Furthermore, since the mid-thirties a marriage boom has occurred in the United States and other Western industrialized countries which is changing the pattern towards earlier marriage and, according to Hajnal, this tendency is greater in urban than in rural areas. J. Hajnal, 'Changes in the Marriage Pattern', in *The American Sociological Review*, 19(3): 295–301, June 1954, pp. 300 ff. Cf. Bogue, op. cit., p. 215. Ireland has shared in this general development.

[69] *v. Census of Population, 1936,* Vol. V, Pt. I, Table 5, p. 16; and *Census of Population, 1951,* Vol. II, Pt. I, Table 4A, p. 9.

internationally in regard to class differentials in the age of marriage for both men and women. In Dublin, as in London, Paris or New York, people in the higher classes marry later than those in the lower classes.

There can be no doubt that these class differentials in the age at marriage, the general trend towards earlier marriage and the decline in celibacy in Ireland during the second quarter of this century are, in part at least, directly due to the increase in urbanization that Ireland has experienced since 1926. This period has seen a great growth in the urban population and a decline in the rural population. During most of this period urban people of both sexes married earlier than rural people, and urban men continue to do so. Urban life in Ireland has this effect because, as we shall see, the structural changes it produces in family life in the city on the whole make marriage in general, and earlier marriage in particular, especially for men, economically and psychologically possible and attractive.

Yet it appears that urbanization is not the only direct cause of this development because the trend towards earlier marriage since 1936 has been somewhat stronger in the country than in the city. Why this is so is not entirely clear. One factor undoubtedly is the improved financial condition of the rural populace which we have noted. On the other hand, there does not yet seem to have been any fundamental change in the social structure of the Irish farm family and community, and it is this total structure, as Arensberg and Kimball have so perceptively demonstrated, that mainly accounts for the late marriage of the rural people. This suggests that in the recent increase of earlier marriages even in rural Ireland urbanization may also be a force, but an indirect one. The increase in industries now located in Dublin and other Irish cities has undoubtedly contributed to greater economic prosperity in the rural areas. At the same time, increased urbanization and increased use of the forms of production, transportation and communication of industrial society by rural people have brought them into greater and closer contact with urban people and their ways. If it be true, as recent trends would seem to indicate, that as industrialization advances the age of marriage declines in the cities, it may also be true that this development tends to promote earlier marriage in rural areas as a result of the diffusion of urban outlooks and customs throughout the countryside. It may even be that, within limits, this process in Ireland will in time result in important structural changes in the rural family which will directly promote still earlier marriage.

Finally, although the urban fertility rates in Ireland are notably higher than elsewhere, the fact remains that they are lower than the rural rates. At the same time, though small, class differentials in fertility that are like those found in other urban population appear, the higher classes being less fertile than the lower classes. Even in this sphere, where Ireland is most distinctive, urbanization tends to produce effects similar to those it produces elsewhere.

The statistical uniformities we have considered here in regard to marriage and family practice indicate one general set of differences between the family life of the countryman and that of his city cousin. The differences are such that the migrant to Dublin and even more so, his offspring, the New Dubliner, seems not only to be moving away from the life of the land, but in many basic respects to be moving towards the urban way of life common to urbanized Western society. In most of the matters discussed in this chapter, the New Dubliner appears to act more like his city cousin in Boston than his country cousin in Mayo. To understand how and why this is so we must now go behind these statistical uniformities to that which gives rise to them—the living behaviour of the city people and, particularly, the New Dubliners themselves.

Chapter IV

THE DUNN FAMILY: A CASE STUDY

TO DESCRIBE REALITY is never quite the simple task that it seems. At the very outset one encounters the problem that facts are dumb and never speak for themselves. One observes them and reports them always on the basis of an accepted theoretical position, and I observed the New Dubliners and their family system in the light of a general theory of social systems which has common currency among social scientists.[1] I did so quite consciously and for the very best of reasons; this theory seems to make the best scientific sense. At the same time, this concept of the social system is essentially the same as that in terms of which Arensberg and Kimball described and analysed the family system of rural Ireland. To apply it to the New Dubliners gives us a more continuous view and enables us to compare more closely their family life with that of the countrymen.

Theory inevitably acts as a filter that conditions what a man sees and how he describes it. But theory does not thereby invalidate his observation or description of reality if he abides by two basic rules of the scientific game. He is bound to formulate his theoretical concepts consciously, and constantly to cut and fit them to his data rather than the reverse. And he is obliged to control the conditions and circumstances of his observation to the best of his ability and to state them as clearly as he can. In this way he cancels out, as far as he can, the purely subjective aspects of his experience and he lets reality stand as clear and verifiable as is humanly possible. This is precisely the function of scientific description. For others are then able to climb the same peak in Darien on which he has stood and to check whether they see what he has seen, with or without his own wild surmise.

Where to begin is another problem of description which, perhaps, is best solved by practical considerations. Three such reasons suggest that we begin our description of the family of the New Dubliners by describing families of the artisan class. First of all, it is about families of this class that we have the most information, and it is always a

[1] This theoretical position has partially been discussed in the first chapter and will be the subject of further discussion in the last chapter.

91

good principle to proceed from the better known to the less known. Besides, it is probable that the artisans are the largest class in the Dublin population and by starting here we are coming into contact with the more common form of family life in the city. Finally, the artisan family, because it stands between the class of general labourers and that of the white-collars, has a number of features common to both. In many respects, the family of the artisan lives much like that of the general labourer. Yet it is so situated financially and otherwise that it is in closer touch with the classes above it, and can more easily get some of its members into these classes by marriage or achievement.

A final problem stems from our concern with uniformities, with common and constant characteristics in the family life of the New Dubliners. Because of this we shall have to describe many families. But a general description of many cases, besides being tiresome, often blunts our insight and understanding especially where dynamic relationships are involved. One often penetrates most deeply into this kind of relationship not by a panoramic view of the many, but by a prolonged contemplation of the one. This perception in depth is the greatest justification for the case study which is so widespread in the social sciences. And it is the reason why we shall start our description of the artisan family with a detailed case study of a single, typical family—that of John and Joan Dunn.[2]

But even a single family is so complex that it becomes necessary to dissect it mentally. And so we shall first take a static, or cross-sectional view of the Dunn family. We shall, as it were, arrest it at a moment in time so as to determine the major features of its structure. Then, the better to understand the dynamics of that structure, we shall follow the Dunn family through the stages of its life cycle from the time that John started to court Joan to the time when this study was completed in 1951 when their children were themselves beginning to marry and the family had entered into the final phase of its dispersal.

A STILL SHOT OF A FAMILY

If we turn the clock back to 1951, we find that John and Joan Dunn are fifty-seven years old. They were married in 1923 when both were twenty-nine. When he was fifteen years old, John had started work at Guinness's Brewery as an unskilled labouring man, grade four on Guinness's scale. In 1934, eleven years after his marriage, John was promoted from 'grade four to grade one, being made foreman in

[2] It is inevitable that any single family, however typical, will deviate from the norm of its class in some respects. But one feature that recommends the Dunn family for study is that even its most important deviations constitute typical exceptions.

charge of scaffolding and rigging in the Engineers' Department'. Joan and John have had six children, the oldest of whom, Mona, was killed in an accident at the age of six. The oldest living child is a boy, Peadar, aged twenty-five, who was ordained to the priesthood in Rome in 1949, and is now a missionary in Australia. The other four children live at home with their parents. They are: Maureen, twenty-four; Sheila, twenty-three; Jerry, twenty-one; and Liam, sixteen. None of them is married, but Maureen, now engaged, expects to be married within the year.

Now numbering six at home, the Dunns live in a five-room, two-story house which they rent. Theirs is an 'attached' house—i.e. one of a row of conjoined houses—in an old neighbourhood off Thomas Street, about four blocks from Guinness's Brewery, a block from the local shopping centre and a half-block from the parish church of St. Paul. Joan and John have lived in this house for all but two years of their married life; during those two years they lived in another house in the same neighbourhood. Indeed, the whole of their lives has been spent in this neighbourhood, since both were born and raised on Reginald Street just a few blocks away.

The activities of this family group are many and various but, for descriptive purposes, they can be classified into three general categories: (1) activities directly concerned with making a living; (2) recreational activities; and (3) religious activities. Although these activities intertwine in reality, it is convenient to consider each of them separately.

The marriage of John and Joan Dunn and the manner in which, as man and wife, they have managed to secure a livelihood, have been conditioned by the occupational history, the relationship to property and the inheritance practices of their natal families. Neither John's parents, nor Joan's, had any holding in land, or any share in productive property. They did not own their own home, but rented. The property they possessed was limited to personal effects such as furniture, etc. Consequently, a substantial property settlement upon either John or Joan at any time was out of the question. So, in fact, was a money endowment. John's father earned his livelihood as a labouring man in Guinness's for thirty-seven years, then went on pension five years prior to his death in 1924. Joan's father also worked for Guinness's as a drayman, but he died in 1894 when she was an infant. Thereafter, until her older sister went to work, the family income was based upon a widow's pension coming to her mother from Guinness's and supplemented by her mother's wage for work she did in a draper's shop. Under these conditions, there could be no dowry for Joan at her marriage. That both of her parents were dead at the time of her marriage made no difference in this respect. Their income in any event would not have been sufficient to provide a dowry.

In the matter of dowry, as in the matter of property and inheritance in general, John and Joan in their day were not exceptional, but rather quite typical instances of a general rule. According to Joan: 'Indeed there is no dowry in the city. It is just a case of "my face is my fortune, kind sir". . . .'[3] And John stated: 'Most people around here in my parents' time did not have very much money and most of them rented their homes. . . . They did not have much to leave their children, but there was no practice of leaving more to the older son or anything like that, and so it is today. Maybe people who are in business do things like that. I don't know about them, and can't say. But with people like ourselves, there is nothing of the sort, nor any of the arrangements you might find down in the country. The parents try to give all their children the same share.'[4]

The usual norm, then, is that of equal division. For John and Joan this meant that any possible inheritance they might have received would be so meagre that they could not rely upon it to finance their marriage. Therefore, they had to provide for themselves out of savings compiled from their earnings in their pre-marital years. Before marriage, Joan had worked for about eight years, first as a housekeeper, then as a seamstress in a draper's shop. John had been earning money at Guinness's for fourteen years before he went to the altar. Each of them over these years had contributed a large portion of their wages to the support of their respective families. During their engagement, which lasted nearly two years, both cut the amount of these contributions sharply, and pooled their savings until they had enough to furnish their house and provide for the usual contingencies of childbirth, sickness, etc. In a very minor way, these savings were augmented by wedding gifts from John's parents and Joan's aunt, as well as from other relatives and friends—gifts which were almost entirely in the form of goods, not money.[5] But their total savings were not

[3] 'Fortune' is an Irish idiom for dowry.

[4] John further reported that where a family owned a house or other property, the parents, or in the case of intestacy, the children themselves, will usually sell the property and divide the money equally, or make an equivalent arrangement. There are standardized exceptions, however; a handicapped child, a younger, unmarried daughter, or a girl who had sacrificed marriage to care for elderly parents or orphaned children would receive a larger portion.

[5] Practices serving to finance marriage are basically the same among the younger generation today. And in regard to wedding gifts, there are customs that are not, however, rigidly fixed. Maureen reported: 'The mothers of the couple will help with the main furnishings of the house, and the relatives and friends will give other presents. The girl's mother is expected to take care of the reception after the wedding. And she will, for example, furnish the bedroom, while the boy's mother will furnish the dining-room. As far as the rest of the house is concerned, the couple is expected to furnish it themselves. But the relatives and friends will give them many things. . . .'

enough to enable them to buy their own home even on the 'hire- ⌐
purchase' system, and today they continue to rent their home as they
did in the beginning.[6] Starting as property-less people, such they have
remained.

After the marriage of John and Joan, the history of the Dunn
family breaks into two periods, and the Great Divide—'the hump',
as John calls it—was the entrance of the children into the business
world. There are marked differences in the arrangement of the Dunns'
family life in each of these periods and as this two-phase history is
characteristic of all artisan families, we must see each phase in order.
For the first period, it is perhaps convenient to consider the Dunns
as they lived about the year 1940 when none of the children were yet
at work.[7]

While the financing of their marriage had been a joint venture
between John and Joan, each contributing to it from their earnings,
the character of this joint enterprise changed radically after they were
wed. Joan promptly stopped working at the draper's shop and thus
ceased to be a direct source of monetary income. In 1940, therefore,
John was the only wage-earner in the family, as he had been since
their wedding in 1923. In 1933, John's wage was £4 5s. per week
($20·40 at the exchange rate then current). When he was promoted
to foreman in 1934 his wage was raised to £5 5s. ($25·20) and subse-
quent raises lifted it in 1940 to £6 6s. per week ($30·30) for a regular
forty-four-hour week; 1934 was a lucky year for John, for that year
the government granted an annual pension for military service in the
Irish Republican Army, for which John was eligible. This amounted
to £16, and together with his wage in 1940 gave him a yearly income
of £341 or $1,637.

Save for interest accruing from bank deposits and an insurance
policy, this constituted the total family income. The reliance on John's
wages as the major, indeed virtually the sole, source of income during
the entire period from 1923 to 1943, when Sheila first went to work
for Monument Creameries, is one of the outstanding features of this
first period in the history of the Dunn family. Obviously, it was due
to the fact that the Dunns neither owned nor operated any productive
property. Obvious as it is, it must be stressed that this forced John
to work for a business concern outside of his home, and independent
of his control.

But John's earnings were only one element in the livelihood of the
Dunns at this time. With John working a regular eight-hour shift
from 8.30 a.m. to 5.30 p.m. away from home, and with all the children

---

[6] I.e., instalment buying.
[7] At that time the children's ages ranged from fifteen years (Peadar) to seven
(Liam). All lived at home and attended school.

in school, the Dunns had to co-ordinate their activity 'to make a go of it', and they had worked out a definite and regular *modus vivendi*. The fundamental framework of this is described by Joan in relating her routine in an ordinary day about ten years ago.[8] Long and prosaic as it is, it merits full statement.

> Well, believe me, I have it much easier now than I used to. Now I get up about 8:30, but when the children were younger, I was up before seven, and I would come down here and get breakfast. John would go off to work about 8:30, and the children would be off to school before 9:00 and I would have to see that they were ready. Then I would ordinarily do some of the housework, and I still do this once they are out of the house. I would strip the beds and get the dishes washed. After that, I almost always did my shopping. . . . No matter what happened, though, I had to start dinner about 12 o'clock because the children would start coming in from school then. . . . John also came home for dinner about that time. . . . He could easily get home from the Brewery and get back by 1:30. So I had the whole family home for dinner at noon.
>
> After dinner, I would finish either the housework or the shopping and usually I would then take a walk—about this time in the afternoon. Especially when the children were too young to be in school, I liked to get them out in the air if the day were fine. Or if I had any shopping to do downtown, I would do that in the afternoon. If I did go downtown, I might take the younger children with me, but mostly I would leave them with one of the neighbours to look after till I came back. They are very good and helpful around here in things like that. . . .
>
> Whatever I did, I had to be home here in those days by 3:30 or 4:00 o'clock because the children would be returning from school. If I had any messages to be done, I would send them out on these then.[9] And all the children had chores to do around the house, and this was the time for that. The boys did the heavier things that were mostly outside. They were expected to take care of the yard in back and to bring in the coal. They would do messages, too, but after they get to be eleven or twelve they think that it is a girl's job and they don't like to do it. The girls had certain things to do in the house, although they were too small to do much then. But they would divide up the work, Maureen doing the dishes, and Sheila the sweeping, one day, and then switching the next. And on Saturdays they were a great help. They would do the beds and help me with the meals and the general clean-up.
>
> But the main thing I insisted on when the children came home from

[8] Most of this description was the result of a specific request that Joan describe her routine at this period, but it has been amplified by statements made in several interviews, and has been arranged to give an orderly view of the family's activities. As far as possible, the words are Joan's and this holds for all subsequent quotations. However, not having the ear of Joyce for the quick Dublin idiom, I have had to paraphrase to a great extent, although I believe the phrasing is close enough to the original statement to merit quotation marks.

[9] 'Messages' means errands to stores, etc.

school was that they begin their lessons. It depended on how much they had to do. Usually they had quite a bit and, especially when the days were long, I would make them get started at these first. Then I would have tea for them at five, and let them play outside afterwards.

John would come home from work about 5:30. He always has taken a nap for about an hour before he eats, so I would have another tea for him after that. Then he would sit around here and help the children with the rest of their studies, and then he would put them to bed. That was his job. . . . That gave me a rest, and we were only too glad when they were upstairs so that we could relax and sit around and talk or read, or I'd knit by the fire in the evening. I say it gave me a chance to rest, but really it gave me a chance to work in peace, for usually I got many things done after the children were in bed—knitting, sewing, fixing the children's clothes or doing odd jobs around the house.

Nearly every night, after he got the children to bed, John would go out for a while, and he still does. On Thursdays and Fridays he goes out to meetings. He belongs to the St. Vincent de Paul Society and he goes to that one night. And he goes once a week to a meeting of an organization the men have over at the Brewery. The other nights he usually goes over to the pub for a few jars, and then he comes home. He has always been home early, about 9:30 or 10:00. We sit and talk for a while. Then about 11:00 or so, off we go to bed.

This routine, followed by the Dunns day in and day out through the year, was broken only by two regular variations: the week-end and the summer holidays.[10]

Joan continued:

The week-ends were a bit different, or at least Sunday was. Saturday was not much of a change for me. I would have to do more shopping to carry me over Sunday. . . . Of course, John would be off Saturday afternoon, and he would do odd jobs about the house and take care of the children. On the whole, he was very good about that. . . . Sunday there was only light housework to do and the dinner to prepare. The girls would take care of most of the housework. John and I would always go to 10:00 o'clock Mass together, and after we returned I would start the dinner with the girls helping me, while John usually would take the boys out. We would have dinner about two o'clock, and after dinner we would all go for a walk if the weather did not force us to stay home.

During the summer, before the children started to work, the big event of the year was going away some place for a month. We would take a house down at Bray or Rush, and the children and myself would stay there the whole month. John would be there with us all day for two weeks when he had his vacation, and during the other two weeks he would come down in the evening after work at the Brewery. . . . Of

[10] The pattern of week-end activity described is followed more or less closely on other holidays of the year, with certain customary variations during the Christmas holidays.

course, I had all the children on my hands during the summer, and while it was good and even helpful in one way, it was harder in another. They would be able to help me around the house, especially the girls, but I also had to keep my eye on them more. I loved to have them around, but still I was glad when school opened again.

This familiar routine with its familiar variations sketches the main lines of the Dunns' occupational activities, but it does not tell the whole story of the division of that activity among the members of the family. John, whose occupations at home are narrowly limited by the requirements of his job at the Brewery, performed virtually all the repairs needed around the house such as 'the papering, the painting, and the carpentry work'. He would hire outside help only for jobs requiring special technical skill beyond his scope, such as plumbing. Otherwise, he managed by himself, aided by 'the boys when they grew up', and on some jobs by Joan herself.

Apart from work of this nature, John and the older boys had nothing to do with domestic labour. Sheila claimed, without demur from her brothers, that the mothers spoil the boys and will not force them to share in the housework. And Joan herself testified: 'The men would starve first before they would shop for anything or even be seen in a shop.' None of the women, however, are as emphatic about this male repugnance as John: 'I certainly would not know anything about shopping for the house or for food. The only time I go into a store, except the tobacconist's, is when I am buying clothes for myself. I would not know one thing from another, and I would not know what were the proper prices. The men here leave that sort of thing to the women. For example, they would not be seen wheeling a baby or washing the dishes or anything like that. That is considered a woman's job. In fact, if you saw a man doing things like that, you would consider him a traitor.'

To Joan, then, with some assistance from the girls, belonged virtually all the domestic work, and all the shopping for the family. Her shopping practices are of two kinds that differ significantly. For the ordinary provisions, such as food, Joan not only patronizes the local shops in the neighbourhood, but gives her trade exclusively to certain shops for reasons that are more than economic. She says: 'I have been dealing with the same shops since I got married. For example, I have dealt all the time with the same butcher, even though he has moved from one place to another. He is still in the neighbourhood, but his place is a bit farther away than it used to be. Still I go to him. I would not go to another shop for the sake of a bargain. . . . I don't know—I feel there would be something wrong about that. These people—well, they are our friends. . . .'

For more unusual items, such as clothes and furniture, Joan goes downtown and there, she says, '. . . it is entirely different. I am out for bargains and good quality and service. Usually, I go where I think I can get the best bargain on a particular day. I keep my eyes open for sales, and so does my sister, and we let each other know about them. . . .'

Besides performing most of the domestic tasks and doing all the family's shopping, Joan has also been the main handler and manager of the family finances. In making financial decisions and in acting upon them, Joan has a wide sphere of independence, and the first to acknowledge her success as a manager is John. Speaking of the period after Peadar went to the seminary, he said: 'From that time on, things became a bit tough, with everything rising rapidly as they generally do while the war lasts. But, as you know, God specializes in making good mothers, and in our particular case He went to great pains in sending us a particularly good one. How she made ends meet left me guessing.'

Of his weekly salary, John has always given Joan '. . . all but a little spending money he keeps for himself, and he has always said: "Do what you want with it." ' Out of this, Joan buys everything for the family and pays for everything.

> I not only pay the bills for the food and clothes, I also pay the rent, coal and light bills. In fact, all the bills for everything. John pays only his fees in the organizations he belongs to, and I should have said that he keeps enough money to pay for his own clothes. Even if it is a question of buying extraordinary things like furniture, I am the one who decides that. And I am also the one who has to provide the money. If I were thinking of buying a dining room set, I would not have to consult John about it, though most of the time I would mention something like that to him. But I would just tell him I was thinking of buying a dining room set, and all he would say would be: 'Well, all right, if you have the money.' Decisions to buy things like that are left to me. I am the one who has to manage, and make ends meet and do most of the saving.

However, John also has authority in these matters, and between them he and Joan have struck a balance, or 'partnership', as he put it. When the family cannot come to agreement, according to Sheila and Maureen, it is John who makes the decisions. And John says in a case like that, '. . . it is up to the father to decide. If we are in a discussion around here, and we can't agree, and we have to make some sort of a decision, I finally make up my mind and say, "That is what we are going to do." And that is the end of it. I think that is right and proper and as it should be. Even according to the teaching of the Church, the father is the one who should have the final say in a case like that.'

But in major matters, John and Joan put their heads together and come to a mutual decision. Thus, when it was a question of Peadar going into the priesthood, '. . . it meant quite an expense, especially then. So John and I talked it over, and we decided that we could make ends meet if we planned carefully and shaved our expenses here and there. It was a matter of both of us agreeing on this after we talked it over.'

During this first period, the Dunns were a family with a single income and to secure this was John's responsibility entirely. To do so, he had to spend the major portion of his time and energy away from home with the result that direct domestic responsibilities primarily devolved upon Joan. As it has ever been, domestic labour—housekeeping, provisioning, cooking, care of the children—was her responsibility. John's share in this was altogether minor, as was the children's although the girls assumed an increasing portion as they grew older. More significantly, the functions and responsibility of management were also predominantly Joan's. She not only handled the family's finances, but she made most of the decisions about its distribution and use even in relatively major matters. In things affecting the family's livelihood, Joan had a wide sphere of authority and even autonomy.

Still, authority in this respect, especially in crucial issues, was more or less equally shared between Joan and John. Vital decisions were reached jointly after discussion. In fact, John retained the final authority where agreement could not be reached, and thus was the titular head of the family as indeed he is today. But both he and Joan consider themselves as equal partners, while in actual practice Joan appears as the principal manager and executive.

The transition to the second period in what might be called the economic history of the Dunns began in 1943 when Sheila, the third oldest child, first went to work. She was fifteen and had completed one year of secondary school. A year later, Jerry, after two years in Technical School, entered Guinness's as an electrician's apprentice at the age of sixteen. Meanwhile, Maureen continued in secondary school until she received her 'leaving certificate' in 1945, whereupon she took the job she presently has as stenographer with the Dairy Disposals Co. attached to the Ministry of Agriculture. The entrance of these children into the occupational world has had important effects upon the family as an economic unit.

The most obvious effect of the children's employment has been to reconstitute the Dunn family as a joint financial unit. Maureen, Sheila and Jerry now all contribute to the family funds as well as John. From a family of single income, the Dunns have become one of multiple income. So it is likely to remain until all the children are married and the family is finally dispersed.

100

The Dunn Family: A Case Study

The resulting financial improvement is quite palpable if we compare the family income of 1949 with that of 1940.[11] Through the 'forties, John's weekly wage has gradually risen 'in an effort', as he said, 'to keep pace with the rising cost of living'. By 1949, it had risen to £10 3s. ($48·75). Together with his pension this gave him an income in 1949 of £533 16s. ($2,558·40), which is an increase of 53 per cent on his income in 1940. But the total family income stood at £1,447 ($6,946) in 1949 which is four times as great as it was in 1940. By 1949, Sheila was making £4 per week as draper's assistant; Maureen was making £5 5s.; and Jerry, now a master electrician, was bringing in £8 per week. Their combined earnings in 1949 totalled £914 ($4,389) which was nearly twice that of John and 63 per cent of the total family income.

Partly as a result of this relative affluence, partly because of their large contribution to it, the Dunn children who are working have acquired a measure of independence, and this has brought about a re-alignment in the management of the family finances. Till about three years ago, Maureen, Sheila, and Jerry handed over their entire weekly earnings to Joan. She, in turn, gave them back a weekly allowance for spending money, but otherwise continued herself to provide for their other needs. Since then, however, the girls have been allowed to keep their pay, and out of it to make a weekly contribution to the family funds, the amount of which they determine themselves.[12] At the same time, the girls are now expected to manage their own financial affairs. They purchase their own clothes and other personal articles, provide their own spending money, and determine their own margin of savings. Thus, the total family income indicated above is no longer, as it was previously, under the virtual sole control of Joan, although the major portion of it still is. As a result, the range of financial problems and decisions incumbent upon her has been reduced. The girls now share these, and they also have assumed some of the shopping activities which were formerly Joan's sole responsibility.

It is interesting, and perhaps significant, that Jerry, at twenty-one,

---

[11] In 1949, the Irish pound was devalued to maintain parity with the English pound. For this reason I have compared the family income in 1940 with its income in 1949 rather than in 1950. For real value, of course, the comparison is not valid as it disregards the great price changes occurring in the intervening years. Nevertheless, the sheer monetary terms indicate graphically the great importance of the children's employment for the Dunn's family income.

[12] This constitutes a great change from the practice common when Joan was a girl. 'When I was a girl working, you simply gave everything to your mother right up till the time you were getting married; and you received an allowance back from her. That was true of almost all the girls. Now, most of the girls do as Maureen and Sheila do.'

101

although this privilege is open to him as well as to the girls, 'simply turns in all his money [to Joan] except for a small amount of spending money'.

The Dunns can also now afford conveniences and moderate luxuries previously out of their reach. John no longer does house repairs. 'Since he is getting along now and finds these jobs a little hard on him', he hires help for them. And John and Joan last summer were able to take a trip to Rome for Peadar's ordination there. Of greater importance is the fact that they are now in a position to finance Liam through the University if, as they hope, he can qualify and desires to attend. While Joan and John, as we shall see, have always placed a high premium on education, a university course for Maureen, Sheila or Jerry was financially out of the question.[13] This was due, partly to the positive expense of tuition, partly to the potential loss of the children's income. Now, due to the contributions of the older children, they can absorb both losses and so exempt Liam from the obligation to help support the family.

Finally, because the children are older, they are able to take care of themselves and the girls especially are able to assume a greater share of the domestic tasks, thus giving Joan a bit more leisure. But since they are away at work most of the day, the major portion of these are still Joan's responsibility, as is the management of the family budget. The entrance of the children into the occupational world, therefore, has caused a shift in the distribution of those activities whereby the Dunns make their livelihood, but this shift represents a change in degree rather than in kind. The main features of the system of co-ordinated activities that obtained before the children went to work—the dependence of the family upon wages earned outside the home and the assumption by Joan, not only of the greater share of domestic labour, but of responsibility for, and authority over most of the family's economic decisions—these remain substantially the same.

The maturing of the children and their entrance into the occupational world has had an even greater effect upon the recreational habits of the Dunns. Until they reached the age of fifteen the children were almost entirely 'kept at home', playing around the house together or in the immediate neighbourhood with children of other families whom John and Joan knew and approved. Their recreational activity was thus under the constant supervision of their parents. Indeed, in great part the entire Dunn family took their recreation together as a unit and in simple forms, such as a walk, a picnic on

[13] Peadar is something of a special case, for, on completion of secondary school, he entered a religious congregation which assumed the cost of his formal professional education.

week-ends, a visit with relatives and the annual summer holiday at the seaside. Even when Peadar and Maureen were able to care for the younger children, Joan and John went out together very infrequently, 'never to the movies and only rarely to the Abbey or a pantomime or an occasional concert'.[14] Despite John's hours with his pals in the pub, he spent the major portion of his free time with Joan and the children, the Saturday afternoon and Sunday family walk being 'almost a ritual'. These outings were supplemented by occasional, but regular parties or 'hooleys' that were primarily 'family affairs, though the neighbours are often in on them too'. The Christmas holidays with their round of mutual visits were the high season for such gatherings.

This latter form of communal recreation is the only one to survive now that the children have grown. Now, the children have their own recreations, for the most part separately, away from the home and indeed outside the neighbourhood altogether. This is true even of the summer vacation. 'The boys belong to hiking clubs and I hear them talking of going some place this summer together. It is the same with the girls. When they get to be that age [about sixteen] the children usually go on holidays with their friends and so there is not much fun for John and myself in going away. So we have not had summer holidays away for the last few years. . . .'

The Sunday walk is now a ritual only for John and Joan. In fact, there was always a tendency for John to recreate mostly with his men friends, and Joan with her women friends, especially her sisters and neighbours. Restrained in earlier years by the requirements of the children, this tendency is now much more pronounced, and it is a common tendency among the families the Dunns know. 'After they are married, the men very definitely take most of their recreation with the men,' says Maureen, 'and a man and his wife do not go out together often.' John simply says: 'The men just like to be together, that's all.' Since the children have reached their 'teens, then, the family has broken up as a recreational unit and recreational activities have become scattered and dispersed.

To a certain extent, however, the Dunn family has been and continues to be a religious community. Their home itself reflects this. In the dining-room, where the family spends most of its time at home, there is a small shrine to the Sacred Heart, and in the sleeping-quarters upstairs one to the Blessed Virgin. Before each of these a vigil light burns all the time, and they are surrounded with flowers and additional vigil lights on special feast days during the year. Throughout all the rooms of the house there are religious articles—crucifixes, a papal blessing which John and Joan brought back from

[14] That is, Dublin's famous Abbey Theatre.

their pilgrimage to Rome, statues, paintings. Generally, these are items of mass-produced devotional art. At Christmas, the Christ Child crib is a more important decoration than the Christmas tree. When the Assumption of Mary was defined in Rome in August 1950, a statue of the Blessed Virgin, lighted by candles, was put in the front window, joining the circle of similar statues which gleamed from virtually every window in the neighbourhood. And that evening, the Dunns, like their neighbours, knelt by their wireless set and joined with the Pope in the recitation of the Rosary for peace.

The ordinary speech of the Dunns, both men and women, is heavily laden with religious expressions and references. The common 'please God', 'thank God', 'God willing', 'God rest him' and the standard farewell, 'God bless you', are entirely spontaneous and unaffected. Equally so, is the frequent conversation about religious events and personalities, matter for which is abundantly furnished, not only by specifically Catholic publications, but by the daily newspapers, as well as by the whole texture of their contacts with other people, lay and religious. Yet the conversation of the Dunns, so pregnant with religious allusion, so given to religious event or personality, seldom turns to discussion of doctrinal points, either among themselves or with friends. Exception to this must be made when doctrinal matters become involved in public events and policies; but in the normal course of events such discussions of doctrine are rare among themselves and their friends. 'For instance,' said John, 'the Catholic Young Men's Society tried having a discussion club here a couple of years ago, and the thing fell through because the lads would not attend. The priests were anxious to have it and they used to get good lecturers, but you would be ashamed, so few would turn out. They finally had to discontinue it.'

The Dunns are deeply conscious that their family is a religious society of a sort. It began as such when Joan and John were married at a nuptial Mass in the local parish, fully aware that the contract they made was a religious and, indeed, a sacramental one. As the children were born, they were incorporated into the religious life of the family by the rite of baptism. And each major stage of their physical and social growth has been made to coincide with religious development in the reception of the Sacraments of Penance (their first confession), first Holy Communion and Confirmation. In preparation for each of these events, the children were instructed in the basic beliefs and obligations of Catholics, not only by religious teachers in school but at home by Joan and John, who have also been the prime movers in habituating the children by training to the fulfilment of their religious obligations and to the exercise of non-obligatory religious practices. Not only has Peadar chosen a religious career, but Joan thinks that Liam may follow his example. When Maureen marries, she will begin her own family life with the same rite and the same mentality as her mother before her. When John and Joan die, they will, barring unusual circumstances, receive Extreme Unction and viaticum. Even though lay people, they will be clothed with a religious habit—a universal custom with Catholics in Ireland —be waked one night at home, and one night in St. Paul's Church. There a requiem Mass will be offered for them, and thence they will be taken for burial in the consecrated ground of the Glasnevin Cemetery.

Thus, religion infiltrates into all phases of their activity and binds together their life as a group. But the crucial sector of formal religious behaviour for the Dunns is what John and Joan refer to as 'religious duties'. By this they mean, first of all, behaviour to which, as Catholics, they are obliged under pain of mortal sin. But they also mean regular behaviour to which they have pledged themselves on joining a religious organization, such as the St. Vincent de Paul Society or the Sodality; and even behaviour which is habitual, but in regard to which they have no real obligation at all. 'Religious duties' as they use the term connotes all these types of behaviour, although John and Joan are quite clear where the line of strict obligation begins and ends. One of their major concerns has been to make this line clear to their children. 'First and foremost,' said John, 'we wanted them to be very clear on what is sinful and what is not sinful.' But the Dunns nevertheless feel that a 'good Catholic' has a general obligation to do more than what is strictly required and these extra activities, especially when they are made routine, take on the aspect of 'duties'.

In the daily round, these 'duties' involve, not only morning and evening prayers and grace at meals, but Mass and Holy Communion for all the Dunns except Sheila, who attends only twice a week. Though Joan could not attend Mass every day while the children were young, daily Mass has been 'a custom with John all through our married life'. During the day all the members of the family 'make a visit to the Blessed Sacrament'—Joan, on her way to or from the shops and the rest on their way home from work. And each privately recites the Rosary. 'Somehow or other,' says Joan, 'we just never got into the habit of the family Rosary, although almost every family had that practice in my parents' day.'[15]

With such a daily routine, the obligatory attendance at Mass on

---

[15] 'The family rosary' means the recitation of the rosary by the family in common. A widespread practice in Ireland, it seems to have been given especial impetus during the penal days when the celebration of Mass and other public acts of Catholic worship were proscribed. It is commonly said, as it was by one of my informants: 'It was the family rosary that kept the faith in Ireland.'

Sunday is secured almost automatically, but with the Dunns Sunday Mass is not a group function. The members of the family go to Mass at different times 'largely because we have to get breakfast for each other, since we would be fasting too long if we all went together and had to wait for breakfast when we came back'. Everybody goes to Confession once a week. And there are various personal devotions which entail going to church one or two evenings a week for various family members.

It is to be noted that the Dunns do not consider religion the special preserve of the women. In the fulfilment of religious 'duties', in the religious instruction of the children, and in enforcing on the children the observance of their obligations, John is as active as Joan and the boys are as responsive as the girls. Thus when they were young it was John's job to 'go upstairs with the children and see that they said their prayers and tuck them in'. Joan, indeed, feels 'that the boys are just as religious as the girls. In fact, I think they are more religious. . . .' The only exception to this is the matter of 'devotions'.[16] In regard to these, 'the women are definitely much more keen than the men'. While Joan, Maureen and Sheila regularly attend the Miraculous Medal devotions on Monday night, Liam is the only male of the Dunn family who accompanies them.

Daily and weekly religious behaviour is supplemented by regular monthly and yearly practices. Many of these functions are those of religious organizations to which the Dunns belong. For example, membership in the Men's Sodality for John and the boys, and in the Women's Sodality for Joan and the girls, requires attendance at a monthly devotional meeting and Mass and Communion in common on one Sunday of the month. Other yearly variations, which are numerous, are summed up in Joan's account:

> We all attend the annual Mission in the parish church. When that is on there are very few families around here who do not go every night. . . . There are several Novenas during the year here, but the main one for us is to Our Lady of Good Counsel. We all go to that. And unless something special comes up, we nearly all go every night to the May and October devotions. . . . During Lent, many of the girls and the men too, will go to Mass every day, and besides that, many will make the stations of the Cross every day—at least, everybody in our family does. And of course, we all give up something during Lent besides observing the fast— smoking, drinking, candy or movies, or something special.

There is a marked individual note in the religious behaviour of the

---

[16] The term 'devotions' as commonly used in Ireland has a quasi-technical meaning. It refers to special prayers and rites, normally conducted in church and usually in the evenings, either as a special direct act of worship of God, or as an act of honour to one of the saints.

Dunns. Of course, the Dunns perform many acts of religion in church together with other parishioners, and the religious ideals and behaviour common to all the members of the family and their friends give support, direction and sanction to the religious observance of each. Still, to a remarkable degree the actual performance of religious actions is an individual, rather than a group, matter. Indeed, it is not often that the Dunn family, either at church or at home, worship and pray together as a family group. And besides promoting individual performance of religious duties, religious training, although it stresses the dangers of private judgment by itself alone, nevertheless lays strong emphasis upon the responsibility of the individual and upon personal devotion and sanctity.

Although we have thus far been principally concerned with relationships existing between the members of the Dunn family themselves, we have had constantly to refer to relationships that obtain between the family and other groups outside of itself. By such relationships the family is integrated into the community. In the rural community, as we have seen, the most important of these relationships are those that bind the family to other familial groups. The familial groups with whom the Dunn family interact most closely are families related to them by kinship, neighbourhood families, and families that are neither kin nor neighbours but just friends. We must now take a closer look at the web of relationships that bind together the Dunn family and those other families to all of whom, unless they are required to specify them, the Dunns are likely to refer simply as 'close friends'.[17]

The parents of both Joan and John died shortly before, or shortly after, their marriage. For almost all of their married life the only relatives of the Dunns resident in Dublin have been two brothers and a sister of John, and two sisters and two first cousins of Joan. Of these all are married and have children, except John's oldest brother who is a bachelor. Between the families of John's first cousins and the Dunn family there are certain obligations that, as we shall point out in a moment, generally apply to all these kin and to others even more remote in kinship. But the amount of interaction between these families, though regular, is quite infrequent. While this in itself is significant, it enables us to leave aside this set of interrelationships and to concentrate upon those that exist between the Dunn family and the siblings of Joan and John. For these are the kinship families with whom the Dunn family interacts most intensely.

---

[17] The use of the term 'friends' seems to be analogous to its use in the country. The difference is that in the country it is applied almost entirely to kin, whether close or remote, while in the city it is extended to neighbours and others as well. *v.* Arensberg and Kimball, op. cit., pp. 71–81.

These siblings' families on both sides are in roughly the same social and economic category as are the Dunns themselves. John's brother-in-law is a foreman for the Board of Public Works; one of Joan's brothers-in-law is a cooper at Guinness's, while the other is an order clerk at Jacobs's Biscuit Company. Both of Joan's brothers are labourers at Guinness's and, thus, occupationally a cut below the rest. This difference is a small one,—a case of 'tuppence ha'penny looking down on tuppence'—and generally speaking, class differences do not seriously affect the interrelationships of these families. Residentially, the Dunns are nearer John's married brother and sister, both of whom live in the same neighbourhood as the Dunns themselves; Joan's sisters live farther away in different directions. Distance, however, does not appreciably affect the amount of contact between these families and the Dunns. More important in this respect is the size of the family. Joan stated: 'We are about equally close to all these families. We have weekly visits from all my sisters and from Jim [John's bachelor brother]. And we see Frank and Mary [John's married brother and sister] fairly frequently, but not as often because they have families to take care of and we have ours, while my sisters have small families. But we have steady contacts with John's relatives through someone in the family, and we see someone of their families every day.'

We have already seen some of the regular forms this constant interaction takes, particularly when discussing the recreational activities of the Dunns. There are other forms that are perhaps much more important. As might be expected, co-operation between these families is most striking at times of crisis, during confinements, sickness, death, financial difficulties, unemployment and periods of 'trouble in the family'. The Dunns have not had any such 'trouble' but they reported that among people like themselves the relatives are expected to do all they can to help the afflicted family economically and in other ways, and generally speaking they live up to these expectations. To a widow, or a wife and children who are being neglected by a husband, they will contribute what they can in the way of comfort and goods and even, though to a lesser extent, of money. Joan's description of what happens in the period immediately surrounding childbirth indicates the usual practice for all other times of crisis.

> You bank on your relatives to take care of the other children and the running of the house. Your mother would come in, or your mother-in-law, and they would cook the meals and tidy up the house. Or, if your parents are dead, other relatives will do that. And maybe there will be shifts of them coming over at a time like that. Or what might happen is that one relative will take one child into her family and another will take

108

another child for the time being. The same thing happens if there is sickness or death in the family. Your relatives would take care of everything. . . .

Naturally, this is a mutual matter, the Dunns in turn being bound to similar service for their kin. In these contingencies there is normally no need to hire someone for services, nor even make a formal request of the relatives for such aid. Such assistance is spontaneous and the knowledge that it will be forthcoming when needed is a source of security to these related families.

Besides such assistance, which is in great part psychological, the Dunns and their relatives also have assurance of co-operation that is more directly economic. If relatives are in a position to do so, they are counted on to use their influence to obtain for other relatives housing quarters, admittance of children to a special school, and above all employment, or, if a relative is in business, to steer trade his way. 'If a relative had a shop,' said John, 'you would certainly deal with him yourself and try to influence your friends to deal with him. And you certainly would bank on your relatives for help in getting jobs, particularly for the children. Relatives help each other in that way all the time.'

The importance that the Dunns and their relatives attach to this type of co-operation between kin is revealed by the sanctions that would be invoked against the individual or family who would neglect it. For example, if John's brother, Frank, were to refuse to help one of John's children to get a job when he could do so, or were to give preference to a friend's child, said Joan, 'There would be a family feud over a thing like that. We would simply ostracize a man who would do a thing like that if we found out about it. That is very common here and it was common in my parents' day. The family has always been very clannish in Ireland. They stick together and they are expected to help one another out. If they do not, if they give a job to friends of theirs rather than a relative, even if the friends are really closer to them than the relatives, the family dislikes it and shows that dislike very clearly.'

Similar group sanctions would also be imposed upon an individual who violated the group's ideal of family behaviour. Describing what would occur if a man were given to excessive drinking and as a result were neglecting his wife and children, John stated:

. . . you would certainly let him know what you thought about that. If I were carrying on like that, for example, I would certainly get a good talking to from my brother. And if that did not work, why, he would start snubbing me and ignoring me. His family would help Joan as much as they could, but they would show their disapproval of me in no uncertain terms. I know I would tell my brother, if he were acting like

109

that, that he need not come around here until he changed his ways. In fact, I might even go to the priest about something like that. You would wait quite a while before you would go that far and you would try everything else first. But if nothing happened, you would go to the priest and get his advice about what to do. And if you thought it might help, you might suggest that the priest have a talk with him. We have never had anything like that happen, but if it did, that is the way it would be. And most of the people around here would act in the same way in that kind of situation.

Next in importance to critical co-operation of the kind described comes the weekly visits of the Dunns and their relatives. The prime function of such visits is to maintain interfamilial communication. While they also provide a means of recreation, such visits are secondary in this respect to independent types of recreation. But normally, mutual economic assistance is very meagre and easily dispensable. The Dunns and their relatives obtain their livelihood independently of each other and their household economies are not co-ordinate. In the ordinary run of things, exchange of goods is limited to occasional exchange of gifts and to Joan's donations of clothes outgrown by her children to her sister. Exchange of services hardly goes beyond caring for each others' children when the need arises. In the background, of course, is the assurance of co-operation in times of crisis, but in the usual round the Dunns and the families of John's and Joan's siblings make their way in relative isolation from each other.

Between the Dunns and their kin who live in the country co-operation is much less than it is between the kin families who live in the city, largely because of the element of distance and the disparity between city and country life. Thus, Joan and John have first cousins with families who live, respectively, about thirty-five miles from Dublin City in County Wicklow, and about 150 miles from Dublin in County Tipperary. While the Dunns will see Joan's cousins in Dublin several times during a year, contact with these rural families, even those in Wicklow, is much more rare. The most regular form of communication is the annual exchange of cards at Christmas time. In twenty-eight years of marriage, John and Joan have visited John's cousins in Wicklow only three times, and the Dunn children have never spent their summer holidays with their country cousins. The only time the Dunns actually see their country kin, according to John, '. . . is when they come up to Dublin for the All-Ireland match or on occasional business. We write at Christmas and that about finishes it.'

But despite this, certain obligations of kinship still bind the Dunns and their country kin. In particular, were one of his cousins' children to come to Dublin in search of a job, John would be expected to put him up if he could, and also to use whatever influence he might command to get him a position. This expectation would be entertained, not only by the country family but, more pertinently perhaps, by the Dunns' kin in the city who would take a dim view of his failure to live up to it. Distance and the diverse ways of life in the country and the city reduce the bonds of kinship to a few thin threads, perhaps, but do not break them altogether.

The relations of the Dunn family to neighbourhood families are on the whole deeper and more vital than their relationships to kinsfolk in the country. From the context of their speech, it is clear that by 'the neighbourhood' the Dunns mean a continuous territory immediately surrounding their home that, while not precisely defined, is smaller than the local parish and yet not confined to the parish. Thus the parish is not identified with the neighbourhood and parishioners are not necessarily neighbours. In contrast to the neighbourhood, as a territorial unit the parish has precisely defined boundaries. Furthermore, while relationships between neighbours are highly informal, the parish is a formal organization established by ecclesiastical authority and embodying a formal system of mutual rights and obligations between the parochial clergy and their parishioners and, indirectly and to a much lesser extent, between the parishioners themselves. The parish also maintains supplementary organizations to which parishioners belong. In the case of the Dunns' parish, St. Paul's, such organizations are almost exclusively devotional and charitable, like the sodalities and the chapter of the St. Vincent de Paul Society. Naturally, on the basis of these formal relationships informal relationships between parishioners have developed and, as we shall soon see, the parish also performs certain functions for the neighbourhood besides strictly religious functions. But, on the whole, the parish does not closely integrate families of parishioners in the sphere of action, nor make all its parishioners neighbours. For, according to Joan: 'The families in the parish who get to know each other well, do so outside the church and not through the church. For the most part here it is just a question of going to church for the sacraments and devotions.'

The Dunns' neighbourhood therefore includes the parish church, another religious church and school nearby, the local shopping and entertainment centre on Thomas Street, and Guinness's Brewery where not only John but many of the residents near the Dunns are employed. In turn this territory is a segment of a larger area adjacent to the ancient site of Dublin City. From the Dunns' it is but a ten-minute walk past historic Christ Church, St. Patrick's Cathedral and Dublin Castle to the portion of the city's main business and shopping district that centres on Dame Street and the vicinity of College Green.

The 'neighbourhood' thus shares with the general area the feature of being old in the sense of having long been settled. It is also old in a wider sense, since in this neighbourhood there are many families who have resided there through many generations. For this is one section of the city where old Dublin families, or colloquially, 'the jackeens', are relatively numerous. Other families trace their residence here back to three generations; and there is also a large scattering of families like the Dunns who span only two generations, the present spouses' parents having moved into the neighbourhood from the country as young people.

While there are varying degrees of intimacy among these neighbours, on a general level the Dunns and all the neighbours interact in such constant and regular ways as to be in fact a real social group. Moreover, the high degree of generational continuity in the neighbourhood has led to continuity in social interaction and tradition. Because it is old, the neighbourhood, in John's words, is

> . . . very close. Practically all the people here now were here when I was a boy except, of course, the ones who have died. But the people I grew up with are still here. Most of the boys I can remember going to school with married girls in the neighbourhood whom I knew. They still live here, and we know each other well and we can depend upon each other.

Interaction between these neighbours, with certain exceptions to be noted presently, is generally the same in kind as that which prevails between the Dunns and their kinsfolk resident in Dublin. Virtually all the forms of co-operation between kin-families that we have seen are found also among the Dunns' neighbours: care of each others' children, help with exceptional work such as preparation for a party, and above all assistance in time of crisis. Speaking of the confinement period, Joan said that, while her own relatives took care of her house and family,

> If a person has no relatives living in the city, the neighbours will do all that. . . . I do not think that anyone around here who had no relatives in Dublin would ever hire a nurse or maid to cook the meals or care for the children if the mother was expecting. The neighbours would care for everything.

This sense of solidarity and of mutual obligation explains Joan's reluctance to buy her ordinary provisions from shops other than the neighbourhood shops. Thus her grocer and John have been friends for years and,

> We know his family and they know ours. You feel that you are helping them a bit by going to them. And we could bank on him to help us out

if anything went wrong and we were short of money. We have an account over there, and though we pay it off regularly, if something came up we would have no trouble keeping it open . . . they would carry us even for quite a spell. And this is the common practice around here. The neighbours have their friends and they deal with them in the same way we do.

As an effective social group, the neighbourhood naturally has its established means of communication. Among the neighbours in general, most of whom have not the convenience of a telephone, there are two outstanding channels. The first, mainly used by women, is the daily gathering of the housewives on their way to the shops outside the church after the ten o'clock Mass, which one of Joan's women neighbours said is locally called the 'gossipers' Mass'. The counterpart of this for John and the men is the almost nightly visit to the pub and its aftermath, which Maureen described rather graphically:

> Father comes home from work, and he will stay around the house for a while, and then he retires to the local pub, do you see? He is down there with his pals until closing time at ten o'clock. When he comes home, we will all be sitting here waiting for him. He will tell us all the tales of what has happened at the pub—what so-and-so said, and who has done this or that. We get nearly all the local gossip from the men's side through him.

Sanctions also are invoked against neighbours as against relatives, and usually they are the same for the one as for the other and are imposed for the same type of misbehaviour. The drunkard who would neglect his family would also receive friendly admonitions and, failing amendment, would find his neighbours severing relations with him. 'He would', said John, 'receive the same treatment as a drunken relative.' Still, there are notable differences between the relationships of kinship and those among neighbours. The Dunns' relatives have a certain priority over their neighbours, both as to claim and as to obligation. Thus, in the matter of obtaining employment, help may be accorded to neighbours only when there are no similar family claims. Indeed, the neighbours themselves would disapprove of John were he to favour a neighbour over 'one of his own' in such circumstances. Similarly, the obligation to help in time of crisis falls first upon relatives, and secondarily and less forcefully on the neighbours.

On the other hand, the Dunns have more frequent interaction with their neighbours than they have with many of their city kin. This is due in part to simple proximity, and in part to the relationships that naturally have sprung up between the Dunn children and their peers in the neighbourhood over the years. It is obviously related to the possibility of the Dunn children intermarrying with the neighbours

113

which, of course, is ruled out in the case of the Dunn children and their cousins. We shall deal with this matter later. But we must note here that the neighbourhood performs a very important function for John and Joan in regard to the upbringing of the children. It makes possible a detailed and intimate knowledge of the families of their children's associates and thus gives them a measure of selection and control over the social environment in which their children act. In the control of the children's behaviour, John and Joan receive much more assistance from their neighbours than from their kin.

Within the neighbourhood, however, there are families who are closer to the Dunns than others and interaction with these families has special features. The Dunns rate six neighbourhood families in this category of special friends. Between these families there are more regular visits and parties than with other neighbours, and a great deal more informality. 'We drop in on each other whenever we feel like it,' says Joan. These families would be the first to know of sickness in the family, the first to be in to offer their services. They are the neighbours who would give John a hand with any job he had to do about the house. And with the mothers of these families, Joan goes downtown to shop and have tea, and generally does with them 'the same things I do with my sisters'. Nevertheless, though all neighbours and all special friends, they are all 'separate friends' of the Dunns. Though all know each other, 'it is never a case of all of us getting together regularly. Each is a close friend of ours without being a close friend of the others.' Taken all together, then, they do not constitute a special group within the neighbourhood; but rather each, with the Dunns, forms a series of family dyads between whom the interaction common to the neighbourhood in general is more frequent and intense.

This neighbourhood way of life is a traditional one. 'When I was growing up here as a girl,' says Joan, 'it was the same in the neighbourhood as it is with us today.' Later on we shall see that this manner of life is quite common to the older neighbourhoods of Dublin, but that in the new neighbourhoods that have sprung up with Dublin's recent growth the interfamilial relationships prevalent here have changed considerably.

Besides kinsfolk and neighbours the Dunns also have other friends. These are families of people with whom Joan and John worked or attended school, and according to John, . . . 'in every case I can think of they are people that we knew before we were married'. The Dunns, however, have relatively few contacts with these friends now, largely due to the distance separating them in the city.[18] They exchange visits

[18] Thus, of a former neighbour who was a very close friend, but who moved to another part of the city, John said: 'We had all the intentions in the world of

once or twice a year and occasionally individual members of the families encounter one another on the street. 'Of course, if you hear there is sickness or trouble in their family, you drop around to see what you can do to help.' But actual contact with their friends is so infrequent that ordinarily the Dunns would have to ask them for help at such times. By the same token, friendships of this sort are less subject to sanction and more easily broken. If one of these friends were drinking and carrying on, . . . 'why, you would just leave him go and not have anything more to do with him'. In short, the life of the Dunn family is not closely integrated with families of such friends, however great may be the sentimental attachment between them. They are peripheral to the central core of families related to the Dunns by kinship and neighbourhood.

Although it has been necessary to note certain vital changes that have occurred in the Dunn family as the children have reached maturity, up to this point our focal centre has been generally the enduring relationships that exist between the family members, and between the family as a unit and other groups, particularly other family groups. But the family is not static and in its development passes through successive stages in accordance with which the relationships between family members also undergo change. We must now centre attention upon these dynamic aspects of family life.

THE LIFE CYCLE OF THE DUNNS

As marriage starts the life cycle of a conjugal family we must return to this primal event in the history of the Dunns. It will help us to recall certain objective facts about John's marriage to Joan. First, they were neighbours whose families had known each other well for a long time; this remained so even after Joan's mother died when Joan was only eighteen, for Joan then came under the care of two aunts who likewise lived in the neighbourhood. Further, both John's father and Joan's, like John himself, had been labourers in Guinness's. Finally, John and Joan were both twenty-five years of age before they began to go together steadily, or 'do a line'. They did not become engaged until they were twenty-seven and they were married only when they were twenty-nine. Both the length of their 'line' and of their engagement was, they say, the common practice among their contemporaries; so, too, was the age at which this occurred. What were the factors that account for these features of their marriage?

They were in part the result of economic and religious considera-

keeping in touch with Mrs. Wyndham, and I am sure she had, too. But she is over in Oxmantown and she does not get over here very often and it is hard for us to go there. So we have gradually drifted apart.'

tions that we have already seen. Both John and Joan considered the married state not merely as a contractual but as a sacred, indissoluble, sacramental one. Both were also obliged, because of the economic position of their respective families, to contribute for some years to the support of their families. Neither could expect a substantial endowment for their marriage and each, therefore, had to help finance their marriage by their own earnings. Both economic and religious factors, however, had further effects upon the marriage, and still other important considerations also affected it. We can perhaps best gain an understanding of all the factors involved by examining the attitudes of the parties principally concerned, namely, John and Joan themselves, John's parents and Joan's mother and aunts. Because of the marked difference in regard to John, as a boy, and Joan, as a girl, we must consider each case separately.

In respect to his marriage, there existed between John's father and mother an area of general agreement, and at the same time a wide divergence of views. Both of his parents were very much concerned about the character and background of any girl John might marry and about the possibility of any premature entanglements before marriage. This concern they shared with the general run of parents in the neighbourhood. As a result, John's conduct was under rather strict surveillance. While, once he had started to work, he was allowed out in the evenings, '. . . I always had to be in by ten o'clock sharp. And most of the time I was out with the other boys. You might take a walk with a girl, but that was very rare and you kept that very quiet. I certainly never brought any girls into the house and none of my brothers did either. It just was not done in our day.'

Furthermore, parental concern about the family background of their children's associates which, on the whole, limited children's associations to the neighbourhood, intensified greatly when the children reached marriageable age. When a boy and girl began to take serious interest in one another, their parents, according to one of the Dunns' neighbours, would investigate each other's family 'root and stock, seed, breed and generation'. This concern, according to John was '. . . not so much about how much money people might have, but what sort of people they were, because parents were mainly concerned about the character of their children's friends, and especially of a girl or boy whom they might marry'.

Despite the general agreement between John's father and mother on these counts, John's father had a significantly different view of John's marriage than his mother did. His father believed that once John had come of age marriage was a matter of his own decision. 'My father had the idea that, I think, most fathers have:—that is no matter what they themselves might think or like, when a boy gets to

116

be twenty-one, it is his life and he has got to lead it. If he has a decent job and he wants to get married then, or if he wants to wait and get married at twenty-four or later, well, that is up to himself.'

On the other hand, despite his father's 'hands-off' policy, John said that for a very long time he was afraid to mention the question of marriage in the family circle and

> . . . that was mainly because I knew my mother would take it pretty hard. I only got around to it when I was fairly well along. But I really had to pluck up my courage to tell her. I remember I just walked in one night and sat down in a chair by the table and said: 'Mother, I am going to get married.' Well, I was nearly twenty-eight then and by that time she must have suspected what was up, so she did not say anything. But I really feared she would create a scene. . . . I think most of the boys in my day definitely had that feeling about the question of marriage.

Joan emphatically agreed that while mothers tried to marry off the girls, 'they tried to hang on to the boys'. And while both John and Joan reported that this common reluctance of the mothers to see their sons marry was undoubtedly connected with the pay cheque a son might be bringing home, this was by no means the only consideration. Even where there was no real economic need for a son's income, mothers quite commonly discouraged their sons' marriage on a number of grounds: that no girl was good enough for their son, that marriage might mean bringing a daughter-in-law in on the mother, that a son should stay with his mother in her old age. Both Joan and John cited several instances of men they had known who, under this pressure, had postponed their marriage until their mother's death. And John reported that 'some of these men were fairly old when their mothers died and as a result they have not married at all'. Both John and Joan, finally, agreed with Maureen's description of this process of obstruction which she claims continues in operation today: 'The mother completely spoils the boys and the boys are afraid of hurting her. They know if they get married their mother is going to feel hurt. The mother in many ways makes them realize that and so, though she might not come out directly and say, "no, I don't want you to get married," yet the boy will feel that if he goes ahead he is going to hurt her and break her heart. So frequently he just doesn't.'

It is hard to assess the individual influence of each of these factors upon John's own attitude towards marriage. By the time John was twenty-one, three of his brothers were working while his father was receiving a pension, so that his contribution to the family income was not indispensable. Financially he was in a position to marry at any time thereafter. Yet, undoubtedly due to the combination of factors listed above, John gave no serious thought to marriage until after he was twenty-five. 'Whether it was due to the influence of my parents or not, I was just not interested in marriage myself until I was twenty-five. I was much too taken up with sports and I was always engaged in things like that and had no time for it until then.'

Many of the parental attitudes towards boys' behaviour at the marriageable age applied to the girls also especially, as we have seen, their concern about the family background of the girls' associates, and the surveillance of their activities. Indeed, a girl's activities were more carefully watched and restricted than those of a boy. Joan stated:

> Parents were more strict with their children, both boys and girls, than we are now, but I certainly think that they were much more concerned about the girls than the boys. After a girl reached the age of fifteen, mothers particularly were more worried about letting girls out than the boys . . . because they feared a girl would get a bit giddy and might get into trouble and if she did, it would be much harder on her than on a boy. . . . I know my mother had absolutely no trust in a man. She had no trust in mankind at all, and she was very much afraid of what would happen to a girl if she stuck her nose outside the door. My aunts felt the same way. . . . I was not allowed to go out in the street after the street lights were lit even after I was twenty-five. . . . Even when John and I were courting, on Saturday I'd have to be in the house to make the tea, and usually I'd have to leave him standing at the gate at six o'clock and it was rare that I was allowed to go out with him again after that. . . .

According to both John and Joan, parents were more nearly in agreement about a girl's marriage than they were about a boy's. They considered that, apart from a religious vocation, marriage was the only legitimate, or at least the only safe, career for a girl. They were deeply concerned, therefore, in getting her married, and they entertained little ambition that a daughter improve her social position by marriage. Both of them, but especially the mother, were quite set against a daughter marrying beneath her. But both were primarily interested in their daughter marrying a man of good character who was steady, had a secure job, would treat her well and provide for her at least in the same manner as they themselves had done. Yet, although exception might be made if this type of husband were available, they felt that a girl should not marry before she was twenty-five. Joan reported: 'Certainly, with my mother and my aunts you did not dare speak of marriage until you were twenty-five at least. Till then they thought you were too young and marriage was out of the question. Their attitude was "ah, sure there's time enough"—how often I remember them saying that. . . . Both of my cousins, for example, were in their thirties before they married, and they weren't allowed to show much interest in marriage until they were twenty-eight or twenty-nine. . . .'

118

While economic considerations again were active in fostering this attitude, Joan claimed that the main factor was her mother's and her aunts' fear of her youth and inexperience. In contrast with this, the girls themselves were eager to get married to get away from the drudgery of their parental homes, even though they usually could not fly in the face of parental disapproval of a young marriage. In this respect, the girls were much more eager for marriage than the boys. For a girl, marriage, though it terminated a girl's employment in shop or factory, generally meant greater freedom, and marriage was their only ambition.

> There was in my younger days no question, of course, of girls going into business or the professions. For girls, the main thing they looked forward to was marriage and you never thought of marrying above your class. The girls then mostly worked in factories. There were few office jobs open to them such as the girls today have. If you were working in a factory all you would do was look for a good man who could support you. You were not in a position to meet a man above your class, and you did not have the education for that sort of a match. There used to be an old saying around here when I was a girl: 'Make sure you get a Guinness' man, he's money dead or alive.' That was because Guinness' gave a widow's pension. That was the idea that we girls here had when I was young, and that was the idea the mothers had then, too. . . .

The aspects of the Dunns' marriage to which we have called attention are largely understandable against this background of attitudes that mainly centre on the preparation and initiation of marriage. Other important attitudes principally concerned post-marital conduct. Pre-eminent among these was the attitude of John and Joan towards having children. For them, as for the society in which they live, to beget children and to raise a family were of the essence of marriage and simply a matter of God's will. There was never any question of thwarting or controlling the natural processes that normally lead to that end. This did not mean, however, that children were accepted as something inevitable. John and Joan positively desired them and wanted as many as God would send them. Undoubtedly, one of the reasons why they did not marry sooner was their desire to be secure enough financially to be able to provide for whatever children they would have. And this, together with other factors that resulted in Joan marrying only when she was twenty-nine, did in fact put a limit on the number of their children, whether the Dunns realized this consciously or not. But it was partly in the expectation of a full brood thereafter that Joan stopped working at marriage. If they had had only one or two, they would have felt disappointed and somehow frustrated. To have had none would have been stark tragedy and a matter of commiseration by their friends and neighbours. It is this latter possibility, not the possibility of having a large number of children, that the Dunns would have had to accept with resignation.

Despite this positive orientation towards having children, Joan and John entered marriage with a rather remarkable ignorance of the sexual and birth processes. Neither of them had received instructions in these matters from their parents, nor did they seek such instruction from a physician prior to their marriage. They had to make shift with the haphazard knowledge of marriage which they picked up from their contemporaries at work. During her first pregnancy, this was supplemented by information and advice which Joan got from her female relatives and neighbours, and towards the end of that period from the doctor who attended her.

Furthermore, one cannot escape the strong impression that towards sex John and Joan have a sense of danger and even evil. This is indicated in their case among other things, by their extreme embarrassment and their reluctance to discuss the subject. Asked whether he and Joan had given instruction in the matter of sex to their own children, John said very brusquely, 'No, we leave them to find out for themselves just as our parents did.' Joan and John refer to immorality in such a way as to imply that they think of it almost exclusively in terms of sexual irregularities. 'When you talk of morality or immorality', said John, 'people almost always mean violations of the sixth Commandment.[19] I know I do and I think most people do too. You don't usually think of dishonesty or things like dodging the income tax or dealing in the black market, even though you know, of course, that these things are wrong.'

When Joan's time came, like her mother before her but in contrast to most mothers today, she delivered her children at home, not at a hospital. With women of her age this was the common procedure, and while it was, in part, due to the then current shortage of hospital facilities . . . 'actually—I don't know why—we always had a sort of dread of hospitals and never wanted to go there. I don't know the reason for that, but that was the way it was.' Joan also nursed each of her children herself and claims this was not only a universal practice in her parents' day and with her own contemporaries, but is the common practice today.

During the years of infancy, the most notable feature of John's and Joan's attitude towards the children was the strong affection which they openly manifested at every turn. As might be expected, Joan indulged all the fondling and terms of endearment for which the Irish mothers are famous. But this also seems to be true of John to a remarkable extent. Joan maintains that the fathers she has known

[19] The seventh Commandment in the King James Version of the Bible.

... are all very affectionate towards babies. To tell the truth they are really crazy about infants. Certainly, John here was. He was always bouncing them and playing with them, and he spent a great deal of time with them. And he was always very proud of them. Once they were able to walk, he would never miss a chance of taking them out and showing them off. The men here are all like that about their children and it comes out especially at the time they make their First Communion. Even though they may be pretty poor, a father will go out of his way to dress them up beautifully and he will be as proud as Punch of them.

After that, however, with the beginning of adolescence John said, 'You have to start checking them up and laying down the law once in a while.' The relationship changes, and largely because he was working away from home, the change affected John more than Joan. Although Joan had to undertake most of the discipline, she had constant chances to manifest affection. John became more remote to the children as Maureen described it:

From the time we were seven until we got out of school, Daddy wasn't quite as close as he had been. It is hard to describe. It would be best to say that he seemed a bit more remote than he used to be. I think that is true of fathers in general. I don't think a father loses his affection for his children, but he just doesn't show it as much. And I don't think he has much time. He is away from home all day and when he comes home he is tired and just can't devote as much time to the children as he would like. When we were younger, we would be sitting around doing our lessons when Daddy got home from work, and even though he would help us with our exercises a bit he was very tired and he would like to take a rest and then go out for a while with his friends. And besides, the children have themselves to play with, and the father thinks that they have their own interests. So at that age a father and his children are not as close as they used to be, nor as close as they are after the children are grown up.

Generally speaking, however, the Dunns and their children are very close to each other. John and Joan are emphatic in saying that this is in striking contrast to the relationship that existed between parents and children in their childhood. John reported that then children would never be allowed to sit in on conversations such as we were having; 'a boy Liam's age [16] there wouldn't be in it . . . he'd be outside the room someplace'. Joan describes the present relationship as one of confidence, and attributes it to the fact that parents grant their children much more freedom.

In my parents' day, children were much more in fear of their parents than they are now. There is no doubt about that. Parents and children today are much more like pals. Parents have authority, but the children are not afraid of them. I know my girls will come in here and tell me things that I would never dream of telling my mother or my aunts. And that is even truer of both boys and girls confiding in their father. . . . We have given our children much more freedom than we ever had when we were children, and as a result the children trust us and when they have a problem, they consult us and confide in us.

Joan goes further and assigns the main reason for this transformation to the change in the relationship between husbands and wives.

Everybody in the family is much more closely knit now than they used to be. And that is especially true about the husbands and wives. Today they are much closer than they ever were in my parents' day. . . . There is no doubt about it, then the women were the slaves to the men. . . . They simply did the drudgery of the housework and the men kept a tight hold on the purse. They were allowed a certain amount of money to run the house and if they wanted more they had to go and ask for it. The father was really the boss and the mother was subject to him . . . and I think many of the mothers were afraid of their husbands. I knew many families where the mother was always hiding things from the father and trying to keep him pleased because she was afraid that he would be hard on the children.

Change in these relationships has been accompanied by a great change in the régime of disciplining the children. Most notable in this respect is the decline in corporal punishment. John and Joan rarely used the rod and then mainly as a threat. Although they kept one on hand, '. . . we burned them more than anything else. If we ran short of kindling we would secretly break the rod up and use it to start the fire.' To a certain extent, reasoning has replaced the rod, although John has not found reasoning always effective. Sometimes rewards for appropriate behaviour are effective but in the long run, 'I found it better to deprive them of something that they really wanted,' says Joan, 'and that has worked best of all.' At times, too, Joan has found it effective to threaten the children with a visitation from John. 'When he acted, he was more severe than I was and more decisive.' But, again in striking contrast to most fathers of her parents' generation, 'It was very hard to get John to do anything in the way of discipline and I really was the one who had to do most of it. I'd have to get after him to speak to the children. And most of the time he would pass it off and say, "O, that is not very important." He has always wanted to leave the discipline to me, and as far as I can see in families around here all the men are inclined to let the women carry the burden of disciplining the children. . . . And that is a great change from the days when I was a girl.'

Through the medium of these relationships the Dunn children have learned the basic ideals, standards of behaviour and obligations proper to members of a family, and have been prepared for the roles

122

they are expected to assume in adult life. In this process, John and Joan have constantly striven not only to endow the children with their own basic ideals, but also to enable them to realize a better life than John and Joan themselves have had. That they have, generally speaking, been successful, is indicated by the children's occupations and prospects.

Where John started as an ordinary labourer and worked his way up to foreman, Peadar, his eldest son, as a priest, is a professional man; Jerry, the electrician, is starting out as a skilled craftsman; and Liam is heading for a clerical or professional career. While Sheila is presently a draper's assistant as Joan herself had been before her marriage, Maureen has a secretarial job; and more important, Maureen is to marry a university man who has an excellent position as a customs and excise officer.

These accomplishments have been made possible, in part, by the modern development of Dublin which, besides generally raising the standards of occupational skill, has had two consequences of especial significance for people like the Dunns. First, it has opened important occupational positions to women. Thus when John first went to work at Guinness's there were hardly two dozen women employed there, most of them 'widows who had a family to support'. He added:

> Today, there are at least three hundred women in Guinness'. . . . The reason why girls today have better jobs is women's emancipation and women's suffrage. When we were young, women had no rights. They had no vote. They were not allowed to go to universities, and good clerical jobs were not open to women, but only to men. Besides, ordinary people like ourselves could not afford to give the girls a good secondary education. There were only a few schools for girls and they were mostly expensive finishing schools. They trained a girl to be a lady, but they gave her no training that would help her in a job because a lady was not supposed to work.

The second important consequence has been a parallel breakdown of class barriers to occupational preferment and advance. When John was a boy, clerical jobs were reserved to the sons of clerical fathers and a working man's son could rarely gain entrance to this circle. To illustrate this, John told the story of the son of a friend of his, a working man. The lad had the qualifications for a clerical job at the counting house, had applied for it, was given an interview and had done very well in it.

> But just when he thought that he had the job, the man who was interviewing him asked what work his father did. The lad said that he worked at Guinness'. 'Well,' said the man, 'what does he do at Guinness'?' 'He's a labouring man there,' said the boy. The man who was interviewing him paused a moment and then said: 'I see. Well, I am very sorry, but we

123

cannot take you.' He would not give him the job because he was a son of working class people. He would have got the job if his father had been on the staff at Guinness' . . . but that sort of job was not open to our kind of people, that's all. . . . Well, all that is changed now. Boys from our class of people, if their parents can put them through secondary school or even technical school, have a real opportunity to get jobs like that. . . .

In order that their children might exploit these new opportunities as well as meet the higher standards of skill, the Dunns have followed a policy that has produced yet another change in the parent-child relationship. To a far greater extent than their own parents, John and Joan have encouraged their children to move on to a level of life that is different from their own; and in order to provide the children with the training necessary to make this transition they have relied to a greater degree than their own parents upon outside agencies. Thus, although John as a boy received most of the technical training required for his job from men other than his father at Guinness's, yet, entering Guinness's as a common labouring man, he was following in his father's footsteps and shared with his father a common context of experience. John's father was in a position personally to teach him not only many of the technical, but also many of the social, skills necessary for success on his job. In regard to his own sons, however, John himself can transmit to them neither the technical skills nor, save in a very general way and especially in the case of Jerry, the social skills required in their occupational environments because he has little direct experience of life in these spheres. To fit his sons for adult roles in these new fields he has had to depend mainly upon the school.

Whatever he may have taught them about general principles of manly behaviour, John has been of little assistance to his sons in their studies since they have gone beyond the level to which his own education was limited. Here he has been able to give them only strong moral encouragement. Technically, he has been able to teach them only the few odd tricks that are involved in doing minor house repairs. And even this has been limited by a notable attitude on John's part that is similar to the attitude of his father to himself. In these small tasks around the house John has taught his sons by example rather than by encouraging active participation and initiative. Joan related:

> John had the idea that the boys could never do anything right. He would have them stand around and watch him do a job rather than show them how to do it and then let them go ahead for themselves. John's father had the same attitude towards him and as a result, when I married John he hardly knew how to do a thing and he had to learn everything himself

as he went along after we were married. I think most of the men I know act the same way towards their sons. They have the idea that the boys are children even after they are grown up, and they won't let them take the initiative even on small jobs around the house. The result is that the boys get fed up and do not want to help their fathers on such jobs.

In looking to the school for the education their sons need, the Dunns are faced with a dilemma that is common to all people in their economic bracket. Unless a boy has really outstanding ability in school, there is always a question that, if he should go for his 'leaving certificate', he may not be good enough to pass either the civil service examinations or the entrance examinations to the University since the competition in both cases is very keen.[20] If he fails these, his chances of getting a good clerical job are sharply diminished and, of course, a professional career is then out of the question. At the same time, he now finds himself in an unfavourable position as far as the crafts go. Apprenticeships are rather limited in number, and since an apprenticeship usually lasts for about seven years there is a tendency in the trades to take boys at the age of fifteen or sixteen. A boy of eighteen is a good deal less desirable, and even if he is fortunate enough to be taken as an apprentice he has the disadvantage of being two or three years behind in a world where seniority is a big factor in the wage scale.

Furthermore, boys who go to secondary school in Dublin may not work part-time and thus help to finance their own schooling. There is no law against this, but it is simply not done. For people like the Dunns, in a country where there are no free secondary schools, this results in an economic consideration that is not negligible. To send the boys to secondary school requires payment of tuition and at the same time results in the loss of potential income that a boy might bring if he went to work. Although tuition for the technical schools is low and there exist secondary schools, especially the Christian Brothers' schools, where fees are moderate, nevertheless the cost of schooling, when coupled with the loss of potential income, entails a sacrifice and a risk for people like the Dunns. Thus, on the completion of primary school, the question of a son continuing in school or going to work is a crucial one.

John and Joan have adopted the policy of taking the risk and making the sacrifice. They strongly encouraged the boys to continue their schooling, and yet they left the final decision in that matter to the boys themselves. Thus, at considerable economic inconvenience

[20] A 'leaving certificate' is the equivalent to a high-school diploma and signifies the successful completion of a four-year secondary curriculum. It is distinguished from an 'intermediate certificate' which is given after the completion of two years of secondary school.

they underwrote Peadar's decision to study for the priesthood. Jerry and Liam represent the two alternative responses that are common in this situation. Jerry declared for technical school and a trade, and although both Joan and John wanted him to go through the full secondary course, they gave him his wish. Liam, meanwhile, although he was not yet decided on a precise occupational field, is following his parents' advice by going for his leaving certificate; and if he continues to follow their advice, he will try for a university degree. Both John and Joan think that 'it is very hard now for a boy to get a really good job unless he has Honours or at least a pass degree from the university'. They are therefore prepared to stake him to a university education even if he can secure only a pass degree, provided that he wants it. The choice between work or school, as well as the correlative choice of the type of work the boys are to do, has primarily been the boys' own responsibility. Their parents' influence upon this decision has been great, but it has been the influence of persuasion and advice that they are free not to follow.

The question of marriage does not enter to any important extent into these considerations of the training and education of the boys. It has the central place in the training and education of the girls, for the role of housewife and mother is the desirable and likely life career for them. The most notable effect of this consideration is that the basic technical and social training for this adult role is directly given to the Dunn girls by Joan. They have learned the domestic skills, the art of management, and the comportment proper to a wife and mother from Joan by directly participating with her in the daily routine of domestic duties. Here the function of outside agencies, such as the school in domestic sciences Maureen now attends in the evenings, is merely supplementary. Even though Maureen, as we shall see, will move into a slightly higher social level after her marriage, the context of her life will remain essentially the same as that of Joan, as the context of Joan's life is essentially similar to that of her mother. In the vital process of training children for their life work there is not the same gap between Joan and the girls that exists between John and the boys.

Considerations of marriage, however, also act to extend the training and education of the girls beyond the limits of domestic training at home. John and Joan have been eager to give the girls a good education in order that they might be able to obtain good jobs before they marry. While they have been motivated in this policy partly by the prospect of financial help to themselves, they have also adopted it because it would better enable the girls to provide financially for their own marriage and would put them in a position to meet potential husbands who could improve their position in life. Furthermore, the

126

possibility that a girl may not marry at all has also influenced their educational policy; for in that event, a good job would stand a girl in good stead throughout her life. We shall see the full import of these views more clearly in a moment when we consider attitudes concerning the marriage of the Dunn children. Their significance here is that they have led the Dunns in the training of the girls as well as the boys to depend upon outside agencies, the school and the apprenticeship.

The question of work or further schooling once primary school is completed is not as acute for a family of the Dunns' means in the case of a girl as it is in the case of a boy. It reduces itself largely to the matter of financial sacrifice since the risk of losing critical occupational opportunities is not as important. As a result, while Joan and John have given the girls the same encouragement to continue their schooling, they have granted them an even greater measure of freedom in deciding the matter for themselves. Thus, even though Maureen is the older, they put her through secondary school till she received her intermediate certificate, and then through business school. On the other hand, they '. . . did not think it a good idea to force Sheila to continue in school . . . because she did not like it and was unhappy there'. And as with school, so with the kind of work, Maureen and Sheila were allowed to choose what they liked.

Joan feels that her neighbours and friends generally share the attitude of John and herself in educational matters for both boys and girls. In fact, as we shall see later, the Dunns are rather exceptional in their willingness to make financial sacrifices for this purpose. Joan herself admits that while parents are eager to give their children some post-primary education, '. . . still, they do not press their children to go on to school very much. If they show a desire for more schooling, most of the parents I know will send them on. But they will not force them.'

Among the children themselves, the boys avail themselves of the opportunity to go to school, especially to technical schools, to a greater extent than the girls. According to the Dunns, most of the girls in the neighbourhood do not go to secondary school or technical school but prefer to go to work in a factory. Here again, the marriage prospect is important. 'Most of the girls, I'm sure, feel that they want to be married and if they can get a good job at a department store like White's, for example, they will have a better chance to marry young and will be better off financially because they will have a longer time to save.'

In the matter of education and the children's careers, however, the attitude of the parents and the amount of freedom enjoyed by the children is in marked contrast to what it was when John and Joan were children. In John's words:

> Everything was entirely different in these matters in my parents' day. Most of the parents then were just waiting for a boy—or a girl for that matter—to get through primary school to send him to work. In most cases the boy didn't have a choice at all, or very little choice. His father would get him a definite job in a definite trade, if he could, and that was that. There was no arguing or objecting about it on the boy's part, because it wouldn't get him very far. Of course some did, and some might even leave home because they did not want the sort of work their father selected, but most of them didn't because the father ruled them with a pretty tight hand. . . .

With Maureen's engagement and the advance of all the children save Liam to marriageable age, the Dunn family today approaches the last stage of its cycle. The conditions affecting the marriage of the new generation and the attitudes towards it differ in many respects from those that prevailed when John and Joan were married; but in many important respects they remain the same. Of the similarities, the most important by far concern the economic aspects of the children's marriage. For them, as for their parents, there is no possibility of a dowry or of a substantial inheritance after their parents' death, and each must also finance his marriage out of his own and his partner's resources. Thus Maureen and her fiancé, Sean, who is a neighbourhood lad, are today following the same policy of mutual savings that John and Joan followed in their day.

Among Maureen's neighbourhood contemporaries who are now engaged the common practice in regard to future living-quarters is also basically the same as it was in the generation of their parents. While they aspire to own their own home, '. . . their ideal is to start out without debt. But most of them cannot afford to buy a house, even by hire-purchase, and at the same time stay out of debt, so the majority are forced to rent a flat.' On the other hand, whereas flats were plentiful in their parents' day and most of John's contemporaries settled in the neighbourhood where they were raised, Dublin's housing shortage forces most young couples today to settle elsewhere, usually in new housing developments quite distant from their parental home. Thus, Maureen and Sean plan to live in another neighbourhood after they are married. This movement, which seems to have started in the generation between John and Joan and that of their children, is one of the processes whereby the new neighbourhoods of Dublin have been peopled.

Maureen and Sean, however, differ from the general run of their contemporaries and from their parents by reason of the fact that they command enough resources to be able to buy their own home, and they plan to do so. Although it is also difficult to purchase a home, Guinness's has an interest in a corporation of builders among whom John has a couple of friends, and he intends '. . . to put in an application for Maureen through Guinness's and I feel pretty sure that they will be able to get a house for me'. Sean's ability to afford a home is due to his relatively high-salaried job. According to John, Sean, a neighbourhood boy whose family has been friendly with the Dunns for years, and whose father works in a factory, '. . . is one bright lad'. He won a scholarship to secondary school, emerged with honours, attended the National University where he took a degree in public accounting, and passed the civil service exam '. . . against tremendous odds' for the position of customs officer. Sean himself revealed that the wage scale for the officer's grade in customs and excise '. . . starts at £340 per annum, rising by annual increments to £1047 after twenty-four years for married men'. Married men also receive a children's allowance of £25 annually per child up to school-leaving age, or until their education is completed if they attend university. Obviously, through her marriage to Sean, Maureen will move on to a higher class level than that of her own family.

Social advance through marriage was extremely rare for a girl when Joan was young, as we have seen. Among girls of Maureen's class and generation it is a fairly common event and an even more common aspiration. Because they have a better education, better jobs and greater opportunities, girls today, says Maureen, '. . . are very much concerned about marrying up the scale. They are always trying to land the lad with a good clerical salary . . . and few of the girls around here are willing to marry a fellow who does the same sort of work as their fathers. They are on the lookout for the lad who is a clerk or in a high-salaried position.'

So, too, are their parents and particularly their mothers. The father who, according to Sheila, 'usually believes in the child's independence a good deal more than the mother does,' is more willing to accept as a son-in-law a lad who is starting married life on the same level as he did himself. But the mothers are very eager that the girls better themselves by marriage. Maureen said:

Suppose a daughter of a working class man had a job in a good office downtown where she was mixing with white-collar people and, when she was twenty-three or twenty-four, she started doing a line with a working class boy. Her mother would discourage her from getting too serious about him even though he might be a good lad, because she would hope that the daughter might in the long run marry one of the boys in the office. That goes on all the time. . . . The mothers throw cold water in a situation like that in the hope that the girl may yet make a match that will better her socially.

Partly as a result of this attitude towards marriage, John says that there are in Dublin a great many 'career girls, as we call them down at Guinness's'. While girls generally consider marriage as the sole desirable career, increasing numbers of them are making relatively good money, enjoy a relatively high standard of living, and are therefore increasingly reluctant to enter marriage if this means lowering the standard. Of the numerous women working at Guinness's, John maintains that: '. . . a very small proportion of them—less than a hundred—are married or ever will be married. . . . They have a good job, they are getting good money, many of them have their own car and they get a lot of fun out of life. So they don't want to leave the job, and they are not going to settle for a fellow who is only making eight pounds a week when they are making five or six pounds themselves.'

The effect of these developments is a curious shift in the attitude towards the proper age of marriage for girls. Parents today no longer feel, other things being equal, that a girl is too inexperienced to marry in her early twenties. 'I think that twenty-three is a good time for a girl to get married,' said Joan, 'and most of the parents I know feel about the same way.' But hope for a good match often leads a mother to indulge in delaying tactics and the girls themselves are no longer eager to rush into marriage as an escape from the confinement of the parental home. Marriage and a home of their own is no longer, as it once was, the only release into freedom. More and more it is beginning to be considered an ultimate responsibility and a 'bit of a drag' that girls are inclined to postpone.

But if parental attitudes about marriage have changed in regard to the girls, generally speaking they have remained unchanged in regard to the boys. Parents like John and Joan do not look to marriage as a means of social advance for their sons. And while the father continues to consider that marriage is for his son to decide for himself, the mother is just as reluctant as she ever was to see him get married. All of the Dunns, parents and children alike, as well as their friends that I met, agree about the fact of this reluctance. Joan says of most of her women friends: '. . . when their sons get married, sure they will be lamenting it for a long time and saying: "Ah, 'tis a shame to see him married, and him so young." The usual complaint is that he is too young even though the lad may not be young at all.'

But they disagree sharply as to the power of the mothers to prevent or postpone a boy's marriage. Thus one of Sheila's friends, a lad named Seumas, maintained that the mother's attitude and obstructionist tactics '. . . doesn't hold up a boy's marriage too much these days. It did in the old days and it may in some cases today. But personally I think that is dying out. If a fellow wants to get married today, he is going to go ahead and do it despite the fact, I will admit, that the mother usually lets him know that she does not like the idea and would like to see him remain unmarried for a while yet.'

Nevertheless, the boys themselves are generally very wary of marriage and inclined, even where it is financially feasible, to put it off as long as they can. This is reflected in the common attitude and behaviour of boys towards girls. Even though, in contrast to the days of John and Joan, boys and girls mingle constantly at parties and dances after they have reached the age of seventeen, and even though a boy may be doing, according to Seumas, 'several light lines at one time,' boys up to their middle twenties and often later rarely become seriously interested in a girl and definitely prefer the company of their men friends. As an indication of this all of the Dunn children and several of their friends stated that it is quite the common thing that a boy, when the chance to have a bit of fun with his pals suddenly develops, will not let a date with a girl stand in his way. Quite frequently he will break it, often without notifying her. According to Sean: 'This goes on all the time. I even know a fellow who broke seven dates in a fortnight. A bit extreme, I admit, but many lads will do that once or twice a fortnight.'

Even more significant is the fact that, while the number of girls who refuse to acquiesce to such treatment is increasing, still, says Maureen, 'most of them put up with it because there is nothing else they can do'. The Dunn children and the circle of their friends agreed that, speaking generally, the attitude of the boys towards marriage was well expressed by the Dublin lad of twenty-eight who said: 'Most of us put it off as long as possible. A few succeed in avoiding it altogether.'

Naturally enough, in regard to their children's marriage, John and Joan entertain the same general conception and ideals that they held for their own. But changes in the city at large, as well as in the structure of relationships within their own family, have destroyed some of the tactics their own parents used to insure the realization of these ideals. Since the children have reached adolescence, the Dunn parents have been as much more concerned about the girls' activities than about the boys'—and for the same reasons—as were their own parents. But the greater freedom that they have willingly accorded the girls as well as the boys makes the close surveillance of activities, such as their parents exercised, much more difficult. As a means of protecting a girl from life's pitfalls, they rely upon their children's sense of confidence and trust in their parents rather than upon rigid supervision. In like fashion, despite the greater weight attached to occupational and social position, John and Joan still place primary emphasis upon the character of their children's future spouses. Today, however, the children's associations 'reach out all over town'. Their friends are no longer mostly neighbourhood children and intermarriage between neighbours, so common in John's day, has sharply declined. As a result, while parents still lay great store by family background as a warrant of character, they find it increasingly difficult to come by the requisite knowledge of the families of their children's peers. More and more they are forced to judge their children's friends by individual qualities rather than family background.

Environmental and structural changes have also affected the children's ideas about post-marital behaviour. Where women upon marrying immediately stopped work outside the home in Joan's time, among the younger generation today it is fairly common for a wife to continue to work for a while after marriage. Also in contrast to the general practice of their parents' generation, the younger husbands and wives participate together in more social and recreational activities of a non-domestic nature, and wives are much less prone to acquiesce in remaining at home while their husbands 'go off with the boys'. Despite such changes, however, the children retain their parents' conception of marriage in the crucial fundamentals. Because it is a sacred state, heavy with responsibilities, they approach it slowly and with caution. The Dunns say that among children they know, the courting period on the average begins earlier than it used to, but runs as long; and that broken engagements are just as rare. Nor has the attitude towards having children changed. Wives who continue to work after marriage will do so, said Maureen, 'only for about six months because the children usually start coming along then'; and virtually no mother goes out to work after that, except in a strict emergency. For the younger as for the older generation of Dunns and, according to their reports, of their friends, a woman's place is still in the home and a man's prime responsibility is to his family. For they, too, look on marriage as a sacramental, indissoluble state whose primary purpose is the procreation and the raising of children.

In the rural family, as we have seen, the central factor governing the dispersal of the family is the marriage of the son who inherits the holding. At the same time the actual processes of dispersal are the marriages of the children and/or their migration from the countryside. Of the Dunns, Peadar has, in fact, emigrated to Australia, but as he is a missionary priest he is entirely a special case. The rest of the Dunn children and, generally speaking the children in their circle, have never seriously contemplated emigrating from Ireland, and consequently such a prospect has never been a major concern with parents such as John and Joan. Emigration, of course, is always a possibility, but it is not a normal process of family dispersal among people of their class. Normally, the only process of dispersal is the

132

marriage of the children, and here the marriage of a particular child is ordinarily not more central than that of any other. Family dispersal is a gradual effect brought about by the successive marriage of each of the children.

As none of the Dunn children expect either to emigrate or to settle down in the country, after their marriage they will be scattered throughout the city. At the present time we can only conjecture about what will happen before that finally occurs. It is possible, and perhaps likely, that at least one of the three younger children will not marry until John and Joan die but will remain with them in their old age, for their sense of filial piety and its obligations is strong. It is even more likely that, if all should marry before their parents' death, whoever of the parents survives the other will be taken into the household of one of the children, although there is no way to determine whose it will be. In any event, however, because all their children, except Peadar, are likely to remain Dubliners like themselves, John and Joan look forward to continual and direct association with their children's families for care, satisfaction and security in their old age.

Our description of the Dunn family has been long and detailed and, as such, it is justified only because the Dunns are a typical artisan family. But it would be demanding too much of the reader's credulity to ask him to accept the Dunns as typical on our mere say so, or to accept as valid any generalizations we might offer on the basis of this one case alone. We need grounds more relevant than this to show that the Dunns are indeed typical and to describe adequately the pattern of life that is common to the artisan class as a whole. This means that we must move from a study of the one to a study of the many and now turn our attention to the artisan way of life in general.

Chapter V

THE ARTISAN WAY OF LIFE

NOW THE NOONDAY DEVIL of tedium besets us. For the search for features that are uniform and common to a class necessarily tends to be a monotonous business. It requires that with all the artisan families we must cover the same ground that we have already been over with the Dunns and count heads. We therefore inevitably have to work with the same central theme. But, fortunately, the theme is a rich one and we may find that its repetition is far from monotonous if, like a musical composer, we develop the many and intriguing variations that it contains.

For one thing, we shall shift our register and in this chapter treat the data on the artisans from a somewhat different vantage point than that from which we viewed the Dunns. In discussing the data from all the artisans, therefore, we shall stress the major interpersonal relations that make up the network of family life and of the effective community in which the family lives. Furthermore, while we have thus far been listening to a long solo aria sung by the Dunns, we can now let other voices in the chorus be heard. There are important matters on which we could only touch lightly in our study of the Dunns and into which other artisans whom we shall now let speak can give us deeper insight. Indeed, we can also now begin to let New Dubliners from other classes get into the act. For as we shall see eventually, there is a core of relationships in the artisan family that is common to all classes of New Dubliners. And as we might expect, people from other classes, especially from the employer-managerial and clerical classes, often give more graphic descriptions of common practices than the artisans, as well as more articulate expression to common sentiments. Consequently, in this chapter we shall quote people from other classes when they give particularly apt expression to something that is also characteristic of the artisan class.[1] By so

---

[1] The people from the classes other than the artisan will be identified by class in footnotes so that it may be clear when people outside of the artisan class are speaking.

134

doing, we shall begin to break ground for our discussion of the family life of the other classes in Dublin.

But the head-counting is a statistical necessity that still dogs us. We are throughout primarily concerned with the quality of common family relationships. But when we say that these are *common*, we are claiming that they have a definite quantitative distribution and we must justify this claim. At the same time, relationships between people that are common are not all equally common and it is important to determine the varying degree of their currency. We cannot then entirely dodge the statistical issue. Nevertheless, quality is still our central interest and we cannot let it be obscured by a complicated statistical scaffolding. It therefore seems advisable to adopt a simple procedure that will permit a clear and direct presentation of the data on the artisans and one that we can later follow in dealing with the other classes of New Dubliners.

From our sample of New Dubliners we have two kinds of reports. New Dubliners reported about their own personal family life, and they reported about the family life of their relatives, neighbours and friends. Although in our analysis we have given more weight to the first kind of testimony, in order to simplify matters we have combined both kinds of testimony about any given practice or attitude. On this basis we have drawn up certain simple rules of evidence.

First of all, we shall take into account only those items about which 75 per cent or more of all the people in our sample, or in a particular class in our sample, have reported. Then if, with at least 75 per cent of our people reporting, 90 per cent or more of them state that an item is common, we shall rate that item as a *general* characteristic of the New Dubliners. If more than two-thirds, but less than 90, per cent report that an item is common, we shall classify that item as *prevalent* among the New Dubliners. Finally, if less than two-thirds of the people reporting describe an item as common, we shall consider the item as only one *alternative* of several that are more or less equally current. And as we deal with the multiple items of family life in the following discussion, we shall specify them according to this terminology. At this stage of our quest, it is better to overload our sentences with the adjectives 'general', 'prevalent', and 'alternative', and with their corresponding adverbs than with numerous and complicated statistics.[2]

PROPERTY AND THE LAW OF LIVELIHOOD

In the crucial relation of the family to property, two noteworthy

[2] For a more detailed discussion of the technical treatment of these data and, of the precautions needed in dealing with them, *v.* Appendix I, pp. 266–8 below.

changes have occurred in the artisan class in the course of this century. The first of these is the decline in the amount of intestacy. Whereas thirty years ago, 'a man of our class would never dream of making a will,' the artisans unanimously report that this is quite common practice today.[3] This change is undoubtedly related in part to the second change, viz. the increase in the amount of home ownership. There is no published statistical evidence to prove this assertion.[4] But we get some inkling of it from the fact that, while only five out of nineteen immigrant, natal families among the artisans owned their home, four of the eleven New Dubliner artisan families studied now own, or are in the process of purchasing, their residence and two entertain hopes of doing so in the near future. More telling, however, is the unanimity with which the artisans report that home ownership is much more common today than it was when they were children. Thus, typically, one man reported that while people of his class rarely owned their own home in his parents' day, '... a very large number of people are in the process of buying their houses out during the last thirty or thirty-five years, but they are the first of that crowd'.

With these two reservations, however, the relation to property that we have observed in the case of the Dunns is *general* among all artisan families and is *generally* the same as it was in the natal families of the spouses. In both generations ownership of productive property, and especially of property that the family would work as a unit, is a very rare exception.[5] As a result, a central feature in the artisan family is the absence of any need to preserve through inheritance the unity and the continuity of a holding.

This has important *general* consequences in regard to the ultimate dispersal of the family. It makes possible the general practice of equal division of funds and movable property among the children at their parents' death. It makes virtually impossible the practice of dowry.

In regard to marriage, while the children are thereby forced to go it on their own, they come to enjoy a large measure of independence. For they need not wait, as children in the country must wait, upon a son's inheritance of the holding and the subsequent dowering of the daughters, before they can embark upon the marital sea. In view of

---

[3] Several solicitors in Dublin informed me that intestacy is still very widespread among rural people, and most of the rural people I queried on the subject confirmed this report.

[4] *v.* ch. ii, p. 62.

[5] Of the artisan families studied only one had an interest in productive property. One husband had a partnership in a small cooperage, but the time he devoted to it and the income he derived from it are only secondary to his work at, and wage from, Guinness's. The only natal family of our artisan spouses that owned productive property had a small bit of land where they raised pigs for market. On the demise of the parents the property was sold.

136

the wider occupational opportunities in the city, they are thus economically in a position to marry at an earlier age and at the same time remain in their native community. Consequently, under the conditions of relative prosperity that prevailed in 1950–51, pressure upon artisans to emigrate was sharply diminished. Emigration had ceased to have a foundation in the structure of family life and had become more directly a function of general economic conditions.[6]

As a result, our artisans reported that while depression at home will exert a push, or that an extremely favourable labour market abroad, as during the war, will exert a pull, parents as a *general* rule do not expect any of their children to leave Dublin. The following typical statement sums up the position rather well:

> There has been quite a change in regard to that [emigration]. About 25 years ago there was a substantial bit of emigration, not only from the countryside, but from Dublin here, too. But this has stopped more or less now. Parents, of course, don't like the idea. And maybe they always have a little nagging fear that perhaps some of the children will be forced to go if times get hard, and that they won't come back. During the war years the wages in England were very good and many people did go over to work in the plants, and while almost all of them went over with the idea of returning, many of them stayed. So there is always a little fear that one of the children might emigrate, but they don't really expect that any of them will.[7]

The fact that the artisan family, as a group, does not work productive property also has consequences for the internal structure of the family. The family is thereby made principally dependent for its finances upon wages obtained from an agency outside itself. The husband's status is that of an employee of such an agency; and the wife's status is not that of collaborator in a productive enterprise, but simply that of wife, mother and manager of the household. Furthermore, it is *generally* characteristic of artisan families that as regards income they pass through a set cycle from single income to multiple income to single income again. And the cycle is such that in the last

[6] However, since 1951 emigration has become a greater factor in family life even in Dublin. *v.* ch. ii, p. 59 above.

[7] Children of our artisan families who were old enough to emigrate were too few to permit an adequate comparison between their generation and that of their parents. However, analysis of the available data, while it tends to confirm the above statement, is not very convincing. Three children of current artisan families were missionaries; none of the siblings of their parents who had emigrated were missionaries. If we, therefore, discount missionaries, we find that from the natal families of our artisan spouses thirteen children from seven families out of one hundred and nine children from nineteen families have emigrated. On the other hand, of thirty-seven children from eleven contemporary conjugal families, two from two families have left Ireland.

phase the family usually has a somewhat higher income relative to its needs than it had in the first phase, with the result that the standard of living is somewhat higher also.

The most important consequence of dependence on wages, however, is the necessity it imposes upon the husband, and later the children, to work away from home and outside the family circle. Externally, this has a chain effect upon the relationship of the family to other groups in the community. Internally, it affects the distribution of family labour, responsibility and authority and thereby affects the basic interpersonal relationships between the members of the family. Such relationships are the core of family life, and it is time now to take a close look at them in the artisan family.

FAMILY RELATIONSHIPS

One of the phenomena that becomes most apparent from a study of artisan families is the emergence among them during the last thirty years of a somewhat new relationship between husband and wife. Earlier in the century it was *prevalent* for the husband, at least overtly, to be dominant and the wife subordinate; for the husband to be the 'boss' with his wife as his first lieutenant. Today, it is *generally* characteristic that husband and wife are co-partners. 'Partnership' is the usual term artisan spouses use to express their relationship. It refers to a mutual attitude and sentiment they bear each other and also, ideally at least, to a roughly equal division of the responsibilities of family life. This sense of partnership is grounded upon the feeling that the overriding obligation of the husband to earn the money necessary for family livelihood is counterbalanced by the obligation of the wife to run the household; that both share the responsibility of raising and training the children; and that both concur with equal voice and authority in reaching decisions that are crucial to the family's well-being.

It is well, however, to go beyond the explicit formula of 'partnership' whereby artisan spouses summarize their relationship and to consider the specific rights and obligations that comprise it. Naturally, the set of rights and obligations to which spouses must first adjust at marriage are those relating to sex. In this matter, all of the characteristics we have noted about John and Joan Dunn are *generally* true of artisan spouses. First, the lack of parental instruction results either in nearly complete ignorance of sexual matters, or in information, of dubious validity, culled from the conversation of contemporaries at work. This is reported by every spouse and often in much more graphic terms than those used by the Dunns. One husband and his wife were discussing the subject and the wife said:

138

The Artisan Way of Life

I think that it was really sinful that I was allowed to marry as ignorant and as innocent as I was about the whole matter. At that time the only way you learned was from the girls you worked with, but I did not work in a factory and I knew nothing. Honestly, I could surprise you with what I did not know. I used to think of marriage as a mere matter of companionship. I thought the children just came somehow, I knew not how. It never occurred to me that children or the purpose of marriage had anything to do with sex.

Her husband added immediately: 'Even though I was working and knocking around in the pubs, I was just about as innocent as Meg on that subject. People spoke about sex in whispers. . . .'

Similarly, the sense that sex is somehow evil is also an *alternate*, if not a *prevalent* attitude, and it is also expressed quite explicitly. Thus, one wife said:

I think there is something wrong with sex and nothing will ever change me. . . . And I think that is the general attitude. One woman friend of mine who is married told me once that she felt after she was married that the loss of her virginity was the greatest loss of her life. And I felt the same way about it. Even when Brian asked me to marry him, and I love him very much, even though I was glad, I felt very sad . . . just like she did. There is something repulsive about it and nothing will get that out of my system. And the women will tell you that it is the men who enjoy it, not the women—they get no enjoyment out of marriage that way. However, Maura [another close married friend] once told me: 'To tell you the truth, Nell, I do enjoy it.' But I don't and I never will.[8]

But women have no monopoly on this feeling of evil. One husband stated: 'We Irish have very peculiar ideas on the subject of sex, despite what anybody might say. Back of everybody's mind is the notion that there is something wrong with it, something bad. It is deeply ingrained in us. I know that is true of myself and of most the people I know.'[9]

Under such circumstances, spouses are more than usually on their own in learning to adjust to marriage sexually. The one who has a little more knowledge of the matter, and this one may be either husband or wife, has to take the lead in instructing the other. The emotional ambivalence this entails is expressed clearly in the following conversational piece between another artisan husband and his wife. Mihail said: 'When I got married, I was really a babe in the woods. Kate knew more than I did. Of course, nature tells you some things, but Kate had to teach me. When she got pregnant, the first time, she told me she had missed her period and I did not even know what she meant. She had to explain it all to me.' 'That is true enough,'

[8] Clerical class.
[9] Clerical class.

139

added Kate. 'My mother told me nothing, let alone my father. I found it all out from the other girls when I was working. And during our honeymoon, well—I felt that I was being awfully bad because Mihail was so helpless and I had to tell him nearly everything.'[10]

However similar to their own parents the artisan spouses may have been at marriage in their ignorance of sex and in their sense of evil about it, in one respect they *prevalently* differ from their parents. Between husband and wife today 'the subject is much more out in the open'. Where it was previously taboo between their fathers and mothers, husbands and wives discuss sex and pregnancy quite frankly among themselves today, and their frankness 'shocks my mother and people of her generation'. A few artisan people as well as people from other classes remarked a changed attitude on the part of the schools and the Church, and they themselves seem to have learned from experience. One mother said:

> For life in the modern world, I think it is absolutely necessary that the children be told about sexual matters, told young and in a perfectly natural way. I notice that in school they get instruction in their courses, at least about the facts of life. And many of the priests and nuns simply tell the parents they have the obligation to instruct their children. Actually, in my oldest boy's case, we did not tell him. We discussed it and decided not to. That was a grave mistake. But one learns by experiences like that. We did instruct all the other children, and I am certainly glad we did.[11]

Family livelihood is the object of another basic set of rights and obligations between husbands and wives. These, too, result from adjustments worked out between spouses after marriage and are subject to a certain amount of evolution in the course of marriage. However, it is the overall design and not the short-run variations to which we shall attend. Apart from earning the wage that is the major, if not the sole, source of the family's income, and partly because this task monopolizes his energies, the husband contributes little indeed to the domestic services that are such a large sector of family life.

---

[10] Most of this was summarily confirmed by a doctor who is not included in our sample, but whose commentary is worth stating:

> The older people had queer ideas about sex. Most of the older women thought it was a nuisance. They got no pleasure out of it and wished it might happen only once a year. And the refinements of the matter were simply unknown. The husband was the authority and boss in this respect and the wife just put up with it. There was no consideration of the woman's part in it. I know that as a doctor. And that still exists to a great extent among the younger women. They come to me to ask me about limiting the family by rhythm because I am a Catholic doctor. . . . Well, one thing leads to another, and it is surprising how little most of these women know about the matter.

[11] Employer-managerial class.

With the exception of minor repairs around the house, on which a wife helps her husband as often as not, servicing the family is exclusively the wife's job until her daughters are old enough to help her. The artisan wife's routine described by Joan Dunn, apart from minor variations, is *general*.[12] For themselves, artisan husbands *prevalently* scorn housework and fear being ridiculed as a 'molly' if they be discovered at it. The wives themselves are inclined to think the man helpless at this sort of work and the *prevalent* attitude is that of one of them who said of her husband, 'he can wet tea, that's all'. The sons, quick to imitate their fathers in this matter, are *prevalently* exempt from such womanly chores. A woman with three sons and no daughters commented: 'It is taken for granted that the boys won't do household chores when they get to be about twelve years old so that, if you happen to have daughters, you have help; if you don't happen to have daughters, you do the work alone.'

Very similar is the distribution of what may be called the exchange activities of the family: the ordinary and extraordinary shopping and the payment of family bills. Shopping for the family and even for individual family members is almost exclusively the wife's province, at least until the children go to work, whereupon the girls *generally*, the boys *prevalently*, buy their own clothes and other personal items. The men *generally* share John Dunn's reluctance to shop; and in half of our cases the wives even buy all their husbands' clothes. It is also the *prevalent* practice for the wife to pay all the family bills, not only the bills for provisions, but the more important bills for rent, fuel, light, etc. Nor is this just a matter of the wife acting as an errand runner and cashier under the authority of her husband. As we have seen with the Dunns, the husband *generally* gives her his wage, except for a small amount to cover personal expenses, and leaves its administration to her. This money she controls on her own authority determining not only expenditures, but, *prevalently*, the family savings. She is veritably, as one husband described her, 'the Chancellor of the Exchequer'.

While husbands *generally* have the same attitude about sharing in domestic tasks and in ordinary shopping that their fathers had before them, the wife's control over family finances constitutes a revolution in family affairs since the days when our artisan people were children. Then it was *prevalent* for the husband 'to keep a tight hold on the purse, to give his wife an allowance and to hold her to rather a strict account of it'. It was the husband, not the wife, who accumulated the savings and took care of the major bills. Artisan people gave various reasons for this shift, but one of the more frequent and perhaps more significant is the following, voiced by a husband:

[12] *v.* ch. iv, pp. 96–8.

In our parents' generation girls were very sheltered from the world. They were kept at home and did not get out and work as my wife did and as the girls today do. As a result, they did not know very much, and when they got married it was accepted that the wife was innocent and ignorant of business affairs. So the husband expected to manage, and manage he did, often with a strong, hard hand. But today the wives have all worked. They have been around and they definitely know what they want and how to get it. They have a good sense of value and are very shrewd, and so they have taken over the management of the family.

The equality of husband and wife shows to its best advantage in regard to major decisions relative to the children. *Generally* speaking, neither would act in such matters without consulting the other and obtaining the other's consent. Again, however, when it comes to the daily training of the children, advising them and enforcing discipline, it is the mother who *generally* has to take action. One of the most *prevalent* tendencies among artisan husbands is to pass the disciplinary buck to their wives most of whom, while they deprecate the use of father as a threat to the children, are forced constantly to remind him of his obligations 'to speak to the children'. The most common explanation both as to why the burden of discipline for boys as well as girls falls on the mother's shoulders, and as to why husbands tend to shy from their disciplinary role, is the husband's absence from home during the day. One mother stated: 'Usually, if something comes up, I have to handle it on the spot and cannot wait till Jaimie comes home. . . . And I guess because he is away from the children during the day, he does not realize how important some things are, so he is always trying to minimize my concern about them, while I have to tell him that he must take a hand in dealing with the children.'

Once more, this pattern is the opposite of the pattern *prevalent* when our artisan spouses were children. Then the father made the main decisions about the children, while the mother brought influence to bear by the devious ways of cajoling and special pleading. Then, 'the mother was never after the father to discipline the children; rather she was after him to restrain him'.

Beyond the sphere of work, responsibility and authority, the 'partnership' the artisan spouses describe also means increased comradeship and freedom of communication between husband and wife. Fear of her husband, at least an *alternative* wifely sentiment in the old days, has almost completely disappeared. Moreover, there has been a marked increase in social association and recreation of husbands and wives outside the home. Where it was *general* for husbands to recreate almost exclusively with their men friends, today this can only be said to be a *prevalent* practice that seems to be on the decline.

Contemporary artisan husbands walk out with their wives, attend movies with them and go out visiting or to parties with them. Indeed, 'in our parents' day, it was very, very rare that women would go to matches with their husbands. But go out to Croke Park for a match today and a good third of the crowd are women. And a man and his wife will not only go out together more than they used to, but more and more they will go into lounge bars and drink together. That was unheard of when I was young. Women who went into bars then had a very definite reputation. . . .'

Nevertheless, the tendency of the men to recreate together is still *prevalent* and it is worthwhile recording a typical statement which, being more descriptive than John Dunn's, gives us a deeper insight into the relationship of husband and wife. One wife who had been married six years reported:

> I certainly will say that married men are out with single men more than married women are out with single girls. A wife is very definitely expected to be at home, and it is very rare that her husband will ask her to go out. O, I do not mean out to the cinema. A husband and wife will go out to the movies once or twice a week. But for a young married couple to go out regularly together to a party or a dance is almost unheard of. I haven't been to a single party since Seumas and I got married, and we have been to just two dances in six years. Of course, it is true that there are the children to take care of, but often it would be quite possible to get somebody to take care of them. It is just that they don't have many activities or affairs for young married couples. Any organization that runs social activities usually plans for banquets or dinners or affairs that are almost entirely for men and not for mixed company.

It is the flashy talk, the quick witticisms, and the carefree atmosphere that seems to make the companionship of their men friends so attractive, and with it drink, the conversational oil. Thus one man who himself had eventually given up drinking altogether and could claim wide experience, remarked: 'The main reason for drinking, I think, is the companionship. You get down in the pub and you meet the boys and you just keep drinking because of the fun you are having with them. Most men I know would not enjoy a drink at home very much and would not do much drinking at home.'

It is quite consistent with this tendency that the most common source of strain in marital relations is not infidelity, but drinking and its consequences. One husband, in an excellent position to observe people in their relaxing moments, reported: 'There is very little infidelity here in Dublin, at least by comparison with London and Paris where I have worked. Men do not fool around with other women very much. But there is a great deal of drinking and a great waste of

143

time and especially of money that could be used by the family. There are very many husbands who spend most of their time off just sitting and talking in the pub.'

However, since the days of their parents, a decline in this sort of conduct is *prevalently* reported; 'there may be more drinking,' remarked one artisan, 'but there certainly is more temperance.' There is also some indication, although the evidence we have on this is quite small, that among the younger generation, the children of artisan families, a redress in the balance between husband and wife is taking place, at least in certain respects. More and more the younger husbands are willing to lend their wives a hand with domestic chores and even with shopping. 'I am amazed', said one mother, 'at what my daughters-in-law have been able to get my sons to do around the house.' And it is frequently reported that the young wife today is not content to remain at home while her husband goes off with the boys, and indeed that young husbands tend to prefer their wives' company on their recreational ventures. The following account by a young wife may be, perhaps, a harbinger of the future:

> There was never any question of Kevin [her father] and my mother going out together. But my husband wants me to go out with him more. When he goes out, he would rather have me along. He isn't interested in going out with other fellows. He definitely has more interest in me in this respect than Kevin had in my mother. And this is becoming more common now. . . .

In view of all the evidence, a reassessment of the husband-wife relation seems in order. Although artisan husbands and wives may legitimately feel that they are 'partners' and 'pals' and that the obligations of the husband in the occupational role counterbalance those of the mother at home, it is clear that *generally* the major share of actual family labour and responsibility rests on the wife's shoulders. Clearly, the division of labour, responsibility and authority is not equal in practice, and the wife has the central role. There are not infrequent reflections of this unbalance in the mildly resentful remarks of the women that 'the men have it rather easy', and in the increasing number of husbands who acknowledge that their wives deserve more equal recreational activities because they are the keystone in the family arch, though few perhaps would go so far as the husband who publicly confessed: 'I am just the eldest son in the family.'

But despite such inequalities in rights and obligations, the sense of equality between husband and wife is strong, and it is their *general*, clear, unequivocal judgment that the husband-wife relationship is a much better and happier one than that which predominated in their parents' day. New Dubliners consider it so for the most part because of the beneficial effect it has had upon parent and child relationships, to which we must now turn.

In a study the scope of the present one, it is impossible to probe to equal depth into every relationship or even as deeply as we might wish. This is especially true of the relationship between parents and infants. We can only say, therefore, that the features of the parent-infant relationship that have been described for the Dunn family are *generally* characteristic of all artisan families. In addition we may point out that while Irish obstetricians *generally* insist upon mothers breast feeding their babies today, artisan mothers often openly approve of this policy because of the emotional stability they feel it builds up in the child. A not uncommon statement is the following, made by a mother who was able to nurse only one of her three children: 'I was not able to nurse the two oldest boys . . . and I feel they have missed something because of this. But Jim [the youngest] I nursed for twelve months and I notice a great difference in him that I think is due to that. It is not only that he is bigger and stronger, but he is much more affectionate and much more steady than the others. Indeed, there is great nature in Jim. . . .'

It may also be well to underline the *general* affectional rapport that exists between parents and infants of both sexes. There is some evidence of a tendency of both father and mother, but especially the father, continually to favour the younger child. There is not enough evidence to show any definite tendency of the mother to favour infant boys, and of the father to favour infant girls. What is most striking, however, is the father's affection for his infants of both sexes and his often boring pride in them. This is frequently a matter of comment by foreign visitors to Ireland: 'I used to think it was just natural for all men to be very affectionate towards infants, but it is strange how often people coming here to Ireland remark about how we treat them. One Englishman told me that he thought we made a great deal of fuss about the baby and doted on him. "We never do that in England," he said. "At that age my children were considered—well like the furniture. They were just around." '[13]

Reports that this affection for infants is *generally* characteristic are the more creditable in view of the reports as to the nature of the *general* change that takes place in the parental attitude towards the children as they move into adolescence. One New Dubliner daughter, now married, said:

> . . . from the age of eight to eighteen, the Irish are very severe on their children, in my opinion. They seem not to pay very much attention to them. That is, they treat them quite severely, they do not manifest much

[13] Employer-managerial class.

affection, they are inclined to keep them in their place and not to allow them much self expression or initiative. . . . I know when I was a girl I resented this very much. In our family, if you started to express any ideas of your own, or to take on any projects, my father would put a stop to it. He would tell you not to be ridiculous, and he would put you in your place. I am not sure it wasn't a good thing. Perhaps we would have made ourselves ridiculous . . . but sometimes I think we Irish carry it a little too far.[14]

The artisans report that this attitude is *prevalent*. There is some evidence that the mother appreciates the need for discipline in regard to the children, and so changes her attitude towards them, sooner than the father. But once the father takes cognizance of the change in the children, he *prevalently* becomes more 'remote', 'indifferent' or even 'hard'. Justifications for this attitude range from father's exhaustion at the end of a gruelling day to his conviction that life is no bed of roses and that the children must be hardened to it. One father gave this explanation:

After the age of seven, the father hardens towards his children. I think the Irish father tries to make his children hard, particularly the boys. We have been oppressed for so long that the Irish father has the conviction that life is a rather bleak proposition, and he has to make his children realize that. He believes that they are going to be treated roughly, and so he himself treats them rather severely with the idea of making them strong and hardy and able to take any knocks that life can bring.

Whatever the explanation, there can be little doubt about the fact, especially in view of the contrast with the attitude towards children in England or America noted by those who have been abroad. One husband stated: 'When I was in America, I was amazed at the freedom that American children have. I would not say I was shocked, because I don't really know whether or not it is a bad thing. But I was astounded to see the things that children are allowed to do, such as going out on their own dates, and even borrowing the family car for the purpose. Over here the children are much more restricted and quiet. . . .'[15]

However they might fare in an international comparison, by comparison with the preceding generation of parents, the New Dubliner artisans are extremely close to their adolescent children and very liberal towards them. This is one of their most *general* characteristics and it is equally true of both girls and boys in respect to both of their parents, and particularly in respect to their fathers. This is indicated by the *general* decline in the use of father as a threat to the children;

[14] Employer-managerial class.
[15] Employer-managerial class.

in the *general* decline of corporal punishment to the point where its main use is purely as a threat; and in the rise of withdrawal of affection, of reasoning and of the bestowal of rewards or the imposition of deprivations—and usually a combination of these techniques —as the *prevalent* forms of discipline. It is likewise indicated by the *prevalence* of greater participation by the children in adult conversations and in the increased association with their parents in recreational activities, particularly between fathers and sons. Furthermore, although it is far from *prevalent*, children may address their parents, particularly their fathers, by their Christian names. More frequently, children will joke with their parents and tease them. One wife said of her husband: 'All of our children have been close to Dan and have treated him like a pal . . . and there is a deal of good humour between them. The children have never been afraid to joke with Dan, and even to josh him about some of his eccentricities. But my father was very stern, and the children in my family all feared him. . . .'

Intimacy in the relationship of parents and adolescent children is, above all, apparent in this *general* decline in the children's fear of their parents and in their reserve towards them, and in the growth of discussion, consultation and the exchange of personal information between them. Thus, according to one mother:

> . . . the children are much closer to their fathers. Paddy and Liam [sons aged twenty-one and seventeen respectively] are very close to Jaimie here. They will be in here talking to him about where they have been, whom they went to a dance with, who was there and what happened and laughing over the funny things that occurred. Jaimie could never do that with his father. In fact, his father would have a fit if he saw Jaimie with a girl friend at that age. . . .

As the above passage indicates, greater intimacy between parents and children is associated with the clearly wider range of freedom in extra-domestic activities that parents *generally* have accorded their children in late adolescence. In early adolescence, the *general* parental surveillance of the children takes forms that are uniform among the artisans. The limitation of the children's peer group to select neighbourhood children, the supervision of their activities by the parents themselves or by relatives or neighbours close enough to the family to act as parental surrogates, the general requirement that children be in the house and, usually, in bed quite early in the evening—all of these endure roughly until the children are touching fifteen, although there is a gradual relaxation of strictures at the end of that period. Thereafter, at least by comparison with the *general* practice when our artisan spouses were adolescents, the range of independent activity permitted the children is *generally* quite broad.

One of the areas where this increased freedom is most marked is the mingling of the sexes and the type of premarital behaviour that is permitted them. We shall discuss such behaviour in our subsequent discussion of marriage. Here let us note that the relatively closed circle of the parent-child relationship now begins to break down as several *general* and important developments occur.

Parental control over the membership of the children's peer group diminishes sharply. Children make their own friends over whom, if the children are obstinate, the parental power of veto is difficult to exercise. For, secondly, the members of the peer group are now no longer recruited merely from the neighbourhood circle of families but 'from all over town'. At the same time, most peer group activities are no longer based at home or in the neighbourhood as was prevalent in their parents' day, but are scattered all over the city. Parental control over both the children's associates and their activities is not only reduced in amount, it is also forced into new forms. Thus, it is general that now parents base their evaluation of their children's companions not upon knowledge of the families of these companions, but rather upon the personal character of the children themselves. Furthermore, parents *generally* control their children's activities in the peer group not by mandate or by policing, but by persuasion and advice, the effectiveness of which depends upon their intimacy with their children and the mutual trust that flourishes between them. Unanimously, parents greatly prefer this arrangement to the opposite one that *prevailed* when they themselves were young. Trusting their earlier training to have formed proper powers of judgment in their children, they *generally* feel, as one mother put it, that 'children will find their own level and the proper kind of friends'. And as another mother stated: 'We felt that our children should be free to make their own friends outside the neighbourhood and with children of families we don't know. And we always tried to make them feel free to bring their friends home. Indeed, we expected them to do so. No matter who they were, if they were decent boys and girls, they were perfectly welcome and we were glad to have them as our children's friends. This wasn't the case at all in my parents' day. . . .'

It is in this *general* atmosphere of affection and trust that the mutual rights and obligations between parents and children are engendered and developed. Our discussion of the manner in which husbands and wives co-ordinate their activities to secure the family livelihood indicates how artisan parents fulfil their primary obligation to their children in respect to the children's physical well-being—viz. to provide shelter, food, clothes, and physical care. It also indicates the obligations of the children to co-operate in this by domestic activities of various kinds. Furthermore, we have also seen the manner

148

in which the parents fulfil their obligation to discipline the children, a central feature in the process of socialization. But socialization is more than discipline, and parental obligations go beyond the provision of the essentials for survival. Artisan parents also *generally* feel obliged to equip all their children so that they may better their lot socially. This double obligation—to fit their children to survive and to advance—demands the co-operation of the children themselves, and thus gives rise to reciprocal obligations on the children's part. These mutual obligations bear principally upon two central questions that are related to each other: the education of the children, and their careers as adults. Although both of these matters involve considerations of marriage as well as of positions in the occupational world, it will help to deal with marriage separately and to concentrate here upon the question of the children's education and their occupational careers.

Although all artisan parents desire to try to better the lot of each of their children, not every father and mother feel able to encompass this equally for all and at the same time provide for the basic needs of the entire family. In such cases, the desire to advance is necessarily subordinated to the family's need to survive or to hold its own. In many cases, however, artisan parents feel competent to meet both obligations. If we consider only the artisan families actually interviewed and the policies they have adopted in regard to the post-primary education for the children, these two attitudes are strictly *alternative*. In six cases the parents, like the Dunns, have offered, or planned to offer, all their children a full secondary education or practically its equivalent.[16] In five cases, parents did not feel able to offer all of their children these educational advantages. But if we turn to the reports of these people as to what policy in this matter is common among people like themselves, the second of these *alternatives* seems to be more *prevalent* than the first. Because of the importance of the matter, however, it will be enlightening to consider both *alternatives*.

Where the needs of the family are conceived as imposing, at least

[16] Such terminology is required by the complexities of the educational system. Secondary schools give a 'leaving certificate' to students who successfully complete a four-year course. To qualify for the last two years of this course all students must pass an intermediate examination. Students who pass this examination but do not desire to continue are granted an 'intermediate certificate'. Many students, especially girls, take an intermediate certificate and then enter a private business or commercial school for special training. Technical schools normally offer only a two-year course in special fields, but a few also offer an additional year designed to provide advanced specialized training or even to prepare students for matriculation in the University. For our purposes, a student who, by any of these arrangements, goes beyond the intermediate level is considered to have the equivalent of a full secondary education.

upon some of the children, the obligation to work immediately or shortly after the completion of primary school, inevitably and *generally* it falls upon the older children; and, *generally* speaking, upon the older children irrespective of sex. Whatever preferment is made on a sexual basis tends to favour the girls by reason of the greater import of marriage for a girl's adult career and the shrewd artisan calculation that educational background enhances a girl's marital prospects.

> Most people like ourselves, if it were a question of choosing between a boy or a girl for secondary school, would send the girl, because it would give her a better chance for a good marriage. . . . If a girl dresses well and has the background so that she can meet any type of people and talk with them and hold her own, she has a much better chance of making a good marriage and that is much more necessary for her than for a boy. A boy will get along if he has a good trade and the ability. . . . Education means much more for a girl here than for a boy.

How realistic is this appraisal of the social situation is indicated by the following description, given by a professional man, of the *general* attitude on this matter among parents in the employer-managerial-professional class.

> Parents do not let you go around very steadily with a girl who, for example, has not gone to secondary school but has ended up after National School. And if you insisted they would rather raise hell about it, especially your father. They would admit that the girl was a nice girl and a smashing blonde. But they would tell you that if you are going to live with her all your life you have to have more than that; that if you were interested in literature and liked to discuss Dickens and she knows nothing about either literature or Dickens, it would not be long before you would be very bored with her and it would make for a lot of unhappiness.

Apart from this consideration of sex, parents who feel that the older children must work shortly after primary school make two standard exceptions: one *prevalently* made is for a child with outstanding talent; the second, *generally* made, is for a child with a religious vocation.

However, while the older children are often obliged to forgo secondary education in the interests of swelling the family income, it is quite *prevalent* for the parents, once they are over the hump, to allow and even to encourage the younger children to continue in school. The attitude of parents who define the situation in this manner is well summed up in the following statement of one artisan father:

> In families like ours, where there are four or five children, the father has to send the older children to work out of sheer economic necessity. He needs the additional income to bring the family up and so the older boys

and even girls will have to go to work. And most of the time, since good jobs are not easy to get, the father will have to use his influence to get his son or daughter a job and when one comes, he can't let them back out of it. As for letting the children go on for further schooling, the child has to show brightness and real intelligence early on before he will allow him to go to secondary school, because that means additional expenses as well as losing the income that the boy or girl might bring in. In a family this size [seven children] the older children would have to be geniuses and be in line for a scholarship before the parents would consider sending them on to school, at least with people of our means. The younger children get more of a break, because by the time they are out of National School the family is usually much better off and can afford the expense, and they would be inclined to send them to school even though they might not have genius but just normal intelligence. . . . You have a concrete example in Biddy and Eilis right there in front of you. We could not give Biddy [the second oldest in the family] further schooling because things were rather rough then and the family was large, so Biddy had to go to work just as Ned [the oldest] and Steve [the third oldest] did. But now, I myself have advanced in my own work and am getting more money, and with the help of the older children things are much better now. So Eilis [the youngest in the family] is getting what we would like to have given all of them but could not.[17]

Although many Dublin companies have either the formal policy or the actual practice of giving job preference to the sons of their employees, the parental obligation to obtain jobs for their children indicated in the preceding statement, and particularly the father's obligation to obtain a job for his son, is not always easy of fulfilment. This is especially so in regard to many trades where the unions are closed and union membership is largely based upon kinship, need and seniority, as in the case, for instance, of the coopers and the shipwrights. This condition sometimes precludes any choice on the part of the boy as to the kind of work he is to take up. Nevertheless, the *prevalent* practice among artisan families is to give the child, even an oldest boy, occupational option. Thus one of the sons of the father we have just quoted claimed with the agreement of his mother and father who were present that:

. . . most of the fathers today do not put their sons to work or decide what they are going to do simply by themselves. They usually give the boy an option. While many of my friends have gone to work at jobs their fathers got them, in almost every case they were not forced to go but could have refused to take the job if they wanted. In many cases, a lad will take the job and later change to something else if he does not like it. . . . If a father worked for Guinness' and could get his son a job

[17] Eilis took her intermediate degree at a convent school and went on to attend a private commercial school.

L   151

there, but the boy really did not want it, the father would be more inclined to let the lad have his way than in the old days, as far as I can make out. Both parents might argue with him and put pressure on him to take the job, but if the lad did not want that sort of work, he'd get his own way.

In the group of families who offer all their children the equivalent of a full secondary education the dilemma of school or work also crops up, but only at a higher level. It is therefore neither as frequent nor as acute, for it concerns university rather than secondary education. The *prevalent* attitude of these parents towards a university course, especially for the boys, is quite analagous to that just described for the other artisan parents in regard to secondary education. Among families wherein all the children are offered secondary education, the children's freedom of choice in regard to an occupation is, of course, quite *general*. On the other hand, the children's choice in regard to the school-work decision appears to be only an *alternative*. Where some parents insist on the children's continuance at school, others let the children ultimately decide for themselves. The *prevalent* tendency seems to be not to force the children to go to school against their clear will. Joan Dunn's statement on this is accurate and from it it is clear that children in these families have the same sort of option as regards school as most artisan children have about the kind of jobs they are to take.[18]

All of this indicates a widespread and important trend among the artisan families during the last half-century. While not all the fathers of our artisan spouses were themselves in the class we have called artisan, twelve of them were. And yet eleven of the twelve artisan spouses in our sample who are their children unanimously reported that both in their own natal family and among people in their family's circle the children were simply put to work on completing elementary school; that there was rarely question of a child being sent to secondary school; and that almost never was there question of a child having any choice either between school and work, or in working at one kind of job rather than another. This is borne out by the fact that of all our artisan spouses only one was given a secondary education. It may be appropriate, therefore, to quote this woman's description of the common parental practice when she was a girl. After her husband, himself the son of an artisan, had stated that in his youth fathers 'generally just told their sons what they were to do and that was the end of the matter' and that he himself, though he wanted to be a carpenter, was simply put into Guinness's as a cooper without any choice about the job, she added:

[18] *v.* ch. iv, p. 127.

Actually I had a choice about what I wanted to do, both in regard to school and to work, but I was definitely an exception. What Jaimie says was true even for the girls, though the fathers were not as hard on the girls as they were on the boys. The fathers are more reasonable today than they used to be.

We get quite the opposite picture in considering our modern artisan families. Of the eleven interviewed only two put *all* of their children to work after elementary school, and even these gave their children their choice in regard to their jobs.

The varying attitudes of parents in the two generations obviously reflect the general change in Dublin during the last twenty-five years, particularly the expansion of occupational opportunities calling for educated personnel, and the parallel extension of educational facilities that are within range of the artisans' means. But it is intriguing to ask why there should be this difference in educational and job policy among artisans who are all in the same environment and in roughly the same condition. Economic differences, though small, as well as variation in family size undoubtedly influence these diverse policies. But they do not adequately explain them, since families, which are just as large and in which the father's occupational status and income is the same, are to be found in both groups.

At least as important as differences in wage and size of family are the varying ways in which parents define a social situation that is essentially the same for all of them. Some read the situation in such a way as to feel compelled to put the older children out to work. Others read it in such a way as to feel that education for all the children is both feasible and worth the sacrifice entailed. That it is the definition of their life situation that is crucial in this matter appears from the lament of the wife of a carpenter and the mother of twelve children, of whom only the youngest boy—significantly studying for the priesthood—has received a secondary education:

> I never looked to keeping my children in school and I have been very sorry ever since. . . . I've felt bad about it because I realize now I did not put enough value on education. I know if I had to do it all over again I'd send as many as I possibly could to secondary school, especially the girls.

It is significant, perhaps, that this woman and her husband, married in 1910, are the oldest of the artisan families studied. It is also significant that four of the six families who are offering all their children the equivalent of a secondary education are the youngest families in our sample. While this evidence is not sufficient to establish the point without question, it is enough to suggest that with the course of the years, the progressive modernization of the Dublin

153

community in which they live, and the experience of how the educated can exploit its opportunities, artisan families are more and more coming to re-define their situation so as to place higher value on education.

Besides financing their children's education and helping them to secure a job, parents have the obligation to help their children tread their way successfully in the occupational world by counsel and advice, and likewise to help them through school by supervising and aiding their studies at home. Which of the parents assumes the role of schoolmaster at home is an *alternate* pattern. *Prevalently*, however, the parental obligation to help the children with their studies runs into two snags. On the one hand, artisan children who go to secondary school pass beyond the educational level attained by their parents and thereby beyond their help. On the other, even while the children are in the elementary grades, parents *prevalently* cannot help them in those subjects that are taught in Gaelic because of their own in-sufficient knowledge of that language. Whether, as a result, parents condemn the policy of using Gaelic as a medium of instruction as some do or whether, as others feel, they consider it a worthwhile and temporary evil that will cease to exist in the next generation, almost all artisan parents acknowledge that the Gaelic requirement has created a chasm between their children and themselves in regard to studies.

Reciprocal to these obligations of the parents, of course, are the children's obligation to study to the best of their ability and after they begin work, to contribute to the financial support of the family. *Prevalently*, artisan parents do not find truancy a widespread problem and some are explicit in reporting that 'mitching', as it is called, has declined considerably since they were children at school age. *Prevalently*, too, they report that their children are faithful to their school work, with children of neither sex clearly surpassing the other in this respect. In view of the fact that parents are liberal in allowing children who do not like school to stop attendance at secondary school, this is hardly surprising.

The obligation of working children to contribute to the family purse is, of course, strict. But the practice of allowing working children, at least after they reach the age of eighteen, voluntarily to determine the amount of their contribution is *general*. This contrasts sharply with the practice, *general* when present artisan parents were children, of requiring children even in their late twenties to turn in their entire wage from which they then received an allowance, and it is another instance of the increased independence modern artisan parents have accorded their children. Unquestionably, the obligation to contribute to the support of the family tends to delay the marriage of the older children, just as we have seen that it did in earlier days in the case of John Dunn. But it does so now to a considerably lesser extent. Thus, one man, whose work brings him in contact with a great many families, stated:

> You may occasionally get children who have that sense of obligation and who would postpone marriage for some years because of it, but it is a good deal less now than it used to be. And strangely I think it happens more frequently among middle class families who have some sort of social standing to maintain. . . . But most children among working class people today will not stand any argument from their parents to postpone their marriage because the family is hard pressed. They feel that if the father can spend a certain amount of money on drink and sports and things of that sort, he can very well give that up and take up the slack. They are not going to give up married life and the chance to go it on their own because he isn't willing to do that.

Furthermore, parents themselves are no longer as demanding in this respect. With the preceding generation of parents, it was not unusual, if not indeed an *alternate* practice, to keep one girl at home to help the mother. Often enough such a girl found her marriage opportunities reduced, and as her parents aged or died she was expected or felt obliged to raise the rest of the family, with the result that she often remained unmarried. Parents today *generally* consider this unfair to a girl, and in any event the girls themselves *prevalently* refuse to be put in this position under normal circumstances. One man reported: 'In my parents' day, the oldest girl was often kept home to help the mother, and very often she got left. The girls today know that and they want no part of it. So they insist on getting out to work.'

In abnormal circumstances, however, the obligations of filial piety are strong and if either parent of a young family dies or is crippled, someone of the children, usually one of the older children, is expected to assume the responsibilities of helping to raise the family. Usually, it will be a son if the father is incapacitated, and a daughter if it be the mother. This actually happened in all five cases from among the nineteen natal families of our artisan spouses where this condition arose. Naturally, there are no instances of this among our completed artisan families. But the artisans report that this is still *prevalent* practice in their circle of friends and acquaintances, and one that definitely leads the children involved to postpone marriage and often enough to forgo it altogether. The number of instances related of boys who postponed marriage for this reason is very great. As for the girls, we have the following typical account:

> It was quite common when I was a girl for a girl to sacrifice her life to her family. When the parents were old or crippled and there were

younger children around, the oldest girl very frequently would just forget about marriage and dedicate herself to taking care of the family and raising the children, and I could quote any number of cases where that happened. I don't think that is dying out now really. It is still the general ideal and principle that girls will act like that in such circumstances. For example, there is a friend of Eithne's who is in that position, and it is rather sad to see her. She is just about Eithne's age [19], and she is going to be devoted to that family for a long time and probably won't get married or not until late, as a result. There is another girl next door on the other side here who is the same way. When a situation like that arises a girl will give up her job—or at least most girls would—out of a sense of family obligation and just devote her life to taking care of the house and helping the family out. I think it is too bad and I think most people think it too bad that it is not dying out, because after the parents are dead and the rest of the children are grown it is very lonesome for a girl. . . .

In short, the extent of the children's obligation to contribute financially to their natal families has declined and with it, in normal circumstances, its delaying action upon marriage. But the obligation to help raise the family in abnormal circumstances, which is much more than a financial obligation, remains just about as strong today as it was. Moreover, it continues to fall upon the older children rather than the younger, and just as often leads to celibacy for the child involved, particularly in the case of a girl.

The limited obligations of parents to help a son or daughter financially at their marriage which the Dunns have described are *general* although all artisan parents, perhaps, have not the same contacts and influence that John Dunn has.[19] But we have not enough evidence to determine the precise extent to which the obligation to help their parents financially continues to bind the children once they are married. Under normal conditions, of course, it ceases altogether since the parents usually are able to take care of themselves. In exceptional instances where this is not the case their children, though married, will come to their aid, but we have no data on how this burden is apportioned between them. The usual exemption from continued financial aid once they are married reduces children's obligations to their parents almost entirely to obligations of a non-financial nature. Apart from the mutual obligation of parents and married children to help each other on special occasions and in times of crisis, and of the children, if need be, to take their parents into their home in their old age, there is a *general* obligation of children to visit their parents at least once a week while they live.

But obligations of filial piety extend beyond assistance of this sort and beyond mutual economic aid. The obligation of the children to

[19] *v.* ibid., pp. 128–9.

help their parents get to church and to the sacraments when they are old, to ensure that they receive the last rites when dying, and to pray and to have Masses said for the repose of their soul after their death is counterpoint to the primary obligation of parents to impart to their children their religious faith and to habituate them to the observance of their religious duties. The concept of religious duties entertained by the Dunns is a *general* one. Indeed, if exception is made of John Dunn's daily attendance at Mass and membership in the St. Vincent de Paul Society, and of the membership of the Dunn women in various religious organizations other than the Sodality, the pattern of the Dunn's religious behaviour and attitudes can be said to be quite *general* and uniform for all artisan families.

This relieves us of further, detailed discussion. But several things are worth noting in particular. First, the esteem of the priesthood and the willingness of artisan parents, even at great sacrifice, to finance a religious vocation, especially of a son to the priesthood, is *general*. There are two ways, however, in which artisan parents feel that they differ in this respect from most of their parents before them and from the country people even today. The first is their attitude towards former nuns and particularly former seminarians. Towards such, the artisans take a more liberal and benign attitude than people of their parents' generation and, they feel, than their rural contemporaries. *Prevalently*, the artisans consider that a lad who leaves the seminary normally does so because of the conviction that he is not cut out for the priestly life and that this is quite proper and even laudable. In their parents' time a much more severe attitude was *prevalent* and, whatever may be the case with contemporary rural people, this attitude, though no longer prevalent, continues to exist among artisans in the city. Thus one woman, quite spontaneously and without being questioned on the subject, reported on men who leave the seminary and women who leave the convent:

> . . . if you do that, it's better if you don't show your face around at all. For example, there is a girl I know who was a nun for three years and then came out. She told me she never felt comfortable, and was always ill at ease and sensitive. Whether she was in her own home or out of it, she felt that all eyes were on her, which they really were. You would hear people talking of her and saying: 'O, she came out from the convent, you know.' And, 'If I were her, I wouldn't have come back here. . . .' I'd say that while it is not as bad as it is in the country, the attitude still exists here in the city, and the main source of it is the mother. She feels she has done everything for a girl and especially a boy and made very great sacrifices. And so when he comes out it is a terrible disappointment, and she feels very resentful. After all, that is the ambition of every mother, to have a son a priest. And the relatives and neighbours understand it, because they feel the same way, so they will back her up. . . . It is very

157

hard on her, you know. Really, I'd take it bad myself. Of course, I know it may be a better thing if he hasn't a vocation. But still it's natural and understandable why they feel that way. I know a case in the neighbourhood of a son who left the seminary and it changed his mother's whole life. She finally had to move out of here because she could not stand the shame of it. . . . After he left the seminary, why, you wouldn't know her. You'd think she had gone mad. She had a stunned look on her face all the time, especially after he married. I suppose she had the idea that while he might have left for a time, he would go back in. But once he got married, she was simply a broken woman.

The second *prevalent* point of difference, at least with their parents' generation, lies in the more critical attitude artisan people have today towards the clergy. While artisan parents are cautious of voicing such criticism before young children and are not likely to be openly critical of the clergy in their presence, they are more outspoken among themselves to the displeasure of the older people. One mother said:

The older people would never say anything against a priest and would not tolerate anything being said against him. Even today, my mother gets very put out and simply won't stand anybody criticizing a priest, even if it is mild and justified. But the younger people, especially the men, discuss religion more and are more outspoken than the older people. Not that they are very strong in their criticism, but they are not afraid to talk about such things. And if they feel something is not being done rightly, they say so, at least among themselves.

The third notable feature, more a matter of observation than report, is the extent to which religion is taken for granted. Knowledge of defections among Irish people who go to England has made many artisan people aware of this. Awareness often becomes explicit among those who have lived some time abroad, such as the wife who said:

To me it seems that religion here is a heritage and that is the way people accept it. It is something that has been handed down to them and that they have always had. And so it is very easy to practise it. There is no bother, or trouble. As a result, I don't think people here have as much real appreciation and intelligent grasp of it or instruction in it as they do, say, in Australia or America. I can't remember when I heard any real discussion of religion among my friends other than discussion of personalities of people who are religious. . . . If there is a Protestant present you don't discuss religion out of deference to him. And if you are among your own, you don't discuss it because it is just taken for granted.[20]

Fourthly, in direct sequence with this, the fear of an intellectual approach to religion, an *alternative* if not a *prevalent* attitude, affects the artisan people as it does all other classes of people in Dublin,

[20] Employer-managerial class.

158

although the artisans are not capable of describing it as graphically and accurately as the professional man who said:

> ... if you were to advocate an intellectual grounding in the faith, if you were to advocate that people be trained more in the knowledge of their religion and in theology, you'd be accused of being a rationalist and of promoting secularism. You would be creating an intelligentsia who have always caused us trouble here, who have been the ones who have lost their faith and created a good deal of disturbance. You see, the general opinion is that we Irish have been through a tremendous amount of suffering for our faith, and we have stood up to it for five hundred years. Therefore, when you advocate any sort of changes, you are questioned whether or not you can produce men and women as sturdy and strong in their faith as the Irish have proved themselves to be. The attitude is: after all, if a man leads a good Catholic life, if he goes to the Sacraments, if he is faithful to his religious duties, brings his children up well, educates them and sees that they have the faith, that is the essence of life. How do you answer that?[21]

Finally, as the last part of the above passage indicates, the reciprocal obligations of filial piety are founded upon the basis of religion. As this is the source of parental obligations to their children, so it is considered the major motive of children's obligations towards their parents. In various ways all artisan parents give expression to the sentiments of the woman who said: 'The only reason why we are held to anything is because of our obligations to God. If you can make the children realize that disobedience or neglecting your obligations is an offence against Our Lord you have given them the only real and lasting motive.'[22]

A discussion of the generic parent-child relationship such as we have been conducting is, of course, incomplete unless we consider how this relationship comes into play at the marriage of the children. But the question of the children's marriage emphasizes a fact to which thus far we have given only passing notice: within the generic framework of the parent-child relationship there are special relationships between the specific members of the family. We will be better able to discuss marriage if we first attend to these.

In the relationship of father and son we have already remarked two features. First of all the relationship *prevalently* passes from a stage of great affection when the boy is an infant to one of relative indifference in the 'gawky' age of early adolescence. And then, in late adolescence and early manhood, it becomes one of greater companionship which is manifested in the *prevalent* exchange of information and in the mutual confidence between father and son. Secondly,

[21] Employer-managerial class.
[22] Employer-managerial class.

fathers *prevalently* consult the wishes of their sons in regard to their occupational careers. Both of these developments, moreover, constitute a notable change from the relationship current between the artisan husbands and their fathers.

The change has been affected in part by modifications in the husband and wife relationship that have resulted in increasing the weight of the wife's voice in the family council and, partly through her influence, in tempering the father's attitude towards his son. Nevertheless, it appears that what may be considered remnants of the former father-son relationship are still *prevalent*. Pre-eminent among these is the attitude of the father that his sons, even in late adolescence, are boys who cannot do any job right and to whom, in the world of practical affairs, it is folly to give any initiative.

> The fathers have an attitude that the sons are always boys who can't do anything right. I know my boys felt that their father thought they were incapable of doing anything on their own. And so they would not do a thing around the house if their father was home. They wouldn't help him hang paper or paint, or even put a nail in if he was here because as soon as they tried to do a job he'd say: 'Ah, you don't know how to do that. Here let me do it.' But if Frank wasn't home, they would go ahead and do a job. . . . That is very common. My own brother, who has a shop, is the same way with his boys. The oldest boy used to work in the shop with him. My brother was always criticizing him. If he told the boy how to do something, two minutes later he was back doing it himself and complaining that the boy knew nothing about business and did not know how to conduct himself in this particular matter. That continued so long that the son got fed up with it and went over to England and took up the same business. He opened up a grocery store and he is doing very well. There is no doubt in my mind that one of the reasons why he went into the grocery business was to show his father that he did know how to run the business. . . . With the rest of the boys here at home my brother acts exactly the same way and this is fairly common.
>
> The fathers think the boys are children even when they are eighteen or nineteen and they tend to keep them children. They won't let them go off on their own or have a bit of their own head and perhaps make some mistakes, but learn by the mistakes. And I don't think that is very much different than it was in my parents' day.[23]

Consonant with this is an *alternative* attitude of the older men to the younger men at work which one woman, the wife of a foreman at Guinness's and the mother of three sons working there, described as 'the same attitude they had a hundred years ago and as the farmers still have towards the boys in the country'. The father of another family likewise stated that:

[23] Clerical class.

160

Fathers here are inclined to feel that lads are going to make a terrible botch of things if they allow them too much freedom and initiative. I know I have an apprentice under me at work and—well, I feel that if he has a job to do I have to be standing around watching him all the time and correcting him. That is the attitude all right.

A tendency that is at least *alternate* among the boys confirms that this paternal attitude still exists and at the same time shows how it is circumvented. After one father had said that when he was a boy, a father would often have his son apprenticed to himself in a trade and then 'would treat him as if he were a baby', his own son remarked: 'All that is changing now. The sons don't want to go into the same trade as their fathers and one of the reasons is that they are afraid of being apprenticed to him and getting that kind of treatment.'

Prevalently, however, the fathers are also eager, if it is possible, to have their sons take up a better line of work than themselves or follow their own line of work at a higher level. In either case, this means that the son works in a different context than his father and it results in a reduction in the contribution a father can make to the technical training of his sons. Partly for this reason and partly because, even before his sons enter the occupational field, a father must work away from home, the father's contribution to the general, humanistic training of his boys is restricted. To a greater extent, and by the nature of the case less effectively, such training devolves upon the mother. Artisan boys in early adolescence are forced to look more to their mothers, more to their peer group, and in late adolescence more to men other than their fathers for both general guidance and for specialized training. What we have said of John Dunn and his sons in these respects is quite *general*.[24]

Like his own father before him, the artisan father *generally* does not consider marriage as a likely means of advance for his son. He is, of course, concerned about the character of his son's light-o'-love. He is also inquisitive about her family background, though he is less concerned than his own father was about this, and particularly about the girl's family *stock*. But he is not greatly preoccupied either with the economic condition or the social position of his future daughter-in-law's family. His *prevalent* concern is that his son not only have security in his job, but that he should not rush into marriage until he has saved enough to contend with the extraordinary contingencies as well as with the normal exigencies that might befall him as a married man. *Prevalently*, fathers feel that a son who marries before he has achieved such a financial condition will 'always be pulling the monkey by the tail'. Their advice, therefore, tends to be conservative and to delay a son's marriage. However, if a son insists upon marrying in

[24] *v.* ch. iv, pp. 124–5.

spite of his advice, the father will not seriously try to block this marriage on the grounds that the son is too young or inexperienced even though the boy be in his early twenties.

The relationship between mother and son bears an altogether different complexion. While, as we have seen, the mother's affection for her sons and daughters in their infancy appears to be roughly equal, one is inundated on all sides by reports that continuously through adolescence, and especially in its later stages and in adult manhood, the mother favours her sons over her daughters and 'spoils' them. Even in the face of the fact that so many people of both sexes and of all ages and conditions of life bear witness that this maternal attitude is *prevalent*, it will be well to investigate the truth of the assertion because this will enlighten us as to how, if true, the attitude works in practice.

There are certain straws in the wind that, while not proving the point of themselves, may confirm it if other and more valid evidence is forthcoming. Thus, the *general* preferential exemption of boys, even in early adolescence, from domestic chores may be significant, although this might be explained as a survival of the rural sexual division of labour. Another indication of discrimination is the wider range of freedom accorded boys, although this discrepancy today in Dublin is not as great as formerly. A bit more pertinent, however, is the reason sometimes cited for the *prevalent* difficulty mothers have in disciplining the boys and in keeping them out of mischief. Boys, more than girls, feel that their mother is too soft and affectionate to carry out her threats and so are able to get around her more easily. Correlative to this, because it seems to indicate that boys feel more secure in their mother's affection, is the scattered evidence that withdrawal of affection has a quicker and more telling effect upon the girls. One mother, like others, finds it '. . . harder to control the boys than the girls, and I have to get my husband after them. For the best way to control the children is to withdraw your affection from them and be very cool with them. But that works much more strongly on the girls than on the boys. The boys seem to know you really do not mean it and it does not seem to bother them much. But it has a great effect on the girls.'

The evidence becomes more pertinent in the face of the *prevalent* fact that especially in late adolescence and early manhood the mother 'slaves for the boys' and, what is more, makes the girls do likewise. She not only lessens the sons' range of domestic responsibility, but conceives that it is part of her and her daughters' job to provide the sons with special service and comforts. This is so established that the daughters are resigned to it. An excellent description of the situation is the following passage which is notable, not only for its vividness, but also by reason of the fact that, made by a girl of twenty-six before her whole family, it met only with confirmation even from her mother and brothers:

Mammy will serve the boys hand and foot. If Matt is upstairs and he yells down that he hasn't a shirt, Mammy will run into the room here to the hot-press and get a shirt and take it up to him. But if it were myself or Betty that needed something, we would have to come down and root it out for ourselves. If I am sitting in the easy chair there and Matt or Charley come home, I am expected to get up and give them the chair. They just say 'Pardon me' and up I get. Well, I do not mind giving it to them, because I know that they work harder than I do, but that is the idea. There is no use fighting against it. I used to, but I soon found out which way the wind blew—we have to wait on the boys from sole to crown. I do not mean that the boys do not do anything for us. Matt, for example, will always fix my bike. But Mammy is just a slave to them, a willing slave, and we are expected to be, too. And that is general. That's the common attitude.

Furthermore, all the artisan mothers interviewed not only admitted that this 'spoiling' of the boys is quite common but acknowledged that commonly mothers are reluctant to have a son marry, even when loss of his income would not have severe economic consequences for her or the rest of the family. Often, indeed, they hardly conceal their sorrow at a son's marriage, although, as one husband said: 'It is not as bad as it was in the old days when sometimes you'd think the wedding was a wake the way a boy's mother would be crying and carrying on.'[25]

Most artisan mothers interviewed were, understandably enough, very adroit in avoiding a direct statement as to how they themselves felt on this matter. But it may be significant that only one mother openly stated that she would be quite happy to see her sons marry in their early twenties and openly condemned the opposite attitude of many mothers. On the other hand, two mothers admitted that even the remote prospects of a son marrying filled them with sadness. Thus a relatively young mother of two girls and one boy, who was four years old and named Seumas, said: 'The mothers always love the sons and always prefer them to the daughters. And, sure, they shower them with affection and spoil them altogether. . . . I feel the same way about Seumas. I think the world of him, and indeed I can't see anything further than him. I hate the thought of his ever getting married and I simply shudder at it.'

The other mother, whose three sons are aged twenty-eight, twenty-four and twenty-one, have good jobs and are unmarried and also unengaged, after reporting what she considered the common attitude,

[25] General labourer.

163

said: 'However, I often tell Matt [the oldest] that 'tis about time he got married.'

'Yes,' said the husband, 'but the day Matt brings a girl in here it is going to be awfully chilly in this house.'

As the six children [twenty-eight to seventeen] laughingly agreed with their father, the mother said: 'Ah, it's true, I suppose it will be.'

Along with making their son's life at home quite comfortable, mothers prevalently employ obstructionist tactics when their son's marriage becomes an imminent threat. If there are no valid economic reasons, she may appeal to the fact that the son is 'too young', that he is too 'inexperienced' and even that he should get around and have a good time before marriage. If she runs out of reasons, she still makes him feel her reluctance.

> My mother was very reluctant indeed about my marriage, even though when I did get married she really had no defences left. I was thirty, so I was old enough. And I was established in my profession [the law], and financially secure, so that she had no grounds for further objection. Yet, very definitely, she did not like it. She had known Dympna since she was a girl and she always liked her very much. But later on when she found out that Dympna was for me, there was a big change in her attitude. She became very critical. It is the old story, of course. She did not think any girl was good enough for me, or could take care of me.[26]

Meanwhile, the mother is highly critical of prospective daughters-in-law when they are absent, and decidedly cool towards them when they are present. A husband married at twenty-seven said: 'When I was going around with girls with the idea of getting married, my mother was putting obstacles in the way all the time to any girl I was showing interest in. She'd be criticizing them and making remarks about them. "Sure that one is too fond of the boys", and "that one's father is a drunk"—little criticisms that were intended to debase the girl in my eyes. I certainly felt that she was putting obstacles to any girl I began to show an interest in, and I think that is very common.'

Another man summed it up by referring to a song in which a girl expresses her exasperation with her sweetheart, vows she will marry 'a better man than him', and consigns him to his old mother: 'Sure, 'tis as the song has it: "It is fightin' me and spitin' me is all that she has done, since first I started courtin' her great big, ugly son." '

Frequently enough, after a son is married the attitude of the mother to her son's wife continues to be resentful and highly critical. One wife said of a family friend: 'I heard Felim's mother say in his presence, "My seven lovely sons, and what terrible wives they have." Well, you have met Felim's wife. Do you think she is terrible?'

---

[26] Employer-managerial class.

This maternal attitude towards the sons is also frequently cited as the reason why the conflict between the mother-in-law and daughter-in-law is alleged to be more severe than the conflict between a mother-in-law and a son-in-law. A New Dubliner artisan wife who, together with her husband and children, lives with her mother, stated in her mother's presence:

> The Irish mothers, as a result, make very poor mothers-in-law, at least where there is a question of their sons. They are always interfering. They don't get along with the son's wife at all, and they are always criticizing her and claiming that she cannot do things in a manner befitting their son. It isn't the same where there is a son-in-law involved. The mother-in-law does not get in the way so much in that case. I suppose it is natural, since she is her own daughter, and the mother has trained her and they have the same way of looking at things. So there is little friction in that case. But it is quite different where a son's mother is living in with him and his wife. Then, there is all sorts of trouble. . . .[27]

In the long run, however, the most convincing evidence is the fact that every person questioned on this matter referred, like John Dunn, to several individual cases of sons who after their father had died, postponed their marriage and often enough never married, in order to stay with their mother. In every case, they insisted, this was not due to any necessity to support the mother financially, nor to a reluctance to leave her alone since there were other members of the family living with her, but because the son felt that he should not leave her nor bring another woman in on her. To relate all such cases would fill a small volume. But since they are so enlightening, we may consider a series of statements on the matter. The first is by an artisan girl: 'The mothers want to hang on to the boys as long as they can, or at least until they are getting along towards thirty. And frequently a lad will say he will stay unmarried until his mother dies. I know one lad who decided that he was going to wait until his mother died before he got married. But, unfortunately for him—or fortunately, as the case may be—he died before his mother did.'

The second statement comes from a clerical wife.

> I don't think Vincent's brother, Paul [now 36], will ever get married because his mother is against it. She says she wants him to, but I don't think she is sincere. She did not want Vincent to marry me, either, but she could not stop him. For example, Paul about eight months ago met a girl he used to be very keen on, and they started going around again. I think he would really have liked to marry her. Certainly he could afford to, since he makes about £1,200 a year. Well, his mother was frightfully upset, and she was very cool to Paul, and eventually it fizzled out.

[27] Clerical class.

The third comment was made by this woman's husband.

Not long ago Paul wanted to buy a new house which happened to be near a cemetery. He wanted to buy it because it was a new house and a wonderful bargain, while our old place is on the ancient side. My mother's reaction was that he was preparing to bring a wife into the house and she was violently opposed to it. She even told him he was buying the new house: 'Because I'd be a bit nearer the cemetery for you.'

His wife immediately added: 'As a matter of fact, the first time we went to see Vincent's mother after we got back from our honeymoon, Vincent kissed her and told her that she still came first, and this right in my presence. And he still has to do it. Well, I don't mind it any more. But it shows the attitude, and these are only isolated instances, I could go on for hours. . . .'

The last statement was made by a manager's wife who, after acknowledging that financial conditions and the obligation to live up to class standards have a lot to do with it, said:

But that is not the only thing involved as I know from many cases. Take Gerald, whom you met the other night. He has a very good salary and has been making good money for a number of years. [He is an insurance broker.] He is a very well educated lad [Clongowes Wood]. He is certainly old enough [30]. And he is a very good looking, attractive person. But he just isn't interested. I am citing him just as one example. There are very many more. It is quite common. Gerald lives at home with his mother and sister and they do all the housework and make him comfortable. He has no problems. He is out to the rugby matches; he is with the boys all the time. He is, apparently, quite happy and not at all interested in marriage, at least for some time to come.[28]

However, if this relationship is still *prevalent*, it is nevertheless undergoing a change. Roughly half of the people interviewed reported that the maternal tendency to favour the sons, cater to them and obstruct their marriage is not as widespread as it was thirty years ago. Quite significantly, more than half agreed with Sheila Dunn's boy friend in reporting that its effectiveness in delaying a son's marriage is noticeably reduced.

The quotations describing the mother and son relationship were chosen for their vividness as well as their accuracy. It is significant, therefore, that while as many statements by men could have been presented, most of our quotations were from women. For the resentment over the mothers' preference for her sons is clearly marked among girls. It is particularly strong against this maternal attitude because of its tightening effect upon the marriage market. It may even swell to a point of hostility between an individual girl and her pro-

[28] Employer-managerial class.

spective, or actual mother-in-law. Towards her own mother, however, resentment is *prevalently* much more mild and is marked by a perceptive resignation.

For there are several tempering factors in the relationship of mother and daughter. However much she may favour the sons, the artisan mother *generally* also has a strong and manifest affection for her daughter. It is notable that the degree of confidence between mother and daughter, and the amount of consultation and exchange of information between them is *prevalently* no less than that between mother and son. Inevitably, girls are more subordinate to their mother than their brothers both because of their greater obligation to assist her which their father endorses, and because they receive from her a far greater measure of direct training. But *generally* speaking, this subordination is neither harsh nor extreme. On the one hand, such subordination is the more acceptable to a daughter because by it alone can she learn the role so crucial for her adult life. Her mother is virtually the exclusive model, not only of the specialized behaviour necessary for servicing and managing a household, but also of the general behaviour proper to a woman, wife and mother. This is, perhaps, an additional reason why, in early adolescence, mothers *prevalently* find daughters more tractable than sons. On the other hand, girls *prevalently* are not only eager to enter the occupational world, but are encouraged to do so, and once this happens their subordination at home is greatly reduced and their freedom approximates those of their brothers.

It only approximates it because *prevalently* the mothers are concerned about the dangers that may beset a girl in late adolescence more than they are about those that may beset a boy, and this attitude their husbands share. Though both father and mother are much more liberal than their own parents were in granting liberty to their daughters that is nearly equivalent to the liberty granted their sons, they worry more about the girls, and the degree of inequality between boys and girls in this respect is largely dictated by their greater fear that girls may become entangled in a troublesome situation. In part, this is due to the feeling that while boys develop a mature interest in girls much later, have less 'temptations' and are better able to handle them, a girl becomes interested in boys much younger, is inclined to be 'giddy' and may find herself in the classic trouble. Although greatly diminished in intensity, the attitude of Joan Dunn's mother towards 'mankind' still exists. 'When the children reach the age of sixteen or seventeen,' one father said, 'the parents are definitely more concerned about the girls than the boys. . . . I know I feel that a girl at that age has a lot more dangers to face than a boy because a boy can take care of himself more easily.'

His wife added:

With a girl like Eithne [19] now, her ambition, like all the girls', is to have quite a few boy friends. Not serious boy friends, of course, but just boy friends. And you can never tell what type of boys she may get involved with and what may happen. The boys are different, at least ours are. They do not consider girls until much later. Gabe [21], for example, is not bothered about girls at all. But with Eithne I do worry over her companions and frankly I'd like to see her married if the lad was the right type, because then she would be settled and safe from the dangers of the world.

Partly, too, as the preceding remarks hint, this maternal concern relates to the status aspects of marriage. It is *prevalently* considered the mother's obligation to marry off the girls. As a girl reaches late adolescence, this tends to unite mother and daughter since both their desires, on the whole, coincide here. A mother may often discourage a son from marrying out of a desire to retain his contribution to the family income, but she is decidedly less inclined to do so in the case of a daughter if a suitable match is in the offing. Although, in fact, artisan girls today *prevalently* marry later than their mothers,[29] this is due to other factors and not to any fixed conviction among either mothers or daughters that marriage in the early twenties is premature.[30]

The most significant change in the attitude of artisan mothers to their daughters' marriage only indirectly concerns the suitable age of marriage. Directly it centres on the norms for the eligibility of potential sons-in-law. While artisan mothers are just as determined as their own mothers that a daughter should not 'marry beneath her', today they are *prevalently* optimistic about their daughter's chance of improving her social position by marriage, and at the same time they are active in working towards that end. Where her own parents judged a daughter's suitor on his character as indicated to a great extent by his family background and on his ability to provide her daughter the same standard of living as their own, the artisan mother today *prevalently* desires the suitor to be a lad with a higher occupational and social position, either actual or potential, than her husband's. Character is still a basic qualification for eligibility, but of almost equal importance is class standing or opportunity. And family background, hitherto scrutinized as an index to the former, is not studied as a clue to the latter also. A suitor who does not meet both

[29] *v.* ch. iii, p. 78, n. 41.

[30] While Joan Dunn's account of the mother's attitude today in this respect agrees with the majority report, her account of the common attitude of mothers as to the age of a daughter's marriage when she was a girl represents the less *prevalent alternative.* Apparently most mothers at that time were willing to let a girl marry in her early twenties.

of these qualifications, who seems likely only to maintain the same level of life that the daughter's own family has reached, *prevalently* will receive the same treatment as an undesired, prospective daughter-in-law, in the manner Maureen Dunn has described. Although this may be a source of conflict between mother and daughter in individual cases, such conflict is not widespread for the simple reason that daughters *prevalently* outstrip their mothers in their marital ambitions. One father typically reported: 'There is not much question of either the mothers or the fathers having to worry about improving the girls by marriage because the parents can't keep up with the girls themselves on that.'[31]

The *general* changes in family relationships in the last forty years have naturally affected the relationship between father and daughter, though perhaps less so than that between father and son because the former relationship was always a bit more intimate. Nevertheless, daughters also *prevalently* stand in considerably less awe of their father today, deal with him more directly, confide in him more frankly, and not infrequently even joke with him and call him by his first name. There is some evidence that the father continues to favour the girls even during adolescence, even though this does not go to the extent of exempting them from their household duties or of 'spoiling' them in the manner of the mothers with the boys. On the other hand, the fathers *prevalently* are a bit more preoccupied with a girl's future security than with his son's because, as one father stated, 'a girl has a harder time of it than a boy'. It was always the fathers who specified that if a greater share of the parents' goods were to be left to one child, this would certainly be true in the case of an unmarried girl. And the fathers interviewed were more emphatic than the mothers in stressing the greater importance of a secondary education for a girl than for a boy. The importance is based upon the effect of a good education on a girl's marital prospects. Furthermore, fathers *prevalently* are just as strong as mothers against their daughters marrying beneath their station and just as eager to see them make a good match. Apparently even in the preceding generation the social quality of a daughter's marriage was more a matter of concern to a father than to a mother. As one father put it: 'The way it was in my parents' day, the father really thought more of improving the girls by marriage than the mother did. I think that was because he knocked around in his work and he knew how tough things could be for a girl more than a mother did. The mother was interested in marrying them off. That was her main responsibility and she was not as much concerned as the father, I think, in the daughter getting a lad who would improve things for her. . . .'

[31] General labourer.

169

As with the relationship of parents and children in infancy, so with the interrelationships between siblings it has not been feasible to probe as deeply as we might wish. And this is particularly true of relationships between specific siblings such as brother and sister or oldest and youngest. We are, therefore, forced to confine discussion to certain generic aspects of sibling relationships.

In spite of the differences in the obligations and privileges proper to artisan children that have been, or will be, pointed out, the overriding principle *generally* accepted by both parents and children is that of the equivalence of all children in the family.[32] Differences among siblings arising out of ability, age, sex or personality are never structurally so important as to institutionalize within the artisan family any inequality in regard to inheritance, marriage or obligations to the parents or to the family as a whole. Evident from the practice of equal inheritance, from the concern to equalize the lot of children handicapped by disease or extreme youth, or by the need to undertake unusual responsibilities, this is especially clear from the *general* sentiments of both parents and children. Just as wives may recognize that between themselves and their husbands there exist inequalities that arise out of the life situation of the family and yet genuinely feel that they are equal partners with their husbands, so both parents and children *generally* feel that situational inequalities among the children must exist, but do not betoken discrimination as to the relative personal worth of the children, and in the long run usually balance each other out. Indeed, artisan children are quite prone to invoke what one father called 'the law of equal burdens'.

Nevertheless, differences among siblings that are necessitated by either situational factors or cultural definition, entail necessary consequences. Among artisan families the most important difference is that of age, especially in large families and particularly, as we have seen, in regard to education. However, there are other consequences of age differences that are worth noting. *Prevalently* and inevitably, the older children are required to assume greater responsibilities than the younger. This is true not only in regard to contributing financially to the family purse in late adolescence, but also, and even in early adolescence, in regard to non-economic matters.

Thus it is *prevalent* among large families for the mother to delegate to older children authority over the younger. On critical occasions, such as the mother's confinement, the amount of authority delegated to an older child may be extensive. Normally, however, it is limited to having the older children superintend the activities of the younger

[32] *v.* Arensberg and Kimball, op. cit., p. 63. In practice this principle appears to be more completely realized among artisan families in Dublin than in the rural family.

at play and when the parents are not present, and to reporting outstanding misdemeanours. Moreover, the older children are expected to provide good examples to the younger. Partly because of this and partly because parental experience in dealing with children is necessarily less where the older children are concerned, parents tend to demand more of an older child and to be somewhat more severe with him. Among the advantages, real or fancied, a younger child enjoys over his older siblings is the more confident and relaxed attitude of his parents that is based upon their greater experience with children and on their reliance upon the older children to give the younger companionship, example and guidance. A typical comment is that of one mother who, after relating how much more freedom her youngest child has by comparison with his older brothers and sisters, added: 'I think the youngest child gets a better break than the others. Perhaps it is only that the times change as we go along. But I think one reason is that, with the older children grown up, the youngest has them for an example, and you feel more secure because you can rely on their influence on him. At least, I do.'

Significantly, however, artisan parents *prevalently* do not give their older children the authority to discipline the younger. Subordination of younger to older siblings, therefore, is quite limited. At the same time, for reasons the children themselves seem to comprehend, this subordination is not proportional to the larger share of responsibilities the older children must normally assume. This undoubtedly is the foundation for the feeling, often manifested, that parents tend to favour the younger children,—a feeling, incidentally, that tends to confirm the assertion that the familial ideal is sibling equality.

Within limits, the obligations we have been discussing devolve upon the older children more or less irrespective of sex. We have, however, already seen the major differences between siblings to which sex gives rise: the exemption of sons from chores, the moderately greater surveillance of the activities of girls in late adolescence, the tendency of mothers to favour the sons. In view of this, it is notable that normally girls, especially as they reach late adolescence, do not greatly resent their brothers' favoured position. If one may state an impression, the girls seem to appreciate not only that the maternal preference is due to a general definition of things for which their brothers are not responsible, but also that the boys may pay a high price for their position of favour by finding themselves in late adolescence and early adulthood less independent than their sisters. In any event, the relationship between brother and sister is *generally* affectionate if not, indeed, cordial, even though the close association of early adolescence lessens in the later years. Brothers and sisters in the latter period *prevalently* do not have many social activities in

171

common outside of the family circle even when they are close to one another in age, partly because both find their peers in different schools and places of work, and partly because, due to the divergent attitudes of boys and girls towards marriage, a girl is likely to be associating with men older than her brothers' peer group and so not one of them.

As for siblings of the same sex, much the same can be said but with obvious qualifications that age differences introduce. There is some evidence that siblings near each other in age 'incline to pair off', as one father put it, and while this may obtain even between brother and sister, it seems to be truer of siblings of the same sex. Granted proximity in age, there is likely to be more association in social activities outside the home between siblings of the same sex than between siblings of different sexes.

However, it should be clear from the very tone of this discussion that our evidence on these relationships, except where the contrary has been indicated, is relatively thin and that our statements are quite tentative suggestions prompted by the evidence at hand. The same applies to the relationship between siblings after marriage. While we can ascertain important features that mark these relationships in general, we cannot do the same for specific relationships such as that of brother and sister, sister and sister, etc. In reporting on their ties with their siblings' conjugal families, artisan spouses and their children do not give evidence of any clearly marked tendency towards greater rapport or towards special obligations between individuals who stand in these various relationships to each other. This may mean that urban life in Dublin may have altered or reduced the force of such ties.[33] But all that we can be sure it means is that we were not able to compass these specific relationships in a study that had to sacrifice some detail for the sake of the round view.

MARRIAGE AND MOBILITY

If there is one thing more striking during the last fifty years than the decline of parental control and the corresponding increase of freedom given artisan children, it is the virtually unanimous and explicit approval of the present relationship that is voiced by artisan parents. A few parents expressed a desire for more control than they have, but none endorsed the previously *prevalent* relationship. And increased freedom is nowhere more apparent than in the leeway parents grant their children when they reach a marriageable age in respect to activities out of which marriage normally blooms.

[33] Furthermore, no detailed study of these relationships has been made for the rural community either, and so there is little on which to base a comparison. Arensberg and Kimball treat the subject only in a general way. *v.* ibid., pp. 63–9.

Whether prior to a couple's engagement or after it, this is a *general* characteristic and despite greater parental concern for the girls at this age, and despite the daughters' greater obligations at home, the degree of freedom granted to girls is *generally* about equal to that granted the boys. So widespread is the change that has taken place since our artisan spouses were children that there is no need to list all the forms of activity in mixed company that were previously proscribed and are now permitted to boys and girls once they have reached, roughly speaking, the age of seventeen. One statement, which could be duplicated in one form or another from every family studied, will suffice to underline the difference. After describing how, when he was courting his wife, even though she was twenty-three years old, '. . . we would often have to leave the cinema in the middle of the feature and run all the way up the street, because I simply had to have her in the house by ten o'clock,' one father continued:

> Today all that is changed. Once the girls start working, even if they are only fifteen or sixteen years old, they demand a good deal of independence and in nine cases out of ten they get it. That is because they are contributing to the income of the household and because they are supported in their demands by the fact that all the other girls who work also have that independence. As a rule, they go wherever they want to go and they go very frequently, sometimes every night in the week. And they are always out to dances and movies. This takes them all over town and they have friends all over town so that parents can't very well control them. All this is also true of the boys, of course. I think that the reason why it was so different when I was a boy is that any claim to independence a boy or a girl might make then, they simply could not back up because they were not bringing in the money they are today. And the increase in the number of movies and dances and especially the dance halls has had a lot to do with it, too.

Furthermore, artisan children *prevalently* enjoy a greater degree of freedom when it comes to actual marriage, although the change that has taken place in this respect naturally is not as pronounced as it is in regard to pre-marital behaviour. We have seen the most important of the *prevalent* parental attitudes towards the marriage of their sons and daughters. These continue strongly to condition a child's marriage and, on the whole, tend to delay it. But, especially as it touches the marriage of a son, the power of these parental sentiments to influence a child's marriage has decreased considerably. *Prevalently*, both sons and daughters are able more effectively to follow their own judgment in regard to marriage. What sentiments, then, do they themselves entertain on the subject?

Even when they have good jobs, artisan boys *prevalently* do not seriously contemplate marriage until at least their mid-twenties and often later than that. Although after seventeen they are allowed the privileges of mixed company with their peers, they are almost unanimously reported as not being maturely interested in girls until they reach the age of twenty-three or twenty-four or later. Until then, not only are they prone not to date a girl steadily, but they clearly prefer the company of their male peers. In the language of the artisans, although boys of this age may 'do a light line' and occasionally take a girl to a dance or a movie, most of them do so 'just as a matter of form'. To the boys, girls are 'an afterthought' and 'a secondary consideration'. In the words of one mother: 'Ah, the boys rather scorn the girls. Very much so. When they get to be sixteen or so they stay together with other boys and the only way to describe their attitude towards girls is to say that for them girls are an afterthought. They will talk among themselves about everything else first. They will talk about sports and politics and when they haven't anything else to talk about then the conversation turns to girls.'

Indeed, the impunity boys enjoy in cavalierly breaking dates with girls, which the Dunn children have described, is at least a strong *alternate*, if not *prevalent*. Perhaps the most graphic description of the boys' attitude towards girls came from a lad, himself twenty-eight years old and virtually engaged, who said:

> When it comes to girls the boys here are juveniles. There is no doubt about that. For example, I belong to an athletic club and there are fifty boys in it, all about my own age. That is, they run from about twenty-five to thirty-two. And I know that only about half of them have any serious interest in girls or in doing a line with a girl. The rest of them are mainly keen on being with the fellows. On Saturdays and Sundays they are out golfing or at a football match with the fellows and in the evenings they usually play cards or have a session at a pub. They are interested in their own company and in sports and towards the girls they act just like boys of fifteen or sixteen.[34]

One reason for this type of deportment that is frequently alleged not only by the boys but by others also is the speed with which any steady interest in a girl raises strong marital expectations on the part of a girl and her parents, and the fear the boys have of becoming entangled and then of having to dash the lady's hopes. The following are typical remarks:

> Around here if a boy were to take a girl out once a week for a month or six weeks, well the girl and the parents and even the boy's friends would think they were thinking of marriage. . . . The girl would begin seeing little cottages. . . . If you take a girl out five or six times, you are considered as doing a line and some night soon the parents will invite you in for tea, and, believe me, once you have gone in for tea, you have

[34] Clerical class.

had it. They'll want to know what your intentions are. . . . Most of the boys are quite honourable. They do not want to do a line until they are in a position to support a girl because they honestly feel that they might be hurting a girl's chances. They feel that if they are going around with a girl she will pass up other fellows whom she could marry, and unless they feel sure that they can eventually marry her they will stay away from her entirely. There are quite a few boys I know who feel this way. This is one of the reasons, I am sure, that the boys stay so much in cliques with boys.[35]

Quite different in all this is the attitude of the girls. An artisan mother stated: 'O, the girls have the boys on their minds from the time they are eight years old. . . . Seriously, though, the girls are always talking about the boys. They are very much interested in them and when a group of girls are together the major topic of conversation are the boys and the men. And once they are sixteen they are going with the boys as much as they can, though usually in that case it will be with boys older than themselves.'

This interest in the boys, the fact that at this age the girls' criticism of the boys being 'spoiled' becomes more intense, and the gravitation towards older men emphasize the greater importance of marriage for a girl. Religious vocations aside, artisan girls, despite increased occupational opportunities for women, *generally* consider married life as their primary and exclusive career and *generally* stop work at, or shortly after, marriage. Although in this she is like her mother before her, the artisan girl today differs from her mother in many important respects. In most decided fashion she differs from her mother in her *general* desire, whetted by her improved opportunities, to move up socially through marriage, either directly by marrying into a higher class or indirectly by marrying an ascendant star of her own class. She is also *prevalently* unlike her mother, who was 'satisfied with a back room when it came to marriage', in her reluctance to give up her job and its attendant social advantages for married life with a man whose wage is not appreciably greater than her own salary. At the same time, she is coming more and more to consider married life to be a limitation on her independence so that she is inclined to postpone it until she can have her share of a good time.

Concomitant with these attitudes of young artisan men and women towards marriage there is a high and strictly observed standard of sexual morality both before and after marriage. As it concerns post-marital behaviour, this standard probably has some influence upon the conservative approach of young artisans to marriage, although it is difficult to assess this influence precisely. Perhaps a suspicious

[35] The last of these quotations is from a young wife in the managerial-employer class.

attitude towards sex absorbed from their artisan parents also works in the same direction. On the boy's side, while his attitude and behaviour towards girls seems clearly to be connected with his relationship to his mother, it is also clearly related to his fear, shared by both of his parents, that early marriage may result in severe economic struggle and hurt his chances of social advance. On the girl's side, it is certain that hypergamy is a major consideration. But in the long run, the tendency towards late marriage among artisan people is undoubtedly the result not of any single one of these factors, but of all of them working in combination.

Obviously, upward social mobility is an important feature in the life of artisan families and we can now assess the methods whereby it is sought and achieved. The realistic desire to advance socially has been greatly increased during the lifetime of our artisan spouses by extensive changes in the Dublin community that have extended their opportunities to do so. Earlier in the century the limited, and relatively sluggish economy, together with restricted educational facilities and certain current cultural definitions that discriminated against Catholics in the occupational world and excluded women from clerical positions, made the roads to advance few, narrow and short for artisan people. Since the emergence of national government and the expansion of the civil service, the economy has also expanded and with it educational facilities have improved and cultural discrimination has largely disappeared.

As a result, upward mobility among artisan families has increased in the last thirty years. Because not enough girls in our artisan families have married to furnish sufficient data, we cannot show from our sample that, by comparison with their parents' generation, actual hypergamy has increased.[36] We have to rely on the majority report that it is actually more common today than it was when our artisan spouses were children. However, it is possible to compare the occupational movement of the sons of the contemporary artisan families studied with that of the sons of all the natal artisan families in our sample who have remained in Dublin. If we eliminate five younger sons who were able to exploit the expanding opportunities after 1925, only one artisan boy out of twenty-three in that generation was able to start his occupational career on a higher level than his father's

[36] We were able to gather from our entire sample information relevant to marriage about eighteen women whose natal families were artisan. This information concerns not only wives in our sample who came from artisan families, but also sisters, married and living in Dublin, of all the parents in the sample whose natal families had been artisan. It is interesting to record that of the eighteen, four married into the clerical class, ten married artisans, four married into the class of general labourers. Significantly enough, three of the four who improved their class status by marriage were younger women who married after 1930.

initial level.[37] Of the remaining twenty-two, fifteen started on the same level as their fathers, while seven started at a lower level. On the other hand, of the twenty sons in our contemporary artisan families who are working in Dublin, nine have already started on a higher level than their fathers, nine have started at about the same level as their fathers, while only two have had to begin their occupational career below their fathers' level.[38] While the number of cases is too small to be anything but suggestive, these figures tend to confirm the artisans' assertion that opportunity for advance is now more wide-spread, as they also reflect the artisans' efforts to exploit that opportunity.

The avenues of advance, then, are clear. For artisan boys the way up is through occupational achievement. For artisan girls, since an occupational career is normally ruled out after marriage, the way up is still the well-travelled road of hypergamy.

THE WEB OF THE COMMUNITY

The web of community in which the artisans live, and of which they are part, is woven of many strands that are themselves spun out of many threads. Some of these strands are relationships that Parsons has called universalistic because they are based upon objective standards of ability that apply impartially to everybody rather than upon personal considerations.[39] This is the predominant sort of relationship that characterizes business concerns, schools, political organizations, some religious and other social groups. Ties of this kind primarily bind individuals into groups outside of their families and in relative independence of their families. As a result, such ties have a great potential for relating individuals of different classes, and of different religious and cultural backgrounds. They may also serve to bring family groups as such into rapport with each other, but this is secondary and incidental. When this does happen, the ties of which we are speaking are the occasions rather than the cause of such familial interaction. We cannot trace all or even most of these universalistic bonds in the lives of the artisans, but it is important that we be aware

[37] As examples of the opportunities immediately opened up after the Civil War, two brothers of one artisan wife competed in the mass civil service examination of the Irish government held in 1926 and passed it with high honours; both today have good white-collar positions with the government.

[38] Of the nine who began their careers at a higher level than their fathers, five began at jobs that place them in an entirely higher class category. I have omitted four boys too young to work, about whom, however, from an intimate knowledge of their families, I would venture a prediction that certainly three of them will begin their occupational career at a higher level than their fathers.

[39] *v.* ch. i, p. 32, n. 30.

that they exist on an extensive scale in Dublin. For they profoundly modify and in turn are modified by, the other kind of relationships in which we are principally interested.

These are particularistic relationships which are rooted in the personal consideration as to whom the individuals are that are related to one another. Particularistic ties are those that primarily bind individuals as members of families. Thus far, we have considered such relationships in so far as they integrate the various members in single, nuclear families. These relationships between members in a single family, however, as well as certain necessities of the family as a group, lead directly and essentially to the integration on a particularistic basis of family groups as such. Kinship relationships and generally speaking those arising between families in a common neighbourhood are of this nature. Friendship, too, to a large extent is particularistic and apt to interrelate the families of friends in like fashion. Finally, despite basic universalistic characteristics, the parish, as a local organization that in practice often treats the family as the basic organizational unit, also has considerable power to create inter-familial relationships of a particularistic kind.[40] We must now consider how all of these factors serve to integrate nuclear artisan families with other family groups.

The most powerful integrative factor is, of course, kinship. But among artisan families the amount of effective interaction and co-operation between kin families is greatly affected by several factors that are external to kinship itself. First of all, co-operation between kin is conditioned by the difference between rural life and life in the city. Thus, where artisans have relatives of the same degree of kinship in both country and city, they *generally* interact more frequently and more significantly with their city than with their country kin. As has been indicated by the practices of the Dunn family in regard to John's and Joan's cousins in both country and city, this *generally* is true as between kin of the second degree. It is also *generally* true between people who are related in the first degree of kinship. The five artisan spouses who have first-degree kin living in the country (father, mother, brother or sister) are especially relevant here. In every instance, these families have more constant interaction with the families of their own brothers or sisters who dwell in Dublin, or with their spouses' kin of corresponding degree who dwell in Dublin, than with the country people.

---

[40] The basic subject of the parish is the individual who has a domicile, or quasi-domicile (i.e. six months residence in the parochial territory) in the parish. Practically, however, since the domicile of most parishioners is their family residence, parochial authorities deal in organizational matters with families. This is the case, for instance, for Baptism, the assessment of parish dues, etc.

Distance, of course, is a great consideration in this decline of inter-action. Artisan people do not usually have cars. When they do, inter-action between country and city kin increases somewhat. Two of our artisan families happened to have recently acquired cars and both stated that, as a result, they had been able to visit relatives in the country whom they had not seen in years. However, not only distance, but the diverse requirements of life in the city and country contribute to the lessening of interaction. For example, summer, the city dweller's holiday period, is the farmer's busy time. As a result, in the words of one New Dubliner: 'People from the city usually are free to visit the country only in the summertime. Well, in August we would be as welcome as an atom bomb if we were to drop in on our country relatives then, because that is the time they are busy with the harvest. City people don't know how to harvest and they are just in the way then. So the contact is cut down in the summertime and if it is cut down then, it is even less during the year.'

Between families of the same degree of kinship in the city, distance also affects the amount of interaction. *Prevalently*, artisan families and their siblings' families will, within limits, have more interaction the nearer they are to each other. Size of family, when large, also operates to lessen interaction, especially in the earlier years of a family's life. After the children reach late adolescence, it sometimes has the reverse effect of increasing interfamilial interaction. On the other hand, class differences, at least between the families of siblings among the artisans, *prevalently* does not affect their relationships to any great degree. This may be due in part to the fact that such differences between artisan families themselves, and even between artisans and their siblings in the general labourer class below, are not very great. But while the artisans betray an awareness of class differ-ences, their reports do not show any significant difference in their interaction with siblings who are artisans like themselves and siblings' families who belong to other strata.[41]

Effective kinship co-operation among artisans is also conditioned by other factors that are inherent in kinship itself. Relationships between specific kin of the same degree may be among these factors although, as we have said, we have not been able to study these relationships in detail. In this connection, it is sometimes said in Dublin that there is a tendency for the nuclear family to gravitate towards the wife's relatives rather than towards the husband's. What evidence we have, though far from conclusive, does not bear this out

[41] This should not be allowed to discount the possibility of greatly lowered interaction between an artisan family and the family of a sibling who might belong to the employer-managerial class. But no instance of this turned up in our study.

179

but indicates that greater interaction with the husband's kin, and indeed equal interaction between the wife's kin and the husband's kin, are all equally common.

Of much greater importance than such specific relationships appears to be the degree of kinship. Whether their kin families reside in the city or in the country, artisan families *prevalently* co-operate with them less the lesser the degree of kinship between them. As regards related families living in the country, the reports of the artisans show a regular regression in time that is *prevalent*, and that is directly due to a decline, first in the number of ties within the same degree of kinship, and then in the degree of kinship itself. Considering all the artisan families studied, it is clear that the greatest amount of interaction between a city family and all other country kin occurs while the parents of artisans remain alive in the country, and that this drops sharply after both parents die. All the second generation artisans report this decline in their own natal families after the death of their rural grandparents. They also report that this is *generally* true today of their friends who are immigrants.

This is confirmed by the three artisan spouses in our sample who happen to be immigrants. The two whose parents are dead have decidedly less interaction with their rural brothers and sisters than the one whose parents are still alive. One of these two, in relating her own experience, indicates the process of decline:

> I used to go down home every year until four years ago when my mother died. And before that my sister used to come up here to Dublin periodically and stay here with me, so that we used to see one another a couple of times a year. Of course, she used to bring all sorts of things with her from the country, and I'd do the same when I went down. But all that has died down now and we have very little contact except for letters and cards at Christmas, or if they visit Dublin, which is very rare. In fact, it has been more than two years since I have seen any of my relatives at all. My sister has her family and I have mine and it is hard for either of us to get away and that's the way it is.

After death destroys the bonds between siblings, interaction between city and country kin drops again and even more sharply. Among artisan families where both spouses are New Dubliners who have only cousins in the country, interaction is virtually limited to exchange of Christmas cards and to the very rare, and usually short, visits by the rural people to Dublin. This process affects the artisans in their relationships to their city kin also, but to a much more limited extent. For the artisans *prevalently* report that the frequency of actual contact and co-operation between themselves and their brothers and sisters in Dublin decreases after the death of their

parents when the weekly visit, especially to their mother, no longer
has place.

When we have counted and thereby discounted all of these differentiating factors, it becomes clear that for the artisans the interaction
between their families and their natal and sibling families in the city
is the enduring core of kinship solidarity. This does not mean that the
ties binding artisans and other kin families are not strong. Notably,
kinship binds tightly where there is question of helping a relative get
a job. What Joan Dunn describes in this respect is *general*. A man
who would use his influence to secure a job for a friend in preference
to a relative, even though the latter were less qualified, would suffer
the open resentment of all his kin who might be inclined, according
to one man, 'to feel that I had been paid by my friend and had sold
the family out.'

> That is something that is done and is expected to be done, and it is going
> on all the time. If I heard from a cousin of mine of a job that he wanted,
> and that so-and-so was the man to see about it, even though the cousin
> was not particularly close to me, I'd drop in and say: 'See here, I know
> this chap Mulligan. He is a very fine, intelligent fellow, and as a matter
> of fact he is interested in the job. By the way, he is a cousin of mine.' In
> fact if I preferred a friend for such a job and used my influence to help
> him rather than one of the relatives, my father would raise hell about it
> and the whole family would take a poor view of it.[42]

This obligation is by no means confined to securing jobs. It comes
into play in obtaining a relative's admittance to the better schools, in
occupational promotion, and in politics. As a result, the majority of
artisans, as one of them put it, are 'very sceptical' about business and
political practice. This attitude of suspicion is a strong, if not *prevalent, alternative* among them as are the practices upon which the
attitude is founded. The practices the artisans describe in various
ways are graphically summed up by one highly placed man who is not
of the artisan class.

> Most businesses are run on a family basis. And that means the owners
> will run in their own sons and relatives as help, with the result that
> employees who have given faithful service, often for years, feel no
> security. The first thing you know, though they have done well and
> worked hard, they are out of a job because the boss had a cousin who
> wanted a job. . . . There is no such thing as the direct approach in
> business. You don't go to a man and make a straight deal with him
> yourself. You see a friend who may know him and has influence with
> him. Or else you might go to a T.D. and see him, and indicate that you
> will make it worth his while if he will use his influence to get you a

[42] Employer-managerial class.

181

contract or see a deal through for you.[43] And even in the civil service the big jobs are assigned very frequently through relatives or friends of relatives. I know for a fact that the children of higher civil servants get preference in the civil service because of the influence their fathers higher up in the service can bring to bear. These people think in terms of trimming their sails for every wind and they are very alert as to which way the wind is blowing.

But when the strength and extent of this obligation have been taken into consideration, it remains true that artisan spouses and their families *prevalently* have direct group contact with their city cousins and their families only four or five times a year. In the course of an ordinary year co-operation between artisan families and such city kin is peripheral. The core of kinship solidarity is the more frequent and constant interaction between the artisans and their natal and siblings' families. In every respect and with only minor differences, the frequency and the forms of this interaction, as well as the sanctions employed to preserve it, are the same for all the artisan families as the Dunns have described as current among themselves and their city kin. Furthermore, the solidarity of first-degree kin has not diminished greatly during the last thirty years. Greater dispersal through the growing city may have lessened it to some extent. Social mobility may have had a similar effect. A few artisans report in the strain of the woman who commented:

> Somehow or other, parents were not so ambitious in the old days as they are now, and they were more concerned about keeping the family together and maintaining close contact with their own kin than they are at present. I think that parents today are more keen about their own family getting ahead and that as a result they are not as anxious about keeping up the close contacts that used to exist here in the city.

But in view of all the evidence, such a decline in solidarity and sentiment between kin within the first degree has been relatively slight in the last quarter-century.

The strength of these sentiments of solidarity between kin, however, should not blind us to the fact that actual interaction and co-operation even between first-degree kin is quite limited. Control over the behaviour of family members is not detailed and minute but quite generalized. Apart from visits and exchange of news, effective co-operation between families is normally more occasional than constant. This is obviously due to the very nature of city life, especially its population density, and its high diversification of occupations and of classes. But as these features affect not only the artisans, but families of all classes, we had best leave further analysis of the impact

[43] 'T.D.' means a member of the Dail.

of urban structure upon kinship until the other classes of families are heard from.

In discussing the Dunns' neighbourhood, we noted that it was an old neighbourhood and called attention to the fact that there is a difference between such old neighbourhoods and the newer ones. What the differences are becomes clear when we consider all of the artisan families studied. For five of our families live in old neighbourhoods and six in more recently developed neighbourhoods.[44]

One of the greatest differences is that the older neighbourhoods where artisans live are today less heterogeneous in class composition than the new neighbourhoods. The former are populated, on the whole, by artisan families and general labourers, with only a scattering of clerical people; and among these neighbourhoods one can even mark off those that are predominantly settled by artisans from others mainly filled with general labourers.[45] But in the new neighbourhoods artisans, clerical workers and poor labourers are commingled. As a result, many artisan parents in the new neighbourhoods feel constrained to keep a sharper eye on their younger children's companions than do artisans in the old, established neighbourhoods. Thus one mother said:

> In this neighbourhood there are different classes of people all mixed together. For example, we pay twenty-five shillings, six pence rent. The man next door in exactly the same type house pays twelve and six. The reason is the rent is based on a means test and he is not a skilled worker. He is a very nice man, but—well, you do get people in here who are a bit below the standard you set for yourself, and it does create a problem. The row of houses in back of us here on the road below have people who

[44] Our eleven artisan families live in eight different neighbourhoods, and it may be enlightening, with the aid of the map that is appended to the second chapter, to locate them. Besides the Dunns who live in the neighbourhood between 'the Coombe' (i.e. Coombe St.) and James's St., one family lives in Sandymount and three families reside near Dolphin's Barn just east of South Circular Road. Selection of three from the same general neighbourhood was quite by chance; incidentally, though two of the husbands know each other through their jobs, none of these three families are acquainted with each other. These are 'old' neighbourhoods. The six remaining families live in different 'new' neighbourhoods: Kilmainham, Inchicore, Whitehall, Drimnagh, Crumlin and Cabra. In two of these six cases, however, the family has moved to their present residence from old neighbourhoods: one from near Parnell St., the other from Dorset St. Thus we have their reports as to life in the old neighbourhoods to supplement the reports of the artisans who continue to reside in the latter. And, of course, all the city-born artisan spouses as children lived in old neighbourhoods and can attest to the manner of life common there earlier in the century.

[45] E.g. the neighbourhood of Dolphin's Barn is mostly made up of artisans and the better paid semi-skilled and general labourers. The neighbourhoods of Killarney St. and Foley St. and the Quays are peopled mainly by dock workers and navvies.

are not as well off as we are and are a different type of people than we are. And, do you know, you try to keep your children from getting too friendly with people like that. So, in a neighbourhood like this your big concern is to keep an eye on whom your children are going with. . . .

And often, also, parents feel that as the children grow older their neighbourhood peer group associations may work to retard them. One of the more ascendant artisan fathers in a new neighbourhood, who now contemplates moving from his present neighbourhood, states his reason and his dilemma:

> The problem at the moment really is to give my children a good education and opportunity. But I will have to move out of here to give them a chance. It is not merely a question of sending them to a good school. I could send them to the best school in town, but if we stayed here they would be associating with people who were going to a different type of school and it would simply pull them down and keep them on the level where we are now. In fact, if we stay here, they will not get as far as I have and certainly they will not get any farther. The trouble is that when the lads here get through National School, most of them go to work or into the trades, and I know as sure as I am sitting here that my boys will want to do the same thing if we stay here. And the chances are Mary won't improve by marriage if we stay here, either. I am split wide open over this decision right now, because the people here are the salt of the earth. I know them and am very close to them. And the thought of moving hurts me because I don't like to break with the tradition. I was brought up in it myself. Maybe my children won't really be better off by it, but I feel I should give them the best opportunities to make the most of themselves. . . .

The major difference between old and new neighbourhoods, however, lies in the kind of relationships that exist between families in each. In the old neighbourhoods today the pattern of life the Dunns have described is quite *general*. This is true of the distinction, implied in their remarks, between the neighbourhood in general and close neighbourhood friends, as well as of the sort of interaction and co-operation that is characteristic of each. In regard to the neighbourhood in general, what the Dunns have told us receives very little modification from the reports of other families who reside in old neighbourhoods. Thus neighbours in general would not, as a sanction against a delinquent husband or wife, resort to snubbing or ostracism. This is perhaps an *alternate*, but *prevalently* neighbours would 'mind their own business in an affair like that' and not change their behaviour towards the individual involved. Similarly, the degree to which the general neighbourhood co-operates as a group is *prevalently* less than obtains in the Dunns' neighbourhood. In every other respect, however, the relationships extant in the Dunns' neighbourhood between neighbours in general is prevalent in all old neighbourhoods.

In like fashion, only minor details in the Dunns' account of their relationships with those neighbours who are close friends need adjustment.[46] What is especially notable in the old neighbourhoods, moreover, is the number of families that are bound by these ties of close friendship. Like the Dunns, all the artisan families name about five or six such families in the neighbourhood with whom they have special and extensive interaction.

Nevertheless, even in the old neighbourhoods, interfamilial solidarity has declined since our artisan spouses were children, and this decline appears to be prevalent in all such neighbourhoods.[47] The artisans attribute this decline in part to the increased freedom now accorded children, together with the widespread revolution in the forms of recreational activities. All the artisans remark the decline in the recreational self-sufficiency of neighbourhood family groups which previously brought both children and parents of many families together. One wife reported: 'Until I was twenty-three and married I did not really know anything about Dublin except my own neighbourhood and the people in it. I used to hear of various places in the city but I did not know where they were and had never been there. We had all our fun with neighbourhood groups. But now the boys and the girls, too, after they are sixteen are off all over the city to dances here and dances there and to movies and that sort of thing.'

In part, also, the artisans attribute the decline to a twofold movement of people. There has been an immigration of people to the new neighbourhoods especially from the oldest sections where house condemnations have been more frequent. On the other hand, there has been an invasion of the old neighbourhoods by large numbers of immigrant country people. The impact of this invasion seems to have been particularly felt in neighbourhoods that, though old, were capable of further development. One man, born, raised and still living in such a neighbourhood near Dolphin's Barn, speaks thus of the change:

In the old days there were fewer people here than there are now. Beyond South Circular Road there, why there was nothing but fields. The city virtually ended with South Circular Road. As a result, all the people here knew each other. I myself knew not only all the houses, but who was in each house. Well, all that is changed. More houses have been built

---

[46] Thus artisans in such neighbourhoods *prevalently* would not, like John Dunn, go so far as to speak to the priest about a delinquent neighbour even if he were a close friend. *Prevalently*, however, they would admonish him, help his family, and sever relations with him if he did not reform, just as the Dunns would.

[47] In this respect, the Dunns' neighbourhood is a bit atypical.

185

here and more people have come in and the old people have moved out. Now I know where the old houses are, but I don't know who lives in them. Because of this the people in the old days were much more friendly and close. . . .

Despite this decline, old neighbourhood solidarity is still relatively strong and strikingly so by comparison with the new neighbourhoods. Relationships between families in the new neighbourhoods are so markedly different from what they are in the old that it is not too difficult to describe them. We have only to note the few practices and forms of co-operation that survive as *prevalent* in them. Considering the neighbourhoods in general, artisans in the new neighbourhoods report that naturally enough the neighbourhood peer group for younger children continues to function, although 'the parents usually keep to themselves'; that the women, inevitably enough, still gather and gossip after the ten o'clock Mass and on their way to the shops; that particularistic shopping practices still prevail, although more and more the women are becoming bargain hunters, even in the neighbourhood markets; and that death, when it visits the family, '. . . breaks down all barriers, and neighbours who at other times only pass the time of day with you on the street, will be in to offer their condolence and assistance'. Nothing besides remains *prevalent* of all the interaction characteristic of the old neighbourhoods.

We can appreciate the difference better by contrasting the new neighbourhoods with the old on a few key points. Where frequent, informal visiting is quite *prevalent* in the old neighbourhoods, people in the new neighbourhoods do not know one another well enough to just drop in unannounced. Relationships are much more formal. An artisan husband stated:

> You rarely see neighbours going into other neighbours' houses. The informal visiting that used to prevail down in the old neighbourhood does not go on here at all. It is even very rare for the neighbours to visit on formal occasions. Of course, if somebody died, they would drop in and pay their respects, but it isn't very common for them to have parties or anything like that.

Secondly, the amount of assistance during times of crisis, such as sickness and confinement, is notably restricted. It is usually forthcoming only when solicited, and this is rare. Describing what happens during times of confinement, one wife said: 'But if you haven't any relatives available, you just hire someone to come in. The neighbours around here wouldn't help at a time like that. They'd feel they were interfering. O, I suppose if you asked them they might, but nobody would feel like asking them. If one of the neighbours on the road was having a baby, you might like to do something, but you feel you would be intruding. She would not want you walking in unless the house were in great order. She'd be embarrassed and you would feel you were just in the way, so you don't do anything.'

Thirdly, the type of behaviour that calls forth sanction in the older neighbourhoods, although still *generally* disapproved, does not evoke similar sanctions in the new neighbourhoods. The man who carries on to the neglect of his family is still an object of talk, but: 'In a situation like that, you mind your own business. You wouldn't say a thing to him at all and you wouldn't change your attitude towards him or stop speaking to him. Some of the women might cool off a bit towards him, but that is as far as it goes. That's the way we feel and, I think, most of the people here feel the same way.'

Finally, although artisans in the new neighbourhoods also speak of special neighbourhood friends, in every case the number of such friends is markedly less than people in the older neighbourhoods name. In the new neighbourhoods every artisan family mentioned only one neighbourhood family that they considered close friends. The refrain is: 'We are close friends only with a family across the street;' 'We are very close to the family next door, but besides them we don't have much contact with the other families in the neighbourhood.'

The *general* reason the artisans assign for all these differences be-tween new and old neighbourhoods, is the 'newness' of the neigh-bourhood, its size, and the fact that it is composed of people drawn from all parts of the country and from different classes and back-grounds. Summarily:

> The situation here is entirely different than in the old neighbourhood. Down there some of those families had been there for centuries and they knew each other well and knew each other's family history. But this is a new housing scheme. It has been up for about twenty years, if that. And people have come in here from the four quarters of the globe. In the old neighbourhood all the houses down there were fifty or a hundred years old, and the family of some of the people in them had been living in them all that time. Here—well, twenty years is not very long. People are not here long enough to know each other well, so you don't have the friendliness you have in the old neighbourhoods.

Under the impact of these conditions, solidarity between families in the new neighbourhood is far less than in the old neighbourhoods. Where friendly co-operation is widespread in the latter, in a new neighbourhood in the words of one man: 'Here the people are all Sinn Feiners, all for themselves alone.'

Whether the neighbourhood be new or old, however, the local parish *prevalently* is not a centre that serves to integrate parishioners' families by promoting widespread social interaction and co-operation between them. We may better understand this, as well as the actual role the parish plays in the lives of the artisans, if we recall that the parish is a formal organization whose essential organizational features, the basic mutual rights and obligations of people and clergy, are defined by Canon Law. Thus artisans, like parishioners of all classes, are obliged to have their children baptized and confirmed in their parish church, and to have them receive their First Communion there; a bride must be married in her own parish; and needless to say, parishioners are aware of their obligation to contribute financially to the support of the parish. Conversely, parishioners know their own rights and the reciprocal obligations of the clergy: to administer the sacraments to parishioners on petition, to provide for their basic instruction in religious doctrine, to visit them in order to take the parish census, to administer the funds of the parish for the general benefit of the parishioners.[48]

But this is the mere legal framework of the real parish. Within that framework, subject to episcopal approval, the parish priest has wide discretion, though no canonical obligation, to establish and maintain other, supplementary organizations that will foster the spiritual and, indeed, the general welfare of the parish as a whole. He may admit, or continue to maintain, parochial chapters of national or inter-national organizations. He may even originate organizations peculiar to his own parish. Such organizations may be wholly devotional or charitable. But they may also be academic, such as a school or a study club; recreational, such as a boys' athletic club; economic, such as a co-operative or a credit union; or indeed, a general, all-purpose organization, embracing at once all such activities.[49]

The clergy of the parishes where our artisans live *prevalently* have used this discretionary power to put flesh on the bare bones of juridical requirements by creating and maintaining a variety of these supplementary organizations. The most important of these organiza-tions is the school, although not all parishes have schools connected with them. Where this is the case, the school is a National School,

[48] This list of rights and obligations makes no pretence of being complete, nor is there any one place in Canon Law where they are all summarized. For the most concentrated treatment, *v. Codex Juris Canonici* (Westminster, Md., 1942), Lib. III, Pt. I, ch. ix, '*De Parochis*', pp. 146–70.

[49] Such general parochial organizations do in fact exist in Ireland today. These are the Parish Councils, promoted by the late Rev. John Hayes, of Bansha, Co. Tipperary and *Muintir na Tíre* (People of the Countryside), a national organization that he founded. The council is elected by the parishioners on a vocational basis, and promotes co-operation of all the parishioners to implement such projects as rural electrification, land reclamation, scientific farming tech-niques and soil conservation, local industries, recreational and cultural facilities, etc. Directed primarily towards solving the problem of rural depopulation, the two hundred-odd parishes it numbers are almost exclusively rural.

subsidized by the government, and under the management of the local clergyman.[50] Where such a school exists, the parish is an educational centre where artisan children acquire the rudiments of learning. Whether or not the parish has a school, however, it remains a centre of religious knowledge for all the artisans, providing continuous informal instruction through the medium of sermons, missions, homilies given at monthly meetings of devotional organizations, and instruction given in the confessional. *Prevalently*, however, the parishes do not give any further, formal religious instruction to the children after the completion of primary school. They do not conduct supplementary courses in religious doctrine, nor do they promote study and discussion clubs.

On the other hand, the parishes maintain a variety of organizations that are charitable or devotional to which members of the artisan families belong. Thus, membership of both men and women in the Sodality of the Blessed Virgin Mary is almost universal among the families studied. And membership in some other parochial organization of this type, such as the Altar Boys' Society for the boys, the St. Vincent de Paul Society for the men, the Children of Mary for the mothers and girls, is at least an *alternate*. Such organizations, however, *prevalently* restrict themselves to devotional and charitable activities. Only rarely do they sponsor social and recreational activities such as a tea or a whist party.

Neither do the parishes, according to the artisans, prevalently sponsor other social, recreational and cultural organizations. There are exceptions, of course, usually in small parishes. One mother remarked: 'If we were across the street we would be in another parish and things would be entirely different. In the parish to which we belong, there are no socials, whist drives, dances, carnivals or anything of that sort that would bring the people together. The only organizations are for purely devotional purposes. But the next parish is smaller, and the pastor there is a great one for having things like that going all the time. But that parish is unusual. Most of the parishes are like ours.'[51]

The absence of such broader social organizations and activities in the parish, which was reported for every parish to which our artisans belonged and reported by all for most parishes in the city, is explained in several ways by the artisans. One reason given is the *prevalent* lack of facilities, such as a parish hall. Another reason alleged is that, while parochial sponsorship of such activities depends upon the pastor, and some seem to be eager to promote them, some do not. A

---

[50] National Schools are also established according to the same arrangement in parishes of other religious denominations.

[51] Clerical class.

189

husband related: 'In my old parish down town some years ago the pastor built a hall and encouraged all sorts of social activities. His successor put an end to all that. But recently they had had a new parish priest and he has started to revive the whole thing.'

Furthermore, when our artisan parents were children such parochial activities were *not prevalent* and, although many of the younger curates today are keen on promoting them, they often meet with the disapproval of the older pastors who were schooled in the former tradition. But the reason *prevalently* assigned is the tremendous growth in the size and number of parishes during the last thirty years. In the opinion of the artisans this has so burdened the clergy with work that, except in the smaller parishes, they are entirely too busy with essential parochial work to promote organizations other than the strictly religious ones. Thus, for example, one wife praised the parish priest for his work for the parish, but claimed that he could not develop social organizations because the parish has grown so large '. . . that they have had to make three parishes out of it in the last twenty years'. Another woman summed up the situation thus:

> When we first moved out here, there were only a few families and the parish was much smaller. Well, they used to have all sorts of functions in the little school house they had here—whist drives, musical evenings, teas and things like that. The priests were very much closer to the people. They used to be able to get around and see them often. Then in a short time, people just poured in here by the thousands and we had to build a new church. Now everybody here is practically a stranger. And in a place like this the priests have a hard time getting to know all the parishioners. With the church debt, they haven't been able to build a social hall. Then, a curate comes here for about three or four years and just as he is beginning to get to know the people he is shifted and the next one has to start all over again. And besides housing schemes like this one are so big that the priests are terribly busy and overworked. It is impossible for them to get to know the people well or to run many social functions. It is out of the question.

The parish, then, stands as the liturgical and sacramental centre that effects a strong, over-arching unity among the artisan parishioners in the realm of ideas and ideals. It is the most immediate and articulate source of many of the major values that impregnate its parishioners' lives. From it, the artisans imbibe most of their great definitions of the world, and of their place and meaning in the cosmos. And as a result of this outlook, commonly shared, in thousands of subtle ways they mutually support each other in the face of life. But the essentially religious activities and the devotional and charitable organizations to which the parish is *prevalently* confined, do not offer

190

to its parishioners a scale of interaction wide enough to integrate parish families into an effective closely knit group.

Another category of people with whom the artisan families have important relationships is the families of friends who are neither relatives nor neighbours. The majority of artisan families claim five or six such friendships and a few claim more. Almost all these friends of the artisans are also people in the artisan class, although a few of them belong to other classes, notably the general labourer class. Although there is some evidence suggesting that, when friends move up into classes above the artisans, the amount of friendly contact diminishes, the line of demarcation between artisans and general labourers is not strong and is easily crossed in social intercourse. Advance into the artisan class usually does not break up earlier friendships with general labourers and their families.

This tendency of friendship among the artisans to be homogeneous as regards class, and yet capable of cutting across class lines, is related to another *prevalent* and almost *general* feature of friendship: the artisans' family friends, like the Dunns', are with few exceptions people with whom the artisan spouses became friendly before they were married. Whether these friendships were made at work, at school, or in the neighbourhood of their natal families, they have been formed on the whole when the parties concerned were in their late adolescence and early adulthood. The artisans *prevalently* attest that these are the friendships that endure.

Despite this, it is *prevalent* that an artisan family and its circle of friends do not form a real group who foregather and share activities in common. This does happen, of course, but usually the relationship that exists between an artisan family and the families of these friends does not exist between these other families themselves. From an artisan family, as from a hub, the lines of friendship go out like spokes of a wheel that has no interconnecting rim. If the spokes be conceived as of varying lengths, this figure also represents the geographical relationship of these families. They are scattered, near and far, all over Dublin.

This dispersal affects the frequency of contacts an artisan family has with the families of friends and, thereby, the amount of co-operation that flourishes between them. The frequency of regular contacts ranges from once every month to four or five times a year, with the latter the more usual practice. It is this lesser degree of interaction that constitutes the main difference in the relationships of the artisans to these friends and to those close friends who are also neighbours. In sentiment, the former may be more fondly cherished but in the kind of activity and co-operation it involves, the relationship of artisans to their friends is similar to their relationship with special neighbourhood friends.

While, as a result, the normal activities of the artisans and their friends consist in 'just visiting and exchanging news and views and in having a good time together', they also *generally* afford each other mutual, spontaneous and extensive assistance in times of family crisis. And the virtual sanctions that *alternately* apply to friends in the neighbourhood also apply to about the same extent to friends farther afield. Furthermore, friendship *prevalently* begets obligations to confer reciprocal favours, especially economic favours, of various kinds. The story of friendship that the artisans recite is full of references that 'as a matter of fact, I had occasion to put in a word for him'; and 'through one of our best friends out in Kimmage we were able to get my niece a job'; or 'in my free time I'm mostly off hustling things up for friends of ours, or else I'm out getting them to do something for me'. Although by the unwritten law of the family, a relative comes first, friends come next. And much the same practices in the occupational world are reported of friends that are related of relatives. A man who had a government job described this in the following fashion:

> The old principle—call it graft, if you will—holds in business and in government jobs, too. People who are in position to do so help their friends out. If you know a friend with influence, you speak to him and he will try to get you a job or a promotion. That exists on quite a large scale, and sometimes it borders on open injustice, although usually people are very sly about it and can get away with it.[52]

The view we have here taken of the family life of the artisans has been broad and panoramic. It has enabled us not only to trace the main ties that bind the individual members within a family, but also to discern various lines of relationship that integrate families within the community. Although the artisans have been the centre of attention in all this, the focus has been wide enough to reveal certain points where the family life of other classes coincides with that of the artisans. We must now shift our attention to these other classes in order to determine the degree of similarity and the degree of difference that exists in the family structure of the New Dubliners.

[52] Employer-managerial class. Another man from this class, who had been to the United States, said that when he was there, he was struck by the extent to which a family's friends seemed to be business associates and stated that in Dublin this did not exist to anything like the same degree. Then he added: 'In the United States it seemed to me that friendship follows the lines of business more than it does here. Here, it is rather the other way round: business follows the lines of friendship.'

Chapter VI

THE PRISM OF CLASS

OUR PURPOSE IN COMPARING the other classes of New Dubliners with the artisans is paradoxical. The major differences that exist between the various classes that make up society are of great interest in themselves and class comparisons are normally directed towards highlighting these differences and understanding the causes which produce them. Our goal is just the opposite. Because ultimately we wish to understand the New Dubliners' family in general, we are mainly concerned with class differences in order to set them aside in the final analysis and to see the similarities that exist in the family life of all the New Dubliners regardless of class.

That there is such a root similarity underlying class differences is a logical assumption. For despite their differences, all of these families live in the city and their major problem is to cope with that common environment. But we need not settle for mere assumption. As we shall see, the data from all the families on analysis clearly prove that the similarities between classes are more extensive than the differences.

For that very reason it will be easier and perhaps clearer to present the differences rather than the similarities themselves. We can best do this by taking the artisan family as a norm and basis for comparison. We shall, then, try to show in what respects and in what direction the family in each of the other classes differs from the artisan family. By so doing, of course, we shall also point out, by implication at least, how the managerial and white-collar classes and the class of general labourers differ among themselves.

In this comparison, we shall methodically use the same procedure we have followed with the artisans and continue to designate practices and attitudes as *general, prevalent* or *alternate*. But here we must make a further refinement. An item that is general or prevalent in the artisan class may be only an alternate in another class or altogether missing from it, and vice versa. When this happens in regard to a given item, we shall consider the difference between classes to be *notable*. To take an example we have already seen, artisan husbands

193

prevalently give most of their wage to their wives who in turn handle almost all of the financial affairs of the family, including the family savings. But this is *generally* not the case in the managerial class. A husband who is an employer or a professional man will indeed give his wife a substantial portion of his income for the household budget and she will have as much authority in its use as the artisan wife. But her husband still keeps a large portion of the total family income under his own control and takes a far larger part in making financial decisions and in actually handling the family's finances, particularly in the matter of savings and investments. In respect to financial management, then, the difference between the artisans and the managerial class is *notable*.

Unless we call attention to *notable* differences of this sort between a given class and the artisans in regard to a particular item, that item can be considered as having about the same currency in both classes. Thus, the exemption of boys from household chores, at least after they have reached the age of twelve, is just as general in all classes as it is in the artisan class. We shall refer to such items of similarity as rarely as possible in this chapter, even though for our ultimate purpose they are the most pertinent. Let the reader beware, then, that the most important things in this chapter are often the things that are left unsaid.

There is one sphere, however, that must be exempted from the treatment just described. This is the area of explicit class sentiments. In the course of the interviews I asked no direct questions about this matter on the assumption that I would not likely get reliable answers. Instead, I posed questions that could serve as an occasion for people to voice class sentiments if they were inclined to do so. The tactic was to leave the expression of class sentiments emerge more or less spontaneously, and emerge they did in many enlightening ways. It is difficult, however, to secure uniformity in such circumstances, and we cannot apply the rules of evidence we have adopted to these spontaneous expressions. Nevertheless, they are so relevant to our purpose that it will be worth our while to consider those class sentiments that received the most common expression.

CLASS SENTIMENTS

It would take altogether too much time and space to attempt to compare the nuclear families of the New Dubliners with the natal families of the New Dubliners in each class in the same detailed way that we have made this comparison in the artisan class. It must suffice to say that, broadly speaking, the major changes that have occurred in this period in the artisan family have, with only minor variations, similarly affected the family in all classes. As we have seen, one of the most important changes that is closely related to all other changes in the constitution of family life is the change that has occurred in the class structure of Dublin. Dubliners today have an acute sense of class. It is probable that a strong class system with attendant deep class sentiments is a heritage from ancient Gaelic society.[1] But more immediately, and without doubt more accurately, the Dubliners' sense of class is attributed to the class structure that existed prior to 1922 and that, to a large extent, was due to the prolonged influence of the Anglo-Irish Ascendancy.

We have already described the general lines of that class structure in the days of the Ascendancy, its relative rigidity and the generally subordinate position of Catholics within it. Despite this subordination, if not because of it, among Catholics, and even among the lower classes of Catholics, lines of distinction and their corresponding sentiments existed before 1922 whose strength was quite disproportionate to the grounds upon which they were based. One New Dubliner quite typically reported:

> There were really two complete orders of society. There was the Ascendancy and the Catholics and between the two there was a great gap. But even in the Catholic society there were distinctions we'd laugh at today. I actually knew one family where a lad was thought to have married beneath him because he married a servant girl, and his family was terribly displeased with him. Well, he was a dustbin collector! Now that is getting rather refined in the matter of class distinction, and of course it is extreme. But the lines were drawn very fine and they extended into the working class. There were hierarchies even there.[2]

The changes that have occurred in the last twenty-five years have not only resulted in the development of a new and powerful Catholic segment on the top level of the class structure but, according to very widespread report, they have broken down these finer lines of distinction almost entirely and promoted considerable interaction between classes and more movement from one class to another. One informant remarked:

> Today there is ever so much less of that nonsense. For example, it was unheard of that a shop girl out of Lacey's [a big Dublin department store] would be a member of a tennis club. Now they are members of tennis clubs and nobody thinks anything of it. A girl like that will belong to a tennis club and during the summer will be playing with a doctor's son or a lawyer's son and it's possible she might even be playing with Cooney's [the owner of the department store] son. I personally know an

[1] *v.* S. O'Faolain, *The Irish* (Harmondsworth, Penguin Books, 1947), pp. 33–7.
[2] Clerical husband.

195

engineer who married a waitress, and a lawyer who married his typist not long ago. I even know a University girl—she was from Galway—who married a Civic Guard. Now that would never have happened when we were younger.[3]

This change has been so marked that people perhaps have the tendency to consider that the class system is much less complex and more open, and that class distinction is much less marked, not only than it was twenty-five years ago in Dublin, but also than it is in England and the United States today. Thus a New Dubliner, who is the owner of a large enterprise and a director of the Bank of Ireland, when I had implied that he belonged to the upper class, replied:

> I am amazed at your use of upper, middle, and lower class. We are quite ordinary people. We do not consider ourselves in any way an upper class. We think of ourselves as ordinary middle class people and we don't have any of the activities that are associated with upper class people. There are really only two classes here—a working class and a middle class, although you might say there is an upper and a lower level in that middle class.

Despite such sentiments, which are not uncommon, the sense of class remains strong among Dubliners and there is some evidence that class lines are congealing. The taboo against boys working their way through school and University or even taking summer jobs for this purpose, the widespread observation of the New Dubliners of all classes that people are competing to outstrip each other in the external symbols of class, such as cars, clothes, 'and even prams', and the reports of social distinctions that are made on the basis of rather small occupational differences in the trades and in the professions— all these are evidence of a strong, continuing class consciousness. A master electrician, spontaneously referring to this as 'class distinction', reported as quite common what goes on in his own trade:

> A fellow who is a full-fledged electrician, if he has a fellow working for him who is not as skilled as himself, will boss him around and order him about, and look down on him and treat him pretty badly. There is a great deal of that and a great deal of conflict and bitterness about it.

In the same vein, a doctor described his profession thusly:

> There are gradations in the professions. Among the doctors, for example, there are different levels and the distinctions between these levels are pretty rigidly kept in social intercourse. For example, I am a specialist and I depend for my clientele upon the recommendations of the general practitioners. But between a specialist like myself and a practitioner there is a definite gulf so far as social matters are concerned and this is

[3] Clerical class. 'Civic Guard' is the official title for a policeman.

kept on all sides. If I were suddenly to begin inviting a general practitioner whom I knew fairly well to my house for dinner, not only other people, but he himself, would start to think: 'I wonder what Jim wants.' He'd take it that I had an ulterior motive and was after something. So our friends are mostly doctors who are specialists and friends in business whom I knew when I was going to secondary school. . . .

Pointing in the same direction are the frequent observations of the New Dubliners, again of all classes, as to the contrast between the city and the rural areas in the matter of class distinction. A prominent business man described this as follows:

In the country, neighbourhood obligations cut across class considerations to a great extent. It is true that people are very conscious of different social positions in the country too, and there is a lot of talk about them. But they don't exist on the same scale as in the city. There, even if a man be a big farmer, he is much closer to his farm labourers than an employer is to his employees here in the city. People in the country help each other and are obliged to help each other, even though the one might be a big farmer and the other a small farmer. And those obligations ride over class lines.[4]

But, as might be expected, the most graphic description of class sentiment comes from a New Dubliner who spent some years abroad. After remarking that class strata are definitely marked in Dublin with little movement between them, she explained that she would be conditioned by these considerations when her children's marriage was in question and would insist on their marrying within the managerial class to which she belongs. Then she added: 'I know it's different elsewhere. In Australia, for example, Mr. Frazier who just died, had nothing when he started.[5] He came over as an immigrant from England without a penny. He married very well and nobody thought anything about it, and before he died I imagine he couldn't tell exactly how much money he had. But you can't do that here. It's a small country and the lines are fixed. And so my attitude will be the same as my parents' and aunts'. I don't see how it will change in my lifetime unless somebody drops an atom bomb.'

The contradictions that appear in all this testimony are as important as the testimony itself. For they indicate ambivalent sentiments and attitudes that may be expected to be current in a complex society and especially one that has been changing at a relatively rapid rate. The basic ambivalence consists in criticizing and even overtly resenting the standards, values and behaviour of people in higher classes and, indeed, of people in their own class and, at the same time, in

---

[4] Managerial class.
[5] Mr. Frazier was formerly Prime Minister of Australia.

accepting the same general set of values themselves and in striving to emulate the people criticized.

From the evidence we have, the people in the professional-managerial class, on the one hand, appear to be concerned not to be considered an upper class and especially not to be likened to the Ascendancy of whom they are inclined to be quite critical. They are afraid of being thought snobs and one of their major problems in raising their children is, as one mother put it, 'to avoid appearing to be sententious'. On the other hand, in addition to the attitudes we have already noted, their own testimony about themselves gives voice to several other sentiments that are characteristic of an upper class. They are inclined 'to live to the hilt of their income'.[6] They tend, 'if a man starts from nothing and makes a success of himself, to consider that not exactly as a matter of shame, but as a mark against him'. They praise a place like Lough Derg, but the very praise is illuminating.[7] 'You talk to everybody and there are no distinctions there. And even though you are suffering quite a bit, you have a sense of democracy and freedom with people that you do not normally have.' The greatest problems of one of the most fashionable of Dublin's secondary schools, according to its headmaster, is that, because of the demand coupled with spatial limitations, 'we are forced virtually to admit only the sons of past pupils here'. And finally, '. . . although they don't say so, most of the people in our class have the impression that the old Ascendancy crowd are still a step ahead of them. They look up to them in a way—at least as far as their social behaviour and standards of living are concerned—and that, I think, is why so many live so much above what they can really afford and have such rigid class standards for marriage.'[8]

[6] 'You'd be surprised', said one woman of this same class, 'how many people are on the hire-purchase system. I know that from my own experience and from a man who is in an excellent position to know. There are a great number of people who are continually going into debt and they never seem to be able to get out of it. They have to have all the best things and move with people who have the best things.'

[7] Lough Derg, otherwise known as 'St. Patrick's Purgatory', is a popular place of pilgrimage. A pilgrimage consists of spending three days there performing devotional exercises barefoot on the rocky island; fasting, save for bread and tea once a day, during that period; and going without sleep the first night.

[8] Three of twelve spouses in the managerial class were children of successful publicans. Each of them were apologetic about this fact. This attitude stems from class feeling and is very common. I had the fortune to meet a great many publicans and to attend several meetings of the vintners' branch of a charitable organization known as the St. Joseph's Society for Training Young Priests. The chaplain for this society told me that it was 'notorious' that the successful publicans all sent their sons to the best secondary schools and into the professions and refused to let them succeed to 'the trade'. And the oldest and one of the most successful of the Dublin publicans, whom I interviewed, reported: 'The sons of the men in the

198

The clerical class for their part look on all this with a scorn that ranges from humorous to bitter. One clerk said: 'In the last thirty years there have been a lot of people who have become *nouveau riche* and they are inclined to put on airs and be a bit snobbish. That is very true of the Army, I think, and there is an awful lot of nonsense going on among the wives of the officers. Well, we're inclined to laugh at all that because we knew them all when they were no better than the rest of us.'

Another clerk, who has recently penetrated into an upper class neighbourhood, refers to it as a 'snobocracy' and *'suburbia in excelsis'*. Still another, typically, criticizes the Irish employers and affirms that '. . . the English and Jewish firms are much better to work for, I think. They pay better wages, have better social services and have more concern about their employees and their working conditions. I don't know what is the matter with our Irish employers. To me they seem to be too intent on living up to the limit of their income to think and take into consideration what is going on all over the world.'

And yet, the clerical people also report that 'there are many people in salaried positions who tax their income to the limit as much as the professional people'; that they 'are keen for cars and clothes and the best of everything', and that '. . . a great many of them now belong to golf clubs and rugger clubs'. And as we shall soon see the clerical class is intent on imitating the managerial class in other important ways.

The artisans commonly manifest the same dichotomous feelings. They feel uneasy in the homes of old friends who have moved up into the clerical class and speak of such friends as becoming 'uppity'. Towards siblings who are in the class above them they report feelings of jealousy and a margin of restraint, although sibling relations usually still remain close. They are critical of employers, and also of labour union leaders whom they accuse of looking to their own interests and collaborating with the employers rather than seeking the best interests of the membership. They resent the virtual closing of the better schools to their children.

> If I wanted to send one of my girls out to St. Jude's Convent, well, they'd be very polite. They would say: 'We'll see what we can do for you. But, you know, we are very crowded. If a free space comes up we'll let you know.' And that would be the end of it. I would never hear from them again. But if I were in a little higher bracket and on a little higher

trade get it very easy. The fathers send them to the best schools and colleges and they get ideas in their heads and don't want to have anything to do with the business. But in the last few years I've noticed a change. There is more common sense about this now and, I'm glad to say, more sons are succeeding their fathers in the trade.'

level, everything would be sweetness and light and I would not have much difficulty getting her in there at all.

And some of them feel that while there has been 'a complete revolution' in the class structure, barriers still exist and according to one artisan father:

> While many more children today are breaking through the partitions that separate the lower middle class and the upper classes, those partitions are still strong and it is only few that break through them. And I'd even say that although the partitions are relatively thin now compared to what they used to be, they are getting thicker. The people who have reached the top are trying to consolidate their position and twenty-five or thirty years from now I think it will be harder for children to advance from one class to another than it is at present.

But another artisan father was 'shocked to learn that my grandfather had been a higher civil servant and had slid down the scale'. And artisan parents give expression to the value they place upon class when, as we have seen, they voice their concern about the possible effect upon their children of the mingling of the classes, particularly in the new neighbourhoods. Indeed, in regard to the artisans we need not rely only upon formal expressions to sound their sentiments about class standards. Their concern about their children's education, their attitudes towards their daughters' marriage, and the attitudes of the children themselves, particularly of the girls, are all clear indices of the class values they accept.

Finally, the general labourers who have steady employment and wages manifest sentiments that are much the same and display the same ambivalence as the artisans. Paradoxically, on the lower edge of this class, among the most unskilled labourers, whose wages are low and who are more continually threatened with unemployment, sentiments tend to be less ambivalent. Even here, however, the children and especially the girls, tend today to be ashamed of their homes, to seek friends among people who are somewhat better off and never to bring these friends home. More and more they, too, refuse to start marriage from scratch, or at least they are inclined to postpone it until after they have had their fling at a good time on a level they will rarely be able to visit after marriage.

But on the whole the poorer labourers' sentiments are more consistent. Their poverty, which they freely acknowledged without harping on it, enervates class ambition and they are simply critical of the forces they feel are responsible for their condition—the employers, the labour union leaders, and government agencies. They are inclined to criticize the clergy for being 'stand-offish' and having it too easy these days; and the doctors in attendance in the tenement sections for being 'snobbish'. '. . . imagine a doctor when he leaves the room covering his hand with his coat which this boyo did with the people next door.' A good many feel that there is little chance for the children in Dublin. 'Serving time is bad now. If you get apprenticed to the Corporation you won't be received unless you belong to the union, and it's very hard to get into a union unless your father is a member. The trouble is the young people don't have a chance any more and that's why they're leaving the country. A lot of the parents tell them to get out of here, that there is no chance for them here. And they are not very worried about what might happen to them in England. They think it is all right over there.'

Such, in general, are the more common sentiments associated with class that overtly intruded themselves into our study, and of themselves they give us a certain insight into differences in the family structure of the various classes. Let us now bring these differences more sharply into focus.

GENERAL LABOURERS

As we already have implied, within the class of general labourers itself, job stability and wages are important differentiating factors. Their effect is directly observable in the type of residence and in the residential districts in which the general labourers live. Labourers with steady jobs and higher wages have an income that is only a small cut below most of the artisans. As a result, they reside in houses that are hardly distinguishable from the homes of the artisans. The description we have given of the Dunn home with certain modifications that, significantly, would also apply to some artisan homes, is a fair description of the dwellings of these labourers. Moreover, though labourers may tend to be concentrated more in the older neighbourhoods, they are also numerous in the new neighbourhoods. And in both they are fairly well interspersed with artisan families.

The lower fringe of this class is forced by lower and less steady wages to live more in the poorer, crowded quarters of the city. Although 'corporation flats' have been built in the newer, as well as in the older, neighbourhoods and some of the poorer labourers whose old quarters have been condemned have moved into these newer neighbourhoods, probably the greater portion of them still dwell in the eastern portion of the old city. Here, even in the more recent corporation flats, let alone the older tenements, families live in extremely crowded quarters.

One such typical dwelling is that of a dockworker. He is the father of eight children of whom five live at home. At the time of this study he earned a weekly wage of £5 10s. The flat, rented at 6s. 9d. weekly, had three small rooms and a small scullery. There was a toilet outside of the scullery, but no bath. Besides the parents' bedroom, the other rooms are used also for sleeping purposes. The furniture is minimal and in some instances makeshift, although this family has a wireless set. Such flats are not centrally heated and, as coal is relatively dear, cold and dampness in Dublin's dank weather are characteristic of these quarters, and tuberculosis is fairly common.

Between families living in such conditions and those of the more prosperous labourers there are many differences, largely stemming from economic disparities, to all of which we cannot attend. We shall therefore confine ourselves to pointing out a few important differences as the occasion demands. For the rest we shall treat labourers of both types as one class group.

Economically, the main distinction between the artisans and the general labourers lies in the more meagre income of the latter. As a result of this home ownership is *notably* less among the labourers. On the other hand, important as this difference in wages is for the people involved, it on the whole is a small one. Furthermore, the manner by which both labourers and artisans secure their livelihood is essentially the same. In both cases the family depends upon wages earned by individual family members who work separately away from home for a non-familial organization. In both cases, too, the family characteristically passes through the same single income phase, during which it is dependent solely on the father's wage, to the multiple income phase when the father's wage is supplemented by that of the children who are at work.

As a consequence, the way in which the families of labourers co-ordinate their activities to secure a livelihood is similar to the system of co-ordination characteristic of the artisans. And since these conditions also obtained for the natal families of general labourers who are New Dubliners as well as for those who are artisans, the factors surrounding the establishment of the families of New Dubliners in the labouring class are similar to those affecting the artisan parents at their marriage. In regard to the marriage of New Dubliners of the labouring class, the only *notable* differences reported were a tendency towards shorter engagements and earlier marriages, and lesser opposition on the part of the immigrant parents to a girl marrying beneath her. These features, moreover, were found more among the poorer labourers than the others. Between the more secure general labourers and the artisans there appeared to be little difference in this respect.

Once the family has been established, the relationships between its members in the labouring class are also essentially similar to the artisans. As far as the division of labour and responsibility among family members is concerned, there are only two discoverable differences between the artisans and labourers. First, there exists a tendency on the part of the husband among the labourers to leave an even greater share of the management of the family's finances in the hands of his wife. Secondly, there is a tendency for the parents, particularly the mother, in the labouring class to delegate to the older siblings a wider range of authority over the younger siblings. In neither instance, however, is the tendency widespread enough to be considered *notable*. Generally speaking, spouses in the labouring class have the same sentiments of equality, and the same practical inequality whereby the wife shoulders the greater share of domestic responsibilities. And they report, as do the artisans, that this constitutes a significant change from the relationships prevalent among spouses of their parents' generation.

This change between husbands and wives has had the same effect upon the relations of parents and children that it has had in the families of artisans. But among the labourers, particularly among the poorer labourers, the effect has been even more pronounced. While the degree of affection and confidence between parents and children in labouring class families is no greater than in artisan families, the amount of parental control over the children is *notably* less and in the raising of the children this makes actual and acute problems that, for the artisans, are more remote and mostly potential. Thus, especially among the boys of the poorer families, truancy is quite common; and where artisan parents are mainly worried about their sons causing property damage out of innocent exuberance, labouring-class parents are hounded by the fear of thievery, delinquency and the reform schools.[9] These parents complain that, even when quite young, the children roam far afield outside of the neighbourhood and the boys, especially, form gangs that get involved with gangs of older boys who lead them into serious trouble.

Labouring-class parents are in disagreement as to whether delinquency is greater now than it was when they were children. Most of them think that, considering the city as a whole, delinquency has declined because of increased occupational opportunities and improved living conditions. On the other hand, they feel that among people who have not benefited from these improvements, decline in parental control over the children, and the growing tendency of parents to find their recreation outside the home and to leave the children more to themselves, have intensified the problem. This is confirmed by the fact that it is in the labouring class neighbourhoods, in the areas around Dorset Street, Killarney Street, and around the Quays, that the various boys' clubs are concentrated and flourish.[10]

[9] Often called 'Industrial' schools.
[10] Some of these are parish-based, while others are associated with a religious church or school, such as the famous Belvedere Newsboys Club.

Labouring class parents are in general accord about the beneficient effects of these clubs in reducing delinquency.

As the girls, who in early adolescence are more amenable to parental control, move into late adolescence, they also present a problem to labouring parents that is more widespread the lower down the scale we move. Mixed activities between boys and girls *generally* begin with labouring class children at an earlier age than with the artisan children,—as early as the age of thirteen or fourteen. Frequently enough to make it a common source of parental concern, girls find themselves in the classic trouble. When this happens, the labourers report that people usually blame the girl for such a turn of events. In any case, both the family of the girl and the family of the boy move to secure the quick marriage of the couple. Usually the boys are quite willing to co-operate, but if either party is reluctant the parents will usually have recourse to the priest. Although there is some evidence that many of these marriages are not too felicitous, most of the labouring people who discussed the case felt that on the whole such marriages turn out as well as the more regular ones. The following account by an artisan girl and her father is typical: 'If a girl got into trouble,' said the girl, 'the boy who was responsible would always marry her. And if he didn't, nobody would have anything to do with him. Even his own parents would make it hard for him. So the boy usually does marry the girl.'

'The parents', said the father, 'would bring it to a head. They'd see that the girl and boy got married and married fast, and in a situation like that they would go to the priest, especially if the lad showed signs of balking. . . . I think these marriages turn out all right afterwards. I think they turn out as well as other marriages, and I don't think most fellows would feel resentful that they had been forced into a marriage they did not want.'

The most notable difference between the labourers and the artisans concerns education. The children of labourers, both boys and girls, receive *notably* less secondary education than the artisans' children. Even among the more prosperous labourers, the maximum level of education tends to be a two year technical school course, and in any given family it is unlikely that all of the children will go as far as that. An intermediate certificate from secondary school is possible, but rarer; a full secondary school education is quite the exception. This is partially a matter of policy on the part of the parents, who require the children to work to supplement the family income. It is also in part due to the *prevalent* desire of the children themselves to go to work. Labourers also differ from artisans in so far that parents, when they feel they can afford to send one or more children into the secondary grades, usually choose the boys in preference to the girls on the grounds that education is much more important for a boy than a girl.

In regard to jobs and the choice of their occupation, however, both the sons and daughters of the labourers are allowed about as much freedom of selection by their parents as artisan children. The range of opportunities, of course, is narrower. But despite the fact that parents in the labouring class out of necessity may bring more influence to bear, they find it equally difficult to control the children in this respect, and the children usually get their own way. Because of the restriction of the labour market, getting their own way may often entail emigration which, as we have already pointed out, is one of the most *notable* distinguishing features of the labouring class. According to the labourers' reports, emigration is common among both girls and boys, with a tendency in recent years for the girls to emigrate even more than the boys.

These patterns of behaviour in regard to education and occupation reflect, as they also influence, attitudes and behaviour towards marriage, which is another area where *notable* differences between labourers and artisans exist. Despite the fact that, as we have pointed out, labouring class girls also aspire to better themselves by marriage, and despite the reports of the labouring class people that girls tend to marry somewhat later than girls of their parents' generation, by comparison with their artisan contemporaries this aspiration of girls in the labouring class is decidedly less effective, and they marry *notably* earlier. Marriage at twenty or twenty-one is fairly common, and earlier marriages are more frequent in this class than in any other. In short, compared to those in the artisan class, girls in the labouring class are more nearly in the position of girls in both the artisan and labouring classes thirty or forty years ago. Although we must constantly remember that this is less true the nearer the general labourers come to the artisans in income, labouring class girls on the whole are more willing to settle for a good man with a steady job and their parents normally go along with them in this respect.

Where the boys' marriage is concerned, however, the labouring class is much more remarkable for its similarity to the artisan class than for its difference from it. From the reports of the general labourers it appears that labouring-class boys do tend to marry a few years earlier than artisan boys.[11] It is also clear from their reports that the fathers in this class are even more inclined to adopt a 'hands-off'

---

[11] Although neither specified ages at marriage with exactitude, the whole tenor of the remarks of the artisans and general labourers about the age at marriage, both for girls and boys, *generally* conforms to the actual pattern of age at marriage in the urban population as revealed by the statistics of the Central Statistics Office. *v.* Appendix I, p. 257.

policy in regard to a son's marriage than are artisan fathers. But the attitude of the boys themselves towards marriage, their attitude towards girls, and especially the attitude of the mothers towards their son and his marriage is *notably* the same as it is in the artisan class.[12]

In the internal relationships between family members, these are the most *notable* differences between the artisans and the general labourers. As for the relationships of the family as a unit to other groups in the community, the differences between the two classes are even fewer. The most pronounced differences of this kind occur, first of all, in the relation of the families of the labouring class to the neighbourhood families. Five out of six families in this class that were studied lived in old neighbourhoods and the kind of co-operation and the type of sanctions neighbours mutually invoke are, according to their reports, the same in kind as those described by artisans who dwell in old neighbourhoods. The only difference discernible lies in the greater degree of co-operation that obtains between neighbourhood families of the labouring class, and particularly between the poorer families. In the slum areas ordinary, daily exchange of services, as well as co-operation at times of crisis, is even more marked than among the artisans; particularism in regard to shopping practices is even more pronounced; sanctions against behaviour contrary to the neighbourhood code are, on the whole, more extensive and more strongly imposed. The experience of the one family that had moved to a new neighbourhood is too limited to be a basis for generalization, but it tallied with the reports of the artisans in similar neighbourhoods in indicating a decline in neighbourhood solidarity.

Secondly, the labouring-class families have more contact with the clergy and rely upon them more for help in getting jobs, for assisting them in solving family problems and in bringing pressure to bear upon delinquent family members. This likewise is more common in the old neighbourhoods than the new, and even more common in the poorer neighbourhoods. However, even here parochial and religious organizations are primarily directed towards helping the children, while clerical action necessarily is limited in large part to aid in times of family crisis. With few exceptions, the parish, or social organizations conducted under religious auspices, do not achieve the integra-

[12] Thus eighteen out of twenty adult individuals of both sexes who reported on this matter said that even after allowances have been made for the income a single son may bring his mother, the labouring-class mother dislikes and tries to obstruct a son's marriage. One father's testimony is worth quoting: 'I know many instances where the boy isn't making much money and whatever he is making, he is keeping for himself and not giving her much. And yet the mother doesn't want to let him go. When he gets a girl on the string, she does everything she can to discourage the girl or at least to delay the marriage as long as she can.'

tion of families of the labouring class any more than they do in the artisan class.

In regard to families of friends and especially of kin resident either in the city or in the country, there appear to be, as far as we could probe, no *notable* differences between the families of general labourers and artisans. The average general labourer's family tends to have fewer immediate kin in the city outside its own class. Kinship relations therefore are usually more homogeneous class-wise and less subject to strain on this account. Furthermore, the general labourer is likely to have less contact with country kin than the artisans, largely because he cannot as easily afford to visit the country during the summer. Again, this statement is susceptible to considerable modification. Those among the general labourers who have more secure incomes do not appreciably differ from the artisans in the amount of their contacts with their country kin, and this is especially true in the case of labourers who have first-degree relatives in the country. Apart from these differences, however, the relationships between labourers' families and those of their close kin and close friends are much like the artisans. Among the general labourers and the artisans the weave of the community web follows the same pattern.

THE WHITE COLLARS

If in the externals of life the distinction between the artisans and general labourers is small in one direction, between the artisans and the white collar or clerical class the distinction is also rather small in the other direction. In these matters, apart from the higher reaches of the clerical class and the lower reaches of the labouring class, the descriptive phrase of one artisan woman is quite apt: 'It is just a question of tuppence ha'penny looking down on tuppence.' While, in contrast to artisan families, clerical families *prevalently* own their own homes and are more likely to be found in the newer and more modern residential districts, their quarters are only slightly more commodious than those of the artisans. Typically a clerical family also lives in an 'attached' house of six or seven rooms with a kitchen and bath. The rooms are somewhat larger than those of the artisans, and the furniture more modern and of better quality. Usually there is a larger garden or lawn in front or back. But it takes a sharp and practiced eye indeed to discern the difference between clerical homes and the homes of those artisans who reside in new neighbourhoods.[13]

[13] A comparison of all of the clerical, artisan, and labourer's families in regard to certain commodities, though not conclusive, is enlightening. All but two of our families were selected on the basis of the husband's occupation. And yet, of six families of general labourers, only one owned his home, none had a telephone, none had a car. Of eleven artisan families, four owned their homes, one had a

The more favourable economic position of the contemporary clerical family is related in part to the earlier, more favourable economic
position that the parents of the clerical spouses enjoyed over the
parents of the artisans. Thus seven out of twelve of the fathers of the
clerical spouses interviewed had been managers or owners of small
business enterprises. As a result, most of the clerical spouses interviewed entered married life with a better educational background, a
more secure financial status and, as far as the husbands are concerned, a higher occupational position than the artisan spouses.

These advantages at the start of marital life, however, have not
been secured without a price. *Notably*, the clerical spouses have had
longer courtships and have married later than the artisans, and according to their reports this is characteristic of people in their class.[14]
According to the reports of clerical people, girls of their generation,
by comparison with girls of the same generation who have become
artisans' wives, were more intent upon improving themselves by marriage, and they judged a boy's social status as important as his
character in rating his qualifications as a husband. And where the
parents of the artisans *prevalently* despaired of social improvement
via marriage, the parents of the clericals' wives *prevalently* supported
their daughters in their hypergamous aspirations. On the other hand,
where artisan people more commonly assign the need of the men to
support their natal family, the clerical people usually refer to the
men's desire for 'financial security', for a good time, and the ubiqui-
tous maternal displeasure over a son's marriage as the main reasons
for their relatively late marriage.

Although, as a result of this conservatism towards marriage, clerical
spouses usually start and continue their marital life on a more secure
financial footing, the division of familial labour between the members
of the family does not appreciably differ from that of the artisan
family. Almost all of the characteristics of the artisan family in this
sphere are equally *prevalent* among families of the clerical class, with
one exception: the single income phase among the clerical families is
prolonged for some years by the fact that *prevalently* all the children
in these families attend secondary school. The clerical family, therefore, typically enters the multiple income phase of its cycle some two
or three years later than the artisan family.

phone, two had cars. Of six clerical families, six owned their homes, three had
phones, and two had cars.

[14] Though randomly selected in this regard, the average age at marriage for our
six clerical husbands is thirty-four years of age, and the average of the wives is
over twenty-nine years of age. This is just about par for the clerical course;
v. Appendix I, p. 263. This increases credence in the reports of these people as to
the conditions and even more, as to the attitudes, that underlie the marital
practices of this class.

As this fact indicates, it is in reference to the socialization of the children that clerical families differ most *notably* from the artisans. The differences do not occur so strikingly in the earlier stages of socialization. *Generally* speaking, in the clerical family parent-child relationships, as well as the modes of discipline, are quite the same as in the artisan family. But the content of the process is somewhat different and this appears particularly in the standards and expectations set for the children in late adolescence.

This is most obvious in regard to education. Clerical parents *prevalently* insist upon all their children attending secondary schools. In this matter, children have less freedom of choice than artisan children, and on the parents' part there are no selective practices based upon age or sex. Not only is education given more extensively to clerical children, but the level of education for all the children is *notably* higher. For boys in the clerical class a full secondary education is *prevalent* and a university course is a more widespread *alternate* than among artisans. In like fashion, though many clerical girls may combine an intermediate certificate with a business-school course, many more complete the full secondary-school course before entering the occupational world. By one or the other of these procedures, almost all girls in the clerical class receive the equivalent of a full secondary education, and the possibility of a university course is much more real for them than for artisan girls. Furthermore, children in the clerical class are given much more supplementary education in matters such as music, art, and domestic science.

As these more rigid demands in the matter of education imply, parental control is somewhat stronger in the clerical families than among the artisans, although the form of control, like that of the artisan parents, remains one of affection and reason rather than show of force. The recreational activities of the children remain home-based for a longer period; their peer group associations are more closely supervised; and the association of boys and girls in unchaperoned activities occurs somewhat later than in the artisan class.

What applies to school applies with modifications to the question of the children's careers. Here, as with the artisans, the central question is the occupational career of the boys. While the principle of allowing a son to choose his life's work obtains as in the artisan class, it does so within narrower limits. There is considerable parental pressure exerted on a son to do better than enter a trade, although most clerical parents are realistic enough to accept this eventuality with good grace in the face of inferior talent or temperamental incompatibility for a white-collar job.

As a result of these educational policies and parental pressures, the *general* run of clerical children, both boys and girls, enter the occupational world at a higher level than the children of artisans. Like the artisans, they enter it with the obligation of contributing to the support of the family, but 'support' has a slightly different connotation for clerical people. It means much more than helping to provide the necessities of life for the growing family. It also means helping the family to live up to the accepted class standards. As clerical families tend to be smaller than those of the artisans, and clerical fathers are usually able to maintain these standards without making great demands on their children, the obligation to help support the family is normally neither as widespread nor as prolonged as among the artisans. But when circumstances bring it into operation, this obligation tends to have more drastic effects than among the artisans. Clerical children are more likely to postpone marriage not only to support their parents as do artisan children, but also to prevent their natal families from the necessity of settling for a lower level of life.

Thus late marriage of people in the clerical class is undoubtedly due in part to the influence of class standards, but normally this influence is not directed back to the natal family so much as forward to the conjugal family that the children will establish. The fact that class standards are somewhat higher for clerical people than for artisans accounts for the *notable* differences that exist between the two classes. The remarkable feature is that these differences are not more numerous. As regards the marriage of the girls, there are no great differences either in the attitude of the girl or her parents. The clerical fathers are perhaps more concerned about the social status of a prospective son-in-law than artisan fathers, though they would not object to an artisan boy who is occupationally situated so as to move up into the clerical class. But the clerical father need not be greatly concerned since his daughters, firmly backed by his wife, are quite determined not to marry beneath them. The refusal to start marriage at a lower level than that to which she is accustomed, the refusal to forgo the material advantages and enjoyment her wages and her liberty bring her, the need to save to buy a home—all these are as *prevalent* among clerical girls as among artisans. So is the desire to improve her social position by marriage although, as she is already on a higher level than the artisan, the opportunity to do so is perhaps more restricted. And, as we have seen, clerical girls also encounter in the men the same, and perhaps an even greater, coolness towards marriage.

For clerical boys are even more preoccupied than artisan boys with achieving financial security before embarking upon the marital sea, and in this they are more strongly supported by both of their parents. On the other hand, reports indicate that the men of this class are just as loath as the artisans to give up the independence and joys of bachelorhood, and that maternal reluctance to lose a son by marriage is not only just as strong but is buttressed by additional arguments. For clerical people are also more reluctant to have a son marry beneath his class, although this is not as strong a standard for a boy as for a girl.

Furthermore, it is significant to note that clerical people more frequently than the artisans reported the practice of family limitation, although sufficient evidence is lacking to warrant any firm generalization. These reports referred to people in the clerical and managerial classes today without distinction between second-generation Dubliners and others. The youngest couple among our families of New Dubliners in the clerical class simply stated that they practise birth control, and the husband added: 'People have to curtail their families. If I were to have another baby this year [he has one] I'd be down to my uppers. The cost is terrible and this business about free maternity service is bunk. It is inefficient and no one is going to avail himself of it unless he is a pauper.'

Another wife reported: 'O, I think people practise family control. The women talk about it quite a bit and I know several girls who say they do. They'll often mention the fact that they are trying to limit the family and that they will be disappointed if they have another baby too soon. I don't know how general that is, but it goes on, and I think people in our class do it to a fair extent.'[15]

These features in the internal structure of the clerical family whereby it tends to diverge from the artisan family are partially related to other differences that are to be found in the family's external relations to other family groups and non-familial organizations in the city. Although clerical families may have slightly more contact with their kin both in the country and the city because they are more likely to have conveniences for communication such as cars and phones, kinship interrelationships in the class are not *notably* different from the relationships we have seen in the artisan class. In this respect, the most *notable* feature is the relative inability of class differences to seriously affect kinship ties between the families of siblings in the artisan and clerical classes.

Clerical families, however, are *notable* for having a much lesser degree of co-operation with the families of neighbours than the artisans in general. This is in great part due to the fact that they live in newer neighbourhoods where neighbourhood solidarity in each of the

---

[15] Besides the doctor previously quoted, several priests also confirmed that control by rhythm and continence is practised in the managerial and clerical classes, and voiced the opinion that it is increasing. They and others likewise, asserted that contraception is virtually non-existent and I believe they are quite creditable witnesses in this matter.

211

three class levels we have studied is lower than in the older neighbourhoods. The interfamilial relationships that artisans in the new neighbourhoods have described are quite typical of the neighbourhoods where the clericals live. It is noteworthy, however, that clerical spouses who have come, not only from artisan, but also from clerical natal families, report that their neighbourhoods during their childhood were characterized by the more extensive co-operation that is typical of the older artisan and labouring neighbourhoods today. This would seem to suggest that the decline in neighbourhood solidarity has affected each of these classes to about an equal degree; and that it is due in part to the geographical re-shuffling of the city's population and in part to the opening up of the class structure.

In another respect, moreover, clerical families *notably* differ from the artisan families in a manner that bears out the preceding statement. Clerical families tend to have more family friends than the artisans and at the same time more family friends who belong to different classes. As with the artisans, strong friendships between families mostly grow out of friendships the clerical spouses made in their late adolescence. More than the artisans, however, clerical people made friends, both at this period and since their marriage, through membership and activities in clubs and associations of a social, but not noticeably of a business, nature. These two facts may account for the greater class heterogeneity of their circle of friends. While there is no more tendency than among the artisans for the clerical family and its circle of friends to form a real group, their interaction and co-operation is *notably* both more intense in kind and more frequent in amount than the artisan family and its friends achieve. Indeed, in all but frequency of contact, it is similar to the interaction of special neighbourhood friends of the artisans in the old neighbourhoods, and often such bonds approximate in strength the ties of kinship that bind together the families of siblings. Kinship is still the strongest bond, but more than one clerical person remarked in the same strain as the husband who said: 'Ah! You'd bank on these people more than anyone else—more than other friends, more than neighbours and more than your relatives. I'd definitely say that. We share nearly everything with them. They are the type of people you can confide in. You'd tell them any trouble you were in. You'd go to them for advice and you would rely on them to stand by and help you. There are many things we have told them that the rest of the family has never heard and, believe me, never will hear either.'

THE MANAGERIAL CLASS

The widest range of variation from the artisan norm is, of course, found in families of the managerial-professional class. The diversity is immediately apparent to the observer in the mode and style of life of families of this class. Their dwellings are single, large houses of two, and sometimes three, stories. One, for example, has thirteen rooms: a living-room and dining-room, both of which are very large; a reception room, a library, a kitchen and auxiliary dining-room, a nursery and five bedrooms. The furnishings of these houses are quite ornate and tend to be late Victorian, although among the younger families the trend is to modern furniture. These homes are staffed usually by one maid and one cook and, if there are younger children in the family, there is likely to be a governess or 'nanny'.[16] They are usually located in the fashionable neighbourhoods that were established before the Irish revolution such as Rathgar, Ballsbridge, Donnybrook and Terenure. Indeed, many of them were formerly residences of the old Ascendancy.

People in the managerial class have phones and cars which are likely to be American or the larger style of English cars. They are very well educated, especially in a literary way, and are extremely well-read. Along with literature, their tastes run to music and art, with considerable interest in modern art, on the one hand; on the other, to golf, riding, hunting, race meetings and rugby football in almost exclusive preference to Gaelic football or soccer.[17] They are also well travelled. They are quite as likely to fly to London or Paris for an international rugby match as their American counterparts might fly from Chicago to New York for a World Series. Many of them have studied abroad in England and the Continent and, since the end of the war, many of them have vacationed on the Continent at resorts such as Lake Como, Villefranche and Biarritz, often combining these excursions with a pilgrimage to Rome or Lourdes.

Both men and women are quite active in social clubs and organizations, and both are *notably* active in charitable organizations. Politi-

---

[16] Retaining servants constitutes an acute problem for families in this class today. Girls come into the city and take jobs as domestic servants until they can find positions in business concerns. Independence and increased marital opportunities that factory and office jobs provide appear to be the motives for this practice rather than better wages or conditions. As a result, one husband asserted, 'large houses such as this one are on their way out. The maid problem is too great and people cannot manage them by themselves. Actually, most of them would be gone now except that the newer houses that are available are so much smaller that it is impossible to get all the furniture in them. But even so, many of them are being sold and turned into flats.'

[17] This may be true not only of the second generation, but also of the first. Thus one immigrant father of a New Dubliner, besides having many irons in the business fire, and being active in politics, was a well-known art collector, a philatelist, a connoisseur of wines, and a patron of music, one of whose sons was talented enough seriously to consider a career as a concert pianist.

213

cally, they are inclined to be conservative. And by their own account and stated preference, they are less intense and more leisurely than Americans and Englishmen in the conduct of their professional and business affairs.

Ownership of property or of a professional practice that is productive of the basic family income is the *general* economic feature that marks off families of this class from those of the other three classes. Furthermore, early in its existence, if not immediately at its inception, the managerial family *prevalently* reaches a position of multiple income through investments made not only from the earnings of the husband, but also from the substantial sum of money the wife usually receives from her parents at marriage. The possession of income-producing property, or of a professional practice, *notably* modifies the principle of equal inheritance common to all the other classes. Where the father owns a business, it is *prevalent* for him to leave the controlling interest to one or some, though not to all, of the children, while the remaining interest as well as the other properties of his estate are equally divided among the other children. A similar procedure occurs where a son follows his father into a professional field, an occurrence that is quite common. The father's practice is left to this son and the remainder of the estate is equally divided among the children. Under this policy, according to people of the managerial class, there is a tendency for the older children to come off best. One case, which according to managerial opinion, is typical, illustrates this last assertion as well as it describes the *general* procedure. The father in this case had made an earlier will leaving everything, including the business, to his wife. Though he had planned making a new will to secure the business to the children, he died suddenly without doing so. His oldest son reported that his mother has now acted as she believes her husband would have:

> Mother has made a will that leaves control of the business jointly to the three oldest in the family [two boys and a girl in a family of eleven]. That is, they receive the majority of shares in the company, and we are doing this to keep the company stable and to insure that it is properly run. Apart from that controlling interest, all the other members of the family receive equal shares in the business. And the rest of the property and money that mother has is also to be equally divided. As far as people in business are concerned, I think provisions similar to this are quite general.[18]

As might be expected, the financial condition of their natal families

[18] From the context of this informant's remarks, and those of others, it is clear that such a policy is usually adopted by business people whether they be immigrants, New Dubliners or Old Dubliners. The parents in this case, as a matter of fact, are both immigrants into Dublin.

makes the marriage of the New Dubliners in this class *notably* different from that of the other classes in its financial aspects. Moreover, this factor has the same differentiating effect on the marriage of the New Dubliners' children. The most *notable* of these differences is the endowment of the girls at marriage—a practice that is *prevalent*. This endowment consists in a substantial sum of money, to which may be added the gift of a house, and to which are always added substantial gifts in the form of furniture, etc. The money endowment is not a formal part of the marriage contract, nor consciously conceived as corresponding to the property the husband provides at the formation of the new family. It is given because, as one woman put it, 'parents want their daughter to have an independent income'. For these reasons it differs from the dowry that is involved in rural marriages.[19] Nevertheless, it has some likeness to a dowry, and perhaps, could be called a quasi-dowry. One wife, describing current practice, said:

> The parents do help at marriage. Actually it is the old story: they are living up to the limit, too, and they can't help much. Everybody thought it was terrific during our engagement that we already had a house. Well, that house came from our parents. The girl's parents have to finance her marriage because, with prices so high, it is difficult for a couple to set out on their own without help. And I don't merely mean wedding gifts. Of course, they give these—especially the more substantial furniture a house needs. But besides these, they put down money. I know the parents of my brother-in-law's wife put down £2,500, and money was put down in our case, too. Certainly, I'd say it is common for the parents of the bride to put down £500 to her. Of course, it is in the form of a gift, but actually it is almost a dowry. It may not be in writing as it is in the country, but practically it is a real dowry. And the parents plan on this and save for it.

Despite this endowment, among the most common reasons assigned for delaying marriage on the part of both the girls and the boys of this class is the need of the children to save to finance their marriage. Partly for this reason, it is almost as common for girls in this class to work before marriage as it is for girls of artisan and clerical classes. This is a great change from the earlier years of the century when it was thought unladylike for even unmarried women to hold positions in business and professional fields. 'The need to save in order to finance marriage', however, is a quasi-formula that the artisans also use today and almost as commonly, but though the words are the same, their meaning is *notably* different in each case—as different as the meanings the clericals and artisans attach to the word 'support'. As in the latter case, so for people in the managerial class

---

[19] Cf. Arensberg and Kimball, op. cit., pp. 113–17.

the need to finance their own marriage means to accumulate enough money to live reasonably near to the standard of their natal families. And what we have seen of that standard is enough to indicate that this ideal would, indeed, have a delaying effect.

Class considerations *notably* have the same effects on marriage in this class as in the clerical class and to a much greater extent. A girl is even more strongly expected to marry within her own class not only by her mother, but by her father. Even more completely must a boy qualify for a girl's hand by reason of his social position and family connections, as well as by reason of personal virtue and character. Furthermore, the girls are quite as intent as their parents upon holding their own or 'even pushing the standard a little higher' by their marriage. What is even more *notable* about the managerial class, however, is the degree to which parents cling to the same set of standards for their sons as for their daughters, although they may be less concerned about the social position of a daughter-in-law's family if she can meet their standards of education. The attitude of the managerial father quoted in the preceding chapter, and that of the managerial wife quoted in our discussion of class sentiments, are both typical and sufficiently enlightening to dispense with further description.[20] As between generations, there appears to be little change in these parental attitudes towards the marriage of their children. But, on the other hand, it is *notable* that the degree of parental control in this respect, especially in regard to the boys, has declined in the last thirty years, as we have already seen. This may, perhaps, presage a change towards greater liberality on the part of the parents of the next generation. But the fact that more than ever before men are able to disregard parental objections and marry girls from lower classes is a corrective for any temptation to think that the managerial class has a quasi-caste mentality towards their children's marriage, as it is also an index of the progressive opening of the class structure.

Generally, people in the managerial class marry later than any other class and *prevalently* they have longer 'lines' and engagements. As in every Western country, the various class considerations we have discussed are partially responsible for this tendency. But class influence should not be permitted to obscure the fact that the same forces that we have seen to be operative in other classes, especially maternal resistance to a son's marriage and the men's attachment to the blessed state of bachelorhood, play just as strong a part as in other classes. In few places in the Western World among people on this level is one likely to hear an account such as the following, which was given by one of the younger managerial wives:

[20] *v.* above, pp. 196–7; ch. v, p. 150.

I know at least five girls, friends of mine, all of whom are about my own age [30] and all of whom are single and now working. They are normally attractive girls. They have had the best in education and they certainly would qualify from the class point of view. And they have money. They have money they have saved from their own earnings and, besides that, money from their parents. So there is no question of finances. They could start out well enough, just as well or better than I did. And furthermore they are eager to get married. Well, I've asked each one of them why they haven't married, and in each case they have just come out and stated that no boy was sufficiently interested in them to ask them.

That is quite common. The boys are simply not interested. They will not face up to responsibility. And when they do get engaged, they seem perfectly happy and content to go along that way for years. I don't know, but they just don't seem to have the urge. And I also personally think that in school, and in retreats and sermons the priests do not stress a man's obligations in this respect. I think they should tell them that unless they are to be priests they ought to be married and not just be useless parasites in the world. And they ought to talk about the sacramental benefits of marriage, too, but that side of marriage is almost never discussed.

Although the New Dubliners in the managerial class received no more instruction in sexual matters from their parents than people in other classes, they are *notable* in that they have imparted such instruction to their own children in contrast to parents of other classes. And according to their reports, birth control, at least among the younger families, is more widespread than on the other class levels.

Within the managerial family, once it is established, the division of labour between family members is, within limits, *notably* different than in the other classes. Despite the growth of the servant problem, the family is assisted, normally, by hired help and the best of domestic labour-saving devices. The boys, as always, are exempted from household chores. The girls are exempted to a lesser extent, but more so than girls in any other class. Despite the fact that the discrepancy has *notably* diminished in the last thirty years, the managerial wife *generally* has more outside activities and decidedly more recreational outlets than the wives in other classes, although she still lags far behind her husband in this respect. Furthermore, as we have remarked, the managerial husband has a larger share in the financial affairs and decisions of the family than in the other classes. For all of these reasons, in the managerial class the ideal of equality between husband and wife comes closest, perhaps, to practical realization. And yet, as far as the sphere of domestic responsibilities goes, an analysis of the routines of the wife reveals that in the ordinary management of the family's affairs, in the disciplining of the children and, though to a

217

lesser extent, in the representation of the family to the general community, the managerial wife, as much as the wives of other classes, has much greater obligations than her husband.

Although the relationship between parents and children in this class has undergone as radical a change as in any other class, there are certain *notable* differences between managerial people and the people on other class levels. In the managerial families, there is more supervision of the activities of children when they are young. Movie-going and play with neighbourhood children are more restricted; parental control over the children's peer group associations is greater; and in mid-adolescence the 'trouble' that parents fear the children, especially boys, may get into is of a more sophisticated sort than in the other classes. During their children's adolescence managerial parents, in contrast to artisan parents, are *notably* less inclined to fear romantic entanglements for their daughters than similar entanglements for their sons. Consequently they are more of a mind, at least relatively, to grant to the girls at this age as much freedom as to the boys. In short, the demands made upon children in this class, if lesser in regard to supporting the family and forgoing educational opportunities, are much greater in regard to maintaining the class standards of the family, which in themselves are considered sufficient compensation for this greater demand.

It goes without saying that the educational standards held up for managerial children are higher than those required for children of any other class. Children of both sexes receive a full secondary education, many of them at expensive and exclusive boarding schools. This is *general*, and the children have virtually no choice in the matter. University education for the boys and, to a lesser extent, for the girls is virtually *prevalent*. Furthermore, the range of choice in regard to occupation, at least for the boys, is narrower than it is in the other classes.

Parental pressure on sons to choose an occupation compatible with their class standing is strong and commonly takes the form of pressure, especially on the oldest sons, to succeed the father in his business or profession. While, therefore, by comparison with sons in other classes, the sons of managerial families in early adolescence may have less intimate contact with their fathers than artisan boys, the older sons especially have the advantages of intimate personal and technical direction from their fathers in the field of their life's work. On the other hand, between mother and daughter in the managerial class the relationship is much like the one that prevails in the other classes. Even though this relationship is likely to be somewhat attenuated by the daughters' attendance at boarding schools, on the whole the managerial mother, both in regard to broad, humanistic matters and

218

in regard to the specific role of housewife, is the major model for her daughters.

In religious observance and practice the managerial family is not *notably* different in any way from people in the artisan class except that, because of a higher level of education, they have more extensive knowledge in this matter. Nevertheless, religious education for these people stops at the secondary level and those who go to the University do not receive an intellectual training in religion that is in any way comparable to their training in other fields.[21] The fear of an intellectual approach to religion is at least an *alternate* among adults in this class and, as we have seen, this fear receives more explicit expression. On the other hand, criticism of the clergy is also more widespread. One man said, 'there is hardly a night when we have friends in that sometime or other during the evening the conversation does not turn on the clergy and becomes a bit anti-clerical'.

Yet the managerial family has much more frequent and closer contact with the cloth than any other class. While its relationship to the parish is much the same as that of the artisan family, greater organizational activity brings them together. Furthermore, the remark of one wife is almost literally true: 'There is scarcely a family that hasn't a priest or religious in it somewhere.' Managerial people quite commonly acknowledge that their more relaxed attitude towards business activity stems from their religious outlook on life. In the words of one husband: 'I think we Irish are quite different from the English and the Americans. The ones I've met seem to me to be wrapped up in the almighty pound or dollar. I've dealt with many Englishmen and my impression is that money and what it brings are their God. But we cannot get as concerned as they over business and material things. We are less active in these matters because always in the background of our minds we are concerned with a more fundamental philosophy.'

But if religion has a restraining effect upon business activity, its positive influence on the conduct of business and political affairs is not great. The *prevalent* opinion among managerial people is well expressed by one of them:

It is amazing how people can divide their lives into two sectors in one of which religion has little or no influence. I would say that generally in business matters here, although the people are Catholic, their faith has a very limited influence on their actions. It does not, for example, influence their decisions in business. You just don't seem to think about it much and you don't feel that it should be a decisive factor in any policy you might follow. It is extraordinarily true, and exceptionally

21 *v.* ch. ii, pp. 44–5, 63.

sad, that Catholics to a great extent can be very good Catholics in their private lives and in everything that does not involve business, but when that comes in their Catholicity wanes rapidly.

The relationship of the managerial family to the greater community is *notably* different from that of any of the other classes. The basis for this, of course, is the relation in which the family stands to the organization that is the source of its income and livelihood. The difference lies not in the fact of dependence upon such an organization, which is common to all urban Dubliners, but in the mode and degree of dependence. In the other classes without exception, the father is in a subordinate capacity in the concern or, in the case of civil servants, in the department, and because of this fact, the family as a group has very limited control over the organization in regard to matters that may affect it vitally. What control it has, furthermore, is largely indirect and is exerted through other organizations such as unions and the government where again family influence is restricted. In the managerial family, on the other hand, the father is in the position of command. His control is, of course, subject to the objective requirements of his business or professional practice for survival in a competitive economy. But within these limits he has a wide range of autonomy and through him the nuclear family as a group can and does exert direct influence upon the concern for its own interests. Indeed, because of the linking of the concern or practice with other concerns, it can bring similar influence to bear upon other organizations on the same high level. What we have seen about the policy of parents in regard to inheritance and the occupational careers of their children, as well as the charges of nepotism we have heard from people in other classes, are largely the effect of this relationship.

At the same time, the position of the father in the occupational world has other effects that expand the ties of the managerial family to the wider community. These are *notably* the social obligations attendant upon business and the professions. Even though the Irish may separate business and friendship more than people of other nationalities, these obligations bring the managerial family into contact, and often close contact, with other families to a far greater extent than on other class levels. Furthermore, by cultural definition, the family's position entails greater civic obligations that are reflected in the more widespread membership of managerial adults in charitable, cultural and political organizations.

As a result, the tendency we have noted in the clerical family to have a greater number of family friends than the artisans, is *notably* more pronounced in the managerial class. To a far greater extent than among clerical families, this circle of family friends is homogeneous in its class composition. To a greater extent, too, this circle tends to be a real group in which not only contacts between individual families, but collective gatherings of families are more frequent. Thus, although reports indicate that it is dying out, it is still a common practice for families in this class to have an 'open house' on Saturday or Sunday evening when any or all of the friends of the family may drop in. When allowances are made for the effects of class upon the type of activities in which people engage, however, the sentiments and the kind of co-operation that prevail between these families on the managerial level is much the same as it is among the other classes. Even the sanctions they mutually impose on each other are similar, though managerial people have a tendency to be more restrained in this matter.

Interaction among families on a neighbourhood basis, however, is as much, if not more restricted in this class than in the clerical class, and here the distinction between new neighbourhoods and old makes little or no difference. All of our families live in well-established neighbourhoods and two children from these families live in new neighbourhoods. Uniformly, all report that the relationships they have with their neighbours are restrained and quite formal. They commonly speak of a few formal invitations to visit the neighbours after they had been in the neighbourhood for a considerable length of time. Even the younger children play little with neighbourhood children, the peer group here being mainly composed of school mates, relatives and children of family friends. Except where such friends happen to live in the same neighbourhood, neighbourhood families in this class *generally* 'keep a respectful distance'.

The ties of kinship do not vary *notably* in kind among managerial families from the *general* pattern we have encountered in every other class, but they tend to be somewhat stronger. This is partly due to the fact that the managerial people *generally* command more effective means of communication. *Notably*, this makes contact with relatives in the country more frequent than in the other classes. It is also due to class considerations, however, for association with the families of relatives gives a warrant, particularly where the children are concerned, that they will associate with the proper type of people. Furthermore, as is evident from the patterns of inheritance current in the managerial class, common business interests and the social activities they entail make interfamilial interaction between kin a necessity. To the families of kin, especially of siblings but also of those further removed, one can well apply the description of one managerial husband speaking of his natal family: 'The family is the rock upon which all of life is based. That was our fundamental philosophy.'

The class differences in the family life of the New Dubliners, then, are many. Yet, surely, the judicious eye can discern beneath the differences a wide range of similarity on all class levels in the internal structure of family relations and in the family's relations to the larger community. We are, therefore, now in a position to bring this fundamental and common structure into focus and, by comparing it with the basic structure of the rural family, to appreciate more fully the effects of urbanization upon the structure of family life in Ireland.

Chapter VII

THE IMPACT OF URBANIZATION

THE CONCRETE AND OFTEN COLOURFUL details of life we have observed among the New Dubliners reveal the results of urbanization in Ireland. People who migrate from the countryside to the city change. They reorganize their lives, modify their behaviour, sentiments and values, and thus adapt themselves to the new and distinctive urban way of life. On the family level these changes are complex and pervasive, touching not only the structure of relationships between members of the nuclear family itself, but also the relationships that the family as a group has with other groups in the community. But this process, though complicated, is clearly not a haphazard one. A high degree of recurrence is observable in the patterns of change that have taken place in family relations within the span of two generations. Regular changes in one sphere of the New Dubliners' family life have quite consistently resulted in regular changes in other spheres so that the total design of the New Dubliners' family is clearly different from that of the countryman's family. In short, urbanization produces in the family systematic and ordered changes which we must now analyse. But certain basic theoretical notions have conditioned both our observation and the preceding description of family life in Ireland, and will govern our analysis. So we will first examine this conceptual framework and then present our conclusions.

THE THEORETICAL FRAMEWORK

The first concept is that of a social system. The idea of system has been current in the social as well as in the physical sciences to such an extent that it needs no further elaboration here.[1] But it is pertinent

[1] *v.* George C. Homans, *The Human Group* (London and New York, 1950), chs. 4–6 and *Social Behaviour, Its Elementary Forms* (London and New York, 1961), pp. 8–11; Talcott Parsons, *The Social System*, pp. 3–36; Pitirim A. Sorokin, *Social and Cultural Dynamics* (4 vols., New York, 1937–41), I, ch. 1; Nicholas S. Timasheff, *Sociological Theory, Its Nature and Growth* (rev. ed.; New York, 1957), chs. 17, 18, pp. 304–5.

to point out that a *social* system such as the New Dubliners' family—or any other human group we have encountered in Dublin—has essential properties that make it a specifically different kind of system from any physical system whatsoever. The behaviour and the attitudes of the Dubliners we have studied show that they are persons endowed with intelligence, and powers of abstraction and reflection. These penetrate and condition all their sensory perceptions and feelings, as their intelligence and reason in turn are drenched and conditioned by sensation and emotion. Because of this radical capacity they are capable of symbolic expression and they have, within limits, powers of volition, choice, creativity. As a result, they can construct between themselves sets of relationships that are subjectively meaningful to themselves and, in good part, willed by them. In short, precisely because of their distinctively human mental life with which we have become acquainted, the systematic relationships that exist between them are meaningfully and creatively interpersonal, and this makes them specifically different in kind from any of the systematic relationships that exist between things below the human level. This, of course, is true not only of the family, but of the Dublin community as a whole. This community, which constitutes the immediate environment of the New Dubliners' family, is a social and cultural reality because it is the work of men interacting meaningfully and wilfully in this fashion.

All this is evident even from those *general* practices about which we find nearly unbroken conformity among the New Dubliners. As their comments on such matters indicate, the New Dubliners have a rationale for such behaviour. More significantly, they are concerned with transmitting that rationale to their children and giving them strong motivation to conform to these norms, for they appreciate that conformity demands effort and to that extent is subjectively a dynamic habit.

But the meaningful and volitional nature of the relationships we are studying is even more clearly demonstrated by the many practices of the New Dubliners which are *alternative* or *prevalent*. These are the result of varying definitions and responses which different people make to a social situation which is objectively the same for all of them. To take but one example, parents in the artisan class with virtually the same background, income, and number of children have divergent policies in regard to the secondary education of their sons. A few practically force their sons to work immediately after they complete primary school. A few more, like the Dunns, leave the decision ultimately to the son but exert strong persuasive influence upon him to complete secondary school and even to proceed to the university. Most artisan parents, however, simply let the boy decide for himself without putting positive pressure on him to continue his education. Similar differences of policy exist between these families in regard to a boy's choice of occupation; the social sanctions the family will or will not impose upon delinquent neighbours; the pre-marital attitudes and behaviour of men towards women, etc. In a wide range of matters, there not only is no rigidly fixed response to their common social environment but, as their explanations of their conduct make clear, their policies in such cases spring from meaningful appraisals of their environment and active decisions in regard to it. Here their responses are creative. And some of them may be true innovations which through acceptance will in time become common practices and produce significant changes in the family in Dublin. For this reason, although our central concern has been with behaviour that has become institutionalized, we have been vitally interested in behaviour below the institutional level that may be pregnant with the future.[2]

The social nature of the groups we are examining is the basis for further analytical distinctions which undergird this study. First, precisely because of the specific characteristics just mentioned, families as well as other types of groups in Dublin are not limited to root needs over which they have no control, but have the capacity in some measure to expand these ends beyond the requirements of sheer necessity. Even the many families in Dublin which are barely able to maintain themselves at the subsistence level are not content with mere survival. They conceive, desire and in some measure achieve things that enrich them and foster the good life, however modestly. The struggle is not merely to survive but to survive at a given level.[3] These higher goods, of course, include material things which we may call welfare values. But, partly because they profoundly influence the determination of such welfare values, the order of goods and values which we have called ideological also have crucial importance.

This leads us to distinguish in group life between the level of ideological values, and the level of organization and organizational values.[4] It is obvious that to survive and attain some higher standard

[2] Homans calls such behaviour subinstitutional and very perceptively discusses the relationship between it and institutional behaviour. *Social Behaviour*, p. 6, and ch. 13.

[3] *v.* Homans, *The Human Group*, pp. 108–10.

[4] Cf. John Thomas, SJ, 'The Catholic Family in a Complex Society', *Social Order*, IV, No. 10 (December 1954), 451–7. Values, as we conceive them, are things—objects, persons, relationships—towards which a person has an observable emotional orientation because he considers them in some way good or bad, and by no means just morally good or bad. Values and sentiments are correlative. The term 'value' stresses the cognitive, meaningful content of that which is emotionally felt as sentiment. This definition abstracts entirely from the source of this cognition and from all its other qualities except that it is evaluative of goodness or badness and is accompanied by an emotional reaction. Values are

of life, order is a prime necessity and hence a group must organize its activities and interaction into standardized and integrated patterns. It is equally obvious that the members of the group must entertain those sentiments and values which are necessary for the maintenance and functioning of that organization. There are innumerable instances of this direct connection between organization and such organizational values in our data on the New Dubliners. None more graphically illustrate it than the sentiments of equality and partnership between husband and wife, and the greater freedom and initiative that is given to youth in the family as well as in the business world, both of which contrast sharply with the attitudes of the country folk in these matters. Equality between husband and wife in Dublin is a value because in the economic organization of the family the husband's occupation away from home has lessened his authority over domestic affairs and thereby has understandably increased his wife's authority and freedom of action and decision. In like fashion, the organizational structure of Dublin's business concerns in a competitive situation perforce puts a high premium on youthful initiative and achievement, and in response to this the family in Dublin has modified its organization in definite ways.

But alongside this level of organization, there exists another level of goods and values which are basically ideological. These are the fundamental beliefs and convictions that people entertain about the nature of the universe and of man and his place in it. They are rarely formally reasoned among a people, but still they are ideas accepted as being true definitions of reality and, as such, the basis for evaluating reality. Such values are, therefore, not primarily instrumentalities for organization, but rather ends in themselves. They in their turn modify group organization profoundly since the organization of a group and, indeed, of society as a whole is in good part structured to secure these ends. The struggle is not only to survive at a given level but to achieve certain ideals.[5]

thus emotionally toned convictions, whether these convictions be objectively verifiable or purely subjective; whether they be intuitive or reasoned on common sense, scientific or philosophic grounds, or accepted by faith in divine or human authority; whether they exist on the conscious level or on the level of the unconscious.

[5] In making the distinction between the organizational and the ideological level, and particularly in studying their interrelationships, I have been influenced by Homans's discussion of the 'external' and the 'internal' systems. But these are not the same. The organizational level includes some of the elaborations that comprise the internal system. And the ideological level, while including certain elaborations of this sort, contains ultimate and religious ideas and values which have some range of force independent of the external system. Homans seems to imply a similar distinction in his discussion of W. Lloyd Warner's technical, social and religious systems; *The Human Group*, p. 129. Cf. Leslie A. White, *The Science of Culture* (New York, 1949), pp. 364–5.

The complete organization of any group is the result of the mutual relationship between sheer organizational demand and those ideological values which set up the ideals and style of the entire social life. Thus the Irish urban family has the same organizational needs as the urban family elsewhere in the industrialized West, and so in radical respects it is like the urban family in industrialized centres elsewhere. A family in Coventry or in Los Angeles would easily recognize its counterpart in the families of the New Dubliners we have met. But because of its own characteristic ideological values, the urban family in Dublin observably differs in other important features from the urban family in other industrial cultures. The Irish religious conception of the purposes of human existence; the premium it places on religious, particularly sacramental, activity; the tempered importance it attaches to business activity as a result; the strong code of sexual morality bearing on pre-marital relations; and the mode of family limitation and the manner of dealing with irreconcilable conflicts between spouses—all these ideological elements clearly affect its organization and distinguish the typical Irish urban family from typical urban families in societies where different ideological values prevail.

This integration of sheer organizational needs and values with values that rest on ideological grounds constitutes the objective purpose of the group—that is, the goal towards which the co-ordinated activities of the group are demonstrably directed, whatever be the subjective interpretations of individual group members about the nature of that goal or their subjective motives in striving for that goal through group participation.[6] As this objective purpose is the central factor which determines the group's total organization, so it is also the decisive element which differentiates groups in a given community. In our view, the same system of ideological values is almost universally accepted by all the component groups in Irish society, and the main source of differentiation between them lies in their objective organizational purposes. On the basis of these organizational purposes we can distinguish in both the rural and the urban community *familial organizations* and *non-familial organizations*.

Modern discussions of the organizational purpose of the modern urban family claim that it has changed radically under the impact of industrialization. The extent to which this is true is a subject of investigation in the present study to which we shall return shortly. But about the organizational purpose of the family as it is found in primitive society and in advanced rural society, and as it existed in urban society at least until the advent of industrialization, there is

[6] *v.* Chester I. Bernard, *The Functions of the Executive* (Harvard, 1947), pp. 86–9.

227

general anthropological and sociological agreement. In non-industrial society everywhere the objective functions of the family 'are commonly held to be seven: (1) reproduction of the population; (2) protection and care of the child; (3) economic production of family goods and services; (4) socialization of the child; (5) education of the child; (6) recreation; and (7) affectional interaction.'[7] From these stem the distinctive organizational features of the family: its division of activities on the basis of age and sex, the co-ordination of activities through parental authority, the existence of a regular family cycle and of personal, particularistic and diffuse relationships between family members. From these also there arise the ban against incest and its extension with the resulting formation of the kinship system.[8] Through ties of kinship and those stemming from other sources such as neighbourliness, congeniality, etc., nuclear families formally and informally co-ordinate to form larger organizations that are also familial in character. Such organizations not only seek to secure and foster the organization, the ideals and values of the individual nuclear families comprising them, but they model their organization on the same broad principles as the nuclear family itself and incorporate a similar division of activities by age and sex, as well as similar types of relationship and modes of social control.

In contrast to these familial groups, there exist in the rural as well as in the urban community groups whose objective purposes, whether relatively simple or complex, clearly differ from those of familial organizations. They therefore operate on quite different organizational principles. The purposes of these groups—the government, business enterprises, the church, schools, etc.—are so diverse that it is difficult to subsume them under one positive term. It is more convenient for our purposes to refer to them as non-familial organizations. Though the term is negative, the major features such organizations have in common are positive. Generally speaking, all these organizations have as their function the production of goods or services according to the rational canon of efficiency we have discussed in the first chapter, and hence possess a bureaucratic form of organization with the impersonal, universalistic relations characteristic of it. In industrialized society the primary locations of such organizations, of course, are urban areas where co-ordination between them gives rise to the extremely large non-familial organizations that make up the occupational complex of the city.

These concepts of familial and non-familial organization, obviously, are ideal types. In reality there is much penetration and

[7] Howard Becker and Reuben Hill (eds.), *Family, Marriage, and Parenthood* (2nd ed.; Boston, 1955), p. 47.
[8] George P. Murdock, *Social Structure* (New York, 1949), pp. 41–2, and ch. 10.

modification of one type by another. This is evident from the importance of non-familial organizations in determining the class status of
the family and in providing favourable marital opportunities for
women, as well as from the reports we have of nepotism in business,
the unions and government in Dublin. Indeed, the changes that have
occurred in family life as a result of urbanization are largely the
result of the interplay between these types of organization.

All these properties, which are characteristic of the family and
other groups as social systems, impose certain requirements upon the
analysis of the changes urbanization produces in family life. Because
the elements that make up these groups are systematically inter-
dependent, variation in one or more of the parts or in their relationships always results in some degree of variation in all the parts and
in their whole interrelationship. Change in family structure, as in any
other system, is therefore total change in the sense that all the com-
ponents of family life are somehow affected by it. Such systematic
change, however, is not a simple substitution of one thing for another.
Rather, it is a continuous process involving a unit that in some
manner or degree persists in the passage from one state to another
state. In this process, some of the original elements endure, even
though in the end the entire pattern is new. Furthermore, change in
any social group has points at which it starts and from which it
proceeds in some sort of order throughout the whole system. The
starting points of change may be predominantly in the environment
outside the group to which the group responds in observable ways.
On the other hand, they may be developments originating mainly
within the system itself that occur while the external environment is
relatively constant. Or finally they may be a simultaneous combination of such environmental and immanent changes.

As a result, there are three essential steps that we must take in the
analysis of changes that, as in the present case, occur in a given
family system during a definite period of time. First, we need to
identify all the essential variables in the environment and in the
family system and to understand how they are related to each other
at the moment before the change begins. Since at that moment the
particular state of a social system is inevitably the result of previous
changes it has undergone, we must know the fundamentals of its
historical development. That is why the condensed history of Irish
society during the last one hundred and fifty years is so important for
our analysis. Second, we must not only determine what elements and
relationships in the family and its environment alter in the course of
the transition from the rural to the urban community, but what do
not. When change has run its course the *whole* family system is
something new, but it is imperative to understand to what extent the

new whole is a combination of the new and the old. Finally, in order to understand how the family system changes and thus to understand why it changes, it is necessary that we fix the starting points of change and from these trace the progression of change throughout the whole family network. We have to spot the features in the urban environment that most profoundly affect family life, and at the same time to determine the areas in its life which the family first alters and which lead it to make subsequent alterations in other spheres of living.

In trying to ascertain the effects of urbanization upon the Irish family, then, we are confronted with three basic questions. In the transition from the rural to the urban community, what in family life remains the same? What changes and what is the new pattern of family life as a whole? What are the particularly crucial areas in the environment and in the family itself where change starts, and how do changes in these areas account for changes in other spheres of family life?

CONCLUSIONS

Let us answer these questions in summary fashion now, and then proceed to substantiate our argument. In Ireland urbanization involves a move from a community that is relatively stable and in which power is centred in the family and in familial organizations to a rapidly changing community wherein power is centred in non-familial organizations. It also effects a transition from a community where a single, traditional ideology holds virtually unquestioned sway to one in which people are brought into more direct contact with other divergent ideologies. The changes that occur in the structure of the family and in its relations to other familial organizations start simultaneously and, to a certain extent, independently in both the area of organization and the realm of ideological values. But the ideological changes and the effect they have upon family organization are in general very small and secondary in Dublin. The major and primary changes take place directly in the organization and the organizational values of the family and of the major familial groups as a result of the impact of non-familial organizations upon the whole family system. The starting point of this change lies in the manner in which the family must make its livelihood in Dublin due to the economic and occupational organization of the city. The transformation we observe in the family of the New Dubliners is thus mainly the result of an adjustment on the level of organization rather than the effect of any profound ideological shift.

These organizational adjustments in family structure do not destroy the basic objective purpose, or with one exception, the traditional functions of the family, but they modify them in many ways. They come about through four crucial processes that constantly centralize power in the large non-familial organizations of Dublin. These are: (1) the concentration of the ownership and management of productive property and activity in the hands of the relatively few individuals who control the major corporations of the city; (2) the concomitant geographic concentration of productive facilities and services and of the labour force in the central urban area; (3) the bureaucratic structure of the non-familial organizations themselves; and (4) the multiplication of class levels due to the increase in occupational differentials, and the increase in social mobility which largely results from occupational mobility. Simultaneously, four parallel processes operate within the urban family which account for its decline in power: (1) the loss not only of ownership but also of control over productive property and activity, so that the nuclear family is no longer a collective, domestic unit of economic production; (2) the consequent decline in its capacity to act as a unit in other, non-economic respects; (3) the individualization and dispersal of the activities outside of the family group; and (4) the decline of interfamilial solidarity which produces increased dependence, economic and otherwise, of the family on non-familial organizations.

The greater ideological diversity in Dublin as compared to rural areas is clear enough. The New Dubliners' activities and the reports they have made on their life in the city clearly indicate the many channels through which, in differing degrees according to their class status, they come into contact with various ideologies of the Western world and particularly with modern secularism. In business and, to some extent, in union activities they associate with people from other countries, especially from England. English and American newspapers and magazines are quite common in Dublin. *The Irish Times,* a powerful journalistic voice, is owned and edited by members of the former Ascendancy and often expresses disagreement with ideas and values that are traditionally Irish Catholic. The New Dubliners are avid movie-goers and, like all Dubliners, have a notable love for the theatre. Irish censorship is not completely effective and the literature of the West pours into Dublin from abroad. Indeed, New Dubliners of the clerical as well as the managerial class frequently travel in England and on the continent. Moreover, not only is education generally more extensive in Dublin than in the rural community, but from the intellectual activity that goes on in University College, Dublin, and in Trinity College ideas seep more widely and deeply into the city at large than into the rural community. Through these many agencies and associations the New Dubliners have become more intimately acquainted than the countryman with views of life that are quite different from, and often in open conflict with, the traditional Irish Catholic concept of life.

But continuing contact with such ideas, as well as engagement in a rationally organized economy, has not brought about any profound transformation in the ideology of New Dubliners which remains substantially the same as the countryman's. It is true that in the midst of this clash of ideas New Dubliners show some tendency to modify certain views and attitudes that are Augustinian, and perhaps even peculiar to Irish Catholicism, and to replace them with views that are more consistent with other theologically orthodox Catholic positions. The most marked alteration is the development of a more informed and reasoned orientation to ideological values that the rural folk accept almost wholly on traditional grounds. This is particularly evident from the increased emphasis New Dubliners place upon reason rather than upon force in the socialization of their children, and in their treatment of sexual instruction. It is also the basis of their increased questioning and critical appraisal of the clergy.

Religious activity seems also to be more individualized in the city than in the rural community. The New Dubliners report that collective family devotions characteristic of the rural family, especially the daily family recitation of the Rosary, have declined in the city. They also attend religious services individually more often than as family groups. On the other hand, they avail themselves of the easy access to church that the city provides, and probably more frequently receive the Sacraments and attend Mass and other church devotions than the members of the rural family.

It is thus quite clear that as a result of urbanization ideological changes are relatively few. The ideological continuity between New Dubliners and the countryman is striking. Their religious behaviour and their participation in various religious organizations give strong testimony to the great value they place on supernatural grace and sacramental activity and this is buttressed by their expressed views and sentiments. The emergence of a more inquiring approach to religious truth, while discernible, significant and apparently increasing, is still slight. Nevertheless, criticism of the clergy largely concerns their economic and administrative policies and rarely their doctrinal statements. The New Dubliners, as we have seen, still voice a strong fear of a positive intellectual orientation to religious truths because they feel it may lead to complete rationalism. Though more open than the countryman on the subject of sex, they too feel that sex is somehow evil and suspect. And like the countryman, though to a lesser degree, they still incline to give the sphere of private morality priority over that of civic and public morality.

On the other hand, the evidence that urbanization produces its major transformations in the family on the level of organization is overwhelming. Critically important here are the great and relatively rapid changes in the organization of the community as a whole that have been going on in Dublin since 1922. As our historical study of the city has revealed, the change in Dublin consists in its political transition from a provincial city to a national capital; in its economic development from a predominantly commercial centre to an industrial metropolis; and in the rapid expansion of its population and of its geographical territory. This has produced the increase and centralization in Dublin of relatively large government agencies and business concerns that in technical equipment, in organization, and in the employment, even on the staff level, of female as well as male personnel, are modern, though not always the very latest models. It has also brought to the city an expansion of modern communication and trade on an international scale.

This continuing change in the city's character accounts for one important universal effect of urbanization upon family life. Migration from the country to the city in Ireland, as elsewhere, is not a transition from one stable community to another that, although structurally different, is equally as stable and subject only to slow change. On the contrary, it is a transition into a community that by comparison with the rural community, is in a state of relatively rapid flux. Involvement in a rapidly changing community is part and parcel of the process of urbanization, and one of its prime effects is to produce as a constant feature of the urban family a higher degree of adaptability than is to be found in the rural family. This greater adaptability of the urban family is clearly demonstrated by the fact that between the present generation of spouses who are New Dubliners and the generation of their immigrant parents—that is, precisely during the period when widespread political, economic and demographic changes were occurring—great changes have also occurred in the structure of family life in Dublin, while during the same period the rural community and the structure of the rural family have remained relatively the same.[9] Although we have limited the description of these intergenerational

[9] This is not to say that the rural community is completely stagnant and altogether impervious to change. But changes that have occurred there have been either the results of processes that have been going on there for the last century, such as continued depopulation; or counter changes, such as rural electrification, increased land reclamation, etc., that at the time this study was made had not yet affected the internal structure of the rural family and community which was basically the same as it was when Arensberg and Kimball described it twenty years before. In three months of field work in rural areas of four western counties I could find virtually no change in family structure. And this is confirmed by the statistics which show that Irish agricultural productivity did not appreciably improve during the middle quarter of the century, and which indicate the continued high incidence of depopulation, celibacy and late marriage.

changes to the artisan family for reasons of space, they have taken place, as we have noted from time to time, in families of every class to about the same degree and always in the same direction.

In addition, the indications are that the changes occurring in this period have affected the families of all Dubliners regardless of their generational distance from the country. It is notable that no one in Dublin clearly distinguishes between New Dubliners and other Dubliners. Some sense of difference is felt on both sides between immigrants and Dubliners, though it is much less marked now than earlier in the century. Aside from this, there is little feeling of distinction between Dubliners based on the length of time their family has lived in the city. New Dubliners certainly do not think of themselves as *New* Dubliners, much less associate as real groups on this basis, and the absence of such a feeling in itself is one measure of the degree to which they have been urbanized. On the other hand, people interviewed who were old enough to recall life in Dublin before 1935 reported a very great difference between the contemporary Dublin family and the family as it was when they were children. According to their evidence, the change in family life has affected all Dubliners so that the differences existing at present between an Old Dubliner family and even an immigrant family are far less than those to be found between an Old Dubliner's family today and an Old Dubliner's family a quarter of a century ago. Therefore, the rapid change in family structure and in the relations of the family to the larger community is a function of the latest phase of Dublin's evolution as a city. It is itself a primary effect of urbanization and is obviously mainly organizational in character.

But in the midst of all this change there is a radical continuity between the general pattern of the family in Dublin and the rural community that it would be fatal to overlook. From an anthropological point of view, the family in the course of urbanization clearly has retained most of its major traits. One very significant exception to this statement relates to residential practice. Where the Irish rural family is generally patrilocal, the family of the New Dubliners is normally neo-local. But for the rest, among the New Dubliners the family continues to be, like the Irish rural family and the family throughout Western Europe and America, monogamous, independent and bilateral (or multilineal) in matters of descent, and it continues to express kinship relations according to the system of terminology that is common to peoples of Western European culture.[10]

[10] *v.* Arensberg and Kimball, op. cit., pp. 80, 97. Technically, this system of terminology has been designated as the Eskimo system by G. P. Murdock. Among anthropologists terminology in regard to these matters often differs. Rather than attempt to reconcile these differences, I have followed one authority and used

The Impact of Urbanization

One might well conclude from this that the internal structure of the family in Ireland retains most of its basic features and functions in the city, and the New Dubliners' behaviour clearly substantiates this inference. Their definitions of behaviour that is properly male and female, of the roles of father, mother and children, and of the obligations of filial piety show that the urban family retains all but one of the main functions of the rural family, and that its division of activities has an essential similarity to that of the rural community in form, and to a considerable extent in content. In the economic sphere, the urban family continues to be a major unit of economic services, exchange and consumption. It continues to perform its essential functions of the reproduction, care and socialization of children and of providing secure affection. And while non-familial organizations have greater influence on the education and especially on the recreational activities of the children in Dublin than in the countryside, the Dublin family still plays a most crucial role in both of these areas.

Yet the changes that do occur around this central core of enduring elements produce a significant variation in this common family system. Within the family itself as it reacts to the urban environment the starting point of change occurs in the organization of those activities whereby the family makes its livelihood. The change that takes place in this sphere is the first and most radical adjustment that people must make in family life when they come to Dublin from the countryside, and it triggers a chain reaction of adjustments that affect the entire internal organization of the family. For the loss of the family's function as a collective unit of economic production causes a significant alteration in the form of organization whereby it fulfils its remaining economic and non-economic functions, and it abolishes the virtual monopoly the rural family and familial organizations have in these latter respects.

The loss by the family, as a unit, of control over activities that produce income, and the resultant individualization and dispersal of these activities throughout the urban community, is almost universal among the New Dubliners. The one apparent exception to this statement is families in the managerial class, and they are exceptional only to the extent that they retain a greater degree of direct control over the non-domestic economic activity that is the main source of family income. Whereas families in other classes do not own property requisite for production, utilities or services, the managerial family or some member of it usually does. In this respect the managerial family

Murdock's terms for the sake of consistency. *v.* Murdock, op. cit., pp. 1–3, 14–17, 96–100, 223–8. The suggested substitution of 'multilineal' for 'bilateral' in describing principles of descent is Parsons' *v.* Parsons, *Essays in Sociological Theory*, pp. 178, 184.

approximates the rural family. But in all other respects its economic organization differs from the rural family and is like urban families of other classes. For it does not work its productive property as a group, and the activities of its members which produce income take place outside of the home in separate enterprises or in separate sectors of the same enterprise. In all classes, therefore, activity productive of income, no longer domestic and collective in character, becomes individualized in the sense that it is subject to the individual's choice, depends for its successful performance upon the responsibility of the individual rather than upon that of the family group, and usually is performed in separation from other family members.

The effect of this upon the form of family organization on every class level is twofold. First of all, it splits off activities which produce income from others that are essential to the family's well-being. In all of our urban families the father works separately, away from home. He cannot therefore contribute as much or as effectively as the farmer working on the homestead to other domestic activities such as the management of the household, domestic service, and the socialization of the children—all of which are concomitant and interwoven with productive activity in the farm family. The second effect, stemming directly from the preceding, is a change in the age-sex division of direct family labour and responsibility. While age and sex remain as the major basis of this division in all the families of the New Dubliners, the traditional balance between the sexes, characteristic of the rural family, is upset in the city. The greater share of direct domestic responsibility and labour falls upon the wife rather than the husband, and generally upon the women rather than the men. At the same time, a marked decline takes place in parental power and in the power of the aged in general.

The first chapter of this book has described this shift in the sexual division of labour and in the range of parental control. The data we have subsequently presented on the New Dubliners not only confirm what we said there but afford us even deeper insight into that transformation. The change in the sexual division of labour is verified by the fact that, while unmarried women in the family of the New Dubliners may be engaged in the same general occupations as men, unlike the rural wife none of the wives in these families participated directly in activities that produce income. But in regard to all other activities the change that occurs is in the opposite direction. Economically, the family's exchange activities which are more or less equally shared by the rural husband and wife, and the management of the rural family budget by the husband, become in great measure the urban wife's responsibility. This is true even in the managerial family. However, here again the fact that the husband in this class tends to retain a larger share of control over family finances corroborates the interconnection between the division of labour and the family's relationship to productive activities. The managerial family is somewhat closer to the rural family in the first respect because, by reason of its more direct control over productive activities, it resembles the rural family a little more in the second respect.

The increase of the responsibilities of the urban wife is even more convincingly apparent in the non-economic activities of the family, particularly those relating to the socialization of the children. In every family among the New Dubliners, the ability of the father to act as an effective role model for his sons either in technical or in broad humanistic matters has clearly declined mainly because his occupational activity normally separates him from his sons for the greater part of the day. This is confirmed, as it is intensified, by the increasing tendency for all sons to receive their specialized training from the school and usually, even where they succeed to their father's business or profession, from experienced men in the field other than their father; and by the entrance of the sons into occupations that differ from their fathers.[11] But perhaps its most significant effect is the much greater authority the urban wife must exercise over all her children than the rural wife. Where the rural husband and wife, especially after the children's infancy, equally share the responsibility of training the children, in the urban family of every class the greater portion of this responsibility observably devolves upon the mother. We have seen the ambivalent position in which this places the mother in regard to all her children, and the particular difficulties and anxieties it causes her in the raising of her sons.

There is also evidence that despite this increase in her domestic responsibilities, the wife's status has not increased correspondingly, and that the status of the Dublin family is rated principally on the husband's occupational position, income, and factors attendant on these, while the wife's contribution tends to receive less acknowledgement. In every class the girls among the New Dubliners manifest a marked tendency to try to penetrate occupational fields that have been traditionally male, to prolong their occupational careers, and to

[11] In this connection the rural father faces a similar difficulty in regard to those of his sons who are to migrate from the land. While in the daily contact of farm life he can be a living model to his sons in a very general way, by his example he can scarcely be a guide for the behaviour that will be required of them in a social and occupational environment that is beyond his experience. This was rather poignantly expressed by one Kerry farmer who remarked: 'Ah, the place is so small that only one can have it, and the rest will have to go. And sure, it's little one can do for them, for you don't know what to tell them. You can only teach them to be good men and to be true to their faith, and hope that, if they do that, they will be all right.'

consider marriage somewhat of 'a drag'. At the same time, especially among the younger wives, there is a growing demand for greater social and recreational equality with their husbands. These developments appear to spring from dissatisfaction with the general failure of the urban community to reward a wife's role sufficiently. There also seems to be an attempt by women at once to equalize family burdens and to participate more fully in those activities upon which, according to the standards of industrial society, status is principally based.

This unbalance in respect to direct family responsibility and to the relative status of husband and wife is clearly related to the decline in the range and intensity of parental control over their children which is equally characteristic of the New Dubliners' family. The most obvious evidence of this are two statistical indices. First, even the children who are the longest delayed in achieving adulthood in their occupational careers—namely, those who go into the professions— are usually established on their own at twenty-six or twenty-seven years of age, a full ten years earlier than the average young farmer. Second, the urban children who marry latest—again the managerial-professional people of both sexes—marry about three years earlier than their rural contemporaries.[12] Now, however, we are in a position to understand the system of patterned relationships which underlie and account for these occupational and marital practices of the New Dubliners.

On every class level, the New Dubliner's family, because of the internal modifications in its mode of making a livelihood which result from its relationship to the wider Dublin community, has had to yield to non-familial organizations a far greater role in regard to the economic and recreational activities and the socialization of its children than the rural family. The clearest indication of this is the degree of freedom of choice which the New Dubliners accord their children as to schooling, occupation, association in teen-age and premarital activities and the selection of a mate. Such freedom is far greater than rural children enjoy currently and even greater than the New Dubliners themselves enjoyed in their youth in the city. This is the result of a change in the form of parental control which urban life produces. The urban family has much less support from familial organizations than the rural family in the enforcement of norms of behaviour, must impose a behavioural code that is more generalized and less specific, and must perforce adopt a mode of control that is much less authoritarian. On the one hand, particularly in later adolescence, children's associations extend far beyond the effective circle of neighbouring and kinship families with which their own family is related. Hence,

[12] *v.* Appendix I, p. 257, Table 4.

urban parents, unlike parents on the farm, cannot rely upon extensive supervision of their children from this source. On the other hand, children act in contexts with which their parents are often not intimately acquainted and which are so diverse and changeable that a host of minute rules of behaviour is impractical, if not impossible. This accounts for the concern of the New Dubliners to instil into their children a set of general norms of behaviour and for their trust that their children, acting on their own, will interpret and apply these general principles to shifting circumstances as they meet them. It likewise accounts for the decline in the use of corporal punishment among the New Dubliners, for their tendency to appeal to reason as the undergirding ground for patterns of behaviour, and in great part for the greater intimacy, confidence and more open discussion which exist between parents and children.

This change in the general mode of parental control is further substantiated by corresponding changes in the control parents exert specifically over their sons and daughters. Although, as we have seen, fathers among the New Dubliners prevalently conceive of their sons as juveniles in the practical affairs of the household, it is well to note that the sons on their side usually refuse to accept this definition. They tolerate it only in regard to minor matters, and effectively disprove it by their early independent achievements in the occupational world where all along the line they are contending on constantly more equal terms with the older generation. Neither the young men themselves nor the community at large consider that they are 'boys' until they are thirty. The attitude that they are juveniles, since it has little functional basis or justification in Dublin, is clearly in decline, a dying remnant of a social heritage from the country. By the same token, the marriage of any urban son does not disrupt the balance of the family as a productive group enterprise which is a major source of prolonged parental control in the rural family. This is undoubtedly why the urban father in regard to a son's marriage is decidedly less concerned than the farmer about the financial condition of his daughter-in-law's family; is less inclined to object to an early marriage; and, even if he should object, is less able to block it.

For the same reasons, there is obviously no longer a functional justification among the New Dubliners for the mother's preferential affection for her sons. Yet on every class level this affection is clearly still quite widespread and, in the devious ways affection can work, it has important effects in delaying the marriage of the sons. It is quite understandable that women who are New Dubliners should have absorbed this attitude from their immigrant mothers who, in their childhood, acquired it from their own mothers on the land. Since the mother-son relationship in infancy and early adolescence undergoes far less palpable change than the relationship of father to son in the city, it is also understandable that maternal affection and its restraining power upon marriage should decline less rapidly than the subordination of son to father. But ultimately its power in this latter respect also appears to be a survival of a rural pattern. This is confirmed by the fact that urban mothers have to assume a greater part in the disciplining of the sons which reduces the strength of the silver cord of affection, and by the clear evidence on all sides that the mother's affection, strong though it still may be, is more and more unable to obstruct or postpone the marriage of her sons. While maternal attitudes, therefore, may partially explain why the degree of difference between Dublin and the rural areas is not greater than it is, the pronounced statistical difference both as to the greater extent of marriage and the earlier age of marriage among men in Dublin, as well as the oral reports of the New Dubliners, attests to the decline in their power of restraint.

The effects of the basic structural change in the family upon the relationships between parents and their daughters are also noteworthy, although they are not as profound as those bearing upon the relationships of parents and sons. The mother-daughter relationship, particularly, is not subject to the same distension as that between father and son. It is true that a great many girls are now working in occupations requiring specialized training that their mothers never knew and this lessens her educational influence. But a mother can still be an effective role-model to her daughter who normally will marry and assume the same adult role as herself, and who is in a better position to observe her mother as she fulfils this role in an adult context. In like manner, the structure of the urban family does not change the affectional relationship of the daughter to her father save, perhaps, to make them even more intimate than in the rural family. Moreover, as the New Dubliners testify, parents *generally* are more fearful of premature and embarrassing romantic entanglements where girls are concerned, and they normally exert more stringent control over the girls than over the boys during later adolescence. Despite such strictures, however, the same forces within and outside the family that bear upon the boy also tend to thrust the girl into the occupational world of the urban community in an individual capacity and thus lessen and restrict her subordination to her parents at home. This accounts to a considerable extent for another major difference between rural and urban girls in their relationship to their parents and indeed to their brothers. For in regard to their marriage, girls in Dublin are no longer dependent upon the dowry that rural parents provide their daughters. This means that the average girl and her fiancé have to finance their own marriage. But a community that provides relatively great occupational opportunities for unmarried women and at the same time wide marital opportunities as well, also enables her to act more independently in respect to her marriage. In short, the structure of the urban family on the whole is such as to encourage the girls, as well as the boys, to assume adult occupational and marital roles at an earlier age than in the rural community—a benefit, especially as regards marriage, that is particularly important for girls. Despite derogatory rural opinions about girls' motives for yielding to the lure of the city, this increased freedom, coupled with enhanced marital prospects, is undoubtedly the main reason why women exceed men in the sex distribution of the Dublin population and why, except from the most depressed level of the labouring class, relatively few Dublin girls emigrate.

The decline in parental control is, by comparison with the rural family, characteristic of the families of the New Dubliners of every class but it is somewhat less marked among professional-managerial families. This appears to confirm its organizational roots. Parents in this class exert much greater pressure on their children than parents in the other classes in Dublin to pursue higher education, to seek superior occupational levels and to select mates from their own class. They supervise their children's activities and associations more closely than families of other classes and in this they receive more effective support from the greater kinship solidarity that exists between families on this level. Here a father generally has closer occupational rapport and influence over his sons who are usually expected to follow him in the professions or in business, and parents are consistently as vigilant against liaisons that are *déclassé* for the boys as they are for the girls. In considerable part, this concern and supervision stems from the desire to maintain within the family control of the productive enterprises and services which are the major basis of the family's class status, and if possible to extend it to their children's families as well. Because the managerial family in certain limited respects approximates the rural family in the manner in which it secures its livelihood, the pattern of parental control on this class level differs from the rural pattern somewhat less than it does in other classes. Still, the degree of similarity in the organization of livelihood activities between the managerial family in the city and the rural family is obviously far less than the degree of difference between them, and parental control in the managerial class tends on the whole to follow the pattern that is common to all urban families.

Along with earlier social adulthood, the structure of relationships in the urban family also permits, if it does not positively promote, a high degree of social mobility within the community. In contrast to the rural family, the absence of the need in the urban family for any

241

son to succeed to the holding and to his father's status, the possibility of neo-local residence at marriage, the decline in subordination and the consequent increase in initiative and responsibility, the financial independence of sons and especially daughters in respect to marriage —all these enable the family to respond to the opportunities and incentives for occupational and social advance that the larger Dublin community offers. This complex of factors clearly facilitates hypergamous marriage on the one hand and occupational achievement on the other, and these two procedures, as we have seen, are the avenues of advance characteristic, respectively, of women and men on all class levels.

The educational policy of the New Dubliners is largely motivated by the desire of the parents, as well as the children, to exploit one or the other of these possibilities, and this is the more significant inasmuch as secondary education in Dublin is not compulsory but voluntary. It is clear from the evidence that the ability to respond to the opportunities varies from class to class and is modified by the greater or lesser pressure of the need to survive. It is also clear that the actual response varies according to various definitions of the situation that people evolve. Making allowances for these differences, however, the general preoccupation of the New Dubliners to have their children not merely hold their own, but to advance to a higher level in the community is decidedly more marked than it is in the rural community. And this is evidence, as it is the partial result, of the fact that the structure of the urban family embodies a far higher potential for social mobility within the local community than that of the rural family.[13]

But the opportunity for social advance through occupational achievement and marriage in the city, together with the structural changes in the family which attend it, has certain paradoxical effects upon the age at marriage that are worth noting. Elsewhere in Western society the impact of urbanization on the age at marriage seems to have varied with the stages of industrialization. Until the late thirties urban populations generally tended to marry later than rural populations. Since the late thirties, however, as industrialization and urbanization have increased, the age at marriage has been lowered in general and the trend towards earlier marriage is stronger in the urban than in the rural population. This suggests that as industrialization has

[13] 'Within the local community' is an important qualification, for obviously emigration is an important road to social advance for rural people. If it be alleged that mobility within the local community is greater in the city than in the country because of the greater opportunities in the former, this is conceded. The point made here, however, is that in adapting to such a community in the sphere of livelihood, the family is constrained to alter its structure in a manner that not only makes mobility possible but actually promotes it.

advanced it has eliminated conditions in urban life which worked to delay marriage in the early industrial period. In Ireland, on the other hand, urban people of every class have consistently married earlier than their rural contemporaries throughout the first half of this century. This tendency, however, stems from circumstances peculiar to Ireland since marriage in rural Ireland, for the structural reasons we have indicated, is so extremely late that it can scarcely be maintained in the city. As a result, the national decline in the age at marriage which occurred between 1926 and 1946 is accountable largely to the decline in the rural population and the correlative increase in the urban population during the same period.

Yet the statistical data presented above show trends in the urban population that are tending to change this situation. First of all, the national trend towards later marriage which prevailed in Ireland prior to 1936 was more marked in the cities than in the country. Second, since 1936 the national trend has swung in the direction of earlier marriage but this trend has been less pronounced in the urban than in the rural population.[14] In short, urbanization in Ireland since at least 1890 has had the effect of lowering the age at marriage, but it also produced developments which tend steadily to raise the age at marriage for the urban population itself and to reduce the gap in this matter between the city and the country.

These developments may stem from the fact that industrialization in Ireland is not as advanced as it is in many other Western countries. In any case, the analysis we have made of the urban family in Dublin throws some suggestive light upon this curious inversion. The structure of the urban family facilitates earlier social adulthood and at the same time promotes greater upward social mobility. Yet the latter tends to restrict the former where marriage is concerned. Urban children are free and strongly motivated to shoulder occupational responsibilities at an earlier age than in the country and are thus sooner able to support a family and have greater autonomy in the decision to marry. But considerations of social advancement on the part of both boys and girls effectively and increasingly operate, according to the testimony of the New Dubliners, to delay marriage on all levels except among the poorer labourers. The structural change that urbanization produces in the family in Ireland therefore has effects upon marriage which are somewhat ambivalent.

The combined effect of all these changes in the internal organization of the nuclear family in Dublin, which stem for the most part from the mode in which the family organizes its livelihood activities, is to reduce the power of the individual nuclear family in relation to the community at large. At the same time these internal changes also

[14] *v.* ch. iii, pp. 76–8.

weaken the solidarity between families based upon kinship and neighbourliness, which are the cement of the rural community, and greatly reduces the power such non-familial organizations wield in the city.

Once more it is necessary to beware of exaggerating the loss of power and function in such familial organizations and to perceive the degree of continuity which exists here between the urban and rural populations. The ties of kinship and of neighbourhood that bind families together remain important in Dublin, and they retain many of the traditional functions they fulfil in the rural community. For purposes of recreation, social control and aid in times of crisis, kinship in Dublin is still a reliable bastion for the family. It also serves as a basis for economic co-operation, even though its importance in this area is notably less than in the rural community, and the forms of such co-operation necessarily differ. At the same time, relations between families living in the same neighbourhood continue to be significant sources of support in Dublin, though to a much lesser extent than those springing from kinship. On a class basis there is also much less neighbourhood co-operation between families in the managerial and clerical class than between families of the artisans and the general labourers, especially between those in the older neighbourhoods where interfamilial ties are particularly strong by urban standards.

Nevertheless, urbanization produces a decline in interfamilial solidarity founded on kinship and neighbourliness which is comparatively extensive and fraught with significant consequences. As far as kinship is concerned, the families we have studied are virtually unanimous in reporting the decline of interaction between city people and their country kin that progresses steadily as degrees of kinship become more remote until in the New Dubliners' generation it is virtually limited to an exchange of seasonal cards strung between very rare visits. This is both notable and important, but it obviously affects the countryman as well as the citizen and reflects the differentiation of two communities. It is the decreased degree of interaction between kindred in the city, common to all classes though less so in the professional-managerial class, that distinguishes the urban from the rural community. Our data reveal that the daily, and especially the regular seasonal, co-operation in productive activities and the exchange of goods and services that is widespread among rural kin is minimal in Dublin. The 'cooring' relationship so important to rural people is reduced in the city to the special co-operation that the critical events of life, such as grave sickness or death, call forth.[15] The forms of co-operation which persist are predominantly non-economic, and even these have lesser force than in the countryside. The reduced

[15] Arensberg and Kimball, op. cit., p. 75.

capacity for kinship groupings in Dublin to exercise co-ordinated control over their younger members, which we have already noted, is matched by a decline in the effective social pressure they are able to exert upon errant adults. And even visiting and recreational inter-action between kin is more limited than in the country by reason of the more extensive social obligations Dubliners have to people who are not kin.

In great part, this decline in the co-operation of kinsfolk in the city directly derives from the different relationship kindred in the city, by comparison with rural families, have to property and the different manner in which they secure their livelihood. Because families in Dublin normally do not collectively own and operate productive property, a whole host of kinship relationships that exist in the country wither away. The importance of economic co-operation as a basis for wider social co-operation in the city as well as in the country seems to be substantiated by two contrasting situations. First, kin families long resident in the old neighbourhoods, and especially those in the neighbourhoods of the general labourers, interact more fre-quently and extensively than the artisans and clerical families who live in new neighbourhoods. Prolonged residential proximity permits more extensive economic co-operation and produces it especially where there is severe economic need.[16] At the other end of the class spectrum, among the New Dubliners the managerial families, who have common interest and activities in regard to productive property, are more closely knit along kinship lines than others, probably even the general labourers. For the rest, however, the very manner in which families make their livelihood, each being dependent upon wages or salaries earned by individual members for specialized work done for an impersonal organization, radically reduces the oppor-tunity for economic co-operation in the rural style. It is significant that the greatest economic obligation of kinship in the city is not to collaborate in common economic enterprises, but to get a relative a job. In short, it is the opportunity for extensive economic co-operation that the occupational structure of the city first kills rather than the desire for it.

The density of the city's population, and the multitude of im-personal, segmental contacts and obligations this creates, compounds this segregation of kin. Class differences further tend to weaken kin-ship solidarity. Because its industrial development is relatively recent and its economic and demographic ties with the country are still

---

[16] This seems to be the case between families of general labourers in old neighbourhoods in contrast to those in the new housing estates in London. *v.* Michael Young and Peter Willmott, *Family and Kinship in East London* (London and Glencoe, Ill., 1957), pp. xvi, 81–9, 121–40.

great, class differences in Dublin probably diminish effective kinship relations less than in most cities of the West. Nevertheless, as we have repeatedly seen, class differences supplement the aforementioned factors which reduce co-operation between kin. Obligations a family contracts with other families on its own class level diminish inter-action with relatives who are on a different class level, and certain class standards bar some kinds of co-operation. Typical is the remark of one artisan woman: 'The children outgrow their clothes and they would suit my brother's children. But, you see, he's on the staff at Guinness's and a little bit above me and . . . well, they feel it is beneath them to take such things. So I give the clothes to the St. Vincent de Paul Society.'

New Dubliners commonly complain that more frequent interaction even with relatives in the first degree is curtailed by 'distance'. Since spatial distance may really be as little as a half-mile with modern transportation available, they clearly refer to the increased social distance between kin. In short, the organization of the city reduces the formal co-operation between kin upon which informal co-operation normally grows, so that the New Dubliner family has to go out of its way, as it were, to maintain rapport with relatives. The inevitable result is that the relationships between them are notably weaker than in the countryside.

The same set of factors, although in a slightly different combina-tion, account for the lesser degree of solidarity between neighbour-hood families which also differentiates the urban from the rural com-munity. In the city, interaction and co-operation between families is at its maximum in the slums, that is, in the oldest and poorest neigh-bourhoods which are also the most homogeneous in class composi-tion. Yet even here, where class differentials are virtually eliminated, social distance is at a minimum, and economic reasons for co-operation are the most pressing, group interaction and co-operation fall below the rural scale for the simple reason that the essential mode of securing a livelihood narrowly limits the degree of economic co-operation that is possible and thus confines co-operation to other kinds of activity. Class differences, where they exist, aggravate this basic situation in various ways. Thus, in the newer neighbourhoods where labourers, artisans and clerical people are likely to be mingled indiscriminately, we have seen how considerations of class status impair neighbourhood solidarity and make it notably less than in the older, more homogeneous neighbourhoods. At the same time, ir-respective of the age of the neighbourhood, our data reveal a steady decline in neighbourhood interaction and co-operation as one goes up the class scale from the general labourers to the managerials.

But before we can assess the general effect of urbanization upon familial solidarity, we must appraise another development that we commonly find among the New Dubliners. On every class level New Dubliner families are integrated with other families on the basis of friendship rather than kinship or neighbourliness, and these groupings have a tendency to be homogeneous as to class. In the small rural community such friendships are relatively rare and their cohesive power much weaker than the strong bonds of kinship and community residence. By contrast, the city provides the urban family with a wider variety of family associations, although, as might be expected, bonds of friendship are inclined to follow class lines. But the data we have seen indicate that on the whole the solidarity that exists between such status friends does not equal the two more traditional forms of solidarity even in the city. With the exception of the managerial class, in Dublin the families of these friends do not normally form a group and their interaction is never as strong, frequent or extensive as that, say, of neighbours in the rural community. It is true that friendship solidarity in the clerical class and much more in the managerial class at times tends to surpass that of the neighbourhood, but the reverse is the case in the other two classes. And on no class level does it normally reach the intensity of kinship solidarity.[17]

If we consider all interfamilial relations in the city, then, whether they be between families of kin, neighbours or friends, it appears clear that, because co-operation in regard to income-producing activities is more restricted than in the rural community, other types of economic co-operation and non-economic co-operation are also there less extensive. This is true on all class levels, but it is intensified by class standards on the upper levels that, except in regard to kin, often proscribe more types of formal interaction between families than they prescribe. It would also appear that urbanization by reducing the degree of co-operation between families in the city increases the load of responsibilities that the nuclear family must bear alone, and it is possible that this load is so heavy as to make the decline in interfamilial solidarity disproportional to the need for it. The practice of late marriage with its postponement of family obligations and the increasing practice of family limitation in the city may well be tactics designed to lighten this load. Increasingly, the urban family depends upon the impersonal organizations in the community wherein power is centred—the company, the union and the state—not only for its basic income, but for other benefits such as health insurance, retirement and old-age pensions, and other forms of social security. This

---

[17] The consolidation of families on the basis of status friendship during recent years reported for the United States has not developed to any notable extent in Dublin. *v.* Carl C. Zimmerman and Lucian F. Cervantes, S.J., *Successful American Families* (New York, 1960), especially pp. 82–7, 214–18.

growing dependence is an important index of the isolation of the family from familial groups that formerly supplied freely aid that must now be purchased.

Two final considerations confirm our conclusion that the change urbanization produces is predominantly organizational and principally originates in the reorganization the new urban family undergoes in its manner of making a livelihood. The first of these are the differences in family organization observable on the various class levels. It is true that in every class the New Dubliners' family differs from the rural family in its essential form of organization because, regardless of class differences, all are subject to the same general organizational requirements that the urban environment imposes upon them. But the differences that do exist between families of various classes appear to substantiate the point that the changes urbanization produce in family life has its main source in the economic reorganization of the family. As we have noted from time to time, this is especially true of families in the managerial class. For their general family pattern differs from that of the rural family less than the pattern of urban families on other class levels because the managerial manner of making a living more closely approximates that of the family in the countryside. We can now summarize, and at the same time add to, the evidence the managerial families provide in support of our analysis.

Because the managerial family owns and controls property productive of income, even though it normally does not work it as a collective unit, the husband is like the rural husband in that he retains a much greater measure of control over the family's finances than husbands in other classes. Direct financial responsibilities are thus more equally divided between husband and wife. By the same token, practices concerning inheritance are closer to those of the rural family. Usually one son will inherit the controlling interest in his father's business or his professional practice, and there is no established custom defining which son this shall be.[18] As a consequence, the son's marriage is of greater economic importance to the managerial family than to other urban families. For this reason, as well as for other class considerations, the managerial family generally exerts stronger control over its sons, especially in their association with girls. For the same reason, a son is somewhat like the rural lad, because normally he will receive more occupational and technical training directly from his father than other urban boys. Similar considerations also lead the managerial family to endow their daughter at marriage, though this does not take the form of the rural dowry.

[18] However, sometimes not one, but several children may share control. *v.* ch. vi, p. 214, above.

All these factors contribute to the later age than other urban children at which managerial children marry and in which they are again more like their country cousins. Finally, their means of livelihood, along with other class ideals, make ties of kinship the basis for broader social relations and firmer social control between managerial families than those of other classes in the city.[19] Clearly, the managerial form of family organization for economic purposes is the major source of their similarities to the countryman's family and of their differences from other urban families.

The ultimate evidence for the pre-eminence of organizational change in the family that urbanization produces, to which we inevitably had to come, is the changes we have observed in the family life of the New Dubliners as compared with that of their natal, immigrant families. Both the differences and the similarities between these generations are of equal and critical importance. The structural features that, despite the differences, are found in the immigrants' family and the family of the New Dubliners on the one hand, and that consistently differ from those of the rural family on the other, indicate the starting point at which urbanization begins to work its ferment in the family. For, granting that the immigrants' family naturally retains more structural elements and attitudes characteristic of the rural family than the family of the New Dubliners, these distinctive similarities between the two generations clearly are the structural areas that are first affected by the transition to the city. Conversely, the differences between these two generations show the subsequent mutations that have followed as a result of these initial changes, as well as of other environmental developments within the evolving Dublin community. The comparison, therefore, gives us some idea of the order and sequence of change.[20]

One major difference between these two generations that our data reveal is the very strong authority the father exerted over the immigrant family. This usually extended to his wife who was clearly subordinated to him and sometimes lived in a bit of fear of him. He had a big hand on the family purse strings and a large share in administrating family finances. The subordination of the children to their father was even more severe. Their attitude towards him was one of formal respect, restraint and often fear in contrast to the virtual

[19] *v.* ibid., p. 221.

[20] The sequential nature of the comparison between immigrants and their New Dubliner children is crucial. Immigrant families today may, and probably do, incorporate more quickly a wider range of structural characteristics common to urban families than did the immigrant families of twenty-five years ago. A comparison of contemporary immigrant and New Dubliner families would be most enlightening, but it would not so clearly indicate the order of changes produced by urbanization.

camaraderie and open discussion characteristic of urban fathers and their children in contemporary Dublin. This was part and parcel of the stronger parental control of children the family generally exercised not only in matters of recreation and peer associations, but particularly in regard to decisions about school, occupation and marriage. At the same time, although relations between families of kin were only slightly stronger than at present, neighbourhood solidarity was notably closer and contributed substantially to the support of each individual family and to the social control the family exerted over its members.

On the other hand, the major area of similarity between the two generations in which they both differ from the countrymen is the manner in which they gain their livelihood and, with few exceptions, the way in which they co-ordinate their activities to secure a livelihood. The most important exception is the wider range of administration of family finances the immigrant husband retained, although his wife had a larger scope than the rural wife even in this sphere. But the lack of productive property, and the basic division of labour, economic and otherwise, is the same in the immigrants' and the New Dubliners' generation, and it radically differs from that prevailing in the countryside. In the face of this latter change, the other attitudes and relationships we have mentioned as differentiating the immigrants from the New Dubliners could not be sustained. Among the immigrants, they appear as residues of a rural family system not cut out for modern urban life. Among the New Dubliners the evolution of the relations between spouses to the point of equal authority; the concomitant change in parent-child relations and in the content of filial piety; and the decline in kinship and neighbourhood solidarity —all appear to be the systematic and inevitable consequences of the initial organizational change on the level of livelihood which has constantly been reinforced by the growth and modernization of the city. In short, this organizational transformation has led to change in the total family and interfamilial organization within the urban community.

In analysing the effects of urbanization on the family and familial organizations in Ireland our main objects of comparison have been the Irish rural and urban families, and international comparisons have been secondary. Cross-culturally, the urban family and familial kinship and neighbourhood groupings in Dublin are undoubtedly among the very strongest in solidarity and power to be found in urban communities in Western societies. Our study, therefore, suggests certain reservations in regard to generalizations about the effects of urbanization on the family. Significantly, the changes we have seen in the process of urbanization in Ireland have not been primarily ideological. The New Dubliners' family has not become secularized and shows little sign of moving in that direction. It thus seems reasonable to infer that secularization is not *per se* inevitably associated with modern industrial urbanization and that ideological values in their own right are critical factors in its development.[21] The change the Irish family has undergone in the shift from the rural to the urban community is principally organizational. Even here the organizational continuities we have noted are substantial and caution against exaggerating the loss of functions the family sustains as it becomes urbanized.

Granting all this, however, urbanization in Ireland has brought about in the family and in familial organizations profound changes similar to those that have occurred in other industrial societies.[22] Although the family retains other very important economic functions, the loss of its productive function has effected a decline in interfamilial solidarity and in the power and functions of the family and of familial organization in general. In Dublin, as elsewhere, it has lost the virtual monopoly of some functions, notably socialization and education; and it has had to reorganize itself internally in order to fulfil these and the many other important functions it continues to perform. As a result, in the rapidly changing environment of the city the urban family, in contrast to the rural family, has become highly adaptable, although its ideological values place limits on its adaptability that are not so extensively found in other Western countries where other ideologies prevail. But, especially in view of the essential ideological continuity between the Irish rural communities and Dublin, and the structural consistency our analysis reveals, it would appear that at least the organizational transformations we have observed in Ireland are, indeed, universal and inevitable effects of industrial urbanism in Western society.

[21] Cf. Redfield, op. cit., pp. 229–69, 362–9.

[22] *v.* William F. Ogburn and C. Tibbits, 'The Family and Its Functions', in *Recent Social Trends in the United States* (New York, 1933), ch. 13. Ernest W. Burgess, 'The Family in a Changing Society', *American Journal of Sociology*, LIII, No. 6 (May 1948), 417–22. W. F. Ogburn and Meyer Nimkoff, *Sociology* (New York, 1940), pp. 708–17. Ernest W. Burgess and Harvey J. Locke, *The Family: From Institution to Companionship* (2nd ed.; New York, 1953), pp. 462–70. Andrew G. Truxal and Francis E. Merrill, *Marriage and the Family in American Culture* (Englewood Cliffs, N.J., 1953), pp. 312–39. Homans, *The Human Group*, pp. 276–80. Talcott Parsons, *Structure and Process in Modern Societies* (Glencoe, Ill., 1960), pp. 301–2. For a different viewpoint, *v.* Carle C. Zimmerman and Lucian F. Cervantes, S.J., *Marriage and the Family* (Chicago, 1956), pp. 64–91, and *Successful American Families.*

Appendix I

STATISTICAL SUPPLEMENT

IN THE THIRD CHAPTER I presented considerable statistical material bearing on marital practice and family life in Ireland, especially in the urban population and among New Dubliners in particular. There are, however, additional statistical data which support and throw further light on these matters. I have likewise at several places discussed the nature of the sample and the methods used in gathering and analysing the data upon which this study was based. But certain technical problems were encountered in sampling and in handling these data which place limitations upon their interpretation. The purpose of this appendix is to present these supplementary statistics, and to clarify my methodological procedures in treating the sample of New Dubliners.

It may be well to begin with a word about the publication of the Irish census material which is the primary source for most of the statistical data presented in this book. For publication of the Irish census has been so affected by the period of adjustment that the nation has passed through since gaining its independence from England in 1922 that there are peculiar difficulties connected with it. Before 1922, the census of Ireland was taken by the Crown as part of the census of Great Britain in the first year of each decade; for example, 1891, 1901, 1911. Because of the Irish Revolution, from 1916 to 1922, no census was taken in Ireland in 1921. And because of unsettled conditions due to the Civil War from 1922 to 1925, the Irish Free State was unable to take its first census until 1926. According to the traditional ten-year pattern, this was followed by a census in 1936 and 1946. All three of these census were published in ten volumes. But as the census of Great Britain continues to be taken in the first year of each decade, the Irish practice left its census five years out of step with the British with obvious disadvantages to both parties. Consequently, in an effort to co-ordinate its census with that of Great Britain, Ireland held a limited census in 1951, and another in 1956. And it has just finished taking a complete census in April 1961. Thus the last complete census presently available for Ireland is that of 1946.

I have discussed these circumstances in order to explain why my use of the census material at times may appear inconsistent, and to call attention to certain limitations that ensue from this state of affairs. In this study, I have used the latest data from the *Census of Population, 1951* wherever possible. But as the 1951 census was not a complete one, it has often been necessary in regard to specific items of interest to go back to the 1946

252

census. For example, the 1951 census presents data on marital conditions but none on fertility, and I have had to have recourse to the fertility statistics of the 1946 census. Furthermore, in tracing trends in the Irish population it has, of course, been necessary to make comparisons between the data from various census. But as the 1951 census was taken only five years after that of 1946, comparisons based on the later material have only limited validity since developments that appear in a five-year period may disappear in the course of the conventional census decade. Indeed this did happen in regard to the size of the total population which, although it increased by 0·19 per cent between 1946 and 1951, decreased by 2·11 per cent between 1951 and 1956. Nevertheless, despite these limitations, I have not hesitated to make such comparisons for it is enlightening to know the latest trends since they may, after all, endure.

Other difficulties arise from our central interest which entails a comparison not only between the town and the rural population in general, but specifically between the rural population and Dublin City on the one hand, and between the New Dubliners and the rest of the Dublin population on the other. Even when augmented by the co-operative contributions by the Central Statistics Office of unpublished data, the census material available does not cover all the specific items for Dublin City our analysis required. As noted above, in such instances I have had to use as the basis for my comparisons the rural population and either the town population or what is called in the Irish census 'the non-agricultural' population on the assumption that the Dublin population is rather similar to the latter two. The assumption is based on the fact that in 1946 the population of Dublin City and Dun Laoghaire accounted for just about half of the town population of the Irish Republic, and for only a little less than half of the non-agricultural population. This is certainly the main reason why, at least in regard to marriage and family life, whenever specific statistics for Dublin are available in the census material, there is always such a close similarity between them and those for the town and non-agricultural population. It therefore seems legitimate to use data for the town and non-agricultural population whenever precise data for Dublin City itself are lacking, and I have done this whenever necessary.

The extent of celibacy as well as the lateness of marriage in Ireland in comparison with Western countries is very graphically indicated by the following table taken from a study published in 1947.[1] (See next page.) Ireland not only had fewer people aged 55–64 who had ever married than any of the other countries listed, but she also had fewer married in every age bracket for both men and women. The 1951 census data for Ireland tend to indicate that she has not significantly bettered her international position in this respect. Among Irish women the percentage ever married between the ages 55–64 actually declined from the 76 per cent listed in the table to 74·4 per cent. The percentage of men ever married did rise from 70 per cent, which is the 1946 figure, to 72·6 in 1951. The latter figure is lower than the percentages ever married in 1926 and 1936, however, and

[1] Taken from The Metropolitan Life Insurance Company, *Statistical Bulletin*, Vol. 28, No. 2 (February 1947), 'Americans Marry Young', p. 9.

Table 1

Per cent of Population Who Had Ever Married, By Sex and Age Periods, In Specified Countries According to the Latest Census

Age Period Years	Country															
	United States	Canada	England and Wales	Scotland	Eire	Sweden	Norway	Denmark	Netherlands	Germany†	Belgium	France	Italy	Portugal	Australia	New Zealand
Males																
15–19	2	*	*	*	*	*	*	1	*	*	1	1	*	*	*	*‡
20–24	28	16	14	12	3	8	7	16	10	5	20	21	9	15	13	10
25–29	64	50	53	44	17	41	35	55	51	45	62	64	46	53	44	44
30–34	79	71	78	69	36	65	64	77	79	75	82	80	73	73	67	70
35–39	85	79	86	80	50	75	77	85	87	86	88	87	85	81	79	80
40–44	87	83	89	83	60	80	82	89	89	92	89	90	89	85	84	85
45–49	89	86	89	83	66	83	85	91	89	94	89	91	90	88	85	86
50–54	89	87	89	84	67	85	87	91	89	94	89	92	91	89	85	87
55–59	89	87	90	85	69	85	89	92	90	94	89	92	91	90	85	87
60–64	89	87	90	85	70	86	89	92	90	94	89	92	92	90	83	86
Females																
15–19	12	6	2	2	1	2	1	3	2	1	4	6	4	4	4	3‡
20–24	53	39	26	23	12	28	19	40	25	23	41	49	31	31	31	28
25–29	77	67	59	50	36	61	48	72	62	64	73	77	62	60	62	62
30–34	85	79	75	68	56	73	67	81	78	80	83	84	76	72	77	77
35–39	89	84	79	74	65	75	73	83	83	83	85	86	81	78	83	83
40–44	90	87	82	77	71	77	76	84	84	85	86	87	84	80	85	85
45–49	91	89	83	78	74	78	77	85	85	86	87	88	86	82	86	86
50–54	91	90	84	79	74	78	79	85	85	88	87	89	88	82	86	87
55–59	91	90	84	79	75	78	80	85	86	89	87	89	88	83	85	86
60–64	91	90	84	79	76	79	80	85	86	90	86	89	89	84	85	85

Sources: Statistical Year Books of the several countries; Special memorandum from the U.S. Bureau of the Census; Institut

the increase is hardly large enough to lead us to think that the Irish males have caught up with the Australians who are the next lowest in the table.[2]

But paradoxically, despite increasing celibacy, the marriage boom which has occurred in Western countries since 1936 has affected Ireland to the extent of reversing the previous long-range trend towards later marriage. This is clear from the following table.

Table 2[3]

Single males and females in the Republic of Ireland as a percentage of the total males and females, respectively, in the age groups 20–24, 25–29, 30–34 at the census of 1936, 1946 and 1951

Year	Males			Females		
	20–24	*25–29*	*30–34*	*20–24*	*25–29*	*30–34*
1936	96·2	82·3	63·5	86·4	64·1	44·1
1946	95·0	76·7	61·0	82·5	57·4	38·8
1951	94·9	76·6	57·9	82·3	54·4	36·4
Change	−1·3%	−5·7%	−5·6%	−4·1%	−9·7%	−7·7%

The table speaks for itself, since for both men and women in each of the three five-year brackets between the ages 20–34 there is a decline in the percentage of single persons.

At the same time, comparative figures for the aggregate rural areas, the aggregate town areas, and for Dublin County Borough, as presented in the following table, clearly substantiate the fact that this trend has been more pronounced, especially among women, in the rural population than in the town population in general, and in Dublin in particular. The Dublin data are also interesting in that they show that the rate of decline among single persons aged 20–34 was quite small and, indeed, that within this age bracket there has been a decline in marriages before twenty-five and a shift towards marriage after twenty-five.

[2] *Census of Population, 1936,* Vol. V, Pt. I, pp. 22–7; and *Census, 1951,* Vol. II, Pt. I, pp. 22–33.
[3] The source of this table is *Census of Population, 1951,* Vol. II, Pt. 1, pp. 22–3.

Table 3[4]

Single males as a percentage of the total males in aggregate town and aggregate rural areas, respectively, in the age groups 20–24, 25–29, 30–34 at the census of 1936, 1946 and 1951*

Year	Town			Rural		
	20–24	*25–29*	*30–34*	*20–24*	*25–29*	*30–34*
1936	93·0	71·0	47·9	97·7	88·6	72·8
1946	91·8	68·3	45·4	96·8	85·5	68·8
1951	92·5	66·4	42·2	96·7	84·2	68·0
Change	−0·5%	−4·6%	−5·7%	−1·0%	−4·4%	−4·8%

* Source: *Census of Population, 1936*, Vol. V, Pt. I, p. 32; *Census, 1946*, Vol. V, Pt. I, p. 36; *Census, 1951*, Vol. II, Pt. I, p. 30.

Single females as a percentage of the total females in aggregate town and aggregate rural areas, respectively, in the age groups 20–24, 25–29, 30–34 at the census of 1936, 1946 and 1951†

Year	Town			Rural		
	20–24	*25–29*	*30–34*	*20–24*	*25–29*	*30–34*
1936	84·6	60·9	42·8	87·9	66·8	45·2
1946	82·5	57·0	39·0	82·6	57·9	38·6
1951	83·2	54·4	37·0	81·1	54·4	35·9
Change	−1·4%	−6·5%	−5·8%	−6·8%	−12·4%	−9·3%

† Source: *Census of Population, 1936*, Vol. V, Pt. I, p. 33; *Census, 1946*, Vol. V, Pt. I, p. 47; *Census, 1951*, Vol. II, Pt. I, p. 33.

Single males and females as percentage of the total males and females, respectively, in Dublin County Borough in the age groups 20–24, 25–29, 30–34 at the census of 1936, 1946 and 1951‡

Year	Males			Females		
	20–24	*25–29*	*30–34*	*20–24*	*25–29*	*30–34*
1936	92·1	68·0	44·1	84·3	60·1	42·0
1946	92·1	66·6	42·3	83·8	58·2	39·1
1951	92·4	67·4	44·0	85·2	58·4	40·5
Change	+0·3%	−0·6%	−0·1%	+0·9%	−1·7%	−1·5%

‡ Source: *Census of Population, 1936*, Vol. V, Pt. I, pp. 32–3; *Census, 1946*, Vol. V, Pt. I, pp. 44–7; *Census, 1951*, Vol. II, Pt. I, pp. 30–3.

[4] The sources for the above figures are *Census of Population, 1936*, Vol. V, Pt. I, pp. 32–5; *Census, 1946*, Vol. V, Pt. I, pp. 44–7; and *Census, 1951*, Vol. II, Pt. I, pp. 30–3.

Statistical Supplement and Methodological Procedures

We have stated above that class differences in regard to the age at marriage in the urban population are relatively small and cannot, therefore, alone account for the relative sluggishness of the recent trend towards earlier marriage in the cities. The following table, which gives the average age at marriage of husbands and wives in 1946 in the non-agricultural population according to social groups, substantiates this statement. It was compiled from the actual numbers of husbands and wives from various classes who were married for the first time and for less than a year in 1946 which are listed in *Memorandum on the Age at Marriage*, page 11, published by the Central Statistics Bureau.

Table 4

Average age at marriage of husbands and wives in 1946 in the non-agricultural population according to social groups

Social Group	Average Age at Marriage	
	Husbands	Wives
Employers, Managers and Professionals	33·7	28·4
Working on own account, and salaried employees	31·7	27·5
Non-manual wage-earners and skilled workers	30·9	27·1
Semi-skilled workers and general labourers	30·4	26·9
Total	31·4	27·4

It is well to note that the grand total averages here for both husbands and wives exactly correspond to the averages for Dublin City. We may, therefore, assume that the class differences apparent in the table are very close to those which obtain in Dublin.

The relative smallness of the rural-urban differential in fertility is indicated by the following table which compares family size in Ireland as a whole with that in Dublin and Dun Laoghaire.

257

Table 5[5]

The percentage distribution, according to the number of children, of families of women married thirty years or more in 1946 for Ireland as a whole and for the combined populations of Dublin and Dun Laoghaire

Number of Children	Percentage of Families	
	Ireland	*Dublin and Dun Laoghaire*
No children	10·1	11·2
1–2 children	12·9	16·5
3–5 children	30·3	30·4
6–9 children	33·7	29·7
10 children or more	13·0	12·2
Total	100·0	100·0

It is not possible to present the fertility differentials for the four condensed class categories that we have used in discussing the town population of Ireland because the data needed to standardize the fertility rate for such categories are simply not at hand. However, we can adequately indicate the differences and at the same time avoid bias by listing the total standardized rates for six social groups of the non-agricultural population as classified by the census of 1946. Actually, the census lists seven social groups as comprising the non-agricultural population. But the seventh is that of the 'retired and not gainfully occupied' and obviously contains in unknown proportions people from all the other social groups. Therefore, we have omitted this group from the following table. In listing the rates for the census groups I have grouped together those that comprise the social class categories of this study.

[5] The national percentages are taken from the *Census of Population, 1946, Fifth Interim Report*, Table XXII, p. 10. The percentages for the Dublin metropolitan area were computed from the number of families in Dublin and Dun Laoghaire in 1946, classified by the number of children and durations of marriage given in the *Census of Population, 1946*, Vol. IX, Table 8, pp. 53–70. Only marriages that have endured for thirty years or more and whose families were completed in 1946 are considered here.

Table 6[6]

Total standardized fertility rates per 100 married women for ages of wife 20–34 years at marriage, and for durations of marriage 5–9 years, 35–39 years, 40–44 years and 45 years and over, classified by social group and religious denomination in the non-agricultural population

Social Group	Catholics	Other Religions Groups	Total
(*Class I*)			
Higher Professionals	338	197	286
Lower Professionals	382	223	358
Employers and Managers	383	226	343
(*Class II*)			
Working on own account	403	277	395
Salaried employees	390	237	371
(*Class III*)			
Wage-earners (non-manual)	378	248	362
Skilled wage-earners	412	265	401
(*Class IV*)			
Semi-skilled wage-earners	444	328	442
General labourers	435	369	434

The difference in fertility between Catholic and other religious groups is so striking as to merit a few remarks. This disparity is a national characteristic; the national fertility rate for other religious groups is 35 per cent lower than for Catholics.[7] But the divergence is greater in the non-agricultural population than in the agricultural population. With the sole exception of the class of general labourers in the preceding table, in every class of the non-agricultural population there is a wider range of difference between Catholics and non-Catholics than there is between them in any class in the agricultural population. Obviously, then, the difference between Catholics and other religious groups is not primarily due to class factors. Not only is the Catholic rate higher for all social classes, but in the very group where the Catholic rate is lowest, viz. the higher professionals, the difference in fertility between Catholics and others is the greatest, the Catholic rate there being 42 per cent higher than that of other religious groups. This gives us some indication of the impact of Irish Catholicism upon the modification of family structure that urbanization produces.

Fertility is not the only familial field wherein Catholics and people of other religious denominations vary. Paradoxically enough, late as the Catholic Irishman marries, his non-Catholic compatriot marries still later. In this, other religious groups may be said to be 'more Irish than the Irish themselves'. This is true across the country for both men and women. In 1946 the national average age at marriage for husbands of other religious denominations was 34·8 years and for wives of other religious denomina-

[6] This table is abstracted from the *Census of Population, 1946, Fifth Interim Report*, Table XXVI, p. 13.
[7] Ibid.

tions it was 29·7 years as compared with the respective Catholic averages of 33·0 and 28·0 years. Moreover, this difference was greatest in the Dublin metropolitan area where, on the average, Catholic husbands married about four years earlier, and Catholic wives about two and a half years earlier, than husbands and wives of other denominations. The *Census of Population, 1946*, Vol. IX, pages 222, 224, lists the average age at marriage for Catholic husbands in Dublin City and Dun Laoghaire as 30·8 years and for husbands of other religious denominations as 34·6 years. For wives, the average age was 27·2 years for Catholics as compared with 29·7 years for other religious denominations.

The differences in regard to age at marriage between these groups, however, are probably not due to strictly religious differences. One factor certainly at work in producing them is the fact that the proportion of persons in the upper class, where marriage normally is later, is far higher in the non-Catholic population than it is in the Catholic population, as we have pointed out previously. Of much greater importance from a theoretical point of view is the fact that late marriage in Ireland is characteristic not only of Catholics but of all religious denominations. This clearly indicates that such a common effect cannot stem primarily from religion in which these people differ, but from the general social structure which is the common context of their lives.

We have attempted to compare the New Dubliners with the Dublin population as a whole, but this is subject to reservations similar to those affecting our comparison of the agricultural and the non-agricultural populations. The matter is further complicated by the fact, already noted, that the New Dubliners are not isolated at all in the census material. For statistical data on the New Dubliners we have had to rely on our sample which comparatively is very small and therefore demands very cautious treatment.

The first word of caution concerns the representative quality of the sample. Even when expanded by the addition of the siblings of the people who were the main focus of this study, this group of families cannot be considered as fully representative of New Dubliners in general in the matters of marital practice under consideration. This is especially true of the age at marriage and of the proportion unmarried. In reference to these, there is a bias in our sample because the families in it were not selected at random, but included some individuals, viz. the parents of the families studied directly, who by the very nature of the case were married and often had full-fledged families. A random selection of New Dubliners, therefore, might well reveal a greater proportion married or unmarried than our group, as well as a later or earlier average age at marriage and perhaps different fertility patterns.

Furthermore, the fortune of sampling was such that most of the families chosen from the employer-managerial-professional class were those of couples recently married. This may not be wholly chance since, as just pointed out, the number of Catholics in this class in the first quarter of the century was relatively very small. Indeed, the increase in this class in general, and of Catholics in this class in particular, during the second

quarter of the century accounts for many of the trends in marriage behaviour which we can discern in the urban data. Still, in a breakdown of
the families in the sample according to duration of marriage, the number
of families in this class that were established in the nine years prior to 1946
exceeds its true proportion by about 20 per cent, and allowance must be
made for the bias that is thus introduced into the figures for this later
period.

These allowances being made, the following table indicates that New
Dubliners appear to marry earlier than do Dubliners in general.

Table 7[8]

Percentage of males and females *unmarried* at ages 24–29 in Dublin City
and County in 1926, 1936, 1946, and in our group of New Dubliners in the
years 1925–27, 1935–37, 1945–47

	Males		*Females*	
Year	*Dublin City and County*	*New Dubliners*	*Dublin City and County*	*New Dubliners*
1926	64·7	54·0	56·9	34·6
1936	68·9	66·7	61·1	41·2
1946	67·5	61·5	58·5	31·6

There is a smaller percentage unmarried at this age in the group of New
Dubliners than in the whole metropolitan area in every instance. Among
the men the tendency to marry earlier is definite but not as pronounced as
among the women where the differences between the whole Dublin population and the sample are large. Actually, the differences are probably slightly
less than they appear because of our need here to use data for Dublin City
and County which includes some of the farm populace in the environs of
Dublin City.

That the trend towards later marriage among women in the urban population which prevailed prior to 1936 was more pronounced among the
New Dubliners than in the urban population as a whole is shown by the
following table.

[8] The figures for Dublin City and County are taken from the *Census of Population, 1946,* Vol. V, Pt. I, pp. 26–7. The actual numbers for the New Dubliners are
as follows:

	Males			*Females*		
Year	*Married*	*Unmarried*	*Total*	*Married*	*Unmarried*	*Total*
1926–28	17	20	37	17	9	26
1936–38	8	16	24	10	7	17
1946–48	5	8	13	13	6	19

Table 8[9]

Percentage of Catholic women *married* between the ages 20–34 according to the durations of marriages, represented by the periods of marriage, in the non-agricultural population and in a group of New Dubliners

Period of Marriage

Age of Wife at Marriage	Non-agricultural Population				New Dubliners			
	Before 1907	1907– 1911	1922– 1926	1937– 1941	Before 1907	1907– 1911	1922– 1926	1937– 1941
(1) 20–24 years	55·3	50·6	47·6	41·6	66·7	33·3	42·1	23·8
(2) 25–29 years	32·5	35·2	36·5	39·7	23·8	50·0	40·0	38·1
Total (1) & (2)	(87·8)	(85·8)	(84·1)	(81·3)	(90·5)	(83·3)	(82·1)	(80·0)
3) 30–34 years	12·2	14·2	15·8	18·7	9·5	16·7	17·9	38·1
Grand Total	100·0	100·0	100·0	100·0	100·0	100·0	100·0	100·0

Clearly, in the two earlier age levels combined the rate of decline has been much greater among the New Dubliners than in the non-agricultural population as a whole; so much so, indeed, that in the last period positions in the 30–34 years bracket tend to be reversed. Furthermore, although we have no data from the non-agricultural population to serve as a basis of comparison, in the sample of New Dubliners the men show the same general tendency as the women, as appears from the following table.

[9] The percentages for the non-agricultural population were computed from *Census of Population, 1946, Fifth Interim Report,* Table 30, pp. 39–41. The numbers upon which the percentages for the New Dubliners are based are the following:

Period of Marriage

Age of Wife at Marriage	Before 1907	1907–11	1922–26	1937–41
20–24	5	5	19	14
24–29	8	7	18	5
30–34	8	2	8	2
Total	21	14	45	21

Table 9[10]

Percentage of husbands who are New Dubliners *married* between the ages 20–34 for the durations of marriage represented by the periods of marriage

| Age of Husband at Marriage | Period of Marriage | | | |
	Before 1907	1907–11	1922–26	1937–41
(1) 20–24 years	52·4	33·3	22·2	4·8
(2) 25–29 years	23·8	41·7	37·7	14·3
Total (1) and (2)	(76·2)	(75·0)	(59·9)	(19·1)
(3) 30–34 years	23·8	25·0	40·0	80·9
Grand Total	100·0	100·0	100·0	100·0

In view of the bias introduced into the foregoing data in the period 1937–41 due to the excess of the higher classes in our sample of New Dubliners, it may be well to add that this trend to later marriage holds also for both husbands and wives of the two lower classes considered separately. If these latter classes are combined, the percentages of wives and husbands aged 20–29 years at marriage also drop gradually from the earliest to the latest period and, inversely, rise for those married at ages 30–34 years. Nevertheless, the tendency of New Dubliners of the lower classes to marry earlier than the higher class appears from a comparison of the average age at marriage of husbands and wives in the sample that were married between 1925–27, 1935–37, and 1945–47 as in the following table. In every case except that of husbands in the first period, people in the wage-earning class have a lower average than the average for the combined higher classes.

[10] The actual numbers are the following:

| Age of Husband at Marriage | Period of Marriage | | | |
	Before 1907	1907–11	1922–26	1937–41
20–24	11	4	10	1
24–29	5	5	17	3
30–34	5	3	18	17
Total	21	12	45	21

Table 10[11]

Average age at marriage of husbands and wives married between 1925–27, 1935–37 and 1945–47 in a group of New Dubliners

Husbands and Wives by Social Group	Average Age at Marriage of Persons Married Between		
	1925–27	*1935–37*	*1945–47*
Husbands			
(1) Employer-professional and salaried class	28·2	34·8	35·9
(2) Wage-earners and general labourers	30·7	29·3	34·5
Wives			
(1) Employer-professional and salaried class	25·4	29·3	31·4
(2) Wage-earners and general labourers	25·3	26·9	29·5

Finally, the relative fertility of the New Dubliners and the general urban population, according to classes, is presented in Table 11 to substantiate the remarks made in Chapter III, pages 70–1 above.

[11] The actual sample numbers are:

Persons by Social Group	Married between the years		
	1925–27	*1935–37*	*1945–47*
Husbands			
Employers, etc.	5	6	11
Wage-earners, etc.	13	9	6
Wives			
Employers, etc.	5	6	10
Wage-earners, etc.	13	9	5

Table 11[12]

Average number of children born to wives who are New Dubliners and to Catholic wives in non-agricultural population in 1946, aged 20–34 years at marriage, for durations of marriage 5–9, 20–24, 34–39, and 40 or more years

Social Group	*Average Number of Children Born to Women Married from Years:*			
	5–9	*20–24*	*34–39*	*40 or more*
Employers, managers and professionals:				
(1) New Dubliners	1·5	4·1	—	—
(2) Non-agricultural population	2·5	4·1	4·7	5·7
(Difference)	−1·0	0	—	—
Working on own, and salaried employees:				
(1) New Dubliners	2·5	3·3	3·3	4·0
(2) Non-agricultural population	2·5	4·5	5·4	5·5
(Difference)	0	−1·2	−2·1	−1·5
Non-manual wage-earners and skilled workers:				
(1) New Dubliners	3·0	5·1	3·8	4·4
(2) Non-agricultural population	2·6	4·8	5·7	6·0
(Difference)	+0·4	+0·3	−1·9	−1·6
Semi-skilled and general labourers:				
(1) New Dubliners	2·2	5·0	7·0	8·5
(2) Non-agricultural population	2·9	5·5	6·1	6·5
(Difference)	−0·7	−0·5	+0·9	+2·0

[12] It would be too burdensome to give the actual numbers of families and children in the group which are the basis for the above group rates. The averages for the non-agricultural population have been computed from the actual numbers of Catholic families and children listed in the *Census of Population, 1946, Fifth Interim Report,* pp. 39–41. Again the group labelled 'retired and not gainfully occupied' is omitted.

METHODOLOGICAL PROCEDURES

There remain some final remarks about the sample of the New Dubliners and the methods and principles of interpreting the data gathered from them. One of the most critical features of the sample was its class composition. For the complexity of the class structure in Dublin and the far greater class mobility that occurs there than in the rural community calls for a profound adjustment on the part of the family which, as we have seen, is one of the most striking features differentiating the Dubliner's life from that of the countryman. This made a clear picture of the class structure of Dublin and the class distribution of the New Dubliners of prime importance. There was an additional reason for such a picture. In the long run, our main interest has been in those effects of urbanization upon the family that are common and that cut across class lines. So it was also important to determine class differentials in order in the end to lay these aside and to discover the general and common features of the family life of the New Dubliners so that we could compare it with the common pattern of the countryman's family.

This posed two problems. First, it was necessary to determine the class structure of Dublin as a whole, and then to establish, if possible, the class distribution of the New Dubliners. We have already discussed the difficulties in the way of ascertaining the general class structure of the city.[13] As for the New Dubliners it was obviously impossible to fix their class distribution with exactitude since the Central Statistics Office had no special interest in them and gave them no special treatment in the census material. Still, there were some clues as to the number of New Dubliners in the city which provided a basis for estimating their class distribution. At each census from 1871 to 1926 a full 30 per cent of Dublin's residents were reported as having been born outside the city. Of these, a certain proportion up until 1922 were British administrative personnel and soldiery. But in each of the census years, 1926, 1936, 1946, the percentages of residents in Dublin and Dun Laoghaire who were born elsewhere in all Ireland were, respectively, 27·3, 26·2, 27·5.[14] Since immigrants into Dublin have accounted for more than a quarter of the city's populace for such a long period of time, it seemed to be a conservative estimate that the children of these immigrants, the New Dubliners, comprised at least a good third of the total population. And since they made up such a large portion of the city's population, it also seemed unlikely that the class distribution of the New Dubliners would differ very greatly from that of the Dublin population as a whole, so that the former could be roughly estimated from the latter. Even though, in order to secure sufficient data from each class, the class distribution of the sample was somewhat distorted, the distortion was conditioned by this assumption of class similarity between the New Dubliners and the general Dublin population.

[13] *v.* Introduction, pp. 6–7, above.
[14] These percentages were computed from *Census of Population, 1926*, Vol. III, Table 7, p. 158; *Census, 1936*, Vol. III, Table 7, p. 154; *Census, 1946, Second Interim Report*, Table 13A, p. 30.

The structure of the sample and the nature of the material secured by interview and observation also conditioned the norms of interpretation we have used with our data.[15] These data have not been submitted to stringent statistical treatment for many reasons. The number of families in the total sample, as well as the number of individuals involved in it, is not very large. When the sample is broken down into classes and each class in turn is dealt with separately, the number of families and individuals is quite small. Furthermore, since our objective has been to get as well rounded a view of the family as possible, the items investigated in each family are very numerous. As a result, a thorough statistical analysis would be extremely complicated and cumbersome. Nevertheless, we have made tentative generalizations about the New Dubliners. The frequency distributions of the various items we are treating are thus important and our method of finding them and evaluating them requires discussion.

The data on the New Dubliners derive both from direct observation and from reports about their practices and attitudes or sentiments. By force of circumstance, report was much more extensive than direct observation and constitutes the main source of our information. These reports are of various kinds. In the interviews, the families of the New Dubliners reported on their own practices and attitudes, and also on the patterns of behaviour and the sentiments that they thought were common among their relatives, neighbours and friends. In many cases, we were able to get supplementary testimony from these relatives and friends themselves. In addition to this kind of evidence, there were also corroborative reports from numerous people outside of our sample. Besides, from all these people, but especially from the spouses of the families in the sample and their parents, we sought information not only about family life as current in Dublin, but also as it was when these spouses were children themselves. We did this in an attempt to determine the difference between the family life of the New Dubliners and that of their immigrant parents and so to ascertain the stages of change in family life from one generation to another.

Our procedure has been conditioned further by the varying content of the reports we are discussing. In regard to certain items, some reports refer only to the actual family interviewed with no report from them on common practice in other families. This happened for one of several reasons. A report about common practice was sometimes not sought in a particular case as not likely to be reliable; or it was overlooked in the vicissitudes of the interview, or because the informants said that they did not know what the common practice might be. Conversely, other items were reported only as common and are not reported for the family interviewed. Besides oversight, which again played a part here, such omissions stemmed from the inapplicability of an item to the specific case or from the reluctance of the family to state its own attitude or practice directly.

In regard to the vast majority of items treated, however, we have reports from individual family members both as to what obtains in their own families and as to what is common among the families they know. These reports combine in various ways. At times members of a family agreed in

---

[15] *v.* ch. v, pp. 134–5; and ch. vi, pp. 193–4, above.

reporting that their family group follows a certain practice or entertains a certain attitude, and that this practice or attitude is also common among the families in their circle. In this case, the reports about the family directly investigated and the reports on common practice tally perfectly. In other instances, these reports do not tally and the individuals interviewed acknowledge that in the matter in question their family deviates from the common pattern. Again, family members frequently agree as to an item in their own family, but will disagree about what is common. Conversely, but less frequently, they will disagree about an item in their own family, usually in regard to an attitude, while agreeing that the item is common among people in their circle.

Thus the testimony we have to handle is complicated, but when all these individual reports are collated, the situation simplifies itself to a considerable degree. In no case do the totalled reports of people of any class show clearly that the families interviewed, as a group, differ from what is generally reported as common to people of their class. When we combine the reports about the families actually interviewed with reports as to what is common, we find either that there is perfectly unanimous testimony about a given item or, as might be expected, that there are varying degrees of agreement about it. It is this fact which necessitated working out the rules of evidence mentioned above.

The rule that we shall not consider an item of importance unless 75 per cent of the people in the sample report on it is logical in view of the size of the sample we have drawn. Testimony from fewer people would not be sufficient to merit credence as to the currency of the item in question. Consequently, we have made no statements about items of this sort unless there were special reasons for doing so. And in that case, we have made special note of the amount of testimony and its distribution. This rule, requiring that three-quarters of the people in the sample report upon an item, applies where we have reports only about our actual cases, or only about what is common practice, as well as where we have reports of both kinds.

It also seems justifiable to consider that, when 75 per cent or more of the people report on an item, and 90 per cent or more of them agree as to the currency of that item, the item is generally common to the New Dubliners or to a specific class of New Dubliners. It may be well here to give an example of agreement of this sort. All eleven of the artisan families in the sample reported that, in the matter of inheritance of property, the principle of equal division among the children would be followed in their own case, with standardized exceptions for handicapped children or children who have made great sacrifices for the family. At the same time, the twenty-six people from all these families who report on this matter attest that this is the common practice and attitude among the people they know. Here we have unanimous agreement. Again, in nine out of the eleven artisan families the husbands are reported as giving virtually all of their weekly wage to their wives and retaining only a small percentage of it for small personal expenses. And twenty-one out of twenty-two parents in these families report that this is the common practice with people among whom they

268

move. In the latter case, the agreement is not unanimous, but it is so great that we are certainly justified in accepting this as a general pattern of behaviour among the artisans.

Where testimony about an item is supported by less than 90 per cent of the required proportion of people reporting, the item may reasonably be considered an alternative item among the New Dubliners in the sense that it is one of several items that are significantly current in the population. But there is room here for more precision. For example, the decision as to whether boys who have completed primary school should go to work immediately, or go on for further schooling, is reported as made primarily by the parents and not by the boy, in nine out of the eleven artisan families interviewed. Besides, seventeen out of twenty-one witnesses from all these families report that this is the common practice. This would indicate that the school-work decision is primarily left to the boy to decide often enough to constitute a real alternative practice, but that this alternative seems clearly to be less prevalent than its opposite. On the other hand, six out of the ten spouses in the five families living in the older neighbourhoods of Dublin stated that they themselves would not impose sanctions on a close neighbour who was drinking and neglecting his family by snubbing or ostracizing him. Yet nine out of seventeen adults from these families reported that in such a case their other neighbours would impose such sanctions. In the face of such a distribution of opinion on this point, it seems reasonable to consider that the imposition of this type of sanction is a practice which is no more widespread than its opposite or some other alternate practice. These are the grounds for making the distinction between prevalent and alternate practices or attitudes that we have employed in dealing with the data from the interviews.

Appendix II

CHECK LIST OF GENERAL INTERVIEW AREAS

A. *Marriage*

1. In lieu of the country 'match', what financial arrangements are there in the city when people marry? Is there a dowry? Are there wedding gifts? What happened in your case? Etc.

2. Where did you meet your husband? Where did you meet your wife? Etc.

3. Did your wife work prior to marriage? Did she work after marriage? Why did she stop working? Etc.

4. Depending upon the age at marriage: would you like to have married younger; or are you glad you married that young?

5. Did your parents object to your age at marriage? If so, what were the objections? Which parent, or parents, objected the most? Etc.

6. Did your parents exert much influence on whom you went with in a serious way? What were the grounds for the objections? Who objected the more? How were the objections manifested? [Ask the siblings the same questions.]

6a. Did your parents effect much influence on your choice of a job, education, etc.?

7. Whom did you consult before marriage? What advice were you given?

8. What is your opinion on your children's marriage in regard to age, financial condition, occupation of spouse? Etc.

9. Do friends your own age feel similarly regarding their children?

10. Does your own attitude differ in this matter from your parents? How does it differ? What caused the difference in attitude?

11. In considering marriage, what opinions do lads and girls hold in regard to age, financial condition, type of spouses, living with in-laws? How do they feel about not marrying? What are the differences in the opinions of the lads from those of the girls? Why is there a difference? Etc.

B. *Children and Authority*, etc.

12. What main difficulties do you find in having and raising a family of this size?

13. What are the main compensations?

14. What are the costs of having a child today? What are the hospital costs? What are the nursing costs? Who cares for the other children?

15. Is the baby 'the king of the family'? Is there jealousy from the other siblings? Are people affectionate towards children? When does severe discipline start?

16. How much time does the father spend with the children? What does he do when he is with them? What does he do when he is with the boys? What does he do when he is with the girls?

16a. What are the other consequences resulting from his hours of work?

17. Does the wife do most of the actual disciplining? What disciplinary problems does she refer to the husband? What authority do older children have over the younger ones? (What tasks?) Are older children permitted to punish younger children?

18. What things present the greatest difficulties for discipline—study, work, bad company, etc.?

19. What is the most effective discipline?

19a. How does your method of discipline differ from that used by your relatives?

20. If the grandparents live with you, do they have any authority over the grandchildren?

21. Are youngsters harder to handle today than they used to be? Why?

22. Are boys harder or easier to handle than girls? Why?

23. Are boys over twelve allowed certain privileges that girls are not? Do boys stay out later than girls? Do boys go out more than girls? Do boys frequent places forbidden girls? Do boys have more money than girls? Do boys go with girls at an earlier age than in the past? Do boys go more with girls or with other boys? What are the boys' activities when with boys? What are the activities when the boys are with girls? Do the boys go to clubs? How often do the boys go to the movies? To what extent do the boys listen to the radio, etc.?

24. What occupations would you choose for your sons? What schooling will the boys receive? Will the sons go into business with the father? What technical training will the sons receive from the father?

25. Do you expect any of your sons to migrate to England, America, or back to the land? What is your attitude towards migration for your sons?

26. What do the sons themselves say they want to do later?

27. Do older girls go out much with lads, or with other girls? What are the girls' activities when with other girls? What are the girls' activities when with boys? What are the activities of mixed groups? Do the girls belong to clubs? Do the girls listen to the radio? How often do the girls go to the movies? Do the girls read books? How frequently do the girls go to dances?

28. Have the girls ever expressed any wish for a career later on, besides marriage? What careers are of interest to the girls? What do you think of a career instead of marriage for a girl?

29. Do you expect any of your daughters to migrate to England, America, or back to the land? What is your attitude towards migration for your daughters?

30. Are girls more religious than boys? Why is this so?

31. How frequently do the girls go to the Sacraments? How frequently do the boys go to the Sacraments? Do the girls and boys both attend the

amily rosary? Do the young people belong to any church organizations, such as the Legion of Mary, Sodality, Young Men's Confraternity? Is catechism taught entirely at school? Do the parish priests teach catechism? Who gives the religious training in the home?

C. *Inheritance Patterns*

32. How did your parents distribute their property and money?
33. What is the usual practice in distributing an estate for older people?
34. How will you distribute your estate?
35. How do your contemporaries feel about this matter?

D. *Division of Labour*

36. What is the normal round of duties, tasks and activities of the wife in an ordinary weekday? (Service, Exchange, Production, Authority, Socialization, Religious, Representation.)
37. What are the main weekly variations? What are the main yearly variations?
38. What is the normal round of duties, tasks and activities of the husband in an ordinary weekday?
39. What are the husband's main weekly variations? What are the husband's main yearly variations?
40. What is the normal round of duties, tasks and activities of the older children in an ordinary weekday?
41. What are the main weekly variations? What are the main yearly variations?
42. What does the wife normally purchase on her own authority? What does the husband normally purchase on his own authority? What do the children normally purchase on their own authority? (Budget . . .)
43. What maintenance services and/or other services does the wife do? What maintenance services and/or other services does the husband do? Are any services performed by hired help? Are any services performed by friends, relatives or neighbours?
44. What does the family do together by way of recreation in the evenings? What does the family do together by way of recreation on week-ends? What does the family do together by way of recreation on summer holidays? What does the family do together by way of recreation on religious or other holidays?
45. What productive activity, if any, does the family have? What size is it? Who are employed in the activity? What does it yield?
45a. What are the reading and entertainment habits of the family members?

E. *Kinship System*

46. How often and what contacts do you have with relatives' families in Dublin? Are the contacts made by the family members individually or as a family group? Do you have business relations with your relatives? (Exchange relations [apart from Christmas, etc.]?) Do you contact your relatives in time of crisis? Are there any matters on which you consult

them? Do you have social and recreational activities with your relatives? What contacts do your children have with their relatives?

47. Would you say all these relatives form a sort of circle? How often do all get together, and on what occasions?

48. What action would you or other relatives take if one began to neglect the family or to drink, etc.?

49. How often and what contacts do you have with relatives in the country? (If indicated, repeat the questions in No. 46.)

F. *Neighbourhood*

50. What families in the neighbourhood are closest to yours? What are the occupations of the husbands?

51. How often and what contacts do you have individually and as a family with these families? (Repeat questions in No. 46.)

52. Do the older lads and girls of the neighbourhood go together frequently? Do the young people of the neighbourhood intermarry to any great extent? Do those who intermarry settle in the neighbourhood?

53. Do the younger children in the neighbourhood play much together? (Probe for problems of play groups here.)

54. What contacts do you have with other neighbourhood families besides those especially close? How frequent are the contacts? What are the occupations of the fathers?

55. If the family has moved, the following questions were asked: Do you like this neighbourhood better? Why did you move? Do you keep your contacts with your former neighbours? Do you have as many and as close contacts here as in the former neighbourhood?

56. If one of your neighbours began to neglect his family or to drink, etc., what action would you take? What action would the other neighbours take?

G. *Status-Friends*

57. Besides relatives and neighbours, are there other families in the town with whom you are familiar and friendly? Who are these families? What are the husbands' occupations?

58. How did you become acquainted with these families? Work? School? Organizations you belong to? Other friends? Etc.

59. How often and what contacts do you have with these families?

60. Would you say these families form a circle or group? What action would you take if one of these families began to neglect his family?

61. Of all the above families, to which do you feel closest? How is this manifest? Etc.

H. *Occupational Factors*

62. Among all of these families, have any husbands won promotions in their work? Has this resulted in their moving into new neighbourhoods? How has this affected your relations with them, if at all? Etc.

273

Check List of General Interview Areas

(For employer, or one in his own business)

63. How did you acquire the business? (Did you buy, inherit, or start it?) How much training have you had in the business? From whom was the training received?

64. Have you had other businesses before? What were the prior businesses? Why did you drop them?

(For employee)

65. How long have you been employed by your present employer? What positions have you held with the company? What are the opportunities for advancement?

(For both if employer has held jobs prior to owning business)

66. What other jobs have you had prior to your present one? By what companies were you employed? How long were you employed by the other companies? What positions did you hold? Why did you change?

67. How did you get your first job—through friends, relatives, exam, etc.?

68. Why did you or did you not choose the same trade as your father? If in the same trade, how much training did you receive from your father? How much training did you receive from outside agencies?

(If professional man)

69. Why did you choose your profession? What was your pre-professional, occupational history? What are the main concomitants of your professional activity?

(Non-professional man, whether employer or employee)

70. What is the technical organization of the company—process of production, with detailed description of your own job? Etc. What is the structure of authority? What is the attitude towards job bosses? Etc. What is the company's policy on retirement, pensions, health, accident insurance, and hospitalization, especially as it affects you and your family?

(For employee only—including civil servants)

71. (Here a series of questions was asked to probe for the informal organization of the company and to see if membership in such groups integrates families outside work.) Are you a union member? Why or why not? What is the structure of authority in the union? What is the union's function in the shop? What benefits do you feel you and your family derive from union membership?

(For employer only)

72. Are all employees union members, or some, or none? If some employees are union members, to what unions do they belong? How does the union operate in your shop? (How integrated into technical and authority structure?) What is your attitude towards the unions?

73. Are you a member of a business association? How is it organized? What are its policies? What is your attitude towards the organization?

Check List of General Interview Areas

(For all, if possible)

74. (Questions were asked as to their income, expenses, savings, etc.)

I. *Religion*

75. (Questions were asked as to: (*a*) the religious practices of family and family members and also of kinship and neighbourhood families; (*b*) the organizational aspects, formal and informal, of the parish; (*c*) their views and attitudes: religious, political, class, etc.)

J. *Residual*

76. Other material that emerged over and above that covered by the preceding questions.

VITAL STATISTICS ON THE FAMILY

1. AGE-SEX STRUCTURE

Case No.

Husband
Name:
Present Age:
Birthplace:
Date of Marriage:
Age at Marriage:

Children
How many children ever born:
Name: Age:

Wife
Name:
Present Age:
Birthplace:
Age at Marriage:

Others in Household
Number:
Name: Relationship: Age:

Comment:

2. OCCUPATIONAL COMPONENT

Case No.

Husband
Occupation:
Own his own business?
  What is it?
  Where located?
  What other family members work in it?
  How many other people does he employ?
  What is precise nature of owner's actual work?

Employed by?
  What sort of work does he do precisely?
(If professional man—doctor, lawyer, teacher, general practitioner or
    specialist [doctor, lawyer]?)
Office in home or in town?

Wife

Work outside home now?
  Occupation:
  Concern:
  Precise nature of work:

Comment:

Case No.

Children

Name:	Age:	Name:	Age:
		(If over 18)	
Married/single?		Married/single?	
		(If married)	
How long?		How long?	
Where live?		Where live?	
Husband's occupation		Husband's occupation	
No. of children?		No. of children?	
	(For all over 6)		
Schools attended		Schools attended	
Working (part/full time)		Working (part/full time)	
What job?		What job?	

  (These questions were asked about each cdild.)

3. RESIDENTIAL COMPONENT

Case No.

House (single, duplex, flat)
No. of rooms
Owned or rented?
  If rented, what is rent?
  If owned, what is value?
How far from (how long to get to) work?
  How do you get to work? (Bike, bus, car)
  Have you a car?
How much garden land connected with house, if any?
  Used productively for own use and/or the market?
Have you lived in this house all your married life?
  If not, how long have you lived here?
  Where did you live before moving here?
  Why did you move?

Comment:

4. KINSHIP COMPONENT

i. *Husband's* Family

Case No.

PARENTS living or dead?
  Where do/did they live in Dublin?
  Own house, or rent it?

Father born and brought up where?
  (If outside Dublin)
  Farm?   Size of it, etc.
  Town?
  (If townsman, whether Dublin or elsewhere)
  What was *his* father's (your grandfather's) occupation?
Father's age on coming to Dublin?
Marry before or after coming?
Age at marriage?
Occupation (i.e. get occupational history)
What schools attended? (i.e. primary? secondary? University?)

Mother born and raised where?
  (If outside Dublin)
  Farm?   Size of it, etc.
  Town?

  (If townswoman)
  What was her father's occupation?
  Her age on coming to Dublin?
  Age at marriage?
  Work before marriage in Dublin?
    Doing what?
  Continue work for while after marriage?
    How long?
  What schools attended?
  How many children were there in his family? (I.e. ever born?)

Comment:

Siblings

Name:	Age:	Name:	Age:
Married/single?		Married/single?	
Lives where?		Lives where?	
Occupation		Occupation	

(If married and in Dublin)

Age at marriage?		Age at marriage?	
Wife's birthplace?		Wife's birthplace?	
Her age at marriage?		Her age at marriage?	
Her father's occupation?		Her father's occupation?	
No. of children?		No. of children?	

Comment:

ii. *Wife's* Family

Case No.

PARENTS, living or dead?
　Where do/did they live in Dublin?
　Own house or rent it?

Father born and raised where?
　(If outside Dublin)
　Farm?　　　　　　　　　Size of it, etc.
　Town?
　(If townsman, Dublin or otherwise)
　What was his father's (her grandfather's) occupation?
Father's age on coming to Dublin?
Marry before or after coming?
Age at marriage?
Occupation (i.e. occupational history)
What schools attended?

Mother born and raised where?
　(If outside Dublin)
　Farm?　　　　　　　　　Size of it, etc.
　Town?
　(If townswoman)
　What was her father's occupation?
Her age on coming to Dublin?
Age at marriage?
Work before marriage in Dublin?
　Doing what?
Continued work for while after marriage?
　How long?
What schools attended?
How many children in your family?

Comment:

Siblings
Name:	Age:	Name:	Age:
Married/single?		Married/single?	
Lives where?		Lives where?	
Occupation		Occupation	

(If married and in Dublin)

Age at marriage?		Age at marriage?	
Wife's birthplace?		Wife's birthplace?	
Her age at marriage?		Her age at marriage?	
Her father's occupation?		Her father's occupation?	
No. of children?		No. of children?	

Comment:

278

Check List of General Interview Areas

5. EDUCATIONAL-ASSOCIATIONAL COMPONENT

Case No.

Husband

What schools attended?
  If left school at 14, why?
  If secondary or technical school, why not University?
  If University, what specialization?
What, if any, labour unions—or business associations—does he belong to,
    with description of its activities?
What religious organizations, parochial and non-parochial?
What political organizations? (N.B. Not ordinary party preference—make
    that clear!—but active membership in a political organization.)
What social and recreational organizations?

Comment:

5. EDUCATIONAL-ASSOCIATIONAL COMPONENT

Case No.

Wife

What schools attended?
  If left school at 14, why?
  If secondary or technical, why not University?
  If University, what specialization?
What religious organization, parochial and non-parochial?
What social and recreational organizations?
N.B. Following two to be asked, only if clear from preceding that wife
    works, and has unusual political interests:
What, if any, labour unions, or business associations?
What political organizations?

Comment:

Selected Bibliography

An Irish Christian Brother, *Edmund Ignatius Rice*, Dublin, 1926.
Arensberg, C., *The Irish Countryman*, New York, 1937.
——, and Kimball, S. T., *Family and Community in Ireland*, Harvard, 1940.
Arquillière, H.-X., *L'Augustinisme Politique*, Paris, 1934.
Becker, Howard, and Barnes, Harry Elmer, *Social Thought from Lore to Science*, 2nd ed., 2 vols., Washington, D.C., 1952.
——, and Boskov, Alvin, eds., *Modern Sociological Theory in Continuity and Change*, New York, 1957.
——, and Hill, R., eds., *Family, Marriage and Parenthood*, 2nd ed., Boston, 1955.
Bernard, C. I., *The Functions of the Executive*, Harvard, 1947.
Blunt, W. S., *The Land War in Ireland*, London, 1912.
Bogue, Donald J., *The Population of the United States*, Glencoe, Ill., 1959.
Bonn, M. J., *Modern Ireland and Her Agrarian Problem*, Dublin, 1906.
Burgess, E. W., 'The Family in a Changing Society', *American Journal of Sociology*, LIII, No. 6 (May 1948), 417.
——, and Locke, Harvey J., *The Family: From Institution to Companionship*, 2nd ed., New York, 1953.
Burke, John F., *Outlines of the Industrial History of Ireland*, Dublin, 1946.
Bury, J. B., *The Life of St. Patrick*, New York, 1905.
Butler, H. D., *et al.*, *The Irish Free State: An Economic Survey* (U.S. Bureau of Foreign and Domestic Commerce Trade Promotion Series, No. 62), Washington, 1928.
Cayre, A. A., 'The Great Augustinism', *Theology Digest*, Vols. I and II, 1953–54, Vol. II, 169–73.
Central Statistics Office of the Irish Government, *Memorandum on the Age at Marriage, 1946*, Dublin, 1952.
——, *Memorandum on the Level and Trend of the Population* (unpublished study prepared in Dublin, 1948).
Chart, D. A., *The Story of Dublin*, London, 1920.
Civics Institute of Ireland, *The Dublin Civic Survey*, Report of the Dublin Civic Survey Committee, London, 1925.
Clarkson, J. D., *Labour and Nationalism in Ireland*, New York, 1925.
Codes Juris Canonici, Lib. III, Pt. I, C. IX, 'De Parochis', Westminster, Maryland, 1942.
Cole, William E., *Urban Society*, Cambridge, Mass., 1958.
Connell, K. H., *The Population of Ireland 1750–1845*, Oxford, 1950.
Curtis, E., *A History of Ireland*, London, 1936.
D'Alton, E. A., Rev., *History of Ireland*, 6 vols., London, n.d.
Daly, John, Rev., 'Family Life: The Principles', *Christus Rex*, Vol. V, No. 1, January 1951, 1–19.
dePaor, Máire and Liam, *Early Christian Ireland*, London, 1958.
Dillon, J., 'The Land Rehabilitation Programme', *Economic Survey of the Republic of Ireland*, issued by *The Statist*, London, 1951, p. 14.
Duffy, Charles Gavan, *The League of North and South*, London, 1886.

Bibliography

Eire, *Report of Inquiry into the Housing of the Working Classes of the City of Dublin, 1939/43*, Dublin, 1943.

European Recovery Programme (U.S. Economic Co-operation Administration), *Ireland: Country Study*, Washington, D.C., 1949.

'Europe's New Industrial Annex', *Business Week*, 30 June 1962, pp. 62–7.

Evans, E. E., *Irish Heritage*, Dundalk, 1949.

Feggis, D., *The Economic Case for Irish Independence*, Dublin and London, 1920.

Freeman, T. W., *Ireland*, London, 1950.

Geary, N., *Marriage and Family Relations*, London, 1892.

Geary, R. C., 'Irish Economic Development since the Treaty', *Studies*, XL, No. 160 (December 1951), 399–418.

Gougaud, L., *Christianity in Celtic Lands*, London, 1932.

Grabill, W. H., Kiser, C. V., and Whelpton, P. K., *The Fertility of American Women*, New York, 1958.

Great Britain, Board of Trade (Labour Department), *Abstract of Labour Statistics, Sixteenth and Seventeenth, 1911–1912*, London, 1913, 1918.

——, *First Census of Production of the United Kingdom (1907)*, London, 1912.

——, *Report on Working Class Rents, Housing and Retail Prices in the Principal Industrial Towns of the United Kingdom, 1908*, London, 1912 (?).

Great Britain Tariff Commission, *The Economic Position of Ireland and Its Relation to Tariff Reform*, London, 1912.

Grogan, Vincent, 'Irish Constitutional Development', *Studies*, XL, No. 160 (December 1951), 385–98.

Gwynn, Stephen, *Ireland*, London, 1924.

Gwynn, Dennis, *The Irish Free State, 1922–27*, London, 1928.

Hajnal, J., 'Changes in the Marriage Pattern', *The American Sociological Review*, XIX, No. 3 (June 1954), 295–302.

——, 'The Marriage Boom', *Population Index*, XIX, No. 2 (April 1953), 80–101.

Hauser, Philip M., 'World Urbanism: An Editorial Forward', *American Journal of Sociology*, LX, No. 5 (March 1955), 427–8.

Homans, George C., *The Human Group*, London and New York, 1950.

——, *Social Behavior, Its Elementary Forms*, London and New York, 1961.

Hughes, Philip, *A History of the Catholic Church*, 3 vols., New York, 1934–47.

Ireland (Irish Free State: Saorstat Eireann) (Department of Industry and Commerce), *Census of Industrial Production, 1931*, Dublin, 1934.

—— (Saorstat Eireann) (Department of Industry and Commerce), *Census of Industrial Production, 1937*, Dublin, 1939.

——, *Census of Industrial Production, 1945–1947*, Dublin, n.d.

——, *Census of Industrial Production, 1948 and 1947*, published in *Irish Trade Journal and Statistical Bulletin*, XXV, Dublin (June 1950), 89–99.

——, *Census of Population 1926*, Vols. I to X, Dublin.

——, *Census of Population 1936*, Vols. I to X, Dublin.

——, *Census of Population 1946, Preliminary Report; Interim Reports* I to V; Vols. I to X, Dublin.

——, *Census of Population 1951, Preliminary Report*, Vols. I to III, Dublin.

——, *Census of Population 1956, Preliminary Report; Population, Area and Valuation of Each District Electoral Division and of Each Larger Unit of Area* (only vol. published), Dublin.

——, *Census of Population 1961, Preliminary Report*, Dublin.

——, *Constitution of Ireland*, Dublin, 1951.

——, (Department of Finance), *Economic Development*, Dublin, 1958.

——, (Department of Agriculture and Technical Instruction), *Ireland: Agricultural and Industrial*, William Coyne, ed., Dublin, 1901.

Bibliography

——, (Central Statistics Office), *Irish Statistical Survey*, Dublin, 1949.

——, (Department of Industry and Commerce), *Register of Population 1941*, Dublin, 1944.

——, (Eire), *Report of Commission on Vocational Organization, 1943*, Dublin, 1943.

——, *Statistical Abstract, 1947–48*, Dublin, 1949.

——, *Weekly Bulletin of the Department of External Affairs*, No. 100, Dublin, 3 September 1951.

The Irish Times, *The Liberal Ethic*, Dublin, 1950.

Jesuit Fathers, *A Page of Irish History*, Dublin, 1930.

Johnston, J. J., *Irish Agriculture in Transition*, Dublin, 1951.

Kimball, S. T., 'The Tradesman and his Family in the Economic Structure of an Irish Town', unpublished Ph.D. thesis, Harvard, 1935.

Kiser, Clyde V., 'Current Mating and Demographic Significance', *Eugenics Quarterly*, VI, No. 2 (June 1959), 65–82.

The Lawyer's Digest, Cincinnati, 1945.

Locker-Lampson, G., *The State of Ireland in the Nineteenth Century*, London, 1907.

McCarthy, M. D., 'Some Family Facts in Ireland Today', *Christus Rex*, V, No. 1 (January 1951), 46–64.

McElligot, T. J., 'Decentralization', *Christus Rex*, III, No. 2 (April 1949).

McGrath, F., SJ, *Newman University Idea and Reality*, Dublin, 1951.

MacLarnon, F., Rev., 'The Family, the Great Educator', *Christus Rex*, V, No. 1 (January 1951), 65–79.

MacNeill, Eoin, *St. Patrick*, London, 1934.

Manchester Guardian Commercial (European Reconstruction Series), *Ireland*, Manchester, March, May, July 1923.

Mansbergh, Nicholas, *Ireland in the Age of Reform and Revolution*, London, 1940.

The Metropolitan Life Insurance Company, 'Fertility of American Women in Relation to Husbands' Occupation', *Statistical Bulletin*, XXVI, No. 6 (June 1945), 7–9.

——, 'Early Marriages Most Frequent in South', *Statistical Bulletin*, XXVI, No. 6 (June 1945), 5–7.

——, 'Americans Marry Young', *Statistical Bulletin*, XXVIII, No. 2 (February 1947), 9.

Mogey, J. M., *Rural Life in Northern Ireland*, London, 1950.

Monahan, T. P., *The Pattern of Age at Marriage in the United States*, Philadelphia, 1951.

Morrissey, D., 'Industrial Development in Ireland', *Economic Survey of the Republic of Ireland*, issued by *The Statist*, London, 1951, pp. 15–16.

Murdock, G. P., *Social Structure*, New York, 1949.

Murray, E. A., *A History of Commercial and Financial Relations between England and Ireland*, London, 1903.

O'Briain, F., Rev., 'Rural Depopulation', *Rural Ireland, 1949*, Tipperary, 1949, pp. 73–99.

O'Brien, George, *The Economic History of Ireland from the Union to the Famine*, London, 1921.

——, *The Four Green Fields*, Dublin, 1936.

——, 'The Economic Progress of Ireland', *Studies*, vol. LI (1962), 9–26.

O'Casey, S., *I Knock at the Door*, New York, 1939.

——, *Irish Fellers, Fare Thee Well*, New York, 1949.

——, *Pictures in the Hallway*, New York, 1942.

O'Cathain, S., SJ, 'Education', *Studies*, XL, No. 160 (December 1951), 437–56.

282

Bibliography

O'Donovan, John, 'Trends in Agriculture', *Studies*, XL, No. 160 (December 1951), 410–27.

O'Faolain, S., *The Irish*, West Drayton, Middlesex, Penguin Books, 1947.

——, 'The Browne Case', *The Bell*, April 1951.

O'Farrell, S., 'The Changing Pattern of Irish Life', *Studies*, XL, No. 160 (December 1951), 428–36.

Ogburn, William F., and Tibbits, C., 'The Family and Its Functions', *Recent Social Trends in the United States*, New York, 1933.

——, and Nimkoff, Meyer, *Sociology*, New York, 1940.

O'Rahilly, Alfred, 'The Irish University Question (1) and (2)', *Studies*, vol. L (1961), 225–70; 353–70; 'The Irish University Question (3)', *Studies*, vol. LI (1962), 147–70.

O'Reilly, B., *Life of John McHale, Archbishop of Tuam*, 2 vols., Pustet, New York, 1890.

O'Sullivan, Donal, *The Irish Free State and Its Senate*, London, 1940.

Parsons, T., *Essays in Sociological Theory, Pure and Applied*, Glencoe, Ill., 1941.

——, *The Social System*, Glencoe, Ill., and London, 1951.

——, *Structure and Process in Modern Societies*, Glencoe, Ill., 1960.

Paul-Dubois, L., *Contemporary Ireland* (trans.), Dublin, 1908.

Plunkett, Horace, Sir, *Ireland in the New Century*, New York, popular edition, 1905.

Pokorny, J., *A History of Ireland*, trans. by S. King, Dublin, 1933.

Pomfret, J. E., *The Struggle for Land in Ireland*, Princeton, 1930.

Population Index, XIX, No. 2 (April 1953).

Portalie, E., 'Augustine of Hippo', *The Catholic Encyclopedia*, II, New York, (1907), 84–104.

——, 'Augustinianisme', *Dictionnaire de Théologie Catholique*, Tome II, Part II, cols. 2485–501, Paris, 1923.

——, 'Augustinisme', *Dictionnaire de Théologie Catholique*, Tome II, Part II, cols. 2501–61, Paris, 1923.

Redfield, Robert, *The Folk Culture of the Yucatán*, Chicago, 1941.

Riordan, E. J., *Modern Irish Trade and Industry*, London, 1920.

Ryan, John, *Irish Monasticism*, New York, 1931.

Sanderson, E. D., *Rural Sociology and Rural Social Organization*, New York and London, 1942.

Smith-Gordon, L., and Staples, L. C., *Rural Reconstruction in Ireland*, Yale, 1919.

Sorokin, Pitirim A., *Social and Cultural Dynamics*, 4 vols., New York, 1937–41.

The Statist, *Economic Survey of The Republic of Ireland*, London, 3 February 1951.

Strauss, E., *Irish Nationalism and British Democracy*, London, 1951.

Sullivan, A. M., *New Ireland*, Philadelphia, 1878.

Thomas, John, SJ, 'The Catholic Family in a Complex Society', *Social Order*, IV, No. 10 (December 1954), 451–7.

Thomas, W. I., and Znaniecki, Florian, *The Polish Peasant in Europe and America*, 5 vols., Boston, 1918–20.

Thompson, W. S., *Population Problems*, New York, 1st ed., 1942; and 2nd ed., 1953.

Timasheff, Nicholas S., *Sociological Theory, Its Nature and Growth*, rev. ed., New York, 1957.

Truxal, Andrew G., and Merrill, Francis E., *Marriage and the Family in American Culture*, Englewood Cliffs, N.J., 1953.

United Nations, *Demographic Yearbook, 1949/50*.

——, *Demographic Yearbook, 1952*.

Bibliography

U.S. Bureau of Census, *Population: Differential Fertility 1910–1940, Women by Number of Children under 5 Years Old*, Washington, D.C., 1945.

——, *Population: Special Reports, Age at Marriage*, Series P-45, No. 7, Washington, D.C., 1945.

Webb, J. J., *Industrial Dublin Since 1869 and the Silk Industry in Dublin*, London, 1914.

Weber, M., *The Theory of Social and Economic Organization*, trans. by A. M. Henderson and T. Parsons, New York, 1947.

White, Leslie A., *The Science of Culture*, New York, 1949.

White, T. de Vere, *The Road to Excess*, Dublin, 1945.

Wright, Arnold, *Disturbed Dublin*, London, 1914.

Young, Michael, and Willmott, Peter, *Family and Kinship in East London*, London and Glencoe, Ill., 1957.

Zimmerman, Carle C., and Cervantes, Lucian F., SJ, *Marriage and the Family*, Chicago, 1956.

——, and ——, *Successful American Families*, New York, 1960.

——, and Sorokin, P., *Principles of Rural Sociology*, New York, 1929.

Index of Names

Index of Subjects

Age: attitudes towards, 37; structure, 65–6 and n., 74, 84, 86–7; division of labour, 235–7

Age: at marriage, 68–76; effects of urbanization on, 82–3, 87–9, 116–19, 130–1

Age-sex roles: in rural family, 13–15, 16, 18, 20–2; and corporations, 31; among artisans, 94–107, 138–72

Agriculture: in nineteenth century, 42–3

America, 146, 158, 234

Anglo-Irish Ascendancy: class norms, 37, 195; power, 41–5, 49 n., 52 and (n. 26); and civil liberties, 52 (n. 27); effects of Irish independence on, 51–2; mentioned, 198, 213

Argentina, 65 n.

Artisans: defined, 6; distribution of, 62; property, 92–3; family, 92–115; residence, 93; dowry, 93–4; marriage, 93–5, 115–20, 130–2, 138–40, 154–6, 161–9, 172–7; age-sex roles, 94–107, 138–72; income, 95; division of labour, 95–100, 138–72, 206; husband-wife relations, 95–100, 102–3, 122, 137–45; finances, 95, 100–2; authority, 96–100, 170–2; recreation, 97, 102–3, 143–4; religion, 97, 103–7, 158–9; education, 102, 125–8, 149–54; kinship, 107–11, 177–83; neighbourliness, 111–15, 183–7; friendship, 114–15, 191–2; family cycle, 115–33; parent-child relations, 116–18, 120–5, 131–3, 145–72; sex, 116, 119–20, 138–40; age at marriage, 116–19, 130–1; mobility, 123–4, 172–7; marriage of girls, 126, 129–30;

marriage of boys, 130–1; emigration of, 132–3, 136–7; inheritance, 135–8; father-son relations, 145–7, 159–62; peer-group relations, 148–9; occupation, 153–4; mother-son relations, 161–6; mother-daughter relations, 166–9; father-daughter relations, 169; siblings, 170–2; hypergamy, 172–6; and parish, 178, 187–91; class sentiments, 199–200

Ascendancy. *See* Anglo-Irish Ascendancy

Augustinianism: influence in Ireland, 25–7, 25 n., 232

Australia, 68, 71, 73, 158, 197, 254; mentioned, 132

Austria, 26 n.

Authority: in rural family, 14–15; in rural community, 15–16; in New Dubliners' family, 33–5; among artisans, 96–100, 138, 142–3, 170–2; parental, 237–8

Boston: mentioned, v, 20, 90

Bavaria: mentioned, 26 n.

British Parliament: acts restrictive of Irish trade, 42–3

Belfast, 43 n., 52

British Census of Production, 45

Birth rate, 58, 71

Belgium, 66 n., 254

Belvedere Newsboys Club: mentioned, 203 n.

Bureaucracy, 231

Canada, 72, 73, 254

Canon law, 188 and n.; on marriage, 55

Catholic Church: universal doctrine, 24–6; in Ireland, 25–7;

287